P9-DCL-231

Programming Linguistics

Programming Linguistics

David Gelernter and Suresh Jagannathan

The MIT Press
Cambridge, Massachusetts
London, England

©1990 Massachusetts Institute of Technology

This book was set in Computer Modern.
Printed and bound in the United States of America.

Library of Congress Cataloging-in-Publication Data

Gelernter, David Hillel.
    Programming linguistics / David Gelernter, Suresh Jagannathan.
        p.   cm.
    Includes bibliographical references.
    ISBN 0-262-07127-4
    1. Programming languages (Electronic computers)
2. Computational linguistics. I. Jagannathan, Suresh. II. Title.
QA76.7.G44   1990   90-5485
005.1—dc20   CIP

Contents

List of Figures

Preface

This book is intended to serve several purposes. First, it's a text for courses in the design and evolution of programming languages. The recipe for turning the book into a course is fairly simple: students should read the book *and* all of the "basic" papers listed at the end of each chapter. Add exercises, stir and serve. To get a beefed-up graduate student version, read all of the "suggested" as well as the "basic" papers in the reading lists. None of these are extraneous or strictly for reference; they all play a significant role in the evolution of the field.

The book is designed also to serve as supplementary reading for courses in compiler construction. It's often difficult for a compilers course to leave students with a comprehensive feel for the breadth and variety of language models that compilers are called upon to support. Students sometimes emerge, besides, without a clear understanding of why anybody would want or need some of the features they've learned how to implement. We hope that this book will be one part of an effective treatment plan aimed at the *I-know-how-but-don't-ask-me-why* syndrome that so often strikes down our young people in the prime of life.

Finally, programming languages are an important topic both for computation practitioners and for researchers. This book may be of use to anyone who needs more information on a significant and intriguing area.

Beyond its specific goals as a text and an information source, the book has a more general mission. Computer science seems to be destined for a permanent identity crisis. This holds particularly for the sub-field called "Systems"—the part of computer science that deals with the design and construction of computing environments, encompassing computer architecture, operating systems, compilers, programming languages and program-building methods. The Systems area is the center of computer science, the most specifically "computer-science-ish" part of the field, and there is an ongoing struggle over its basic character.

A large number of distinguished researchers seem to feel that, if this field is ever going to find itself, the only place to look is in the mathematics department. The study of programming languages in particular is imagined in some quarters to be reducible to the study of implementation techniques on the one hand and to the formal or mathematical description of language semantics on the other. Both topics, despite the

obvious importance of implementation and the potential significance of
formal semantics, beg the fundamental questions:

- What do programming languages look like, and what *should* they
  look like?
- Why do they offer the tools and constructs they do, what kind of
  programming styles do they suggest, what do they tell us about
  some particular vision of software structure?
- What light do they shed on the basic, unanswered question in
  Systems—what *is* a program anyway?

Before students worry about topics like formal semantics, they should be
quite clear about what they are studying the semantics *of*. They should
aim to understand the language design field in all its richness and depth,
resisting the narrow outlook that is sometimes imposed in the interests
of formal tractability. And they should keep in mind that programming
languages are synthetic creations, and that language design is properly
an *engineering* study.

We stress this last point on behalf of a larger, more important, often-
neglected consideration: engineering exists at the interface between science and art. Aesthetic issues, the design judgments that are captured
in a programming language and underlie some vision of the shape and
form of software machinery, are just as important to this field as the
theorems that define computation. The beauty and power of the best
programming languages are one facet of a larger topic, having to do
with the sweep and intellectual depth of engineering in general. Unfortunately, this broader topic is simply not on the menu at the typical
fast food-for-thought joint that passes as a modern university (and is
even less likely to be served at the trendiest bistros)—which very likely
contributes to computer science's difficulties in defining itself.

The book's structure is heterogeneous. The chapters vary greatly
in length and will (obviously) require varying amounts of time to get
through. The three Classical Languages (Fortran, Algol 60 and Lisp)
are grouped together in one long chapter, in order to accommodate some
historical background and some exercises relating to all three, and in
deference to the fact that together they underlie most subsequent work
in the field. The Pascal chapter has a prologue dealing with Algol 68
and PL/I; the Simula 67 chapter has a postlude that deals with spec-

ification, abstract types and Ada. Through the Pascal chapter, each language is treated essentially as a whole. Thereafter we assume that enough groundwork has been laid to justify our focusing mainly on specific language features—the class in Simula, the package in Ada and so on. We follow, in a sense, the development of a single "plot" from the Classical Languages through Scheme; the plot has to do with the rise and fall of a virtual structure called the Algol Wall. (Of course there are a large number of other themes under development at the same time.) The final two language chapters, on Declarative and Parallel languages, each represent a digression of sorts after the main story has drawn to its slightly bittersweet conclusion. Two special-purpose appendices, following the Pascal and the Declarative Languages chapters, attempt to place programming language design in a broader intellectual context. Two appendices, following the second chapter, give a summary of and formal semantics for the "ideal software machine" model; they're included mainly for reference use and may be skipped without loss of continuity.

Acknowledgments. The first author thanks the Linda group at Yale, particularly Nick Carriero and Jerry Leichter. I'm grateful to Jerry especially for introducing me to the remarkable work of Billington. I have the distinct impression that, although this book deals only glancingly with the main topic of our collaboration, it could never have been written without Nick's contributions. The Computer Science Department at Yale was a stimulating place to work. It's an honor to acknowledge that extensive and wide-ranging conversations with Alan Perlis contributed a great deal to my own understanding of programming languages. Martin Schultz turned the Department into a place where our work could thrive, and I'm grateful to him for his support. The heart of the ideal software machine model, and the view of language design that underlies the book, goes back to my thesis work at Stony Brook, and to conversations there with teachers and fellow students. Of course I thank my parents, The Sibs and above all my wife—to whom the author hereby gives notice that, several years of work on this book being now finally complete, it may conceivably be possible for him to resume mowing the lawn occasionally.

The second author is grateful to the Laboratory for Computer Science, Massachusetts Institute of Technology, where the semantics and detailed design of the ideal software machine model were developed. The proposition that this model could serve as a viable basis upon which to unify superficially diverse concepts in programming languages formed the centerpiece of my doctoral research. Although I am indebted to all my colleagues and friends at MIT for the stimulating environment they helped to create, I especially would like to thank Rishiyur Nikhil and Bert Halstead for their significant contributions to my understanding of programming languages and systems. I thank David Gelernter for his invitation to collaborate with him on the writing of this book, and the Computer Science department at Yale University for providing the superb resources that allowed us to undertake this endeavor. Most importantly, my contributions to this text were possible only because of the never-ending encouragement and support given by my family—my wife Hema, my parents, and my brother Aravind.

Programming Linguistics

1 Programming Linguistics: Goals and Methods

Programming linguistics studies the design of programming languages and the relationships among them. Its particular goal is to discover the patterns, the relationships and the common antecedents that can make a complicated field rational and graspable. (In this sense it broadly resembles linguistics proper.) We will examine a wide range of language designs, from Fortran to newly-minted research languages, stopping at most of the significant points along the way. Learning the personalities of these languages is important. But the real problem before us is more elusive and deeper: every computer scientist knows what an algorithm is, but what is a program? An algorithm is a series of steps that computes a function. It has a formal mathematical meaning that translates into a clear intuitive one. "Program" on the other hand has no universally accepted mathematical definition. Deciding what programs are and how they should be built has occupied computer science from its beginnings, and still does. In studying programming languages, we are studying a series of informed hypotheses, intuitive leaps, brilliant theories and shots in the dark, all directed at these basic and essential questions.

We begin with a working definition of our topic, including a broad, general definition of "program" that we will use as a starting point for the more detailed definitions advanced by the languages we study. We then introduce the method we'll use to study language design, and discuss the book's organization. We conclude by defining some basic terms that are assumed in the chapters following.

1.1 Fundamentals

What is a program? At first glance, programs have two different sorts of manifestations. On the one hand, they are documents of some kind that give a series of instructions to be executed by a computer. But these passive documents can be turned into active physical processes: when a program is executed, the instructions in the document are carried out. The program text is passive, but the *executing* program is an event in real time. Does "program" refer to the passive text, or the active event? The answer is *both*, because from our point of view in this book, *a program is a machine*. The program text represents the machine before it has been turned on. The executing program represents the powered-up machine in active operation. There is no fundamental distinction between the passive program text and the active executing program, just as there is none between a machine before and after it is turned on.

So a program is a kind of machine, in particular a "software" machine. There is nothing a program can do that a mechanical machine built out of gears and sprockets can't, but the software version can be built using a programming language on a computer terminal.

What is a programming language? It follows that a programming language is a *construction kit for software machinery*. The machines we build depend on the interplay between tools, materials and imagination. Where software machinery is concerned, programming languages define the tools and materials. Theoreticians note that all general-purpose programming languages are "Turing-equivalent." Ultimately they can all compute the same set of functions, so none is more powerful in a mathematical sense than any other. The analogous observation is that all hardware machines must obey the same physical laws. No software machine can solve the halting problem (can compute a mathematically uncomputable function), and no hardware machine can violate the laws of thermodynamics. But the fact that all bridges obey physical laws hardly implies that our choice of steel versus mud as a bridge-building material doesn't matter; programming languages can be nearly as important in the engineering of software machinery. Of course, a large number of generic programming techniques are useful in almost any language. It is also true that for small programs, choice of language rarely has any deep importance. But the larger, more complex and less routine the application, the more central a programming language's influence becomes.

If a program is a machine, and a programming language is a construction kit, where does that leave the computer? Nowhere. The physical computer is nothing more than a (metaphorical) power source for the software machine. A program has to be plugged into a computer in order to execute, but the characteristics of the software machine are directly determined by the language and the programmer, only indirectly by the physical computer. It is therefore possible to study the *design* of languages as distinct from their implementation. Programming language implementation is a different topic: it covers the translation of programming languages into computer-executable forms. It deals with interpreters and compilers, runtime support packages and, sometimes, with computer architecture. We will refer to these topics occasionally, but in most cases they are not central to our topic.

Language designs range over a large field. Some languages closely mirror the design of the physical computing machines. They lend themselves to the construction of efficient software machines (ones that make the most of the raw power available in a computer—programs that run fast); they have been significant, too, in the development of programming language design. Fortran is the most important example.

Some languages were developed with almost no regard for the details of computer architecture. Getting programs in these languages to run efficiently is a harder problem; but many programmers feel that these languages are more flexible, expressive and generally inspirational than others that adhere more closely to existing hardware. The Lisp family is the most important member of this class, and there is a wide range of others. We will take up the most significant, from APL through functional languages, Smalltalk and Prolog.

Between these two camps are the languages that are arguably the most important and influential of all, the Algol-based languages. Some are highly efficient tools, very close to the structure of physical machines; but all differ in their logical structure from mere hardware in ways that are decisive to computer science.

Outside of (but related to) these basic families are languages that have been designed for special purposes. At present the most important special purpose is *parallelism*. Languages designed for parallel computers—computers made up of many sub-computers that are all active simultaneously—must support the construction of programs that do many things at once. Virtually all hardware machines do many things at once, but software machines traditionally have not. These new languages are an increasingly important sub-topic, and we will discuss several of them.

1.2 Studying Language Design: The "Programming Linguistics" Approach

Understanding the personalities of a wide range of real languages is important, but it's not enough. Our aim is to grasp the field as a whole. We need to investigate how the pieces relate to each other, where these languages *really* differ and where they only seem to. We need to distinguish the bedrock from the flounces and throw-pillows of language design. To do this, we lay out an *ideal software machine* model and relate each real language to this simple and stylized ideal.

We might have gone about things differently. Most language design texts recognize the need to abstract and to generalize, but they do so by formulating a collection of "basic concepts" and organizing the presentation around these. They might have a "data structures" chapter, a "subroutines" chapter and so on. For our purposes this approach is rational but unsatisfying. Suppose we were studying flowering plants. Agreed, merely to list and describe them would be incomplete; but it wouldn't be edifying either to start with a chapter on "Carpels," discussing their manifestations from flower to flower, followed by a chapter on "Stamens" and so forth. If it's not enough merely to describe individuals without abstracting, it's also not enough to tease out the basic components and study each in isolation. We need to start out by knowing what a flowering plant is in general and *as a whole*. We need to understand not only which structures are basic to all species, but how they relate to each other: how, collectively, they constitute a flowering plant. Equipped with the knowledge of a "stylized flower" or "model flower" or "ideal flower," we are prepared to understand the ways in which the model is adapted, extended or modified throughout a range of diverse families and species, how the families relate to each other and how they relate to the "ideal flower" that serves as focal point.

This is our premise in programming linguistics. We begin with an ideal model that allows us to study the fundamental structure of programming languages as opposed to merely the surface features that distinguish one from another. Of course it isn't possible to propound a unique ideal software machine, any more than a unique ideal flower. Matters of taste and judgment are involved in boiling a complicated picture down to essentials. The model we come up with is not unique and is not provably the best possible. But it is serviceable, as the text will demonstrate.

1.2.1 Moving from the Ideal Model to Real Languages

In chapter two we present ideal software machines; we move from there to a discussion of real languages. Certain features are particularly important in establishing their personalities. The ideal model sheds light on these features, but we can introduce them independently of the model too, and we proceed to do so here. These three basic features are naming environments; data structures, values and types; and self-descriptiveness.

Naming Environments We've given a broad conceptual definition for "program" (a "software machine"), but operationally, a program in almost every extant language is a *naming environment*[1]: a dictionary that associates names with definitions or values. A Fortran program, a Lisp program and a Pascal program are radically different in many ways, but all three consist basically of a list of names and their meanings—names of subroutines or functions or procedures, of data structures, values or variables, of type definitions and so on. What objects can be named? How are the names organized into groups? How are names made known wherever they are needed? These are fundamental questions in language design.

We will examine many choices and possibilities. In some languages, naming environments must be defined as a unit, all together; in others, a naming environment may be extended incrementally—new names may be tacked onto the end of a growing environment. Generally speaking, the first condition holds for compiled languages and the second for interpreted languages. A program is a naming environment, and in most languages it may contain other sub-environments within it: can we nest sub-environments hierarchically as in Pascal records? Can we build a new environment out of two superimposed sub-environments, as in Smalltalk? Can we selectively hide some names, but make other names visible, as in CLU or Modula-2 or Ada? Can we gather environments into named collections, as in APL? Some languages require certain

---

[1]We will also refer to naming environments as *namespaces*.

objects to have names, where others allow them to be anonymous—in most of the Algol world, a function or subroutine must have a name or it can't exist; in the Lisp world this isn't true, and the difference is a crucial symptom of different philosophies with respect to the allowable world of values. As we proceed, environments will emerge as a central factor in subroutine calling, concurrency, composite data structures and numerous other language facets as well.

Data Structures, Data Types and Data Values   Broadly speaking, a data structure is an organizational scheme for data, a data type is the description of such a scheme, and a data value is a data object to be organized.

Data Structures and naming environments are usually treated very differently, but in fact (as we discuss in the next chapter) it's much simpler to regard them as two versions of the same thing. The elements of a naming environment have names; a data structure's elements don't need names—they can be identified in some other way, usually by position. Thus an "array" is a kind of data structure in which every element can be located by index (*e.g.*, by row and column number in the case of a two-dimensional matrix); a "list" is a data structure whose i^{th} element can be accessed only by traversing the $i - 1$ elements preceding it; a "stack" is a data structure that has some element at the top; and so on.

A stack is more than simply one location named "top of stack," of course. To have a stack, we also need a set of stack operations—we need rules for what happens when we pop the stack or push a new element. When we describe a data structure as an "organizational scheme," then, we refer both to a particular structure and to a set of operations that manipulate the structure.

Languages differ markedly in their approach to data structures, and their personalities are influenced in major ways by this issue. Some languages and families are organized around central or defining data structures—Lisp and APL are important examples. All languages must decide which data structures are primary—supplied as part of the language itself—and which are secondary, to be synthesized by the user. Consider the data structure usually referred to as a garbage-collected heap. In languages that supply one, programmers can create new data objects and never worry about getting rid of the old ones—the language (more properly, the language's implementation) tidies up automatically. In languages that lack one, programmers can implement exactly the same structure—but at the the cost of a certain amount (occasionally a considerable amount) of labor. Why not throw one in as standard equipment with every language? A comparable question—why not equip every car with an automatic transmission and an air-conditioner? Answer: some programmers and drivers are more interested in performance than in comfort, and are willing (in some cases eager) to do things themselves in order to get it.

Data Values are the objects with which a language deals. We can define a "value" as something that can be returned as the value of an expression, stored in a data structure, or passed as an argument to a function. Most languages agree that objects like integers, floating-point numbers, characters and the Boolean values "true" and "false" should be values. But disagreement then arises in (at least) two directions. Are programs *themselves* (as embodied in functions or subroutines) values? This is a disagreement alluded to above also; languages that treat functions as values have personalities that are heavily dependent on this fact. Another direction: an integer is a value, and an array of integers is a data structure; or can we regard an array of integers (or a data structure in general) as a new, compound value? Many languages have trouble deciding.

The worlds of structure and of values meet and interact in the potentially complicated question of *types*. A type is the description either of a kind of primitive value (the type "integer" or "function") or of a kind of data structure (the type "two-dimensional array of integer"). The real significance of announcing the type of a value or structure lies in controlling the kinds of operations that can be performed on objects of that type. If we know the type of every object, we know what operations are allowable over every object: we can prevent a programmer from multiplying two characters, say, which would be meaningless. But suppose a programmer has good reasons for treating an object of type X as if it were type Y? Some languages allow this; most refuse. Suppose that, rather than defining a different set of operations for every type, programmers prefer to make the *same* operation mean different things in different domains: thus adding two integers means to sum them, adding two character strings means to concatenate them. Some languages allow this (Smalltalk is an important example; PL/1 is in in some ways an interesting precursor).

A related (but more general and flexible) type system allows the same function to be applied to arguments of many different types. Thus, a function to reverse the elements of a list may operate over lists of any type; the meaning of such a function in this kind of *polymorphic* type system is the same in all domains even though the types of its arguments (integer lists, boolean lists, *etc..*) are different. Most modern-day functional languages (Miranda[2] and ML are two good examples) support such a type system. Are objects themselves typed, or are variables? These two approaches are an important point of difference between the Lisp and Algol worlds. Can we add new types to a language, and what does it mean to do so? These questions form a major topic of discussion in the context of "abstract typing."

Self-Descriptiveness   The English language (like virtually any natural language) is largely but not completely self-describing. We can write a dictionary and a grammar of English in English; a user would have to know certain things about English before he could understand them, and there are some words that a verbal description can't explain (try defining "red"), but an immense amount of complexity can be described in terms of a small subset of the language.

Programming languages are also to some extent self-describing; the degree to which they are varies, and it's an important (though widely-ignored) factor in determining their personalities. It's valuable to be able to explain as much as possible about a language—both about its operations and its structures—in the language itself, for reasons both of clarity and of flexibility. Clarity—insofar as a highly self-describing language has fewer primitive, basic ideas—makes a language easier to learn, to understand and to use effectively. Flexibility makes it possible to break a complicated operation into simple steps, to rearrange or alter those steps to build variations on the complicated operation. We don't need to accept the operation as-is, take it or leave it. The same holds for structures.

For example: Simula 67 introduced a revolutionary new structure called a "class." But we can't represent an individual class *instance* in

---

[2]Miranda is a trademark of Research Software Ltd.

Simula 67, we can only represent the template that can be used to stamp out instances. (We can describe the cookie-cutter, but the cookies are mysteriously invisible.) This is a loss, because it means that classes can't be used to build modules or libraries—although logically, they are perfectly well suited to module- or library-building. The fact that APL and most Lisps provide interpreter-constructed environments, but no standard *representation* for objects of type "environment," means that programmers can't write routines to examine and manipulate their environments. Subroutine invocation in Algol 60 is a primitive, irreducible to any sequence of Algol sub-steps—and therefore must be explained in English. This fact has a whole series of consequences for later developments in concurrency and modularity.

We will return repeatedly to self-describability because it is crucial to determining if a program (*i.e.*, a software machine) is not merely a disguised version of a mathematical structure (*e.g.*, a function), what exactly it *is*. As we will see, the early language models were all directly inspired by the received language of mathematics.

Some objects (such as integers or sequences) and processes (such as addition or function composition) are part of mathematics. But other objects (such as naming environments) and processes (such as subroutine-call or link editing) are not. Because they are not, because mathematics provides no traditional way for expressing these objects and operations, they were left out of programming's notational scheme at the beginning; and by and large, they remain left out to this day. Inability to express or represent something is often symptomatic of a failure to understand it clearly—and these objects and operations are *precisely* the ones that are crucial to establishing the character of programming in its own right. The strangely halting history of self-describability will be a central theme in our discussion.

1.2.2   The Historical Approach

After chapter 2, the discussion is organized in a roughly chronological way, language by language. We begin with languages developed in the late fifties, Fortran, Lisp and Algol; we proceed to designs of the early sixties like APL and Cobol, and so on. One advantage of the historical approach is that it allows us to treat language designs as wholes (returning in each case, of course, both to the ideal model and to our basic themes). The historical approach has other virtues as well. New language designs have related to each other in fascinating and subtle ways that don't become clear until we consider them in historical context. There are close ties, for example, between the development of recursion in Algol and in Lisp (Lisp-inventor McCarthy, after all, was on the Algol design committee), and Lisp's characteristic data structure was designed and first implemented in the context of a Fortran-based language, FLPL. Only by following the historical record can we track the tidal flows between classical simplicity and rococo extravagance that repeatedly sweep over the field—from the simplicity of Algol and Lisp to the complexity of PL/1 and Algol 68, then back to simplicity in Pascal and Scheme, and forward to a new generation of complexity in Ada. General formulations like this always oversimplify the record to some extent, of course; but we can learn from them nonetheless. Language designers are influenced by the intellectual climate in significant and interesting ways, but they won't always say so themselves. It's up to the programmer and the historian to notice and ponder these points.

It is a corollary of our historical approach that the original research papers, not language manuals, later discussions or current implementations, must be our primary sources. Only by studying the original papers can we grasp what the designers themselves thought was important. We refer to these original papers extensively. All serious students of programming languages should read them.

1.3   Conclusion: Setting the Stage with Some Basic Terms

We conclude by defining a grab bag of basic terms that are used often in the rest of the book: (a) syntax and semantics; (b) formal and actual parameters; (c) compiler and interpreter; (d) compile time and runtime; (e) parallelism. Readers who are familiar with these terms are asked to read this section anyway, because the flavors of the definitions following are important to the rest of the presentation.

Syntax and Semantics

Syntax refers to the form a program takes, and semantics to its meaning. Languages in the Lisp family, for example, have very simple syntax: to get a syntactically-correct Lisp program, write parentheses around a sequence of words, numbers or other parenthesized sequences. Pascal has a much more complicated syntax: a Pascal program consists of a series of sections, which must appear in a particular order, each of which must begin with a particular word and be organized and punctuated in a particular way. In research papers on language design, "syntax" is often immediately preceded by "mere." The fact that Lisp programs are written with lots of parentheses and Pascal programs with semicolons is not a difference of mere syntax: if you dress a Pascal program in Lisp syntax, it is merely a funny-looking Pascal program, not a Lisp program. It is true that syntax is not fundamental, but false that syntax is unimportant. As we'll see, syntax influences the ways in which programmers use and think about a language.

Semantics deals with the meaning of programs. The semantics of assignment statements, for example—what it means to assign some value to some variable—are very different in Lisp and Pascal. It's easy to write down a language's syntax clearly and concisely; figuring out how to write down a *semantics* clearly and concisely has proven to be a much harder problem. Why so? To give the meaning of a phrase in some programming language, we must explain how the execution of the phrase depends on and how it alters the state of a complicated piece of running machinery. What does this Algol statement mean? An analogous question: what happens to this engine if I reset the valve over here or switch these two hoses while it's running? It's fairly easy to get the answers to such questions mostly right. It can be excruciatingly hard to get them completely, exactly right.

A number of techniques have been developed for giving complete and exact descriptions of a programming language's semantics. One, called denotational semantics, is a complex formal system based on a theory of the denotation (or "meaning") of functions over lattice-structured domains; we will not discuss it here. Operational semantics is a useful but less formal collection of techniques for giving semantics in terms of the actual steps executed by some very simple, precisely-defined

computer in realizing each kind of statement in the language. We don't
rely on operational semantics, but we refer to these techniques occasionally. In an axiomatic-based semantics, the meaning of a program is
given in terms of axioms or assertions that describe its expected behavior. The semantics-describing system that has been most important to
date is known as "English", and we will be using this system extensively.
English is a large, shaggy system and it lends itself to fuzzy, ambiguous statements—particularly when used by fuzzy, ambiguous thinkers.
It can also be used with great precision, and in the hands of precise
thinkers, it often has been, as we will see.

Formal and Actual Parameters

Subroutines, procedures and functions—chunks of program text that are
defined in one place and can thereupon be executed any place, repeatedly, wherever and whenever they are "invoked"—are fundamental to
programming, and every programmer knows how to use them. When a
subroutine (we use this term to stand for subroutines, procedures, functions and all similar structures, irrespective of the name given them in
particular languages) is invoked, data of some kind is transferred from
the invocation statement to the subroutine itself. Exactly how this happens is a complicated topic to which we return repeatedly in this book.
We need to define the basic terms first, though. Data objects passed
from the invocation statement into the subroutine are called "actual parameters" ("actuals" for short). If we invoke a square-root subroutine
by executing the invocation statement "`SquareRoot(17)`," the integer
17 is an actual parameter. The names that are given to the incoming
data objects within the subroutine itself are "formal parameters" of the
subroutine. If the definition of the `SquareRoot` routine is given in terms
of operations to be carried out on a quantity called j, then j is a formal parameter. The invocation statement above causes j to be set to
17, whereupon the operations necessary to compute a square root are
executed over j.

There are a number of ways in which the value of an actual can be
transmitted to a formal. In a *call-by-value* parameter-passing discipline,
a copy is made of each actual and it is this copy that is bound to the
appropriate formal. Because the subroutine deals with a copy rather
than with the original, assignments made to a call-by-value formal in

the body of the subroutine are not visible outside of the procedure. If **F** is a procedure with formal **x**, and **F** is invoked using call-by-value with actual parameter **y**, then changes made to **x** within the body of **F** do not affect **y**; **x** is initialized to **y**'s *value* (not its *location*). In a call-by-reference protocol, actuals and formals *share* the same location. Thus, if **F** were invoked using by call-by-reference, any change made to **x** would be visible in **y**; **x** is initialized to **y**'s *location* (not its *value*). There are a number of other parameter-passing mechanisms besides these two which we'll examine later in the book.

Compilers and Interpreters

A compiler is a program that accepts as input a program in some "source language" and produces as output a program in some "target language." A compiler, then, is a *translator*. The target language is ordinarily assembler or machine code for a particular computer. Thus a "Pascal compiler for the VAX" accepts Pascal programs and translates them into a low-level language that can be executed directly by VAX computers. Compilers are usually designed not only for particular computers, but for particular operating systems: a compiler is a complicated program that will rely on an operating system as it runs, and will produce code that relies on the operating system as well, particularly for input and output and for file handling. Thus, for example, "a Pascal compiler for the VAX running VMS."

An *interpreter* is a program that reads statements in some language and executes them. A Prolog interpreter, for example, is a "virtual Prolog machine": it converts a physical computer that knows nothing about Prolog (a VAX again, say) into a machine that understands Prolog and can execute it directly, without further translation. Interpreters make it possible to construct programs incrementally: we can feed an interpreter one function definition, then another, then have it evaluate some expressions, then feed it a third function definition and so on. We can't do this with a compiler. A compiler can translate an arbitrarily small program, but having done so, it's finished and it terminates. It doesn't maintain a growing set of definitions and values the way an interpreter does.

Constructing programs incrementally is extraordinarily convenient and can become addictive, particularly for improvisational types. But interpreters are inevitably less efficient than compilers. A compiler-produced program will execute faster than an interpreted program because the compiler has had a chance to see the program as a whole, and because the compiled program, when it executes, has the whole computer to itself; a program running under an interpreter shares the machine with the interpreter. Languages that are usually interpreted rather than compiled—the Lisp family, for example—are generally supplied with compilers also, so that finished programs can be executed efficiently.

Compile time and Runtime

A compiler translates source into target programs at "Compile Time." The target program is executed at "Runtime." There is a significant distinction between operations that can be done at compile time and those that must be postponed until runtime. An operation that may be done at compile time requires only such information as can be gathered from the program text—from the quiescent rather than the powered-up machine (*e.g.*, a smart compiler might choose to replace the expression $2+3$ with 5; an even smarter compiler would be able to replace $x+3$ by 5 by determining whether x is a variable guaranteed to be 2 at the time the addition operation executes). We can tell a lot about a car's condition by inspecting it with the engine off—but we can't tell everything. An operation that must be done at runtime depends on information that can't be gathered until the program is executed. A program might try to divide by zero, to reference the $n + 1^{st}$ element of an n element array, to dynamically allocate more storage than is available. In general none of these errors can be detected until runtime. A truly dimwitted programmer might of course write an expression like "$x := y/0$"—the compiler, if it were looking for this sort of thing, could point out the error—but programmers are much more likely to write "$x := y/f(a,b,c)$," and not until the subroutine invocation "$f(a,b,c)$" is executed (that is, not until runtime) can we tell whether this is a legal division or not.

Parallelism

Parallelism refers to one program's doing many things simultaneously. A "compute-intensive" program—one that does a great deal of computing, as opposed to (say) a data-processing program that spends most of its time reading and writing files—can be speeded up by having it perform many sub-tasks simultaneously. This will only work if the logical structure of the program permits it, of course. But in practice, it's rare to find a compute-intensive program that can't be made faster in this way.

Parallelism has become increasingly important in computer science. It seems to be an empirical law that the more computing power we have, the further we are from having enough. No matter how fast we make an individual computer, we can get a faster computer by hooking a bunch of individuals together; and as individual processor speeds approach limits set by current technology and by physics, hooking processors together becomes the *only* way of getting more performance out of a single machine. Figuring out how to build these parallel machines and how to program them is, accordingly, a research topic of great importance.

To build a parallel software machine, programmers need a language that allows them to write not only "do A, then B, then C," but also (in effect) "do A, B and C simultaneously." A parallel software machine is in turn a candidate for execution on a parallel computer. If the software machine calls for five hundred sub-tasks to be carried out simultaneously, it will run at maximum speed on a parallel computer that encompasses five hundred sub-computers. But it can also be executed on a smaller machine; if it runs on five rather than five hundred processors, each will be responsible for roughly one-fifth of the total work. The same program can also run on a conventional single-processor computer; the single processor executes all five hundred tasks.

If we have only a conventional computer, there is no speed advantage in running parallel software on it. Parallelism can sometimes be useful, though, irrespective of execution speed. Consider our five-hundred-subtask program. If the five hundred tasks can run simultaneously, then if no parallel machine is available, the order in which they are executed by a conventional machine clearly doesn't matter. Suppose we have a conventional machine only. If we use a conventional language, we'll have to make up an execution ordering for these five hundred tasks even though the order is irrelevant. If we use a parallel language, we can write "do these in parallel—that is, in any order you want; don't bother me about the details." This can be convenient and it is, in a sense,

truer to the logic of the algorithm. Whether parallelism is "natural"
or not—whether it's easy to find situations in which it makes sense to
write "do these sub-tasks in parallel," independent of execution-speed
advantages—is at present a hotly-debated topic in computer science. On
the one hand, algorithms have been described as sequential processes far
longer than computers have been around. But programs, for purposes
of this book at least, are *machines* and not merely algorithms, and no
machine of any complexity performs only one activity at a time. Human
beings do seem to think sequentially (by and large), but nonetheless they
build "parallel" machines. The rising tide of parallelism and the debates
it engenders will be an important topic in this book.

2 The Ideal Software Machine

In describing this model, we're attempting to achieve two goals. First, to lay the basis for a comparison among a series of programming languages and a discussion of some of their basic attributes. Second, to define a large collection of fundamental concepts, not in depth, but in sufficient detail to give readers a sense of recognition when they encounter these concepts in the wild among the languages themselves. We will introduce the following ideas: **scope, block structure, parallel program structure, records, objects, data systems, modules, libraries, linking, templates** and **abstraction devices, application, data structures, data parallelism, systolic programs** and **type systems**.

To describe an ideal software machine, we must answer two questions: (1) What does one look like? (2) What happens when we turn it on? Our presentation will be informal; readers interested in a more formal definition will find one in the appendix at the end of this chapter.

2.1 The Basic Idea

Before we launch into the definition, here is its essence.

An ISM is a structure built out of two interlocking and orthogonal components. The two are called *space-maps* and *time-maps*, broadly speaking because they allow us to specify the arrangement of entities in *space* (*where* things are) and in *time* (*when* they take place) respectively.

"Turning on" or evaluating a time-map causes a sequence of instructions to be executed in a specified order. A time-map is like a sequence of statements separated by semicolons in Algol 60 or Pascal or C.

Now suppose we flip a time-map on its side in computational space-time—we interchange the roles of time and space in the definition. The result is a space-map: the n elements of a time-map execute at n different times (they execute one at a time, in order); the n elements of a space-map execute in n different *places*. Because the elements of a time-map never overlap in time, they can all share *one* place; the elements of a space-map all share one interval of *time*, one lifetime—they all come into being together and disappear together.

A simple analogy, to make the logical structure clear: imagine a group of n workers in a factory. They can execute at n different times (one of them works the first shift, one the second shift and so on); if so, they can all occupy the same *place* on the line. Or, they can share the same "lifetime": they all arrive at the start of the first shift and leave at the end. If so, each one will have to occupy a *separate* place. The separate-times same-places structure is the time-map; it is orthogonal to the separate-places same-times structure, the space-map.

We started with the time-map, an easily understood structure that occurs in one form or another in most programming languages. A simple transformation produced the space-map—but the space-map is a "synthetic" structure. It doesn't occur "in nature"—*none* of the programming languages we will study includes a structure with the characteristics of our space-map. Why bother with it, then? Because the space-map proves to be a surprisingly powerful and general structure. A wide variety of naturally occurring structures will prove, when we examine them, to be in essence special-purpose, restricted versions of the space-map. The space-map will accordingly be a useful tool in our attempt to explain the similarities and relationships between superficially different structures and languages.

In our analogy a space-map is occupied by workers, but the elements of a space-map can be passive objects also—for example, variables or drill presses. If some worker needs to have access to a drill press (or some statement needs a variable), the worker and the drill press should be part of the same space-map (they should share one lifetime, arrive and depart at the same time)—*or* the drill press should be part of a longer-lasting space-map that *includes* the worker's. That way, whenever the worker reaches for the drill press, he's guaranteed to find it. We will also use space-maps to understand the idea of *parallelism*—when two workers who are part of the same space-map execute simultaneously, they are part of a "parallel program."

In a time-map, we don't say merely that n statements execute at n different times; we also prescribe some particular *order* of execution. A space-map, similarly, doesn't merely involve n separate places; the places occur in a particular order, which is determined by the way in which we specify the structure. The fact that space-maps impose a particular spatial arrangement means that we can use them to model the idea of a simple *data structure* as well the idea of a scope or a parallel program. In a simple data structure (like a vector or an array), each element goes in some particular place relative to the others, just as, in a time-map, each element executes at some particular time relative to the others. Returning to our factory, a row of five parts-bins is a data structure, a "vector of parts bins," so to speak; five workers is a parallel program. In short, data structures and programs will be instances of the same kind of structure in the ISM.

We now look at the model in more detail, and in the course of doing so conduct a whirlwind tour of the programming language world.

2.2 The ISM Defined

An ideal software machine or "ISM" is a "space-map," a "time-map" or a simple expression. A "space-map" gives an arrangement of some elements in space; a "time-map" gives an arrangement of some elements in time. A simple expression may be a value or something that produces one, or it may be the "empty region" indicator, or it may be a template that can be used to stamp out new ISMs. "A value or something that produces one" means an element that (a) computes a value and optionally assigns it to a variable (*e.g.*, "$i := x + y$"), or (b) a plain value (*e.g.*, "12"). A value may be an integer like 12, or the Boolean value "true," or an array of real numbers, or (generally speaking) anything that accords with the intuitive meaning of "value" in programming. An "empty region" is indicated by the special element "$*$," meaning in essence that this region of the map is empty, and will have something put in it later. We will refine these definitions as we go along.

When we turn on a space-map machine, all regions of the map are turned on simultaneously and they evaluate together. The result is a new space-map in the same shape as the old one (see figure 2.1).

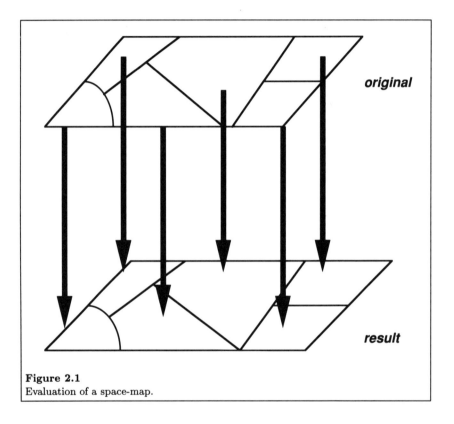

Figure 2.1
Evaluation of a space-map.

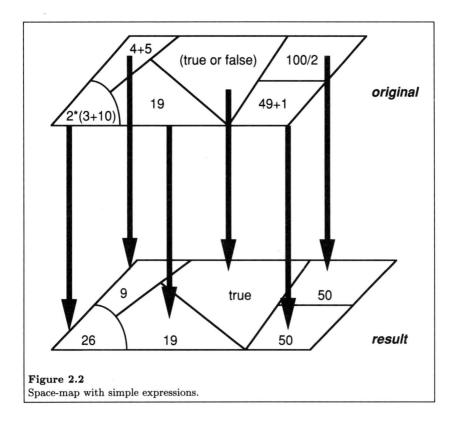

Figure 2.2
Space-map with simple expressions.

What goes inside a region? Any ISM. Thus an ISM is defined recursively:
you build a big ISM out of smaller ISMs. To "turn on" or to "evaluate"
a region means to turn on the ISM that is stored in the region.

Turning on a space-map, then, causes a bunch of ISMs to be turned
on and to evaluate together. In the new space-map that results, each
region holds the result obtained by evaluating the corresponding region
in the original map. Suppose we put a simple expression in every region
(remember that a simple expression qualifies as an ISM): the result is
shown in figure 2.2.

Regions may be given names, and they may refer to each other by name
as they evaluate (see figure 2.3).

The name of a region in the resulting map corresponds to its name in
the original. By referring to X, we mean "the contents of region X *after*

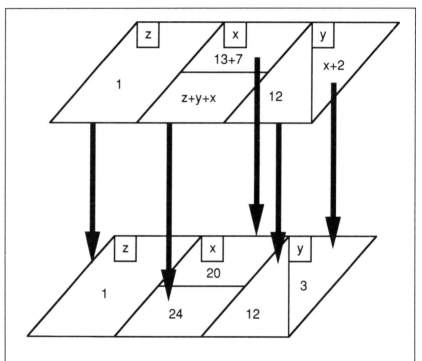

Figure 2.3
Space-map with named regions. Note that regions in the result map have the same
names as their counterparts in the original.

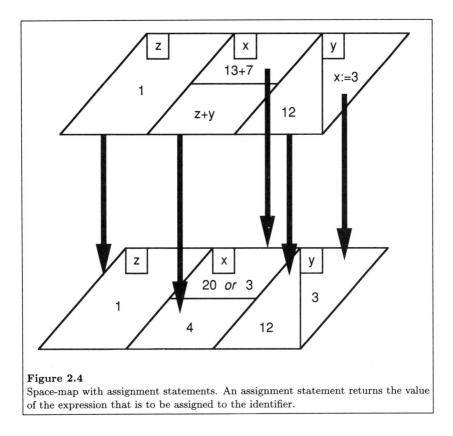

Figure 2.4
Space-map with assignment statements. An assignment statement returns the value
of the expression that is to be assigned to the identifier.

X is done evaluating." During the turned-on period, then, some regions
may have to wait for others. Executing an assignment statement causes
a new value to be dropped into a region (the old one is erased) (see
figure 2.4); the result of the assignment statement is this new value.

Regions may be given names, but this isn't required. We can locate an
unnamed region (if we need to) by position: as in any map, the elements
of a space-map machine have well-defined and unique positions. One element may refer to another by name, or it can refer to another element as
(for example) "the seventeenth element from the left." Space-maps may
be structures in a space of arbitrary dimensions. They may be three-
dimensional, then, or planar. Most of the space-maps we discuss will be
linear since these maps correspond most closely to the structures found
in modern languages. It's convenient to provide a standard graphics-

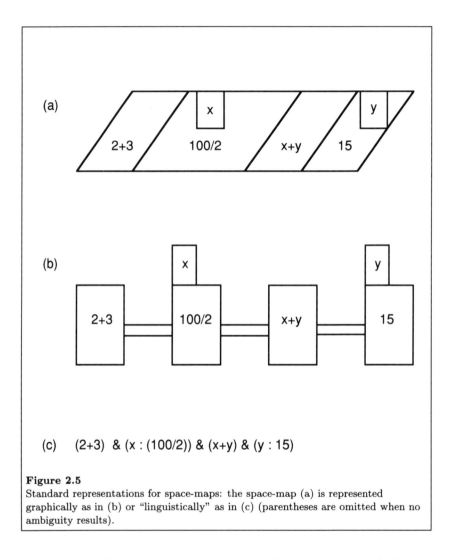

Figure 2.5
Standard representations for space-maps: the space-map (a) is represented
graphically as in (b) or "linguistically" as in (c) (parentheses are omitted when no
ambiguity results).

style and standard language-style notation for linear maps, which we
give in figure 2.5.

The fact that two regions are parts of the same space-map is an important kind of relationship. If two regions C and D are part of the same
space-map (whether or not they are adjacent), we say that "C SSM D
is true," or "C SSM D" for short (in the same way that we can say either

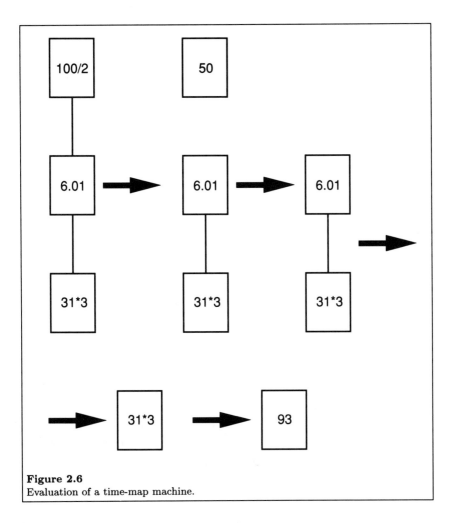

Figure 2.6
Evaluation of a time-map machine.

"$x = y$ is true" or simply "$x = y$"). (Technically, SSM is an *equivalence relation*, like "equals.")

We turn now to time-map machines. When we turn one on, its first region is evaluated and disappears; then its second region is evaluated and disappears, and so on in sequence. The result is the value yielded by the last region (all other regions having vanished) (see figure 2.6).

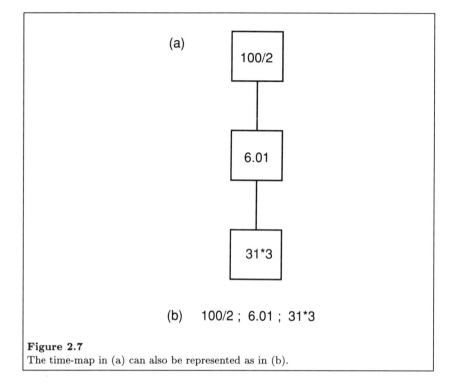

Figure 2.7
The time-map in (a) can also be represented as in (b).

Time-maps may only be linear—if two events occur at two separate times, one or the other is first; there are no other choices. Figure 2.7 gives a standard notation for time-map machines.

It's possible to give names to time-map regions (on analogy with "the seventeenth century," which is the name of a time period, as opposed to "Brooklyn," which is the name of a place). In practice we never use this capability, because real languages have nothing comparable (in the abstract they could, but they don't), and our goal is to model and understand real languages.

An example. Consider a Pascal program that tests Newton's method for approximating square roots. The program generates 100 random numbers, calculates the square root of each and prints out the result. (This example is based on one given in [30].) We'll consider variations and refinements of this program as we go along.)

The program works as follows. The main body executes 100 iterations of a loop. On each iteration, it invokes a function called "random" to get a random number, prints the random number, invokes a function called "Newton" to get the square root of the number, prints the square root, and goes on to the next line of output. One more detail: the random-number generator relies on a variable called "seed." Each time the "random" function is called, "seed" is modified, and the random number returned is based on this newly modified value.

In outline, the program will be

```
Program TestNewton;
    var   the number we want the square root of ;
          the seed ;
          a counter for the trials ;
    function Random;
          update the seed and return a new
              random number ;
    function Newton;
          accept a number and return its
              square root ;
begin
    initialize the seed ;
    for each of 100 trials
          pick a number using Random ;
          print the number ;
          compute and print the square root
              of the number using function Newton
end.
```

The program is shown in figure 2.8. We omit the text of the function definitions. They aren't important here; we consider the text of Random later on, however.

The ISM version of this program is shown in figure 2.9. We have structured it as a space-map with six regions. The first three regions are initially empty; we use the symbol "*" to indicate an empty region. The next two regions hold function definitions. In the ISM, a function definition is a blueprint; to invoke the function means to construct and then

```
Program TestNewton;
   Const initial_value = 10;
         trial_count   = 100;
   Var n, seed, count: integer;
   Function random: integer;
       return a positive pseudo-random integer,
       updating seed;
   Function newton (number: integer): real;
       return an approximation to the square root
       of number, using Newton's method;
   begin
     seed := initial-value;
     for counter := 1 to trial-count do
         begin
           n := random;
           write(n:6);
           writeln(newton(n):12:5)
         end
   end.
```

Figure 2.8
TestNewton in Pascal.

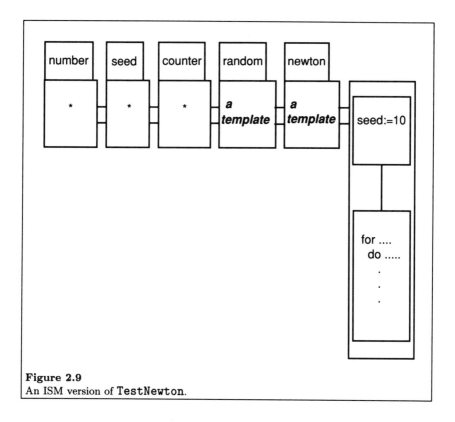

Figure 2.9
An ISM version of `TestNewton`.

execute the blueprinted machine. We discuss this later. The last region holds a time-map.

When we turn this machine on, we evaluate the contents of all six regions simultaneously (figure 2.10). In the first three regions there is nothing to evaluate; these regions sit passively—they serve as empty boxes in which values can be kept. To evaluate the next two regions, we need to "evaluate" two blueprints. An ISM blueprint evaluates to a slightly modified version of itself; the result is a "working drawing" (so to speak) that can be used directly in constructing new ISMs. (We explain the slight alterations in Section 2.3.6.) To evaluate the last region, we evaluate the time-map it holds, executing each instruction in sequence until we get to the end.

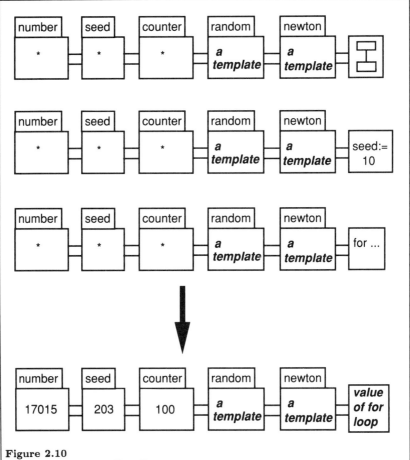

Figure 2.10
Evaluation of the ISM TestNewton program. In the resulting space-map, the
regions named n, seed and count hold the final values of these variables. The
random and newton regions hold the same templates they started out with. The
last region holds whatever values happen to be returned by a for statement.

We insisted that all regions in a space-map evaluate simultaneously—
they are all turned on during exactly the same interval of time. In this
example, only one of six regions actually does anything. But the fact
that the machines are all turned on during the same interval is still
fundamental: it means that the last region can freely refer to the others
and be assured of finding them. It can store values into, or read values
out of, the region named **seed**; it can invoke the function contained in
the region named **random**. All six regions must share the same lifetime
because the first five must be available *for as long as the last region
needs them.*

In the first section following, we define and discuss basic program structures. (This includes such subtopics as scope rules, block structures,
records, modules and concurrent programs.) In the second we discuss
subroutines; in the third, data structures, values and types.

2.3   Program Structure in the ISM Model

We have already shown the basic structure, in ISM terms, of Algol 60
and Pascal programs. In both languages, a program consists basically
of a list of name definitions followed by an executable statement that
draws on these definitions. In Algol 60, the things being defined (the
objects given names) are variables and procedures. In Pascal, we can
give names to constants and types as well. We discuss the meanings of
these different schemes and their implications later. What is important
here is that in the ISM, a series of definitions followed by an executable
statement translates into a space-map. All regions of the map but the
last have names. When we evaluate the map, the named regions sit
passively; the last region, which holds the executable statement, draws
on the named regions as it executes.

ISM translations are *not* identical to the originals. One important distinction is that an ISM program always yields a value. The ISM version
of **TestNewton** yields a six-element space-map as its value; the Pascal
version yields nothing. It is executed only "for effect," for the actions
it takes while it evaluates, namely printing some lines of output. (The
ISM version also prints the lines of output, of course). Another difference is that Algol 60, Pascal and virtually all other languages insist on

distinctions that are not present in the ISM. In Pascal, a variable declaration and a function definition are syntactically very different, and
each can occur only within its own designated section of the program.
In the ISM, variable declaration and function definition are each merely
named regions; they may occur anywhere, in any order.

There are numerous other differences between the translations and the
originals. Despite these differences, the ISM version captures the essence
of the Pascal program. The same algorithm is used to perform the same
computation. The same variables and functions are used; the same
output is produced. The ISM is useful because, though it's not identical
to (say) Pascal, it can be used to capture in a rather simple way a far
wider range of program types and structures than Pascal itself can; and
the same holds for other real languages vis-a-vis the ISM.

The coarse structure of Algol 60 and of Pascal programs do differ in one
obvious way: Pascal programs have names; Algol 60 programs define
a series of names, but don't themselves have names. In the ISM this
distinction is easy to capture. It means that Pascal programs will be
modeled by single-region maps. The name of the single region is the
name of the program; the contents of the single region is the space-map
that defines the program (see figure 2.11).

The coarse structure of a program in Fortran or C is essentially the same
as that of an Algol 60 program, with one minor difference: Fortran and
C programs have no executable statement; they are merely a series of
name definitions. One of these defines a "special name" whose value is
a subroutine. When the program executes, this subroutine is invoked
automatically. In the ISM, this kind of program looks exactly like a
Pascal or Algol 60 program with the last (anonymous) region lopped
off.

2.3.1 Parallelism

Algol 60 and Pascal programs are space-maps with a single active region:
when we turn them on, one region is active and the rest sit passively,
waiting to be useful. Suppose we yank a passive region and replace it by
an active one. For example, we could remove the function called **random**

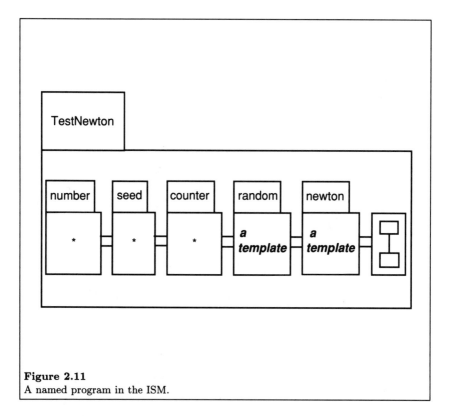

Figure 2.11
A named program in the ISM.

in `TestNewton` and replace it by a loop that calculates 100 random numbers and writes them in a file:

```
begin
    initialize the seed;
    for  each of 100 trials  do
      begin
          pick a number using random;
          write the number in a file
      end
end
```

The `random` function was merely the blueprint for a machine; this loop *is* a machine. Suppose we modify the loop that occupied `TestNewton`'s last region: instead of invoking the function `random`, it reads random numbers from the file (figure 2.12).

We now have a **parallel program**. It performs two activities simultaneously: generating new random numbers, and meanwhile computing the square roots of the random numbers generated so far.

The structure of a parallel program in the ISM is the same as any program's structure. If we remove passive regions and add active regions, we get parallelism. (As this example illustrates, it's not enough merely to create simultaneous threads of activity; the threads need a way to communicate. In the above example they communicate through the file system, but this is rarely an acceptably efficient possibility. In later chapters we discuss better techniques.)

     □ The structure of a parallel program in the ISM is the same as the structure of a sequential program. If every region of a space-map but one is passive, we have a sequential program; if there are at least two active regions, we have a parallel program. If we want A and B to execute in parallel, we can either (a) arrange for A SSM B to be true or (b) arrange for A and B to be regions nested within space-maps M and N such that M SSM N.

(We will use the "□" symbol throughout the book to introduce cases in which two superficially different ideas—within the same language or

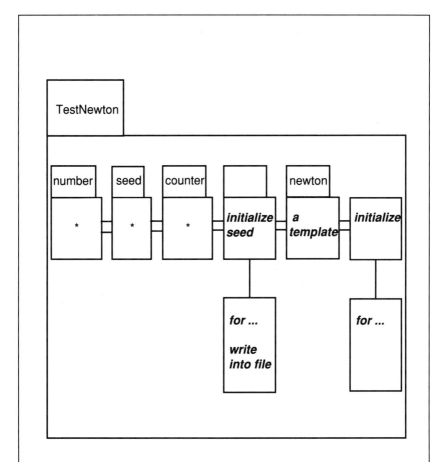

Figure 2.12
Parallel `TestNewton`. The last region must change to reflect the fact that it is now reading values from a file instead of invoking a function, but it might still be structured as an initialization statement followed by a `for` loop.

model or within two different ones—can be understood as variations on a single underlying idea.

2.3.2   Scope and Block Structure

Suppose we replace one element of a time-map with a complete space-map. Why would we want to do this? By nesting space-maps inside time-maps, we can be as specific as we like about the *scope* of a particular name.

The **scope** of a name is defined as the collection of statements that can see the name, hence can use the object it designates. In our original TestNewton, for example, count has global scope: it is visible throughout the program and can be used anywhere. In fact, though, it isn't needed everywhere; it's relevant only to the for loop. Suppose we take out the for loop and substitute a two-element space-map:

```
(    count: *
&    for count := 1 to 100 do loop body)
```

We can remove the original map's "count" region (see figure 2.13).

Given this version, the region called "count" leaps into existence only when we need it, during the execution of the loop. When the loop is complete, count disappears: its **lifetime** (or **extent**) is tied, by the structure of the space-map, to exactly the period of time during which the for loop is active. Its visibility is confined to the space-map containing the for loop.

Here, the practical implications of the change are slight. But suppose that TestNewton were a long and complicated program; it would read more clearly if count were declared where it is needed, and used as soon as it is declared, than if it were declared pages previously. More important, *conservation of names* is a crucial consideration in programming. A complicated program may deal with ten thousand separate objects, but we don't want to make up ten thousand separate names to designate them. There may be dozens of variables that work like counters; it would be nice if we could name each of them "count," and have the right "count" automatically come when we call.

Consider, for example, our parallel TestNewton. It includes two active regions, and each one executes a for loop. Each for loop needs

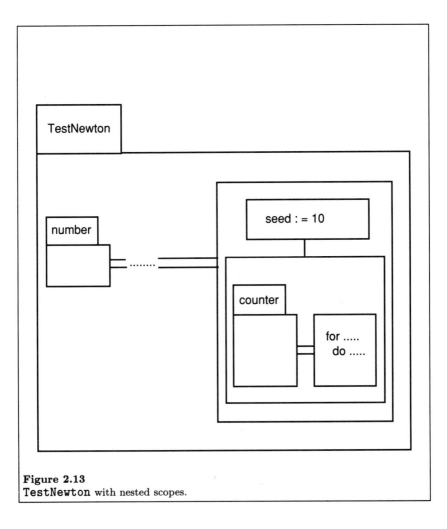

Figure 2.13
TestNewton with nested scopes.

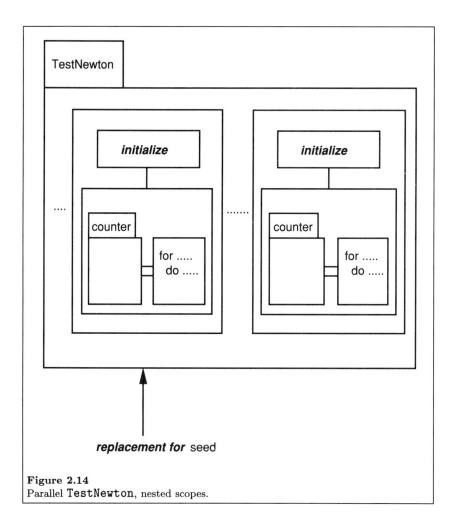

Figure 2.14
Parallel TestNewton, nested scopes.

a counter. We could declare a count1 and a count2; far more convenient, we could associate a count directly with each for loop, giving the
structure shown in figure 2.14.

The recursive definition of ISMs allows us to create named objects at
many levels. In order to take advantage of the ability, we should allow
regions to refer by name not only to regions in their own space-map,
but to regions in any surrounding space-map. Thus we should allow the
for loop in our modified TestNewton to refer not only to count, but

to regions in the encompassing space-map—for example, to the region called **newton**. One way to do this is by adding the following rule to the basic ISMs we've been dealing with:

Definition 2.1 *Name resolution rule.* To ascertain the meaning of name "N," check first for a region named N within this space-map; if there is none, check for N in the space-map that encloses this one, then in the next-enclosing space-map and so on. To override this search sequence— if we need to refer to a name that is defined within an adjacent region instead of within a surrounding one—the notation "X.N" means "look up name N within the region named X."

In general, if e is any ISM expression, we'll write X.e to mean "look up any name N referenced but not defined by e within region X."

This rule isn't a necessary part of the ISM, but it's sufficiently useful for us to assume it for the remainder of the discussion.

We can now use the ISM to model block-structured programs. A **block-structured** program has *hierarchical scopes*—we can declare a variable named N; within N's scope we can declare another variable N, and give this new N a scope that is nested inside the scope of the first Ns, and so on. The extent of each declaration of N is equal to the lifetime of the block in which they are declared; the scope of each N is limited to the expressions and statements found within the block in which it's declared.

Pascal doesn't have this capability; languages like Algol 60, C and Scheme do. Thus consider the C program-fragment

```
{
    int N; /* declare an integer called N */
    N = 5;
    {
        int N;  /* another N */
        N = 10; /* we're assigning to the nested N, */
                /* not the original */
        . . .
    }
    . . .
}
```

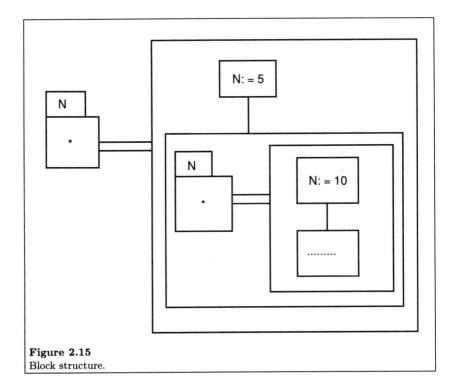

Figure 2.15
Block structure.

This translates into the ISM shown in figure 2.15.

In the ISM, then, we get block structure simply by nesting space-maps inside of time-maps.

In the ISM, to summarize, the regions that are within the **scope** of a name N are the regions whose lifetimes are guaranteed to be included within N's lifetime. These are the regions that are (a) in the *same space map* as the region named N, or (b) within any space map that is nested *inside* a region that is within the same space map as the region named N. That is, region R is within N's scope if

   Region-Named-N SSM R,

or

   Region-Named-N SSM *AnotherMap*,

and R is a region nested within *AnotherMap*. Thus

☐ In the ISM, the relationship between a region and other regions in its scope is the same as the relationship between two simultaneously executing pieces of a parallel program.

2.3.3 Records

If we can nest space-maps within time-maps, we can also nest them within space-maps. This operation might seem simple, but we have just discovered *modularity*, which is another basic crux in language design.

One simple kind of modularity is the sort we discover when we examine structures like the Pascal record. A **record** is a named collection of named fields, where a field can only be empty, a plain value or an expression that evaluates to one—but not a template. Thus in Pascal, we can create a record-structure to hold data on some person:

```
someone: record
            name: string;
            sex: (M,F);
            ssnum: integer
         end;
```

We can then put values in the fields of the record by a series of assignment statements, for example

```
someone.name := "winston";
someone.sex := M;
someone.ssnum := 123456789;
```

The names "name," "sex" and "ssnum" are defined not within the Pascal program at large, but within a special environment-like structure. This special structure itself has a name: "someone." We can find the value associated with the name "ssnum" inside environment "someone" by writing "someone.ssnum."

In the ISM, we would express something like this Pascal record this way:

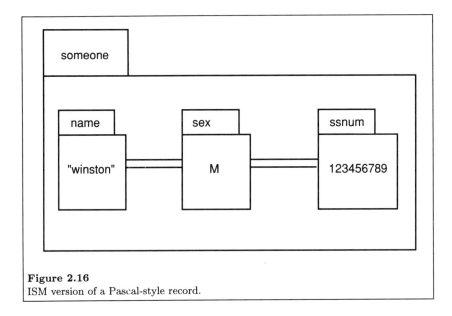

Figure 2.16
ISM version of a Pascal-style record.

```
someone: (  (name: "winston")
         & (sex: M)
         & (ssnum: 123456789) )
```

(See figure 2.16.)

We immediately notice two things. First, in the ISM, a "record" is simply a named space-map, nested inside another space-map. Second, in the ISM, the structure of a Pascal-type *record* is in essence the same as the structure of a Pascal-type *program*. They are both simply space-maps. Pascal didn't acknowledge this fact, and (partly) as a consequence, it allows things in a "program" space-map that are illegal in a "record" space-map. For example, a program can include fields that have procedures or functions as their values; a record can't. This turns out to be a crucial limitation.

☐ In the ISM, a Pascal-style record is simply a named space-map, with certain restrictions on its fields. If K and L are fields of the same record, then K SSM L.

2.3.4   Objects or Data Systems

As soon as we allow subroutines as well as passive data-fields into our records, we get what is usually called an **object**. This idea originated in the important language Simula 67. An "object" is a record that can "do things"; it is an entity that can be instructed to transform itself in a set of well-defined ways.

We will generally refer to this kind of object as a **data system**. A data system includes some variables, some subroutines that are designed to manipulate these variables, and (optionally) an executable statement.[1] The statement is executed when the data system is instantiated; ordinarily, it initializes variables within the data system. The subroutines in a data system are tailored to the particular role the data-system is intended to serve: a "bank account" data system might contain procedures to deposit or withdraw money; a "pushdown stack" data system might contain procedures to push and pop the stack. In the ISM, a data system is simply a space-map that includes both variables and procedures among its fields.

□ In the ISM, a data system or "object" is (another) restricted form of space-map.

Thus, we could rewrite "someone" this way:

```
someone: (   (name: ''winston'')
         &   (sex: male)
         &   (ssnum: 123456789)
         &   (ChangeSex:
                  a function that executes
                  (  if (sex = male)
                     then sex := female
                     else sex := male)) )
```

---

[1]The word *object* is, unfortunately, both useful and ambiguous in discussing programming languages. When we refer to "data objects," we mean *any* value or collection of values that can be given a name—an integer, an array, a record and so on. But *object* is also used within the "object-oriented programming" community to refer specifically to what we've called a data system. Occasionally we will use the word in this special sense; its meaning should be clear from context.

We discuss functions later on, but given this definition,

```
someone.ChangeSex()
```

carries out the necessary operation.

2.3.5   Modules and Libraries

Now that we can include subroutines in our records, we can build records
that consist *only* of subroutines. For example, we can build a "math
library":

```
mathlib: (  sin:   function to compute sin
         & cos:   function to compute cos
         &  so on... )
```

"Module" generally refers to any well-defined piece of a larger program.
A compiler, for example, usually includes a section that performs "scan-
ning," another that does "parsing" and a third that does "code generation." So we might describe a compiler as a program that consists of
three modules:

```
compiler: ( scanner:  ...
         & parser:   ...
         & code-generator:  ...  )
```

A module, again, is merely a space-map. Generally, a data system may
occur many times within some program (you may need to define many
persons, bank accounts and so on), but a module is a named set of fields
that occurs only once. A **module**, in other words, can be defined as *a
named sub-set of related fields* within a larger program. A **library** is a
module that is intended for inclusion within many different programs.

Let's return to TestNewton. In the example given earlier, TestNewton
follows each call to the Newton approximation function with a call to the
built-in routine sqrt that is provided as part of the Pascal library—the
program executes the invocation newton(num) and then the invocation
sqrt(num), intending to compare the two.

What does it mean to call a function that is part of a library? The
programmer is invoking a function he didn't write, whose definition is

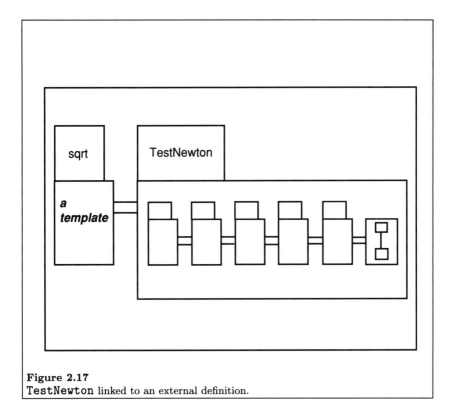

Figure 2.17
`TestNewton` linked to an external definition.

not part of his program. To make the program work, he has to *link* his program to the Pascal library—connect it to another program in which `sqrt` is defined. (He may do this explicitly, or the system might do it for him automatically.) In the ISM, the result of linking a program to an external definition is simply another space-map (see figure 2.17). There's no reason why a statement can't search beyond the bounds of its own program and enter a wider space-map in the quest for a name's meaning; space-maps can properly include programs, as well as be included by them.

□ A module or library in the ISM is a named space-map. To *link* two programs P and Q means to include them in the same space map: if P is linked to Q, then P SSM Q.

Data systems, modules and libraries are often regarded as fairly esoteric
or advanced language features. In fact, they're exceptionally simple and
basic. In studying real languages, we'll follow the complicated variations
and contortions through which language designers have passed in an
attempt to accommodate these simple, basic ideas. The ISM will make
plain how simple most of these seemingly complicated structures really
are, and how closely they are related to other basic language features.

2.3.6   Templates

We know how to build ISMs and evaluate them, but we need more.
Return to `TestNewton`: its space-map has a region named `random`. What
does this region hold? Clearly a *function definition*: an object upon
which we can perform the operation "execute" or "evaluate," just as we
can perform operations like "add" or "multiply" over integers.

In the ISM, a function or subroutine definition is simply a blueprint
for any arbitrary ISM. To invoke the function means to construct the
blueprinted machine and turn it on. We need a notation for blueprints;
we will write

> `template` $(arg_1, arg_2, \ldots, arg_n) < any\ ISM >$

to indicate a template with formal parameters $arg_1, \ldots, arg_n$, whose
body is *any ISM*. We refer to this template as an "abstraction" of *any
ISM*. An **abstraction** of some structure is a reusable description of (or
blueprint for) the structure, a template that captures the structure's
basic properties.

How do we evaluate a template? We've mentioned that a template yields
as its value a slightly altered version of itself. In the ISM that serves as
the template's body (the "*any ISM*" above), names occur; they may be
serving as name tags for regions, or they may occur in expressions. When
a name occurs in an expression—when we try to evaluate `foobar` $+ 3$,
for example—how do we know what the name means? The names that
occur within a template's body are *free*, *bound* or *local* with respect to
that template. A *bound* name is the name of a formal parameter (it
is one of the arg_i's). A *local* name is the name of some region that is
defined within the body of the template. A *free* name is neither. When
we encounter a free name, how do we know what the name refers to?

There are two possibilities: we can decide on the meaning of free names when we *define the template* or when we *apply* it (in other words, use the template to construct an ISM—invoke a function or a procedure). The former is referred to as *static scoping* or *lexical binding*; the latter is called *dynamic scoping* or *dynamic binding*. We'll discuss the implications of these two alternatives later. For now, we'll give a lexical-binding semantics to ISM templates.[2] To evaluate a template, we look at its body, find all the free names, cross them out and replace them with permanent references to the regions designated by the names in the template-evaluation environment.

Note that after a template is evaluated, its body contains no free variables. Besides template evaluation, the only other operation allowed on templates is application; a template, once evaluated, is a constant.

Application. If Q is a template of no arguments, we specify the operation "invoke Q" (that is, "build and turn-on machine Q) by writing Q(). Thus we can write

```
random: template ()
        <  an ISM that computes a random number  >
```

We return later to give a complete definition for random.

What do we do with the arguments to a function? Consider now a very simple parameterized function: say max is a function that, when given two integers X and Y, returns the larger (or returns either one if they're the same).

Suppose we specify a max template that carries out this simple computation. Once we've done this (we discuss how below), what kind of expression should represent the invocation of "max"? In particular, in what kind of structure should the actual parameters be stored? Should they be stored in a bag, a list, an array? The question is hard to grasp at first, because conventional programming languages don't ask it. In Pascal, for example, we would invoke max using the expression:

```
max(xexpr, yexpr)
```

---

[2] Readers familiar with the idea of *higher-order functions* might wonder how the ISM treats template-yielding templates. We'll defer this question for now, but will consider it in detail when we discuss Scheme in chapter 7.

and in Lisp we would write

```
(max xexpr yexpr)
```

but neither language has any conception of "a structure in which you
store actual parameters." The phrase Pascal uses to pass actuals—
"(xexpr, yexpr)"—is a non-structure, meaningless in itself. So is the
phrase Lisp uses. But in fact there are very definite rules that govern the
treatment of actual parameters, and almost all programming languages
agree on them. It is almost always agreed that

1. the temporal order in which actuals are evaluated doesn't matter,
   but

2. the *spatial* order in which they are presented *does* matter.

Suppose xexpr and yexpr are complicated expressions. In most programming languages, these expressions are evaluated before the body of
the "max" function starts executing, but most programming languages
refuse to commit themselves to any particular evaluation order: either
argument might be evaluated first. But on the other hand, it *is* guaranteed that once the two arguments are evaluated, they will be presented
to "max" in the specified spatial order. If they were swapped, "max"
would treat the xexpr as if it were the yexpr and *vice versa*.

In what structure can we embed xexpr and yexpr such that, when this
structure is evaluated, no guarantees are made about the temporal order
of evaluation, but the *spatial* arrangement of fields is guaranteed to be
preserved? The ISM does have such a structure, and it is of course the
space-map. In the ISM, we write

```
max(xexpr & yexpr)
```

We embed the arguments to a function in a space-map because space-
map evaluation imposes no temporal order but preserves spatial arrangement. (xexpr & yexpr) is a *program* that evaluates to

$$(\; value\text{-}of\,(\texttt{xexpr}) \; \& \; value\text{-}of\,(\texttt{yexpr}))\,.$$

We can take this latter space-map and match each of its regions pairwise
with each name found in max's argument list as we describe below.

□ In the ISM, the actual parameters to a procedure or function are regions in one space-map. If X and Y are actual parameters in the application of some function, then X SSM Y.

Note that in the ISM, arguments to a function may be evaluated simultaneously; in most conventional languages they are evaluated merely in unspecified order. This is another respect in which the ISM is not quite faithful to most real languages. But the ISM is a *direct generalization* of real languages, because being informed that "these expressions will be evaluated in some unknown order" is just one logical step away from being told that "these expressions will be evaluated simultaneously."

Most real programming languages maintain a confused silence on the issue of how, exactly, the arguments to a function are evaluated. We ordinarily know that "arguments in language X are evaluated in unspecified order" not because the designers of X stated this fact and explained it, but rather because they said nothing about the topic whatsoever. Lacking data on what the order is, we must infer that there is no order. It's not surprising, however, that most language reports do not tell us that "to evaluate the arguments to a function, we use the evaluation rule that imposes no temporal order but preserves spatial arrangement." The fact is that in most programming languages, *there is no such rule*; the rule has remained hidden, tangled up in the details of function invocation, never isolated and identified on its own; under these circumstances, the importance of the rule and its relationship to the rest of the language can't possibly be understood.

But in the ISM, such a rule does exist, completely independent of function invocation *per se*. The structure of the ISM makes it clear that the *actual parameters to a function* relate to each other in the same logical way as the *bindings that make up a program structure*. Both relationships hinge on *distinctness of place* and *concurrency of lifetime*, which in the ISM are facets of one structure. In most languages, argument evaluation appears to be a special phenomenon unrelated to anything else; this instance of related phenomena being treated as unrelated is evidence of *latent but unrealized simplicity* in programming languages, which will be an important topic throughout the book. But it is also true that, in the ISM, every argument list is a small parallel program. The

idea of concurrent evaluation *almost* exists in nearly every language, by
dint of the widespread use of a no-specified-order evaluation protocol for
function arguments. But it doesn't quite exist; and so we will observe
the phenomenon of conventional languages struggling to accommodate
parallel programming by introducing a galaxy of new structures, when
parallelism in fact lies buried just beneath the surface of structures they
already have. The *latent but unused power* in the structure of most real
programming languages is another central theme of this discussion.

> □ In the ISM, the *actual parameters to a function* relate
> to each other in the same logical way as the *bindings that
> make up a program structure*. (The relationship is SSM.)
> In the ISM, the *actual parameters to a function* have the
> same structure as a *parallel program* (the structure is a space-
> map).

We have resolved the structure of function invocation; what happens
afterward? A function is a *template*. It causes the construction and
evaluation of a particular space-map. This space-map yields as its
value another space-map. But functions are generally designed to return some special, designated value. Many languages use the statement
"return(x)" to designate x as the special value to be returned; we adopt
this same notation for this discussion. Executing "return(x)" causes
the specially-constructed space-map to be torn down and thrown away,
and x to be returned as the value of the function invocation.

Our "max" function can be specified this way:

```
max: template (x,y)
        <if (x > y)
            then return(x)
            else return(y) >
```

When we evaluate max(xexpr & yexpr), xexpr and yexpr are evaluated
simultaneously, and then the following space-map is constructed and
evaluated:

```
(x :  value-of (xexpr)) &
(y :  value-of (yexpr)) &
if x > y
   then return(x)
   else return(y)
```

This is a three-element space-map and (as always) it yields a three-element space-map as its result. But we throw this latter space-map away, and return the value of the expression following **return**. This point is important as we proceed to the next section.

Figure 2.18 gives Pascal and ISM versions of the **random** function.

2.3.7   Data Structures

What is a value? We've said that ISM regions may hold values or expressions, but we haven't said what values are. Clearly a value may be one element drawn from a pre-supplied collection—it may be a single integer, say, or a single Boolean. But there will obviously be occasions when we need multi-element variables too—arrays, records, lists and so on.

The varieties of structured variables supplied by a language, together with the operators supplied to manipulate them, define the language's approach to data structures. We can generate a large collection of possible data structures; each language will have to include some and leave the rest out, for the user to program himself if he needs them. We'll discuss various approaches when we take up the languages they belong to. What we're interested in here is the grand design: how do a language's data structures relate to the rest of the language, and how do they relate to each other? We will approach this problem in the framework of the ISM.

The ISM doesn't need data structures. In the ISM, data structures are merely a subset of program structures. Exploring this contention leads to a final important instance of the latent power and the latent simplicity that lurk unrealized beneath the surface of real programming languages.

---

in Pascal:

```
function random: integer;
  (*   return a positive pseudo-random integer,
       updating the variable Seed *);
  const modulus = 65536;
        multiplier = 25173;
        increment = 13849;
  begin
    seed := ((multiplier*seed)+increment) mod modulus;
    random := seed
  end;
```

---

in the ISM:

```
random : template ()
   <    (modulus : 65536)
     &  (multiplier : 25173)
     &  (increment : 13849)
     &  return (seed := ((multiplier*seed)+Increment)
                           mod modulus)
   >
```

Figure 2.18
Random in Pascal and in the ISM.

We begin with the Pascal record. We've already discussed this structure under "modularity"; we looked at the record as a little module (a named sub-environment within a larger environment), but most languages treat records as data structures. To support records, we didn't need to add a new structure to the ISM; we simply wrote a program that had all the properties of a record. Thus

```
someone: (  (name: "winston")
         & (sex: M)
         & (ssnum: 123456789) )
```

is an ISM *program*—it is an expression, it can be evaluated. It consists of a named machine. To evaluate the machine, we create a space-map and evaluate its three elements simultaneously. Each one evaluates to itself (*i.e.*, "winston" is a constant value of type string, and constants evaluate to themselves, and likewise for each other field). So the whole structure evaluates to itself.

To construct a record, then, we assemble all the necessary fields, line them up and connect them with "&"—that is, we connected them into a space-map. In building a record, the crucial point is the ability to access each record element *by name*; a space-map gives us this power. Now: how should we construct an array? In what structure should we embed the values that make up an array? The crucial point here is that an array structure must hold things in a *fixed, predictable order*. A *space-map* is (once again) the right structure for holding array elements: each element of a space-map occupies a fixed and predictable location. In other words, if Q's value is a vector (or one-dimensional array) of five elements, say the integers 10, 9, 8 , 7, 6, it's natural to represent Q this way:

```
Q: (10 & 9 & 8 & 7 & 6)
```

Given this representation, it's possible to define Q[i] as the ith element of Q—possible because, as long as Q is at least i elements long, its ith element is a fixed, well-defined entity. So a space-map can be used to store an array. But notice that we have once again written a *program*. We haven't introduced a data structure, we've selected a particular *program* structure and used it for storing data.

(Note that it's possible—in fact usual, in formal treatments—to understand the ordering implied by an array in a completely non-spatial sense; we can define set-theoretic concepts of order and sequence that have nothing to do with any physical arrangement of parts. But we are intentionally bypassing this interpretation in favor of a simple physical one. The physical interpretation makes the relationships among data structures, maps, naming-environments and concurrent-execution structures clear. The mathematical interpretation doesn't address these relationships.)

Space-maps serve both for naming-environments and data structures. When we store a naming-environment in a space-map, the fact that the map has a particular spatial layout generally isn't important; we identify elements by name, not position. But it's impossible to write down a map without giving some order (just as we can't write a time-map without giving a temporal order), so spatial ordering is always inherent. We make use of it explicitly in building data structures and in evaluating templates.

In the ISM, then, data structures are the same shape as program structures. A k-element data structure will be represented by a k-element space-map. We can represent higher-dimension structures directly or we can build nested linear maps, which have a more convenient representation (see figure 2.19).

> □ In the ISM, a *program* and a *data structure* are instances of the same kind of structure, namely a space-map. Two bindings within one program structure relate to each other in the same way as two values within one data structure—the relationship is SSM.

Two bindings within one program structure relate to each other in the same way as *two values within one data structure*. Bindings in a program structure have concurrent lifetimes. Values within a data structure occupy distinct and well-defined places. *Distinctness of place* and *concurrency of lifetime* may be understood as two aspects of the same structure—namely of the space-map.

What follows from the principle? If we have a way to connect bindings into programs or modules, then we ought to have a way to connect

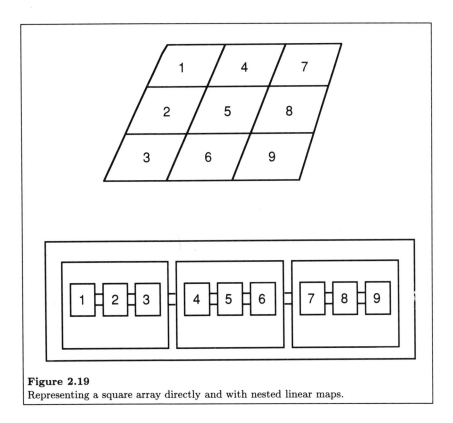

Figure 2.19
Representing a square array directly and with nested linear maps.

values into arrays. Most languages in fact handle the two cases in completely different ways. In APL, for example, bindings are connected
into *workspaces*, but there is no way to express the value of a complete
workspace; values are connected into arrays using an unrelated operation. In C, bindings are grouped into the program structure we described
above, and arrays are specified using a different kind of structure. In Pascal, bindings are connected into *programs*, values into arrays—and there
is no way to express the value of a complete *array*, reversing APL's situation. Inconsistency (as in C) and—more important—incompleteness
(as in APL and Pascal) are important themes in the study of languages
and their development.

Data parallelism. The principle that data and program structures may
be regarded as identical has another interesting consequence. It opens a
subterranean passageway that leads directly from simple data structures
into esoteric territory. *Data parallelism* is a strategy for writing parallel
programs that is usually associated with a brand of parallel computer
known as a SIMD (single-instruction, multiple-data) machine.[3] In data
parallelism, we program with "parallel data structures"; when we apply
an operation to a parallel data structure, that operation is applied to
every element of the parallel data structure simultaneously. Thus, to
take a simple example, if our parallel data structure is a ten-thousand-
element vector, and we choose to multiply it by 3, all ten thousand
multiplications may take place simultaneously. (Whether they actually
do take place simultaneously is irrelevant. The point is that they are
allowed to, if this is possible on the computer we are using.)

In the ISM, data parallelism is inherent in every data structure. Consider
the array we took up before:

    (10 & 9 & 8 & 7 & 6)

What happens when we multiply this array by 3? What does the expression

    3 * (10 & 9 & 8 & 7 & 6)

mean? If we decide that multiplication distributes over &, then

---

[3]The "Connection Machine" [59] is an example of such a computer.

```
3 * (10 & 9 & 8 & 7 & 6)  ⟹
((3*10) & (3*9) & (3*8) & (3*7) & (3*6))  ⟹
(30 & 27 & 24 & 21 & 18)
```

as desired. It is the middle form that is interesting. The middle form is a space-map; by the normal rules, it calls for all five multiplications to be performed simultaneously—as in data parallelism. All data structures in the ISM have data parallelism "built in," because they are represented by space-maps, and whenever we *evaluate* a space sequence, we evaluate all of its elements simultaneously. Adding data parallelism to the ISM would be simply a matter of defining distribution rules over space-maps. In the ISM, every data structure is a latent parallel program.

Systolic programs. We arrive in another esoteric domain when we reflect that, in the ISM, a program is a map of computation activities each with its own definite location. In the ISM model, it's legitimate to discuss programs in which an array Q is three elements to the east of a record R. A program in the ISM is a machine whose working parts are arranged in whatever fashion the programmer has specified. (We discuss the specific syntax used in the ISM to write programs of this sort in the appendix.)

It's therefore possible to use the ISM to express programs that have definite shape; these are usually referred to as *systolic* programs. A systolic program is a variety of parallel program in which many small computing elements work simultaneously; each element reads a series of input values from adjacent elements "upstream," and pumps a sequence of results to adjacent elements downstream. The physical arrangement of the elements is crucial, because elements deal with each other not by name but by *location*.

Most languages stitch programs together without any notion of *parallelism* between the pieces nor any notion of the *physical arrangement* of the pieces. From this point of view, systolic programs are a startling departure. But in the ISM, all elements of a space-map are evaluated in parallel, and the space-map imposes a definite spatial arrangement upon its elements; instead of a startling departure, systolic programming becomes a natural extension.

In sum, program structure (with its concomitant questions of binding, scope, modularity and so on) and data structure aren't really two separate fields; in the ISM, they're aspects of a single underlying structure.

2.4 Types

Programmers often feel the need to describe a value without specifying it; such a description is called a *type*. Types serve two purposes. The first has to do with efficiency and with debugging. If a programmer announces that a particular variable will take on values of type "integer" only, then the compiler knows exactly how much space values associated with that variable will require. It can also mention to the programmer any occasions on which he attempts to use his purportedly integer-valued variable in a non-integer way. A programmer who attempts to reference the fifth element of an integer using an array-style indexing operation, for example, has probably made a mistake in his code, and it is sporting for the compiler to point this out to him before he executes his program and it crashes.

The second reason has to do with replicating structures from templates. If we need to create many different variables with the same structure— all of these variables, say, will be 1000 × 1000 integer arrays, or records with two real-number-valued fields called "re" and "im" respectively— then it's convenient to create a new type and to treat this type as a template. If we create a template called "complex," and the template specifies a two-element structure with elements named "re" and "im," we can create many variables with this same structure by declaring that each one is of type "complex," rather than by spelling out the structure of each.

Languages that support data typing typically include a value-description language *distinct* from the value-yielding one.[4]

---

[4]There is good reason for maintaining such a separation. Consider a language that allows types to be treated as values—a language that permits types to appear as elements of data structures, or returned by function applications. What is the type of type-yielding expressions in such a language? If the type of such expressions is some "super"-type, call it **Type**, and types are themselves simply sets of values, to what set does **Type** belong? Pursuing such an analysis quickly leads to an intractable Russelian paradox—to what type does the type of all types belong? Clearly, we must

To begin with, we clearly need to describe values that are selected from
a pre-supplied set. We'll write

$$(r : *) \ ^{SomeSet}$$

to indicate that values to be stored in the region named r may only be
chosen from *SomeSet*. For example, most languages supply some version
of a set called "Integers" as standard equipment. If **int** is the name of
this set, we can write

$$(r : *) \ \textbf{int}$$

to express the fact that r will hold integers only.

Typed regions in combination with * provides a convenient basis for
a value-description languages, one that will allow us to examine many
typing issues in a uniform framework.

For example, given our type notation and the availability of *, we can
describe a value chosen from among any pre-supplied set, or we can
make up a set. Thus

$$(r : *) \ \{\textbf{red,violet,blue}\}$$

specifies that the value of r will be one of **red, blue** or **violet**, and so on.
Symbols appearing in the specification of one of these sets are assumed
to be constants (in the same sense that "3" is a constant); they evaluate
to themselves. Thus we can execute assignments like

r := red,

which assigns the constant **red** to r.

(Symbols occurring within type definitions can't serve as ordinary
variables—as the names of regions, in other words—within the scope
of the type definition. We can't name a region **red** within the scope of
the above definition.)

---

have such a type since we have expressions which yield types (not values) as their
result, and we must have some way of assigning a type to such expressions. Because
of the semantic difficulties that come from treating types as ordinary values, the
language of type-yielding expressions is usually treated as separate from the language
of value-yielding ones.

We can express structured types in the same way. We dealt above with
a Pascal-style record:

```
someone: (  (name: "winston")
         & (sex: M)
         & (ssnum: 123456789) )
```

Suppose we need to generate many records with this same structure; how
do we describe the structure? Pascal and many other languages have
so-called "record types," which describe the type of a record and allow
us to stamp out many record instances. In the ISM, we can describe the
someone record as one instance of a set of structures, each one of which
can be described this way:

```
(  (name: *) string
 & (sex: *) {M,F}
 & (ssnum: *) int )
```

We can construct a person-generating template by specifying a template
to stamp out this sort of structure:

```
person : template ()
                  <(  (name: *) string
                    & (sex: *) {M,F}
                    & (ssnum: *) int ) >
```

The type associated with this particular template is written thus:

```
() →
      [ name:  string,
        sex:   {M,F},
        ssnum: int ]
```

The → denotes a function type and the square brackets are used to represent space-map types. These operators are known as *type constructors*
because they build complex types out of primitive ones. Function types
range over sets of functions; space-map types represent sets of space-
maps. The particular set these types range over is determined by the
types of their components. We can use the above type description in
any place where primitive type expressions are allowed.

The type associated with **person** is an element of the set of functions which take no arguments and which return a three-region space-map. The first region of this map must be a string named **name**, the second must be named **sex** and its value must be drawn from the set {**M,F**}, and the third must be an integer named **ssnum**.

We create an instance of a **person** by evaluating **person()**. If J is an instance of a person, then the assignments

```
J.name  := "winston"
J.sex   := M
J.ssnum := 123456789
```

are legal, while the assignment J.name := 100, for example, is not.

□ In the ISM, a record-generator is simply a template whose body is a space-map; this space-map has typed fields that obey the general restrictions on the sort of fields that are permissible in records.

2.4.1 Classes

We've described a way of associating a type with a region and a way of generating instances of structure types from template definitions. There's more to typing than this, though. The description of a new value may include not only passive data fields, but a series of operations that may legally be performed on that type of value. Suppose, for example, that we need to introduce the operation **ChangeSex**, which is defined only over values of type **person**. One possibility is to associate this operation directly with each "person"-type instance. Thus we could write

```
person : template ()
              <        (name: *) string
                & (sex: *) {M,F}
                & (ssnum: *) int )
                & ChangeSex: template ()
                        < if (sex = male) ... > >
```

Each person now has a built-in *ChangeSex* field; the fact that templates are lexically-scoped means that the free occurrence of `sex` in `ChangeSex`'s body will refer to the region named `sex` in the instance map of which it is a part. If `FirstPerson` is an instance of this new definition of `person`, then

```
FirstPerson.ChangeSex(),
```

performs the requisite operation.

Our redefined and expanded `person` type is an instance of what is generally called a *class*; classes are templates that are used to stamp out instances of the data systems we discussed above.

2.5   Conclusions

It's not surprising that so many seemingly unrelated phenomena derive from the same deep, simple rules. It would have been surprising had this *not* been the case. For some reason there aren't many conceptual domains that can't be spanned by a fairly small number of powerful rules. They may be natural laws such as the conservation of energy, or engineering phenomena such as the basic energy-transducing mechanisms common to so many organisms, or abstract relations such as the Fibonacci series: superficial diversity should always awaken our suspicions. Programming language design occupies one tiny corner in the grand ballroom of science and engineering. But that corner is an interesting place and becoming more so. On the basis of this broad introduction, we investigate it thoroughly in the rest of the book.

Appendix A: A Micro-Manual for the ISM

The *Ideal Software Machine* (ISM) is one of the following:

1. A simple expression or a primitive value.

2. An assignment operation.

3. The special element, *.

4. A space-map.

5. A time-map.

6. A template.

7. *Grouping*: If E is an ISM, then so is (E).

Space-Maps

1. A space-map is an arrangement of elements in space. Each region in a space-map is itself an ISM. *Notation*:

   R$_1$ & R$_2$ & ... & R$_n$

   defines an n-region space-map.

2. A space-map value is a space-map in which each region is a value.

3. Evaluating a space-map yields the *same* map (with the same structure) except that each region in the resultant space-map holds the value obtained by evaluating the corresponding region in the original.

4. Regions in a space-map share the same lifetime (evaluate concurrently) but occupy disjoint space.

5. Regions may be given names. If N is a space-map, then "$N.x$" refers to the contents of the region named x in map N, *after* the region has evaluated to a value. A reference to a region named x not prefixed by "." is resolved to be the closest lexically-enclosing definition of x. In general, evaluating $N.x$ where x is an arbitrary

expression causes all names referenced but not defined within x to be resolved based on the names defined by N.

```
( x:1 & N:(y:2 & x:3) & N.y + x)  ⟶
( x:1 & N:(y:2 & x:3) & 3)
```

6. Regions may be accessed by absolute position. An n-element absolute address refers to a region in an $n-1$-level nested map (relative to the top-most map in the program).

```
(Program: (z:1 & (x:3 & 4) & [2,1] + [1]))  ⟶
(Program: (z:1 & (x:3 & 4) & 4))
```

The expression "[2,1]" refers to the first region defined in the map that occupies the second region in the program.

7. We can ask for the value of any region relative to any other. The expression ↑[1] refers to the region immediately to the right in which the expression is found; ↑[-2] refers to the region two to the left. Thus if we wrote a program of the form:

```
(... ↑[1].x  ...) &
( (x : 2)  ...  ↑[2,3] ... ) &
( ↑[-1].x ) &
( (f : 1) & (g : 2) & (h : 3) & (i : 4))
```

all four elements work simultaneously; the result after the program finishes would be (assuming that the initial bindings have not changed):

```
(... 2 ...) &
( (x : 2)  ...  4 ... ) &
( 2 ) &
( (f : 1) & (g : 2) & (h : 3) & (i : 4))
```

Time-maps

1. A time-map consists of a collection of regions with disjoint lifetimes (evaluate sequentially) but shared space. Each region in a time-map is itself an ISM. *Notation:*

$$R_1 \ ; \ R_2 \ ; \ \ldots \ ; \ R_n$$

defines an n-region time-map.

```
(x:1 & y:2 & (x := x + 1 ; y := x + 2 ; x + y))  ⟶
(x:2 & y:4 & 6)
```

2. To evaluate an n-element time-map, we evaluate the first region, then the second and so on. The result yielded by evaluating a time-map is the value of its last region.

Templates

1. Evaluating

```
(template (f₁, f₂, ... fₙ ) < Exp)>
```

yields a template with the same structure except that each free variable in *Exp* is replaced with a reference to its absolute position. Thus,

```
(Program:(z:1 & (template ( x ) < x + z >))  ⟶
(Program:(z:1 & (template ( x ) < x + [1]>))
```

2. Applying a template yields a space-map:

```
(template (x,y) < x + y> (3 & 4))  ⟶
(x:3 & y:4 & 7)
```

The actual arguments in an application are stored within a space-map. The actuals evaluate relative to the space-map in which the application takes place.

3. We can extract a specific region in a template application-generated space-map by using **return**:

```
(template (x,y) < return(x + y)> (3 & 4))  ⟶ 7
```

Empty Regions

An expression that attempts to read the contents of a region that contains a * simply blocks until some other expression deposits a value (via assignment) into that region.

(x:* & y:x & x := 10) ⟶
(x:* 10 & y:10 & 10)

Evaluation of the reference to x in the second region blocks until x is assigned a non-* value.

Types

Any region can be superscripted with a type specification that constrains the region to contain only values drawn from a specific type.

(x:* int)

constrains the region named x to contain only integer-type values. A type specification may denote a primitive type (*e.g.*, **int**, **Bool**, or **string**), a function type or a space-map type. A function type is written using →.

(int, int) → **Bool**

denotes the set of functions that take two integers as arguments and return a Boolean as a result. A space-map type is written using square brackets.

[x: int, y: Bool]

denotes the set of space-maps whose first region contains an integer named x and whose second contains a Boolean named y.

Thus, the expression

person : *[name: **string**, sex: {M,F}, ssnum: **int**]

constrains **person** to be a space-map with the type structure specified by its type declaration.

Appendix B: Formal Semantics of the ISM

Readers may skip this section without loss of continuity.

Our intuitive description of the ISM as a physical system with well-defined temporal and spatial characteristics can be made precise by examining the transformations made to the ISM program by an abstract ISM interpreter. In this short appendix, we develop a set of transformation rules that specify the semantics of the ISM. To simplify the presentation, it's convenient to consider a more abstract definition of a map. For the purposes of our formal semantics, we'll consider a map to be a special kind of graph. The structure of this graph (which we'll refer to as a *state-transition* graph) captures the concurrent evaluation semantics of space-maps and provides a simple way of visualizing the evolution of an ISM map-expression into a fully developed map-value.[5] The interpreter is embodied in a set of rules that specify transformations over a state-transition graph representation of an ISM program.

The space-map

```
( (x : 1) & (y : 2) & x+y) )
```

is represented by the graph shown in figure 2.20.

The graph consists of four circle nodes (called *places*), a single horizontal node (called a *transition*) and a set of edges that connect places to transitions. Except for the top-most place (known as the *root*), the places in a state-transition graph correspond to regions in an ISM map. Each non-root place contains a simple expression (*e.g.*, a constant, a variable reference, a template definition or an application) and may optionally be labeled with an identifier. A transition node acts as an interface to the other regions of a map. An s-labeled transition serves as the interface to the regions of a space-map; a t-labeled transition serves as the interface to the regions of a time-map. (There also exist a-labeled transitions that serve as interfaces to template-applications under evaluation.) Each place has a unique parent in the graph, though it may have any number of children. The parent of a place is always a transition and the parent of a transition is always a place.

---

[5] Readers familiar with Petri-net theory [103] will notice strong similarities between state-transition graphs and marked Petri-nets.

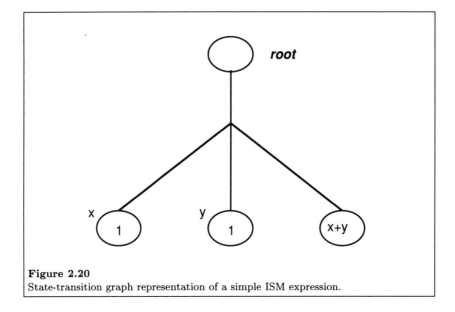

Figure 2.20
State-transition graph representation of a simple ISM expression.

A node whose incoming edge is labeled with a • (known as a *token*) is said to be *enabled* or *covered*. Our abstract interpreter transforms a graph containing enabled nodes by evaluating the expressions found within those nodes based on a set of transformation rules presented below. The semantics of the ISM follows from the transformation rules on state-transition graphs. The set of tokens in a graph defines the set of concurrently evaluatable expressions in the ISM program. In figure 2.21, the top-most transition node in the example graph is enabled; enabling the top-most transition in a graph corresponds to "activating" the program represented by the graph. Evaluating this graph results in the graph shown in figure 2.22; in this graph, the node corresponding to each region in the space-map has become enabled. The evaluation of this graph results in the graph shown in figure 2.23. Evaluating an enabled node that contains a value causes the token on its incoming edge to be removed. A graph whose edges contain no tokens and whose places contain only values corresponds to a fully-evaluated ISM program.

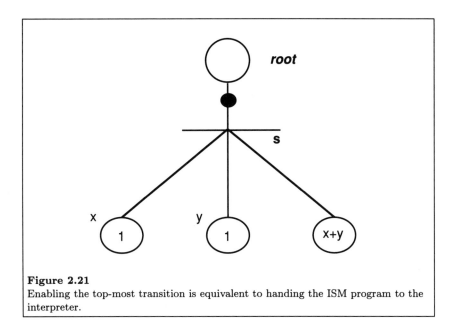

Figure 2.21
Enabling the top-most transition is equivalent to handing the ISM program to the interpreter.

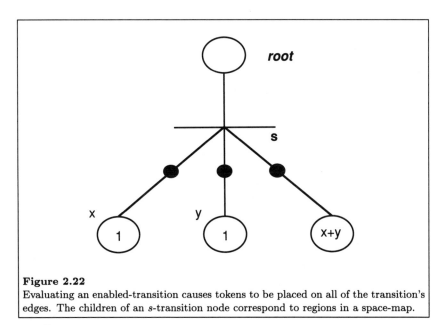

Figure 2.22
Evaluating an enabled-transition causes tokens to be placed on all of the transition's edges. The children of an *s*-transition node correspond to regions in a space-map.

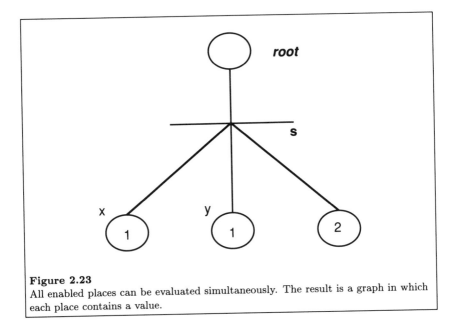

Figure 2.23
All enabled places can be evaluated simultaneously. The result is a graph in which each place contains a value.

Definitions

Before presenting the transformation rules on ISM-based state-transition graphs, we give precise definitions for some of the terms used informally above.

Definition 2.2 A simple expression is one of the following:

1. An identifier.

2. A constant of primitive type, *e.g.*, integer, Boolean, character, strings.

3. An expression of the form $[i_1, i_2, \ldots, i_n]$ where each of the i_k, $1 \leq k \leq n$ is an integer.

4. A template definition.

5. A template application.

Definition 2.3 We say that an identifier *id* is *free* in a phrase *e* if any one of the following conditions hold:

1. $e = id$.

2. $e = (id_1 : e_1)$, $id_1 \neq id$ and id is free in e_1.

3. $e = \texttt{template}(f_1, f_2, \ldots, f_n) < body >$, $id \neq f_i$, $1 \leq i \leq n$ and id is free in $body$.

4. $e = (e_1 \& e_2 \& \ldots \& e_n)$ and id is free in e_i, $1 \leq i \leq n$. (A similar condition holds for time-maps.)

5. $e = f(a_1 \& a_2 \& \ldots a_n)$ and id is free in a_i, $1 \leq i \leq n$.

6. $e = [x_1, x_2, \ldots, x_n]$ and id is free in x_i, $1 \leq i \leq n$.

7. $e = e_1.id_1$ and $id_1 \neq id$ and id free in e_1.

Definition 2.4 We define a value inductively as follows:

- Elements of primitive type are values. Thus, integers, Booleans, reals, *etc.*. are values.
- If $v_1, v_2, \ldots, v_n$ are values, then

$$(v_1 \& v_2 \& \ldots v_n)$$

is a value.
- Let $T = \texttt{template}(f_1, f_2, \ldots, f_n) < body >$. Then T is a value if there exists no variable free in T.

Definition 2.5 A *state-transition graph* (*STG*) is a triple (r, V, E) defined as follows:

1. $r \in V$ known as the *root*.

2. V is a finite set of nodes, $\{n_1, n_2, \ldots, n_k\}$ where each n_i, $1 \leq i \leq k$ is either

   (a) A pair, (l, e) (known as a *place*) where
      i. l is an identifier or the special symbol ϕ.
      ii. e is a simple expression or a value.

(b) An element (known as a *transition*) drawn from the cross-product of the sets $\{\mathbf{s}, \mathbf{t}, \mathbf{a}\}$ and $\{Id \cup \phi\}$, where Id ranges over identifiers.

3. E is a finite set of edges, $\{e_1, e_2, \ldots, e_j\}$ where each e_i, $1 \leq i \leq j$ is a triple, $((v_1, v_2), i, type)$ where v_1 and v_2 range over V, i is a positive integer (known as an index), and *type* ranges over the set $\{\bullet, \psi\}$.

Notation. In drawing our graphs, we will use the meta-variables

- e to range over simple ISM expressions (if e is written within a place) and to range over general ISM expressions otherwise;

- v to range over values;

- x and f to range over identifiers; and

- i to range over integers.

Meta-variables may be freely subscripted. We'll omit drawing the null-labels ϕ and ψ as well as the index label on edges unless they are relevant to the discussion. An expression (or value) meta-variable enclosed by a $\triangle$ symbol denotes the STG graph representation of that expression (or value).

Values

We illustrate the transformation on an STG with an enabled place containing a value in figure 2.24. The transformation does not change the contents of the value-holding place, but does cause the enabled token to be consumed.

Identifiers

An identifier reference reduces to the value to which it's bound in the environment in which the reference occurs. Figure 2.25 illustrates the transformation on an STG with an enabled place that contains an identifier reference. Our figure depicts an STG schema—the dots connecting

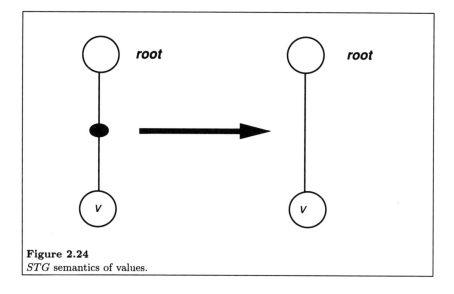

Figure 2.24
STG semantics of values.

the sub-graphs shown in the figure represent an arbitrary sub-graph; we assume that the place labeled x at the top of the graph does not occur in the sub-graphs denoted by the dots that precede the reference.

It's also possible to ask for the binding-value of an identifier in an arbitrary map by using the "." notation. We define the transformation in figure 2.26. The **a**-transition applies the "." operator to the arguments M and x. The value yielded by the application replaces the application graph. (The transition rules for general template application and return is described below.)

Space-Maps

We illustrate the transformation on a general space-map in figure 2.27. The evaluation of an enabled s-transition results in the placing of tokens on the outgoing edges of this transition. This transformation captures the parallel evaluation rule for space-maps—each region in an evaluating space-map executes in parallel.

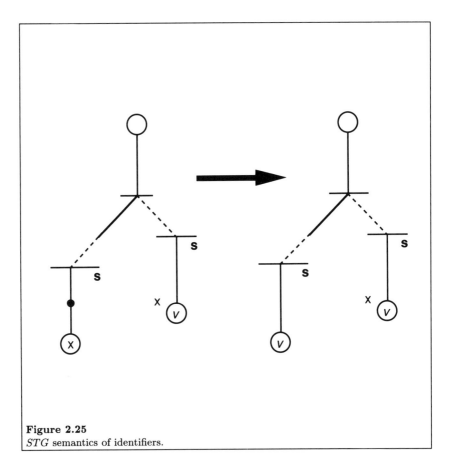

Figure 2.25
STG semantics of identifiers.

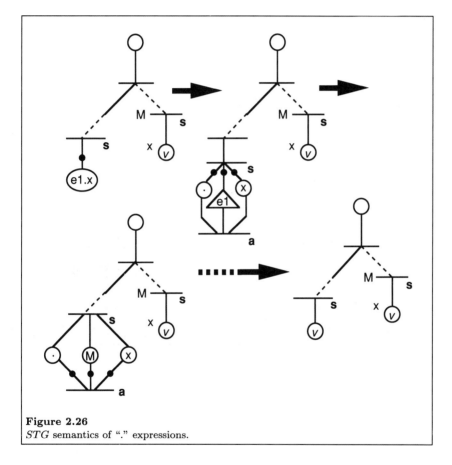

Figure 2.26
STG semantics of "." expressions.

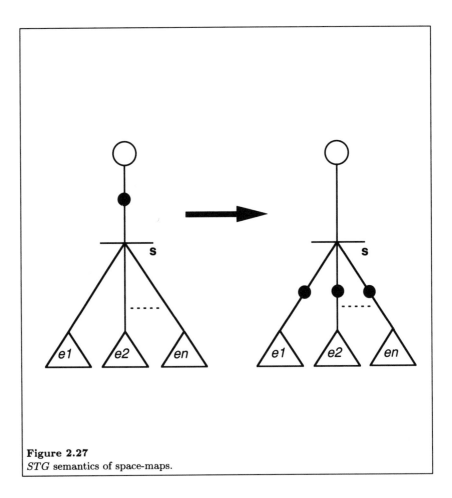

Figure 2.27
STG semantics of space-maps.

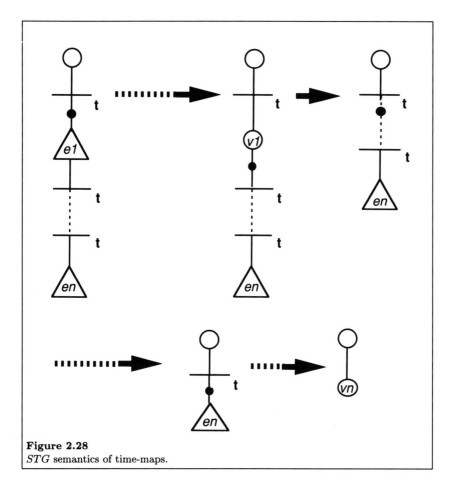

Figure 2.28
STG semantics of time-maps.

Time-Maps

The STG interpretation of time-maps is given in figure 2.28. A time-map is represented as a chain; the ith element in a time-map is evaluated only after the $i-1^{st}$ region completes. When all regions in the time-map finish evaluating, the time-map graph is replaced with the value of the last element in the chain.

Example: Figure 2.29 gives the structure and transformation of the following ISM program:

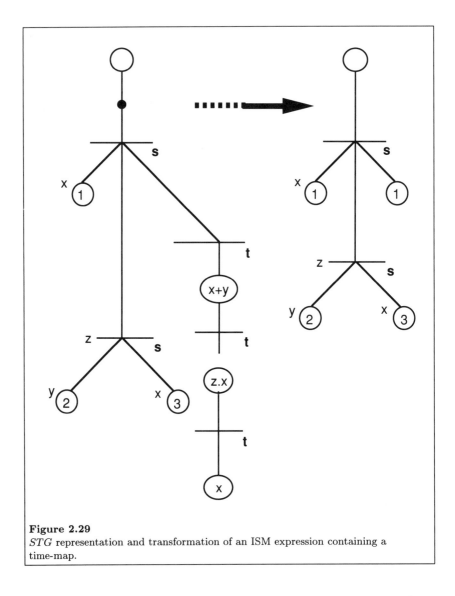

Figure 2.29
STG representation and transformation of an ISM expression containing a
time-map.

```
( (x : 1) &
  (z : (y : 2) &
  (x : 3)) &
  ( (x+y) ; z.x ; x) )
```

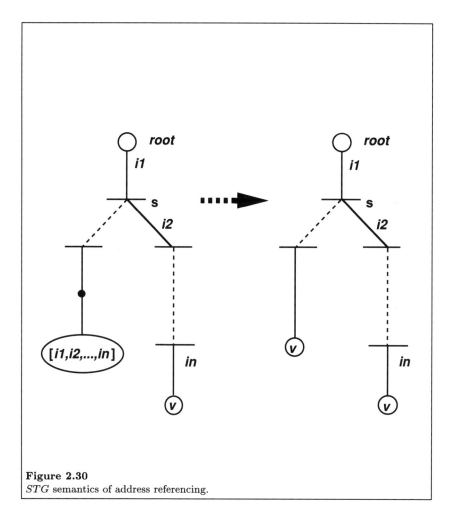

Figure 2.30
STG semantics of address referencing.

Position-Dependent Addressing

The transformation shown in figure 2.30 illustrates the semantics of position-based addressing. To simplify the presentation, we assume that the indices have been reduced to integers.

Template Application

To simplify the presentation, assume that all free variable references
in templates have been suitably transformed into a position-based reference. We show the transition semantics of template application in
figure 2.31; the a-labeled transition indicates that the places it is connected to are evaluating sub-expressions of an application. To evaluate
an application, we first construct a space-map to evaluate the actuals
and the template-yielding expression. Once the actuals and the template have been evaluated, we construct a new space-map whose first
n regions are named with the template's n formals and whose body is
the $n + 1^{st}$ region. The a-transition is used to generate the application space-map when it becomes enabled, $i.e.$, when the actuals and the
template-expression have yielded values.

Return

Recall that the return operator causes the space-map in which it's found
to be replaced by the operator's argument. We illustrate its semantics in
figure 2.32. We treat an expression of the form return (e) as an application, and the rules for its evaluation follow those given for an ordinary
application $except$ that, instead of simply returning an instantiation of
the template in the form of a space-map, we replace the map in which
the expression occurs with the value of return's actual.

Conditional Expressions

The transformation on conditional expressions is straightforward and
illustrated in figure 2.33.

Assignment

We illustrate the transformation of an assignment of an identifier to a
value in figure 2.34.

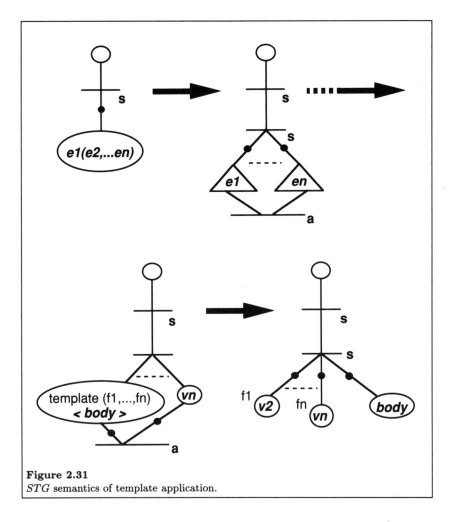

Figure 2.31
STG semantics of template application.

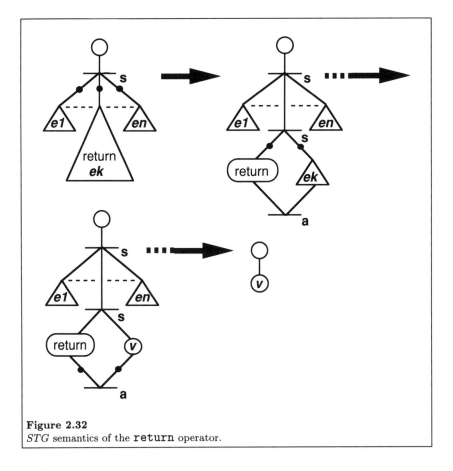

Figure 2.32
STG semantics of the **return** operator.

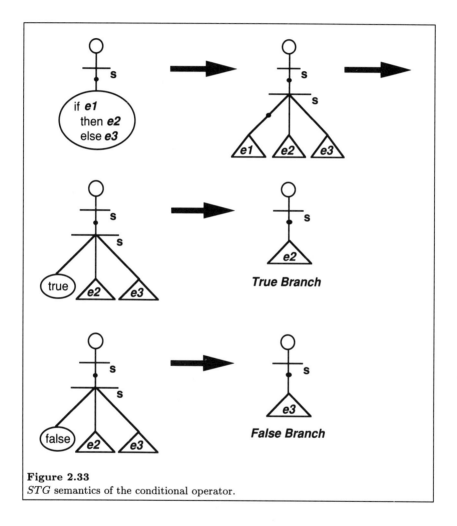

Figure 2.33
STG semantics of the conditional operator.

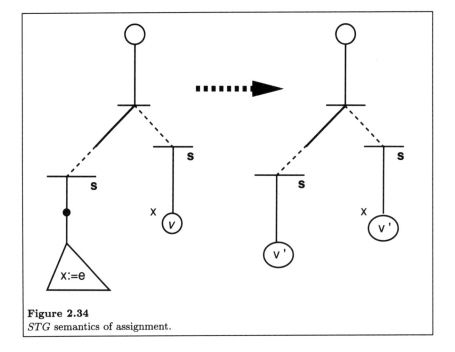

Figure 2.34
STG semantics of assignment.

3 Fortran, Algol 60 and Lisp

These languages lay the groundwork for all subsequent study of our two main questions. First, what does a program do—what are the objects it manipulates, and how does it manipulate them? Second, what kind of structure is a program?

Fortran and Algol 60 agree that a program operates mainly on numbers, often organized into arrays, by executing a list of statements. This is a natural viewpoint given the problem domains, mainly scientific computing in both cases, for which these languages were designed. Lisp originated a surprisingly different view: a program operates mainly on symbols organized into lists, where a symbol is represented by a character string (say `foobar` or `bazball`) which, unlike the strings that represent numbers, are completely arbitrary and have meaning only to the programmer. Lisp programmers manipulate these objects by evaluating expressions that produce new objects as their values.

As for the second question—what kind of structure is a program?— Fortran specifies static, "flat" structures that resemble assembly programs; Lisp, with its interpreter-oriented bias, starts life with a loose and somewhat unclear idea of what a program is. It is Algol 60 that happens upon the remarkable discovery that transforms programming: programs are recursive structures; big programs are assembled, according to well-defined rules, out of little programs.

Fortran was first described in 1957, but the Fortran under discussion here is basically the first version of the language to be standardized (Fortran IV, standardized in 1966); we also refer to Fortran 77, the later version which is today's most widely used Fortran. Algol 60 is the language described in the 1960 report. Many Lisp-like languages have grown from McCarthy's original 1960 proposal. The Lisp we discuss in this chapter is basically the Lisp 1.5 of 1965, although we refer also to "original Lisp," McCarthy's 1960 language. When we use the term "Classical Lisp," we are referring to Lisp 1.5 and all of its direct descendants through the mid-seventies.

3.1   Fortran

We investigate three basic propositions that characterize Fortran:

1. Fortran programs are static and "flat" or non-hierarchical in structure. We need to grasp this in order to understand that the principle of recursive structure discovered by Algol 60 is neither obvious
   nor strictly necessary to a programming language. (Dissatisfaction
   with one aspect of Fortran's "staticness" did, however, directly give
   rise to a new language, FLPL, that was Lisp's precursor.)

2. Fortran struggles toward an understanding of program structure
   from the direction of assembly programming. There are aspects of
   the Fortran design that aren't fully differentiated from assembly
   language.

3. The largest task facing Fortran's designers wasn't to specify an
   ideal programming language, but to demonstrate that the very
   idea of a programming language was plausible: to demonstrate
   that a programming language could be compiled into assembly
   code that was competitive in efficiency with hand-written assembly
   code. Thus (1) the main intellectual effort in the Fortran project
   was devoted to language implementation, not to language design,
   and (2) the language design reflects the central importance placed
   on *efficiency*. Fortran programs were expected, first and foremost,
   to be translatable into efficient object programs.

3.1.1   Fortran Profile

Program Structure. A Fortran program is a collection of subprogram
definitions. Some of the subprograms may be FUNCTIONs (they return
values), some may be SUBROUTINEs (which do not return values), and one
must be the "main program" subprogram, which is invoked first, automatically, when the program as a whole is executed. Subprograms
begin with variable declarations, continue with the definition of "statement functions" (functions defined by a single expression), continue on
to data-initialization statements and "FORMAT" statements (which are
used in conjunction with input and output statements), and then finally
to the executable statements that perform the actual computing.

The main abstraction devices in Fortran are subroutines and functions. A subroutine or function defines a computational unit that may be invoked many times from within the main program.

The subroutine definition

```
SUBROUTINE SWAP (I,J)
    M = I
    I = J
    J = M
    RETURN
END
```

swaps the integer values of I and J. (Fortran's type system has some highly idiosyncratic features, among them the fact that a variable need not be declared, and if it isn't, a type will be associated automatically with it based on the first character of its name. Variables beginning with I, J, ..., M are assumed to be integers unless otherwise specified; variables beginning with A, B, ..., H or N through Z are assumed to be reals.)

A function is structurally similar to a subroutine except for the header specification and a value-returning mechanism.

Arguments to a subroutine are always passed by reference; thus, any assignments to a formal parameter made within a subroutine are reflected in the actual as well. (If an actual parameter is an expression, as in the subroutine call

```
CALL BLAT(X+Y*Z)
```

which invokes the subroutine BLAT on an actual parameter whose value is given by X+Y*Z, the expression is evaluated, the result is stored in a temporary location, and the address of the temporary location is passed to BLAT.)

"Statement functions" are a special type of function: they are defined in a single expression (they have no internal naming environment—no local variables or definitions), and they are defined within and are local to some other subprogram. For example,

```
FUNCTION FOOBAR(X,Y)
   ...
   PLUS2(A) = A+2
   ...
   FOOBAR = PLUS2(X)
END
```

FOOBAR is a function-type subprogram; PLUS2 is a statement function, which may be used only within FOOBAR.

Fortran's subroutines differ in one significant respect from their counterparts in Algol or Lisp (or any of their derivatives): they can't be defined recursively. (That is, a subroutine may not invoke itself either directly or via another subroutine invocation.) This restriction allows the compiler to generate absolute addresses for all local variables and parameters of a subroutine; applying a subroutine with k arguments simply involves writing the addresses of the arguments in the k slots in memory that are to hold the value of the subroutine's formals.

In languages that allow general recursion, each application of a procedure requires the construction of a special-purpose *activation record* to hold the value of the arguments. (Clearly, if a new record were not constructed for each application, the value of the formals would be lost upon return from a recursive call.) In Fortran, on the other hand, invoking a procedure requires only (1) that references to the actual parameters and the return address be stored in the appropriate slots associated with the procedure being applied, and (2) that a jump statement be performed to the first instruction of the procedure.

Because application does not involve template instantiation, values of local variables are effectively preserved across different applications of the same procedure.

Data Types. Fortran supports a range of numeric data types (integer, real, double precision and complex); it also includes logical (or Boolean) variables, and Fortran 77 includes character strings. (Earlier Fortrans relied on something called "Hollerith data" to store characters. Character strings could be represented as constants, but there were no character-type variables; if characters had to be assigned to a variable, the variable would be declared to be some numeric type. The immortal Herman Hollerith is the inventor of the IBM-style punched card.)

The only complex data structure supported by the language is the array (and, in Fortran 77, the character string). Arrays may have up to seven dimensions; the fact that they are stored in memory in column-major order—first complete column, followed by second and so on—is part of the language definition, and is relied upon specifically by many Fortran programs.

Control Structures. Fortran's control-altering statements are simple relative to more modern languages. The main control flow statement in Fortran is the GOTO statement. GOTO l, where l is an integer constant, transfers control to the statement with label l.

More general iteration is expressed using the DO statement and computed GOTO. A DO loop of the form

```
DO 100 I = J,K,L
            statement-1
              ⋮
100         statement-n
```

executes *statement-1* through *statement-n* (K-J+1)/L times; in the ith iteration of the DO loop, I is bound initially to J, then to J+L, then to J+2L and so on, until its value exceeds K.

The computed GOTO statement:

```
GOTO (l₁,l₂,... ,lₖ) J
```

transfers control to label l_i if J's value is i.

Fortran also includes a minor variant on the computed GOTO. Execution of the IF statement

```
IF   predicate lₙ,l_z,l_p
```

causes control to be transferred to label l_n if the *predicate* evaluates to a negative integer, to label l_z if *predicate* evaluates to zero, or to l_p if *predicate* evaluates positive.

Statement labels and GOTO statements are important in Fortran because the language as originally conceived had no "statement bracketing" whatever: there was no way to parenthesize a group of statements and to treat the group as a unit. Accordingly it was impossible to write iteration statements that were expressed as "execute the following statement group n times," or conditional statements phrased as "if b is true, execute the following statement group." Iterations needed to be phrased instead as "do all the statements down to label j," conditionals as "if b, GOTO statement k." Modern Fortrans have added a more structured form of conditional that allows a list of statements to be treated as an implicit group, but the heavy use of GOTO statements remains typical of Fortran programs.

Common blocks. Because of Fortran's emphasis on efficiency, it's not surprising that the language allows programmers to lay out data objects in any way they wish. "Common blocks" are Fortran's way of arranging for globally shared data objects. All Fortran data objects are either local to a subprogram, or they inhabit a common block. A common block is a heterogeneous collection of data objects, which may (although need not) be named. Common blocks are declared in a rather peculiar way. Six subprograms may share access to a single common block named FOOBAR; each of the six must include a declaration for FOOBAR. Thus, although FOOBAR is a collection of data objects that is *external* to the subprograms that use it, it is declared *within* them—FOOBAR has no independent, external declaration. Each subprogram that uses FOOBAR may furthermore view the data objects within FOOBAR in whatever way it likes. If one subprogram includes the declaration

```
COMMON/FOOBAR/I,J,K
```

and another subroutine includes

```
COMMON/FOOBAR/LORK(3)
```

each of the two has access to the same common block, but the first subroutine views FOOBAR as consisting of three variables named I, J and K, the second as consisting of a single three-element array named LORK.

There is no dynamic allocation of data and no pointer type in Fortran.

Naming Environments. We illustrate the structure of the ISM map that corresponds to the Fortran program given above in figure 3.2.

```
PROGRAM MAIN
   ...
COMMON/BAR/X,Y/BLAT/Z
   ...
END
SUBROUTINE N1
   ...
COMMON/BAR/X,Y/BLAT/Z
   ...
END
FUNCTION N2
   ⋮
END
```

Figure 3.1
A Fortran program consisting of three subprograms and two common blocks. The subprogram headed "Program Main" will be invoked first when the program is executed. Common Blocks are global objects, like subprograms themselves; unlike subprograms, they aren't declared separately, merely cited by each subprogram that uses them.

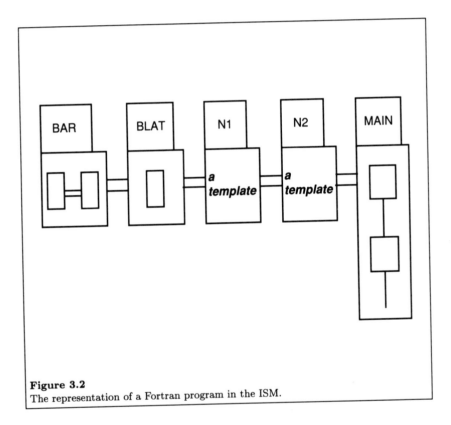

Figure 3.2
The representation of a Fortran program in the ISM.

When a Fortran program refers to a name, the name will designate either a data object that is local to this subroutine or one that is global to the entire program. A locally declared object can be a variable or the definition of a statement-function. A globally declared object is either a subroutine or a "common block." Variables cannot be introduced in such a way that their scopes are limited to one portion of a subroutine (there is no block structure). Furthermore, subprograms can only be defined at the global level, not within other subprograms. As a result there are no local subprograms—every subprogram is accessible to every other. Prohibiting subprogram definitions within other subprograms also prevents a situation in which one subprogram (the inner one) might have been able to refer not only to its own local variables but to the locals of the surrounding subprograms. As is, nothing disturbs the pristine flatness of a Fortran namespace: one variable can never temporarily "shadow" or supersede another.

3.1.2   Fortran Analysis

The static and non-hierarchical character of Fortran programs is a theme that is carried out with remarkable uniformity throughout the language. Program execution is "static" in the sense that Fortran subprograms are fixed objects, not templates: they are permanently allocated, not built to order whenever they are invoked. There are no dynamically created variables. The naming environment is flat (names never shadow other names), and the lack of statement-bracketing means that a group of small statements never coalesces into a single larger statement. In fact the language syntax only grudgingly acknowledges the existence of larger data objects (arrays) that are composed of smaller ones, as we discuss below.

Abstraction Hierarchies   We discuss these issues in turn. But first, why are they important? What does it matter if programs in language X are necessarily "flat"?

Abstraction is a recurrent issue in programming. Programs can be complex objects. To build or to understand them—indeed to build or to understand any complicated object—we often rely on a simple technique which we refer to as *layered abstractions*: first understand *in general* or *in the abstract* what's going on; then worry about the details. The same process can often be applied recursively to the details, until the entire structure has been synthesized (put together) or analyzed (taken apart, understood) down to the lowest level. Software machines can be complex both temporally (What are the major steps to be carried out in performing this computation?) and spatially (What are the major pieces out of which this program is constructed?).

Hierarchies are useful to the technique of synthesis or analysis via abstraction. They allow us to wrap up a collection of details and pigeonhole them within a larger framework. So-called "recursive hierarchies" are best, as we will discuss, but any kind of hierarchy can be useful.

Turning now to Fortran: it is "flat," non-hierarchical, and thus unfriendly to abstraction in our sense. Temporally, Fortran has no statement bracketing. There's no way to express the thought that "these 30 statements are regarded as a single unit." This forces Fortran programmers to rely on labels and branch statements to guide execution. They can't write "execute the following statement group"; they can only write, in effect, "execute the next (single) statement, and keep executing statements—one by one—until you reach label Q, or until a branch sends you off somewhere else." (In Fortran77, new constructs ameliorate this situation partially but not entirely.) There are no hierarchical naming environments in Fortran. Spatially, subprograms can't be nested within other subprograms. A Fortran program, then, is a flat collection of subprograms (subprograms never coalesce into larger groups); each subprogram is defined by a "flat" collection of statements (statements never coalesce into larger groups).

The consistent failure of basic units to coalesce is indicated by small syntactic details as well. To declare a 10-element array of reals, for example, we write

```
REAL BAZBALL(10)
```

The term "array" isn't part of Fortran's vocabulary; an array is merely a bunch of numbers.

A related phenomenon involves an implementation decision with implications for the meaning of the language. The spatial structure of a Fortran program is static. All required variables are arranged at compile-time and allocated when the program is loaded; no variable-creation takes place at runtime. As noted above, the invocation of a Fortran sub-program doesn't require the instantiation of a template. Storage space for each subprogram's parameters and local variables is pre-allocated at load-time. Thus Fortran has no "templates" at all in the ISM sense. This implementation decision affects the language semantics: it means that a procedure may, upon exit, leave values stored in its local variables with the assurance of finding the same values waiting for it the next time it is invoked. (In Fortran77, programmers must state explicitly whether they want local variables to be preserved, but the option is available for any subprogram.)

What's important is the conceptual unity of the Fortran design. A For-tran program is a static sequence of subprograms; execution whizzes back and forth among them, never entering a newly constructed envi-ronment. Each subprogram is a flat list of statements; execution whizzes back and forth among them via GOTO, never entering a "new level."

These facts don't constitute a debilitating problem for Fortran program-mers. A programmer with a hierarchical way of thinking can use Fortran to build a well-structured program. But the language itself won't help. If you choose to synthesize or to analyze a program by means of layered abstractions, Fortran will play the role of sullen bystander.

Fortran *vs*. Assembly Language: the Idea of "Storage" and the Idea of "Variables"   Our most important task in studying program-ming linguistics is to investigate some hypotheses about what a program is—concretely, what distinguishes software machines from hardware ma-chines on the one hand, and from mathematical expressions on the other. Programming language designers have most often worked towards an un-derstanding of programming from the direction of mathematics, and as we discuss in the last section of this chapter, the same is true in a sense of Fortran's designers. But Fortran at a more basic level was influenced by assembly programming more directly than any other language we'll examine—hardly surprising, given that Fortran comes first in the series. Fortran was introduced at a time when almost all programming was assembly-language programming.

In some ways, the influence of assembly language was direct and imme-diate, and tended to disappear as the language evolved. The original

Fortran I of 1957, for example, included statements such as

```
IF (SENSE LIGHT i) ...
IF ACCUMULATOR OVERFLOW   ...
WRITE DRUM i ...,
```

all in reference to architectural features of the IBM 704 computer. (Fortran I, for that matter, had neither subroutines nor common blocks; these made their appearance in 1958 with Fortran II.) In other ways, assembly programming's influence was less immediate, more conceptual, and continues to be felt in all Fortrans down to the present. These cases are of particular interest to us, because they allow us to underline the evolving distinction between hardware and software machines.

One basic aspect of the distinction is that, while a hardware computer has *storage*, a software machine deals with a *collection of data objects*. "Storage" means an undifferentiated series of bits or bytes or words. The assembly programmer, who manipulates the hardware machine directly, is welcome to regard certain of these bytes as storing integers, others as storing floating point numbers or character-strings and so on. But in fact, generally speaking, one byte is the same as another. The assembly programmer can choose to do whatever he wants with his storage space—he can overwrite the third byte in a series of four that collectively constitute an integer, and nothing will stop him. This style of programming is flexible and (as any assembly programmer will tell you) it can be seductively convenient. But it also tends to be difficult and error-prone, and to result in inscrutable programs.

Fully developed software machinery substitutes a different model. Data are stored not in one contiguous set of bits, but in a collection of data objects. The language's type system decides what kind of objects are available and what can be done with each kind. The programmer creates a set of objects and deals only with these objects, and only in the approved ways. The implementation takes charge of arranging the software machine's objects within the computer's physical storage space.

Fortran accepts the data-object model, but with some hesitancy. It allows the programmer to create and manipulate data objects, but allows him also to deal with storage space directly. Consider two examples: if n subprograms share access to a single COMMON block, they may view it in n different ways, as we noted above. A COMMON block, then, is not a collection of data objects; it is simply a storage area, with no intrinsic organizational framework. EQUIVALENCE statements make it possible to neutralize the object divisions in *any* data structure, whether or not it appears in a COMMON block:

```
EQUIVALENCE (BLAT(1), LORK(1,1))
```

makes the first entry in the one-dimensional array BLAT identical to the first entry in the two-dimensional array LORK; BLAT is an array of reals and LORK is an array of integers (we can tell because of the default typing rules based on the first letters of the names LORK and BLAT). This means in effect that Fortran programmers can treat any part of storage in any way they choose. Storage is broken up into objects with type labels affixed; but the *same piece* of storage can be subdivided in as many different ways, and labeled with as many different types, as the programmer chooses. Thus, the Fortran programmer always has a choice: he can abide by the civilizing norms of a collection of separate, typed data objects, or he can tear off the outer layer and get at the raw storage underneath.

Fortran supports this dual view because efficiency is a crucial consideration. Consider the EQUIVALENCE statement. Recall that Fortran has no dynamically created variables: every data object is allocated before execution starts, and stays allocated until execution ends. An enormous array may be important only during the first ten percent of an average program run, but there's no way to reuse the space later on. EQUIVALENCE statements are a way around this limitation: if two data structures are required during two disjoint periods of program execution, we can "EQUIVALENCE" them, and they will share the same piece of storage.

It's widely conceded, on the other hand, that these techniques place a considerable burden on the programmer and can be a major source of Fortran programming errors. Storage as opposed to data objects largely disappears in the languages that follow Fortran. A variety of better methods for efficient space management emerge.

Efficiency   Fortran occupies a special place among the language designs we will consider because, as noted above, its designers were re-

quired not to produce a perfect language but to demonstrate that the
whole idea of programming languages made sense. "As far as we're
aware," John Backus, leader of the Fortran project, writes in 1978, "we
simply made up the language as we went along. We did not regard
language design as a difficult problem, merely a simple prelude to the
real problem: designing a compiler which could produce efficient programs [114, p.168]." Whatever the strengths and weakness of the language design, Fortran passed its most important test with flying colors:
that first Fortran compiler did indeed produce highly efficient object
programs. This is a tribute to the compiler-builders and, to a lesser
extent, a reflection of the emphasis placed on efficiency in the language
design. To Fortran's users, this emphasis is just as fitting today as it was
when the language was first proving itself. Fortran's users have always
tended to concentrate in domains where compute-intensive applications
predominate, and to program with efficiency concerns uppermost.

Selective Access to the Global Environment   Nor is a pragmatic,
efficient design such a bad thing. Consider the COMMON block. In a language in which all namespaces are structured hierarchically—Algol 60,
for example—all subprograms at a given nesting level share access to
the same set of global variables. If subprogram A has access to glob-
als $V1, V2$ and $V3$, then so does subprogram B (if A and B are declared, again, at the same level). In Fortran, on the other hand, subprograms can share access to global variables in a selective, programmer-
determined way. Subprogram A might have access to $V1$ and $V2$ while
B has access to $V1$ and $V3$—the declarations might look like this: within
subprogram A,

```
COMMON /BLOCK1/V1/BLOCK2/V2
```

and within B,

```
COMMON /BLOCK1/V1/BLOCK3/V3.
```

Fortran works this way for pragmatic reasons. Fortran subprograms
are *compiled separately*, then stitched together into a runnable image by
the link-editor program. When presented with a subprogram, in other
words, the Fortran compiler knows nothing about the other subprograms
that make up the program as a whole: it deals only with one subprogram at a time. The link-editor gathers the separately compiled pieces

together and hooks them up. Thus, subprogram J might include the statement `call K`; while working on J, the compiler has no idea where K will ultimately appear, and so this statement must be compiled to an incomplete call, in essence to an instruction that says "invoke the subroutine called K, wherever K happens to be." The link-editor decides where to put K and resolves this incomplete reference. Because of separate compilation, the compiler has no knowledge about a subprogram's global environment. The compiler doesn't remember, from subprogram to subprogram, which variable names refer to which `COMMON` blocks; it must be told, and each subprogram may as well inform the compiler about exactly the pieces of the global environment relevant to it, and no more.

Long after Fortran's debut, however, language designers became convinced that this kind of *selective access to the global environment* was important on grounds of good programming methods. Subprograms, it is argued, should specify explicitly which pieces of the global environment they will use. Requiring explicit specification, rather than granting access to the entire environment by default, helps makes it clear when a subprogram is doing something it was not intended to do. "If this subprogram is only intended to use $V1$ and $V3$," the compiler and the programmer can reason, "then this reference to $V2$ must be a mistake." Fortran's `COMMON` blocks don't offer a fully fleshed selective-access scheme, but when we return to this topic in a later chapter, remember that Fortran was the first language to offer something along these lines.

Vectorization and Parallelism   *(This is a specialized discussion that may be skipped without loss of continuity.)*

One of the many advantages of Fortran's bare-boned program structure and its minimal repertoire of data types is a language that makes a good target for a range of compile-time optimization techniques. The easier a language is to optimize, the faster it can be made to run. The static structure of a Fortran program allows the optimizer to analyze the source code with the assurance that the data structures and subroutines defined within the program are the only ones that will be extant at runtime.

The static nature of the language allows the Fortran compiler to apply complex dataflow analysis techniques to determine how and when data

values are being used. One important application of these techniques involves the transformation of Fortran programs into semantically equivalent programs (programs with the same meaning, that compute the same
thing) that are able to take advantage of vector or parallel machines. A
parallel computer encompasses many subcomputers, all of which can
be focused simultaneously on the same problem. A vector computer has
special hardware that makes it fast and efficient to apply some operation
to a vector of values, by overlapping many of the individual computations. Fortran's simple program structure makes it suitable for a range
of optimizations that take the form "Transform each iteration of this
sequential loop into a concurrently executing process" (for parallel machines), or "Transform this iterative array recurrence equation into an
operation on a vector" (for vector machines).

To begin, consider the following iteration expression that defines an
array A in terms of some array B (assume that both A and B are defined
as 100-element vectors):

```
DO I = 1 to 100
   A(I) = B(I) * 10
```

On a sequential machine, each step in the iteration is performed after
the previous step completes. At the first step, A(1) is assigned the value
yielded by evaluating B(1) * 10; at the second, A(2) is assigned the
value yielded by evaluating B(2) * 10, and so on. But this loop could
be transformed into

```
A = B *ᵥ 10,
```

where $*_v$ is the vector analog of the standard integer multiplication
operator. In the abstract, $*_v$ coerces its two arguments into vectors
of equal length, and performs a piecewise multiplication of the vector
elements in parallel: we get $B_1 * 10$, $B_2 * 10$ and so on. A vector
machine can perform many of these individual multiplications at the
same time.

Eliminating a loop in favor of a vector operation is not always so straightforward. Consider the following code fragment:

```
DO I = 1 to 100
  A(I) = A(F(I)) + 1.
```

The above loop defines a recurrence relation: the value of A(I) is defined
in terms of the value of A(F(I)). Before we can assign a value to A(I), we
need to compute A(F(I)). If we compute A(I) in parallel with A(F(I)),
the value finally assigned to A(I) may or may not correspond to the value
assigned to it under normal sequential evaluation. (Consider the case
when $I = 1$ and $F(I) = 2$; we must make sure that we don't evaluate the
next iteration of the loop (that assigns a value to A(2)) before executing
the assignment in the first iteration.) In other words, because of the
dependencies that exist between different elements in A, we can't apply
the same simple transformation to this loop that we did to the earlier
one.

Optimizing Fortran compilers carry out transformations of the kind described above by using *dependency analysis* techniques. A detailed discussion of the theory of dependency analysis is beyond the scope of this
book, but we'll attempt to convey the basic flavor of the approach. Dependency analysis is concerned with the question: Given statements i
and j, what are the set of data elements V that i and j access? Clearly,
if V is the empty set, there are no dependencies between i and j and
they may be executed in parallel. On the other hand, if V is non-empty,
then the manner in which V's elements are accessed by i and j determines what (if any) transformations can be performed to make i and j
execute concurrently.

Let v be some element in V. There are four ways that i and j can
interact through v:

1. i and j both read v,

2. i writes v and j reads it (data dependency)

3. i reads v and j writes it (anti-dependency), and

4. i and j both write v (output dependency).

We consider each case in turn.

In the first case, i and j do not alter v. Thus, v's value is not dependent upon the order in which i and j are executed. In particular, if v is the only element in V, i and j may be evaluated in parallel. The effect of executing i and j concurrently is no different than if i and j were evaluated sequentially.

Analysis of the other dependency cases is more complicated. If i writes v, j reads it and i logically precedes j in the program, then we cannot evaluate the two statements concurrently—the evaluation of statement j is dependent upon the effect produced by evaluating statement i. Statements i and j have a data dependency with respect to data element v.

A similar restriction applies in the other two cases as well: if j updates v and i reads from it, we must ensure that i sees the old value of v, not the value written by j. Similarly, if both i and j write to the same data object, we cannot arbitrarily interleave their execution.

On the surface, it would appear that various dependencies between statements in a Fortran program would be so extensive that they would effectively prohibit the compiler from extracting any significant parallelism. There are, however, several simple intermediate transformations that can be applied to eliminate many of these dependencies. We describe some of the simpler ones briefly below.

Renaming. A program that uses the same variable in different ways can be rewritten to use different names for each different kind of use. By renaming variables, certain output and anti-dependencies in the source program may be eliminated. Consider the following loop fragment:

```
DO 100 I = 1,N
    X = X + 1
    Y = X + 2
    :
    X = F(Z)
100:  ...
```

The first and second statements in the loop body are related via a data dependency, *i.e.*, the second statement can read X only after the first writes it. Similarly, the first and the last statement are related under

- an output dependency, *i.e.*, both write X, as well as an anti-dependency—the first statement must read X before the last writes it,

- an anti-dependency, *i.e.*, the kth write of X in the last statement must precede the $k + 1^{st}$ read in the first, and

- a data dependency, *i.e.*, the read of X in the first statement must take place before the assignment to X in the last.

In addition, the first statement has both a data- and an anti-dependency on itself. The data dependency results because in a given iteration, the X referred to on the right-hand side must be read before it is written. The anti-dependency exists because the assignment to X in the kth iteration can take place only after it is read in the $k - 1^{st}$. The first and second statements are also related under an anti-dependency, *i.e.*, the kth iteration of the second statement must precede the $k + 1^{st}$ iteration of first—X must be read in the current iteration before it can be written in a subsequent one.

After loop renaming, the fragment would look like this:

```
DO 100 I = 1,N
    X' = X + 1
    Y = X' + 2
    ⋮
    X = F(Z)
100:  ...
```

The output dependencies between the first and last statements are eliminated as is the anti-dependency in the first statement.

Expansion. A variable that is used locally inside a loop is transformed into a one-dimensional array whose size is equal to the number of iterations performed by the loop. The intent of this transformation is to have each iteration of a loop be associated with a unique set of locations; thus, after the expansion transformation, it may be the case that there are fewer dependencies *across* loop iterations than existed before.

The loop fragment shown above (after renaming) could be transformed using expansion as follows:

```
DO 100 I = 1,N
   X'(I-1) = X(I-1) + 1
   Y(I-1) = X'(I-1) + 2
      ⋮
   X(I) = F(Z)
100: ...
```

As a result of the expansion, the data dependency between the right- and left-hand sides of the first statement, and the anti-dependency between the first and last statements, are eliminated.

Loop Distribution. A loop whose component statements are interconnected only by data dependencies can be transformed into a set of loops, each of which is amenable to vectorization. The above loop, for example, could be transformed into the following set of loops:

```
     DO 100 I = 1,N
        X(I) = F(Z)
100: DO 200 I = 1,N
        X'(I-1) = X(I-1) + 1
200: DO 300 I = 1,N
        Y(I-1) = X'(I-1) + 2
300: ...
```

Notice that the order of the statements in the original loop have been changed after the loop distribution. When the second loop is executed, the data elements it reads have already been defined as a result of the first loop. Similarly, the third loop (which requires X') is executed only after the second one (which defines it) completes. Each of the loops can be transformed into a vector operation that computes the elements of the arrays being defined in parallel.

In conclusion.

Fortran was designed for efficiency, and continues to be well-suited on the whole to the needs of the community that values efficiency most: scientists and engineers with large, computationally expensive problems to solve. We need to temper any criticisms of its expressiveness with a a healthy respect for its practicality. (See also the "Discussion" at the end of this chapter.)

3.1.3   ISM Comparison

Fortran's major restrictions compared to the ISM: The named regions of a "Fortran space-map" may hold only templates, simple data objects or homogeneous data structures. Space-maps may not be nested within the regions of a space-map or a time-map: hence there are no records, modules, data systems or local scopes. There are no real templates, hence no recursive subroutines, record types or classes. Fortran has no parallelism.

Major additions, compared to the ISM: Fortran has special visibility rules associated with common blocks and provides type aliasing features via the equivalence statement.

3.2   Algol 60

We concentrate on the following propositions:

1. Algol 60 lays the basis for the entire subsequent history of programming languages by discovering the principle of the *recursive structure of programs*. (We define *recursive structure* and differentiate it from a *recursive definition* later in the chapter.) But Algol 60's realization of recursive structure is *incomplete*, and the omissions in Algol 60 have been as influential as the inclusions. A central consequence of Algol's approach is a complete separation between the structure of programs and naming environments on the one hand and of data objects on the other. This "Algol Wall" becomes a crucial factor in the evolution of programming language design.

2. Call-by-name and "own" variables are Algol 60 features that were *not* widely emulated in its direct descendants, but which have been incorporated in modified form elsewhere. They each hark forward to problems that were increasingly regarded as central: call-by-name relates to the use of *procedures as first-class objects*; "own" variables were a first attempt to deal with the data system problem. A modified form of the call-by-name protocol goes under

the name "lazy evaluation," and "own" variables form the basis
for subsequent work on "object-oriented" programming.

3.2.1 Algol 60 Profile

Program Structure. An Algol 60 program is either a *compound statement* or a *block*. A compound statement is a list of statements to be
executed sequentially, parenthesized within the words begin and end. A
statement may be a primitive expression (*e.g.*, a procedure application),
a conditional or assignment, a jump or a block.

A block is a local naming environment: it consists of a series of name
definitions followed by a *statement*. The execution rule for a block states
that upon block entry, the local objects declared in the declaration come
into existence and the *statement* is then executed. To determine the
meaning of a name foobar within *statement*, we look for a foobar declared within this block or (if there is none) in the closest-enclosing block.
Both a block and a compound statement qualify as "statements"; therefore any element of a compound statement may be another compound
statement or a block.

For example, in the compound statement

```
BEGIN
  INTEGER x,y,z;
  x := 1; y := 2;
  BEGIN
    y := 3;
    z := x + y
  END
END
```

the result of the addition operation is 4. The reference to name y is
resolved by taking its binding-value in the block immediately enclosing
the addition statement. The reference to name x is resolved by taking
its binding-value in the outermost block, since no binding for x is present
in the inner one.

Data Types. Like Fortran, Algol 60 supports integer and real numeric
data. There is a distinguished Boolean type as well. The basic suite of

relational operators $(\geq,\leq,>,<,=)$ and the standard logical connectives (or, and and so on) operate over Boolean values and yield Boolean results.

The only complex data type in Algol 60 is the array. An array is declared using the **array** type declaration.

INTEGER ARRAY A[1:m,2:n]

declares A to be a two-dimensional array whose lower bounds are 1 and 2 respectively and whose upper bounds are m and n respectively.

Unlike a Fortran array, an Algol 60 array may have bounds defined by any integer-yielding expression. Hence, the compiler can't necessarily tell how big an array is by looking at the declaration (the size may be determined by an expression whose value won't be known until runtime), and storage for arrays cannot be pre-allocated. Space must be allocated dynamically when program control enters the block in which the array is defined. (An array bounds expression cannot depend upon the value of names defined within the block in which the array is declared; at the time control enters into the array defining block, the meaning of all identifiers in an array-bounds expression must be known.) In the above example, the value of m and n are resolved relative to the environment within which the block containing the declaration is evaluated.

Algol 60 does not support general character or string data types nor any form of record type. Character strings are available only as constants to be passed to library procedures for output. (There are no input-output facilities in the language; input and output are to be handled by a library of external utility procedures, to be coded not in Algol but in some appropriate machine-specific language.)

Control Structures. Algol 60 introduced a set of control structures that laid the groundwork for a large number of subsequent languages. It introduced the **for** and **while** loops to provide for bounded and unbounded iteration—for iteration some number of times that is decided in advance (bounded) or is determined while the loop executes (unbounded). The Algol 60 **for** statement is actually a rather complicated structure, which later Algol-inspired languages have tended to simplify. It takes the form

FOR *index* := *some values* DO *statement*

Each value in the collection designated *some values* is assigned in turn
to the variable *index*, and *statement* is executed once after each fresh
assignment. To specify *some values* we use a list of value-designators
separated by commas: *index* is assigned the sequence of values specified
by the first value-designator in the list, then the second and so on.
A value-designator may be a `step` phrase like "0 `step` 10 `until` 50,"
which specifies the sequence 0, 10, 20 and so on through 50; or it may be
a `while` phrase like "index*2 while index < 1000," which—if `index`
starts at 1—generates the sequence 2, 4, 8 and so on through 512; or it
may be a single value.

Algol 60 introduced the `if-then-else` conditional which allowed the selection of either of two statements based on a logical test; the fact that a
statement may (again) be a compound statement or a block allowed this
conditional to select among arbitrarily complex alternatives. There are
conditional *expressions* as well as conditional statements (they were proposed by Lisp-inventor McCarthy, who was part of the Algol 60 design
committee during the same period in which he was developing Lisp). A
conditional expression like

```
IF x > y THEN x ELSE y
```

yields the maximum of x and y. A `goto` statement and statement la-
beling are provided, along with a multi-way branch statement and a
method for deciding at runtime on the identity of the labels in the mul-
tiway branch.

Procedures and Functions. Procedures and "function procedures"—
the latter return values—may be defined recursively. Actual parameters
are passed either "by name" (the default) or "by value." Parameter
passing "by name" means that the variable or expression associated at
invocation time with formal parameter F is considered to be substituted
literally for every occurrence of F in the body of the procedure. Stated
another way, the actual expression is *re*-evaluated for every reference
made to the corresponding formal in the procedure body. Given, for
example, the Algol 60 procedure

```
PROCEDURE blat(x, y)
  BEGIN
    x := 1000; y := 1000
  END
```

the invocation `blat(i, A[i])` causes the execution of a statement that is in effect identical to

```
BEGIN
  i := 1000; A[i] := 1000
END
```

1000 is assigned to i and then to the 1000th element of the array A.

Call by name is powerful precisely because it allows this kind of substitution of arbitrary variables into a pre-arranged control structure (we explain further below). The variable names within an actual parameter passed by name are uniformly changed if they conflict with variable names that have local meanings within the procedure.

Naming Environments. The Algol 60 namespace is structured hierarchically. A block defines a namespace; other blocks nested inside a block define their own, inner namespaces. A variable named foobar in the inner namespace "shadows" or temporarily supersedes any foobars that happen to occur in the surrounding blocks. This arrangement is called "block-structure," as discussed in chapter 2.

The objects to which names are given may be either variables or procedures. An object's lifetime is ordinarily determined by the active life of the block in which it is declared: the variable named bazball leaps into existence when execution enters the block in which bazball is declared, and disappears when execution leaves the block. But there is an exception: a variable may be declared to be an own variable, and in this case only one instance of the variable is created during the lifetime of the program. If mybaz is an own variable of block B, then when execution enters B, a mybaz becomes accessible that is exactly the same mybaz that was accessible the last time around. mybaz is discovered holding the same value it held when execution last left B. (Note that we speak only of own variable and not of own procedures: an Algol 60 procedure

is immutable and so it is meaningless to ask whether a given procedure
`blat` is or is not the same `blat` that was available the last time around.)

3.2.2   Algol 60 Analysis

Recursive Program Structure   Algol 60 lays the basis for virtually
all subsequent work in programming languages by discovering that programs may be treated as objects with *recursive structure*.

Recursive structure is a simple idea that is related to but should be
distinguished from the idea of a recursive definition.

Definition 3.1 A *recursive definition* is a definition that refers to the
term that is being defined. We might, for example, define the procedure
factorial in terms of itself:

$$factorial \; n = \begin{cases} 1 & n = 0, 1 \\ n * factorial \; (n-1) & n > 1 \end{cases}$$

A *recursive structure* has sub-components that are structurally the same
as itself. Thus a binary tree is composed of a root and two (smaller)
binary trees.

It had been accepted for centuries that algebraic expressions were naturally treated as recursive structures. We can add two integers, but we
can also replace the integers with two arbitrarily complex expressions;
the addition operation has the same meaning and the same syntax in
either case. Electrical circuits, to take another familiar example, are recursive in structure: two complex circuit elements relate to each other in
exactly the same way as two simple elements within a complex element.

This kind of hierarchical, recursive structure is an elegant and powerful
device for managing and understanding complexity. To synthesize a
complex object, we build simpler objects and assemble them. To analyze
a complex object, we disassemble it into simpler pieces. Hierarchies are
useful because, as we discussed above, they make this process of synthesis
or analysis easier and more natural. Hierarchies built using recursive
structures are best of all: in a recursive structure, the simple, low-level
pieces relate to each other in exactly the same way as the complex, high-
level pieces do. At whatever level of detail we are examining, the rules
that decide how parts interrelate are the same.

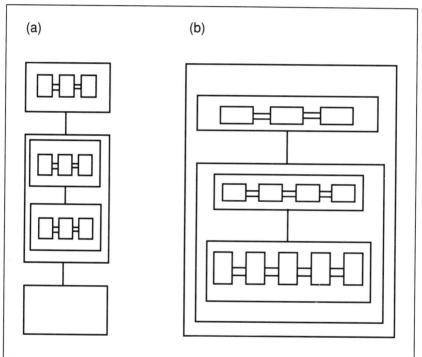

Figure 3.3
Interlocking, recursive structure: A program can be a compound statement (a) or a block (b) with other blocks and compound statements nested within.

The fact that recursive structures were well-known in algebra and engineering didn't by any means make it obvious that *programs* could be understood as recursive structures. Assembly programs are not recursive in structure, and neither are Fortran programs. But the Algol 60 designers realized that big programs can be built out of little programs, just as big expressions are built out of little expressions. They made recursive structure possible by providing *statement bracketing* and two interlocking basic structures—the compound statement and the block—that will work at any scale. This was a fundamental breakthrough. In Algol 60, we can structure a large program as a single 50,000-line block; its last element might be a 200-line compound statement, whose third line might invoke a procedure defined by a 50-line block, whose last element is a 10-element compound statement, whose fourth element is a 3-line block and so on. We can organize massive computations and miniature ones in the same way.

□ In Algol 60, programs have *recursive structure*, just as expressions do. Big programs can be built recursively out of little programs.

But Algol didn't take the recursive-structure principle all the way to completion, and the places where it stopped short are revealing and important. Consider the ISM: an Algol block or compound statement will be a space-map. An Algol block defining n local names and a single statement s will be represented as an $n+1$-element space-map: the ith region in this complex machine will be given the same name as the ith binding in the corresponding block; the last region in the space-map will hold s. An Algol statement containing n sub-statements will be represented as an n-element time-map. Note that because statements within blocks may define other blocks and that blocks within statements may define other statements, the regions within an Algol-60-based space-map may recursively contain other time- or space-maps. In other words, a procedure may define a local block whose name definitions and executable statements share the same lifetime.

Note, however, that an Algol-60-based space-map is a restricted version of a general ISM space-map. *Any* element of an ISM space-map may be either a space-map or another time-map. But it is *not* true that in Algol,

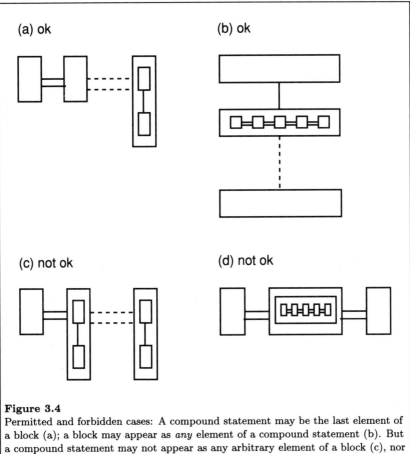

Figure 3.4
Permitted and forbidden cases: A compound statement may be the last element of
a block (a); a block may appear as *any* element of a compound statement (b). But
a compound statement may not appear as any arbitrary element of a block (c), nor
may a *block* appear as any element of a block (d).

any element of a block may be either a compound statement or another
block. Only the *last* element of a block may be a compound statement,
and only the *last* element of a block may be another complete block.

Why does it matter? Because Algol 60 omits from its interlocking
scheme precisely the two cases that would have lead respectively to concurrency and to modular naming environments. If Algol had allowed
any element of a block to be replaced by a compound statement, not
just the last, it would have permitted programs such as

```
BEGIN
  INTEGER i, j;
  BEGIN S1; S2; ... Sn END;
  REAL r;
  BEGIN T1; T2; ... Tn END
END
```

In Algol this is gibberish, but if we translate this to the ISM it's obvious that we have a concurrent program. Just as variables i and j exist during the lifetime of the statement sequence T1 through Tn, the first statement sequence S1 through Sn exists during this same lifetime, and hence the two sequences execute concurrently.

Suppose Algol had allowed *any* element of a block to be replaced by another block, and suppose also that it had allowed sub-blocks to be given names. We might then have had, for example,

```
BEGIN
  INTEGER i, j;
  Person : BEGIN
             INTEGER ssnum, age;
             BOOLEAN sex;
             PROCEDURE changesex(...)... end
           END Person;
  ...
```

Person, in effect, represents a four-field "object" or data system.

In other words, allowing fully recursive block-structure would have provided a general method for introducing named sub-environments— records, modules, data systems.. Both omissions are important, the second even more so, perhaps, than the first. These omissions in a breakthrough language like Algol 60 have had deep implications for the future development of the field.

A recurring problem: how does program structure relate to object structure? To understand a programming language, we need to understand the data objects it encompasses. The sorts of programs we can write in language L are determined in significant part by the sorts of objects L can handle. If we intend to write a linear-system solver in L, L must include real numbers. To simulate the behavior of a

stampeding yak herd, L will probably need objects of type "yak." Two
fundamental classes of object, numbers and logical values, were inherited from mathematics. Numbers are useful to be sure, but suppose
we want our program to parse sentences or to format text for output?
Lisp introduced "symbol" type objects (as we will discuss), and alphanumeric characters gradually made their appearance as well. Good, but
insufficient. As we'll see, *heterogeneous data objects*—records, modules,
data systems—were gradually seen to be essential. How to provide for
such structures was eventually to become a vexed question in language
evolution.

Now consider the Algol 60 design. Algol 60 discovered the principle of
the *recursive structure of programs*. Had it allowed for named sub-blocks,
the second "missing case" discussed above, it would have discovered
something else too: that not only programs but *data objects as well* can
be regarded as recursive structures—in fact, *data objects and programs
can be regarded as two facets of the same structure.*

Consider the basic components of Algol 60 software machinery. On one
side we have program structures; on the other, data objects. Algol
60 program structures are elegant crystalline things, with the sort of
transparent, recursive structure we've described: blocks nested within
compound statements nested within larger blocks and so on. These
interlocking, recursive building blocks are endlessly flexible. The variety
of program shapes we can assemble is limitless. Turn now to the data-
object side. We find a bag of integers, a bag of reals and a couple of
Booleans. These can be assembled into homogeneous arrays. There is
no other way to build larger structures out of smaller ones.

But consider the kind of data objects we'd *like* to have. We'd like
records; in time, we will want data systems. We'd like to be able to
build such objects directly, or create them using templates. *If* Algol
60 had allowed data objects to be assembled according to exactly the
same rules that govern program structure, we'd have all these objects.
Records, data systems, arrays can all be assembled in the same way that
a block-structured program can be assembled: in describing the ISM, we
explained how.

This kind of realization, the unification of object structure and program
structure, would have completed the transformation that recursive pro-

gram structure began, a transformation in the direction of power and
simplicity. Programming languages *in fact* evolved in a way that erected
a wall between data objects and program structures. The wall was
breached in a very limited and *ad hoc* fashion by Lisp (which lacks a
well-developed idea of program structures and has a narrow perspective
on naming environments), and more systematically, although not fully,
by Simula 67 and by Scheme. The wall serves certain (arguably) useful purposes having to do with typing, as we discuss in a later chapter.
At the same time, a natural understanding of the relationships between
concurrency, modularity and basic program structure has continued to
elude language designers.

□ Programs and data objects can *both* be regarded as recursive structures—in fact, as two facets of the same structure
(as in the ISM).

? Algol 60, followed by most subsequent languages, built
a wall between program structures and data objects: these
two basic classes are governed by separate rules. In Algol
60, program structures are governed by simple, flexible and
recursive rules; data objects are not.

(The "?" symbol is the flip side of "□." It designates cases in which
a distinction has been drawn between two concepts or structures that
might have been treated as aspects of the same thing.[1])

Call-by-Name and First-Class Procedures   In a design as enormously influential as Algol 60, our attention is naturally drawn not only
to the features that recur in later languages, but to the few that don't.
We first explain call-by-name and then "own" variables, and discuss the
larger problems that these constructs hinted at but couldn't fully cope
with.

Call-by-name is usually explained by quoting the Algol "copy rule,"
which states that a called-by-name formal parameter behaves, when its

---

[1]The purpose is to induce thought, not to wag the the authorial finger at "design
flaws." The mere fact of a distinction doesn't mean that the distinction is unreasonable or that it serves no purpose. Flaws in language design are subjective things. At
any rate all language designs involve trade-offs; none optimize everything.

procedure is invoked, as if the expression passed as the corresponding actual were substituted literally for the formal in the procedure definition. Note that call-by-name and call-by-value parameters may be combined in a single procedure. Note also that the copy rule is incomplete. The Algol 60 report notes that if names appear in an actual call-by-name parameter that are also defined in the local scope within which the procedure executes, conflict is avoided by "suitable systematic changes" of the conflicting identifiers [98, p.12]. In effect, the meaning of identifiers found within an actual expression used in a call-by-name context is determined in the *caller's* environment, not the procedure's. Thus, given the code fragment

```
INTEGER PROCEDURE f(x); INTEGER x;
  BEGIN
    INTEGER y; y := 1;
    f := x + y;
  END;
BEGIN
  y := 2;
  r := f (y + 1);
END;
```

the application of f to expression "y + 1" in effect causes all occurrences of y in f to be replaced by some new identifier. We can think of the executable statement in the above fragment as being equivalent to

```
BEGIN
  y := 2;
  BEGIN
    z : INTEGER; z := 1;
    r := (y + 1) + z;
  END;
END;
```

What's the point? Call-by-name parameters allow a procedure body to side-effect its arguments. Suppose the procedure "zero" is intended to replace the value of its integer argument by zero. We can write

```
PROCEDURE zero(i); INTEGER i;
  BEGIN
    i := 0
  END.
```

The invocation zero(k) has the effect of making k equal to 0, because the formal "i" is replaced in effect by the name "k" in the procedure body. If on the other hand we had specified zero in such a way that i is a call-by-value parameter:

```
PROCEDURE zero(i); VALUE i; INTEGER i;
  BEGIN
    i := 0
  END
```

the invocation zero(k) has no effect on k. It merely causes the *value* of k to be associated with the name i; the variable named i is thereupon set to zero, which of course has no effect on the variable named k.

Like call-by-reference, then, call-by-name allows procedures to change the values of their arguments. But there's more; it also allows a control strategy to be abstracted from the computation it is controlling, and reused for a family of computations. One standard example involves a procedure to compute the sum of a vector. Consider the statements

```
sum := 0;
FOR i:= 1 STEP 1 UNTIL N DO sum := sum + k
```

The FOR statement causes the assignment "sum := sum + k" to be executed once for each value of i between 1 and N. Suppose these statements appear within a procedure definition, and that i, N and k are formal parameters, passed by name. Suppose that in some invocation of this procedure, the formal k is bound to the actual parameter A[j], the formal i is bound to the actual parameter j, and the formal N is bound to the actual SizeOfA. Executing the above statement is then equivalent to executing

```
sum := 0;
FOR j := 1 STEP 1 UNTIL SizeOfA DO sum := sum + A[j]
```

In other words, we wind up summing the elements of vector **A**. If **M** is
a square matrix, we can sum the elements along its diagonal using the
same procedure—we bind formal **k** to actual **M[j,j]**; and so forth.

There's one other feature of call-by-name that makes it an intriguing
mechanism from a theoretical standpoint. Call-by-name has the interesting property that an expression serving as an actual parameter is
evaluated *only if* its value is indeed required by the invoked procedure.
Consider the following program fragment:

```
INTEGER PROCEDURE f(x,b); INTEGER x; BOOLEAN b;
  BEGIN
    f := IF b
            THEN x
            ELSE 1
  END;
```
If **b** is false, the value of **x** is irrelevant to the computation. Now
consider the function invocation

    f(*Trouble*, FALSE).

Suppose that *Trouble* is a non-terminating computation (at some point,
it gets into an infinite loop). This application of **f** will yield a value
(namely 1) anyway, because it behaves as though the following expression were to be evaluated:

```
IF FALSE
  THEN  Trouble
  ELSE 1
```

The conditional won't try to evaluate *Trouble* because the controlling predicate is false. In short, call-by-name is a minimal evaluation
strategy—it causes an actual to be evaluated only when absolutely necessary.

The importance of being able to defer the evaluation of an expression was
recognized by logicians some thirty years before Algol appeared on the
language scene. One important result in the theory of programming languages states, in essence, that any program that terminates (doesn't *diverge*, doesn't compute forever) under a call-by-value parameter-passing

protocol is guaranteed to terminate with a call-by-name protocol as well.
The converse is not true. (This result, known as the Second Church-
Rosser Theorem, will be discussed in greater detail when we take up
functional languages.)

Call-by-name and the idea of first-classness. The essential property separating call-by-name from call-by-value or call-by-reference is
deferred evaluation of actual parameters until they are needed by the
applied procedure. Stated another way, call-by-name provides a mechanism to *abstract* over an arbitrary expression, to wrap the expression up
into a package or a template that can be evaluated repeatedly. Consider
an Algol 60 procedure definition:

PROCEDURE f () E;

This definition represents, again, an abstraction over the expression E, a
so-called procedural abstraction. E won't be evaluated unless and until
f is actually applied; and E can be evaluated repeatedly whenever f *is*
applied.

One way to understand call-by-name is in terms of a kind of procedural
abstraction. An actual parameter under call-by-name represents the
body of a procedure with no names and no parameters, created on the
fly (rather than pre-defined in the declaration section); this special sort
of procedure is applied every time the procedure to which it is passed
refers to it.

Thus, call-by-name serves as an early and partial attempt to deal with
an issue that eventually gels as the following question: "are procedures
first-class objects?"

Definition 3.2 The first-class objects within language L are the ones
that can be yielded as values by expressions within L.

Thus in Fortran, for example, integers are first-class objects: for any
integer that can be represented in Fortran, there is some expression
with that integer as its value. Common blocks are not first-class: there
are no expressions within Fortran that evaluate to common blocks.[2]

---

[2]The term "first-class" is merely the residue of an inept metaphor. First-class
objects are said to be "first-class citizens" of the language, assuming that a pro-

What exactly does first-classness entail? It's often valuable to be able to envelop the many related elements of some collection of data values in a single wrapper, and to deal with the whole thing as a unit. We can pass such a collection as the parameter to a subroutine; we can return such a collection as the value of a function; we can assign such a collection to a variable in an assignment statement. If an object is *first-class*, all of these possibilities follow. Further, if this set of possibilities is true of some object, that object must (in effect) be first-class, because these possibilities imply that our language includes *expressions* that yield the kind of object in question. A function returns the value of an *expression*; the right side of an assignment statement is an *expression*.

So we might say that the first-class objects in our language are simply the ones that can be treated as a unit in the sense described above. In fact, though, the distinction isn't always easy to draw. Many languages include objects that can be treated as units for some purposes but not for others. The array in Fortran and in Algol 60 is an important example. In both languages, we can pass an entire array as the argument to a function: if A is the name of an array and f is a function, f(A) is possible in both languages. In neither language is it possible to return an entire array as the *value* of a function. In neither language can an expression that evaluates to an entire array appear on the right side of an assignment statement.

This kind of data object displays some of the attributes of first-classness, but can't be considered first-class. First-class objects can be treated as units for any and all purposes.

We now turn specifically to *procedures as first-class data objects*. The underlying question isn't so much whether procedures are first-class data, but whether they can be treated as data at all. If they can, however, it would be nice if they were first-class data objects.

Consider a hypothetical language that includes first-class procedures: it includes expressions E such that E yields a procedure. Just as sin(x) or factorial(y) might be legal invocations, $E(z)$ is a legal invocation, in particular an invocation of whatever procedure is specified by expression

---

gramming language can somehow be compared to a state whose citizens are its data objects—which it cannot, or at any rate just barely. A "second-class object" is any non-first-class object; there are no third or n^{th}-class objects.

E. Several possibilities arise. We should be able to assign procedures to
variables: just as we can write

```
x := y + 4
```

we should be able to write

```
f := E
```

We should be able to pass procedures as parameters to other procedures:
if we can write a procedure invocation like `g(y + 4)`, we should be
able to write `h(E)`. We should be able to write functions that return
procedures as results: again, if we can return `y + 4`, we should be able
to return *E*. We should be able to incorporate procedures into data
structures. If `A` is an array, then we should be able write expressions of
the form `A[1] := ` *E*. All of these capabilities are useful.

Call-by-name doesn't bring about the full power of first-class procedures,
but it provides some of the power of the second case above, passing
procedures as parameters to other procedures. If procedures were first
class, we could write `h(E)`; the body of `h` can evaluate the expression
that defines *E* whenever it wants by invoking the formal parameter to
which *E* is bound. If `f` is an Algol procedure whose one parameter is
called-by-name, we can instead write `f(`*some expression*`)`. The body of `f`
can evaluate "*some expression*" whenever it wants, simply by referring
to the formal parameter to which it is bound. Thus call-by-name in
effect allows the programmer to pass, as an argument, an expression
that behaves as if it were a procedure of no arguments.

A procedure of no arguments constructed by the compiler to defer the
evaluation of an expression is referred to as a *thunk*. We can think of a
call-by-name application in terms of a call-by-value application in which
each of the actuals are unnamed procedure objects.

It's interesting that Algol 60 also allows procedures (more accurately
procedure names) to be passed explicitly and directly as actual parameters. (Procedures are not allowed to be returned as results of an application, however; a procedure definition is considered to be a declaration,
not a value-yielding expression). This is another partial approach to
the freedom implicit in first-class procedures. It allows procedures as
arguments, but requires that they be defined and be given a name first;

they can't be made up on the spot. This isn't quite the same as the invocation $h(E)$, where E is improvised for the occasion and not defined anywhere else, much as in h(3+4), 3+4 is an arithmetic expression that is improvised on the spot. Call-by-name must be used in such cases.

The relationship between call-by-name and first-class procedures is important in our effort to grasp the evolution of programming-language ideas. Call-by-name is a special device that allows certain problems to be handled neatly. As a parameter-passing protocol, it subsumes a call-by-value discipline—any program that terminates using call-by-value will terminate with the same value using call-by-name, but the reverse is not true.

As a mechanism for building unnamed procedural abstractions, however, call-by-name is a very weak form of the more general concept of first-class procedures. In programming-language evolution, special devices tend to be displaced by general-purpose tools. This evolutionary process doesn't always work, and in many cases it has barely begun (programming languages don't have a very long history). But we can observe it working in the disappearance of call-by-name.

Call-by-name has specific drawbacks as well. Algol 60 uses call-by-name as a replacement for call-by-reference: there is no call-by-reference in the language. Call-by-reference is the parameter-passing mechanism to use when actual parameters must be changed by the procedures to which they are passed. In Algol 60, if we need to write a procedure that changes its arguments, only call-by-name is available; but there are cases in which the obvious solution won't work. A classic example is a procedure that is supposed to swap the values of its two arguments. We might write

```
PROCEDURE swap(x, y);
   INTEGER x,y;
   BEGIN
      INTEGER temp;
      temp := x; x := y; y := temp
   END
```

Nice try, but it won't work. Suppose we evaluate swap(i, A[i]). We wind up executing, in effect,

```
temp := i; i := A[i]; A[i] := temp
```

In other words, if i were 17 and we wanted to set its value to the value
of A[17], and the value of A[17] to 17, what we accomplish instead is to
assign 17 not to A[17] but to A[*something else*], where *something else*
is the starting value of A[17]. Had we used call-by-reference instead
of call-by-name, the procedure would have worked correctly. (See the
exercises for a call-by-name version of **swap** that works for this case.)

Own Variables   In Fortran, the local variables of a procedure are
allocated statically and exist throughout the lifetime of the program.
Algol introduces procedures that act like *templates* in the ISM sense;
they are not maps in themselves, but rather map-specifications. The
map described by an Algol procedure definition is reconstructed each
time the procedure is invoked. Suppose, however, that a procedure needs
to refer during its nth invocation to a value computed during its $n - 1^{st}$.
Consider a procedure to implement a pseudo-random-number generator.
To implement such a procedure, we start it off with a **seed** value; each
time we invoke it, it assigns a new, transformed value to **seed**, and
returns this value as the pseudo-random number. Now clearly if **seed**
were a local variable of the random-number procedure we wouldn't get
the desired kind of behavior. Whenever we invoke **random**, a new copy
of **seed** is created, and when **random** completes, **seed** disappears. Algol
solves this problem by including a category of local variable called own
variables. If we write

```
INTEGER PROCEDURE random;
   BEGIN
      OWN INTEGER seed;
      random := seed :=  some new value
   END
```

then **seed** persists between calls. When we invoke **random**, we discover
seed already in existence, holding whatever value was last assigned to
it.

The problem of a procedure needing to retain the values of its local variables is a special case of the *data system* problem discussed in chapter 2.
It's sometimes convenient to think of data objects that aren't merely
passive but are capable of transforming themselves when instructed to
do so. This means, in effect, that when we create an instance of such an

object, we create not merely passive data fields but procedure fields as well, where the procedures are customized to the needs of transforming this particular data object.

This is, in a sense, what we do when we specify the random procedure with an own variable. The variable seed is private to the procedure random; it can't be touched by any other procedure. But we might also say that the procedure random is private to the variable seed: the procedure exists solely to manipulate the variable.

"Own" variables are not, strictly speaking, required in order to solve the "random" problem. We could always have made seed a global variable; the program would have looked like this:

```
BEGIN
    ⋮
INTEGER seed;
    ⋮
INTEGER PROCEDURE random;
    BEGIN
        random := seed := some new value
    END;
    ⋮
END
```

Now, seed lives for as long as procedure random (whereas, if seed were a non-own local variable, it would have lived for as long as one *invocation* of procedure random). But this solution is unsatisfying, because it's unfaithful to the programmer's conceptual design (he presumably thinks of seed not as a global variable, but as a variable that is associated with random), and it allows seed to be toyed with by any routine in the program.

Algol 60 is ahead of its time (as usual) in presenting the solution to a problem that won't be clearly recognized and definitely solved until the design of Simula 67. But there are problems with the solution, as there were with call-by-name. Suppose that an own variable is to be *shared* among two procedures? For example, we might want two random procedures which share the same seed: next returns the next pseudo-random number and toss returns either 0 or 1. Own variables won't

work, and we're back to global variables. We need something more
general.

3.2.3   ISM Comparison

Algol's major restrictions compared to the ISM: Any element of an Algol
60 time-map (namely the compound statement) may be either a time-
map or a space-map (namely a block); but only the *last* element of a
space-map may be a general time-map or space-map. The other elements
of a space-map hold simple values, homogeneous collections or templates.
Algol has no record structure or classes. An "Algol space-map" has no
parallelism.

Major additions, compared to the ISM: Algol 60 provides a call-by-name
parameter passing protocol in addition to a call-by-value one.

3.3   Lisp

We discuss several propositions.

1. Fortran and Algol 60 were each intended mainly for scientific computing; neither was suitable for artificial intelligence programming,
   which focuses on symbolic rather than numeric data objects, and,
   most important, requires data structures that can be improvised
   dynamically as the program runs. Lisp was designed to meet these
   requirements.

2. The fact that Lisp is an *interpreted* language is central to its character.

3. The `lambda` phrase is central to Lisp, and indeed to the whole
   history of language evolution.

   (*a*) `Lambda` forces us to face up to a fundamental issue that Fortran
   and Algol 60 only partially address: *what is a procedure, and how
   do procedures relate to the rest of the language?* This issue returns
   us to the question of procedures as first-class objects.

   (*b*) The way `lambdas` are treated in Classical Lisp violates the design principle of *orthogonality* and becomes a *cause célèbre* in the

evolution of Lisp. We discuss the meaning of "orthogonality" and its significance. This lack of orthogonality reflects the fact that while Fortran doesn't fully distinguish between a program and assembly code, Classical Lisp hasn't completely separated programming from mathematics.

3.3.1   Lisp Profile

Program Structure. A program in Lisp is in essence a collection of function definitions—"in essence" because (as we discuss) the idea of "program" is loosely defined in and somewhat foreign to Lisp. Algol-based languages have some concept of a "statement," an instruction that is executed for its effect on the surrounding program, not for its value. Lisp has no such concept; a Lisp program is defined in terms of expressions only, where an expression always returns a value. Hence an assignment statement in Lisp has a value (the value yielded by the expression being assigned to the variable); Lisp's analog of the Algol 60 compound statement has a value (the value yielded by the last expression in the sequence), and so on.

Function application. The Classical Lisp `lambda` phrase is the representation of a function. Consider the expression

```
((lambda (x y) (+ x y)) 3 4)
```

Its meaning is as follows.

1. To apply function `F` to arguments `x` and `y`, we write

    ```
    (F j k)
    ```

    In the expression above, the lambda phrase `(lambda (x y) (+ x y))` plays the role of `F`, 3 plays the role of `j` and 4 plays the role of `k`.

2. The lambda phrase describes the following function: "accept two arguments; call the first `x` and the second `y`; return the sum of `x` and `y`."

3. When we apply this `lambda` phrase to 3 and 4, the function described by the lambda is invoked; formal `x` is bound to value 3, and formal `y` is bound to value 4.

The result is 7.

Arguments to a **lambda** can be symbolic or numeric constants, variables, lists (described below) or function applications. (A **lambda** phrase itself falls into none of these categories.)

Parameters in Lisp are passed by *sharing*: the same object that is bound to or designated by the ith actual parameter is bound, upon function invocation, to the ith formal parameter. We explain further below.

Data Types. Lisp was designed as a language for "symbol processing" as opposed to numerical computing, and the types and data structures of the language reflect this. The main data objects in Lisp are "atoms" organized into "lists". Atoms are either numbers or symbols, where a symbol is an alphanumeric constant that serves as an identifier or *name-tag* (a symbol that is associated with some object).

Lists are manipulated by the operators **car**, **cdr** and **cons**; a large number of other list-manipulating operators are also part of the language, but they can all be expressed in terms of these three. If a_1 and a_2 are symbols, then the expression **cons** a_1 a_2 yields a list which we represent in the form

$(a_1 \ . \ a_2)$

If this list is called L, then evaluating (**cons** L a_3) yields the list

$((a_1 \ . \ a_2) \ . \ a_3)$

The dot notation is used if one or both arguments to **cons** is a symbol. If *expr1* and *expr2* are expressions whose values are the 3-element lists *list1* and *list2* respectively, then (**cons** *expr1 expr2*) evaluates to a new 4-element list with the entire *list1* as its first element, followed by the elements of *list2* in succession. Thus if the value of *expr1* is the list

(1 2 3)

and *expr2* evaluates to

(A B C)

then (**cons** *expr1 expr2*) is the list

((1 2 3) A B C)

This is a four element list: first element (1 2 3), second element A and so on. (car *expr2*) returns as its value the first element of *list1*, namely the symbol A. (cdr *expr2*) returns a 2-element list that is identical to *list2* with its first element deleted, namely the list (B C). It's possible to combine car's and cdr's simply by juxtaposing a's and d's within a selector: (caddr *exp*) is equivalent to (car (cdr (cdr *exp*))), and so on.

"Atom" betokens an object that can't be decomposed, hence is "atomic" (unlike a list, which can be decomposed into more primitive elements via car and cdr).

These operations allow us to create and manipulate data structures (1) whose size can't be determined until runtime, and (2) whose elements are members of a diverse group with no special rules applying to all of them—each element is identified by a symbol unique to it, not by a symbol that (like a numeral) is "predictable" given the object to be represented. For example: suppose we need a program that reads an English sentence from a file and attempts to parse it. We can model the sentence as a list whose i^{th} element represents either the word or the punctuation mark that was i^{th} in the sentence. We can process the sentence by examining the car of the list (looking at and classifying the head element), then repeating the process on the cdr (the rest) of the list until we get to the end.

Lisp symbols are sequences of characters that can serve as identifiers or name-tags. We construct symbols by using the quote operator: (quote foo) (abbreviated 'foo) means "return the object following quote *without* evaluating it." This expression yields the symbol "foo." We can build lists of objects in the same way: the quoted expression '(blue yellow orange) evaluates to the list (blue yellow orange).

Control Structures. Control in Lisp is built around a conditional expression and recursive function definitions. Suppose we need to perform a group of steps repeatedly for as long as condition B is true. In Fortran, we would write

```
100   IF (.NOT. B) GOTO 200
            the group of steps
      GOTO 100
200   CONTINUE
```

In Algol 60,

```
while B do
    the group of steps
```

The equivalent structure in idiomatic Lisp is

```
(defun some-steps ()
  (cond ((not B) t))
       (t (progn
               the group of steps
               (some-steps)))))
```

We've defined a function; we now need to apply it, by writing

```
(some-steps)
```

The expression beginning "cond," the standard Lisp conditional expression, examines a list of condition-action pairs sequentially, and executes the first action whose matching condition evaluates to "true." Thus some-steps is a recursively defined procedure that checks whether the iteration condition B is true; if yes, it executes the called-for steps and re-invokes itself; if not, it terminates, returning the pre-defined boolean symbol t (denoting true). When this procedure is invoked, the effect is to repeat the called-for steps so long as B is true, as in the Fortran and Algol 60 examples.

The progn form evaluates a sequence of expressions in order and returns the value of the last. Progn is Lisp's version of Algol's compound statement. A progn, unlike a compound statement, however, can contain only constants, applications, or jumps; Lisp provides nothing in the way of an Algol block.

Modern Lisps invariably introduce looping constructs of some kind, modeled generally on the ones in Algol 60; but in the presence of a conditional and general recursion, loop constructs are logically unnecessary.

A function that implements iteration through the use of recursion and
a conditional is said to be *tail-recursive*: the last thing we do (except
when the conditional B is true and execution is finished) is to re-invoke
the same function. An implementation note: in a naive implementation
of tail-recursion, each recursive call would result in the construction of
a new activation frame, and this new frame would remain in existence
until the end of the recursion. Such an implementation is expensive and
extremely inefficient relative to the simple loop that could be generated
using a Fortran or Algol iteration construct. It's easy to see, though,
that the intermediate activations in a tail-recursive call serve no purpose beyond re-starting the procedure—we never need to refer back to
previous activation frames.

Naming Environments. The character of Lisp depends heavily on its
special understanding of *binding*, of the association between names and
values. A name in Fortran and in Algol 60 designates a particular *place*.
To assign a value to a variable named `foobar` means, in effect, to take
some object and deposit it in a box named `foobar`. Whatever *had* been
in the box disappears. In Lisp, on the other hand, "assign a new value
to some variable" means, in effect, "tie a new name-tag to some object."
Names don't designate *places*; they correspond to *name-tags* that can
be affixed to whatever object we choose.

This arrangement has two important consequences relative to Fortran
and Algol: removing a name-tag from an object doesn't change the object; an object may furthermore have many name-tags tied to it. Suppose we execute the Algol 60 statements

```
foobar :=  a red object;
bazball := foobar;
       change the red object to a mauve object;
```

and then look at the variable `bazball`. `bazball` still designates a red
object. But if we execute a comparable series of expressions in Lisp:

```
(setq foobar  a red object)
(setq bazball foobar)
       change the red object to a mauve object,
```

we find that `foobar` *and* `bazball` designate a mauve object: "setq" is
Lisp's assignment expression, and it merely tied the label `foobar` to the

red object; the second assignment tied a `bazball` label to the object
(already) labeled `foobar`—so the red object now has two labels tied to
it—and the last statement changed this same object.

(`setq` is actually an abbreviation for `set-quote`. `setq` doesn't evaluate
its first argument; it treats its first argument merely as an identifier,
which is what we want when we execute an assignment. The primitive
`set` operator evaluates both its arguments. (`setq foo 3`) is equivalent
to (`set 'foo 3`).)

Lisp's understanding of the relationship between names and objects is
important to its object-creation strategy and to its idea of function invocation. As a Lisp program runs, it causes new objects to be created.
These objects remain in existence for as long as they are needed, and
then they are "garbage-collected" and disappear. In Algol 60, on the
other hand, objects are created at well-defined points during the execution of a program (when execution enters a block), and they disappear
at well-defined points (when execution leaves a block).

Lisp's understanding of names means that this Algol approach is impossible in Lisp: Lisp's idea of binding and assignment means that objects
are implicitly *shared* among all variables to which they have been assigned. In the Algol 60 framework, the disappearance of a name (upon
exit from a block or from a procedure) can be taken as permission to
destroy the object that is associated with the name (except in the special
case of own variables); but no such permission exists in Lisp. A name
may disappear, and the object it had designated may still be tagged with
many other names. Only when all name-tags have been removed from
an object itself, and from any other, larger objects in which it might be
included, can a Lisp object be bulldozed by the garbage collector.

Garbage collection. The implementation of garbage collection has
nothing to do with the Lisp design *per se*, but garbage collection is so
important to Lisp that a brief note on how it's accomplished may be
useful. *This section may be skipped without loss of continuity.*

Many Lisp garbage collectors use a *mark-and-sweep* strategy. In the
mark phase, every object in the heap that has a name-tag is marked.
In the second phase, all *unmarked* objects are collected and placed on a
global free list, a list linking all free memory cells together. The mark-

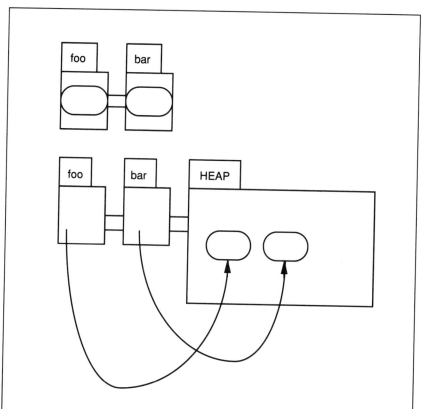

Figure 3.5
Name-to-object binding in Fortran and Algol versus Lisp: In Fortran and Algol 60, names designate "slots" (modeled by regions in the ISM), and objects are kept in these slots (a). In Lisp, objects are generally kept in a *heap*, a large collection of memory cells; names still designate slots, but slots hold *pointers* to objects rather than the objects themselves (b).

and-sweep approach is simple but inefficient: the user's computation must grind to a halt while the garbage gets collected.

A better approach is an incremental garbage collector, a garbage collector that operates in tandem with an ongoing computation. This approach was first described by Baker [8]. The algorithm works by dividing the heap into two equal-sized divisions, known as *tospace* and *fromspace*. Newly created objects are put in *tospace*. The role of the garbage collector is to move some objects from *fromspace* to *tospace* every time an object is created. When all accessible objects in *fromspace* (that is, all objects that have "name tags" or are included within objects that do, and must accordingly be assumed to be still in use) have been moved, the *fromspace* area can be reused. A *flip* occurs at this point: *fromspace* becomes *tospace* and *vice versa*.

Whenever an object is copied from *fromspace* to *tospace*, a forwarding address is left in its place. A reference that reaches its object via a forwarding address is updated to refer to the now *tospace*-resident object directly. Operations that access components of objects (*e.g.*, `car` or `cdr`) check that the object is in *tospace*; if the object happens to be in *fromspace*, it is moved and the reference is appropriately updated. When the head of a list is initially moved from *fromspace* to *tospace*, its tail may still be resident in *fromspace*. A subsequent reference made to the tail (or any of its components) causes the object being referenced to be moved into *tospace*. The process of transplanting the components of an object into *tospace* from *fromspace* is known as *scavenging*. Scavenging is similar to the mark phase in a mark-and-sweep garbage collector— it reaches all accessible objects in *fromspace* that are reachable from *tospace*. By interleaving the scavenging process with other user-specified computation, the garbage collector can be made to work in tandem with the user's ongoing computation.

3.3.2 Lisp Analysis

Research on artificial intelligence began during the late fifties, the period in which Fortran was establishing itself as a powerful programming tool. But Fortran is a poor language for artificial intelligence programming. It doesn't deal conveniently with non-numeric data, and—perhaps most important—provides no good method for building data structures dynamically.

Dynamic data structures (for example, trees and lists) are crucial to programs that eschew algorithms with predictable behavior in favor of heuristics, especially heuristic searches. A *heuristic search* attempts to find the needle in an enormous haystack by using cleverness ("heuristics," good guesses) instead of brute force (an exhaustive search through the haystack). Fortran wasn't adequate for this type of programming. An extended Fortran called FLPL was developed specifically to meet this need. Lisp, which was a very different language, took FLPL as its starting point with respect to dynamic data structures. We pursue these points further at the end of the chapter.

Lisp as an Interpreted Language Early in its career Lisp was implemented as an interpreted language. While a Fortran or Algol programmer would write down a program, send the program to a compiler and then execute the compiled or "object" version, Lisp programmers would type their programs to the Lisp interpreter, which would execute them directly. The middle step—translating a source program to an executable version—is eliminated.

Interpreters are less efficient but more convenient than compilers, as we discussed in chapter one. The stylistic differences—the distinction in feel between the two kinds of systems—are less easy to characterize. The interpreter environment agrees with the improvise-and-polisher.

Behind the difference in personality is a major technical distinction in the way we view a computer. In a compiled language, the role of the physical computer is to embody a series of software machines of the user's devising. In an interpreted language, the computer's role is to embody permanently a *particular* software machine specified by the language designer: to become a "Lisp-executing machine" or an "APL-executing machine."

There are two ways of imagining a user's relationship to the interpreter. Users *might* intend to build software machines for realization by the interpreter. The difference between interpreter and compiler, in this case, boils down to the fact that the interpreter allows software machines to be constructed *incrementally*. Instead of collecting all subroutine

definitions, data objects and so on into a single unit and handing this
unit to the compiler, the user might type his first subroutine definition
to the interpreter, then his second; then, perhaps, he might invoke each
of the two on test arguments to try them out; then he might enter
his third subroutine, and so on. On the other hand, users might be
intended to approach the interpreter as if it were a *calculator* instead of
a computer. A calculator is a machine that reads an expression, outputs
the value of the expression and repeats. From one expression to the next
it remembers nothing. Nothing the user does ever changes the internal
state of the calculator.

McCarthy's original Lisp is in fact a calculator. This is why `lambda`
phrases were an essential part of the original language: a calculator is
immutable. In particular, it can't ever be extended with new function
definitions. The user can't instruct the interpreter to "assign name F
to the function that returns the sum of two arguments," because such
a statement is *not* merely an expression that returns a value; it is an
instruction to *change something inside the interpreter*, to make an entry
in a table somewhere that associates a new meaning with name F. No
such instructions were possible in McCarthy's original Lisp. It follows
that lambda phrases were necessary because without them, only functions whose definitions were wired into the interpreter—functions that
were intrinsic to the language, not defined by the user—could ever be
applied. Note that even with lambdas, users couldn't type "$(F\ 3\ 4)$"
to the interpreter where F was some identifier; what would F mean?
The only choice is to define F on the spot, as part of the application:
"$((\text{lambda}\ \dots)\ 3\ 4)$."

The Structure of Lisp Programs   In Lisp 1.5 this radical limitation
is corrected: Lisp 1.5 includes an instruction called "`define`"[3] that allows the user to add new definitions to the interpreter, and thus to treat
the interpreter as a computer and not merely a calculator. So we turn
to the next question: what kind of structure is a Lisp program? The
Lisp 1.5 manual says merely that a "Lisp program consists of pairs of arguments to `evalquote` which are interpreted in sequence [90, p.203]." In
other words (given the definition of `evalquote`): "a Lisp program consists of phrases of the form (*function-name function-arguments*), which

---

[3]We'll continue to use **defun** in our examples to conform with current Lisp usage.

are interpreted in sequence."

Is this a satisfying answer? We know that a Fortran program is a series of subprogram definitions, and that an Algol 60 program is a block or a compound statement. Lisp programs are specified incrementally, but we'd still like to know *what a Lisp program looks like*. After I've typed (say) fifty definitions to the Lisp interpreter, what do I have? What kind of structure have I built? Can I give a name to the structure? Does the same kind of structure appear elsewhere in the language (do I have recursively structured programs, as in Algol)? Concretely, suppose my program consists of three functions, plus a fourth "main" function which, when invoked, invokes the other three. I use a Lisp interpreter to build this program incrementally; > is the system's prompt. I might enter

```
> (defun f1 (...) ...)
> (defun f2 (...) ...)
> try out f1 and  f2
> (defun f3 (...) ...)
> try out f3
```

What kind of structure have I built? The answer is *no structure* (or at least, no structure that has a meaningful representation in Lisp itself). Evaluating a defun merely changes a table somewhere inside the interpreter.

Lambda-Binding and the Non-Structure of Incremental Programs   It's not very surprising that Lisp has no structure to represent an incrementally built program. In McCarthy's original Lisp and in every subsequent version derived from it, there is one fundamental way to associate a name with a value, namely *lambda binding*. "Lambda binding" refers to binding between *the names of formal parameters and the values of actual parameters*. Other situations in which names and values are associated—bindings between the names of the local variables in a block and their values, for example—are modeled in terms of lambda binding.

Now consider the distinction between the interpreter acting as a calculator and as a computer. As a computer, the interpreter must remember a series of bindings. But an incrementally extended series of bindings is

a poor match to the idea of lambda binding. To carry out lambda binding, we must know all the names to be bound *a priori*; these correspond
exactly to some list of formal parameters. There is no way to alter or
extend a list of formal parameters: whatever it is, it is. Hence there is no
good way to use lambda-binding to model the sort of binding that goes
into the construction of an interpreter's incrementally growing naming
environment. Hence Lisp *has* no good model for this kind of binding:
whatever can't be neatly modeled by lambda binding is handled by *ad
hoc* mechanisms thrown together for the purpose (*e.g.* defun).

Lisp has no model for an incrementally assembled program structure.
Does the ISM? Can we use ISM maps to model incrementally constructed
interpreter environments? The answer is yes; we haven't discussed this
aspect of the ISM, but we'll introduce it here. It will be useful later when
we take up "object-oriented programming." This is the only aspect of
the ISM model omitted from the overview in chapter 2.

Because ISM environments (*i.e.*, space-maps) are objects that can be
manipulated, it's simple to define an operation over two environments.
The compose operation layers a new space-map over an old one (like
installing a new roll of vinyl over an old floor). The layering operation
obeys the following rules: layering map *TOP* over map *BOTTOM* produces a new map *NEW* in which bindings defined in *TOP* supersede
bindings of the same name in *BOTTOM*; bindings defined in *TOP* but
not in *BOTTOM* are simply appended to the end of *NEW*.

For example, given

$$BOTTOM: (\text{(w:1) \& (x:2) \& (y:3)})$$
$$TOP: (\text{(y:4) \& (w:5) \& (z:6)})$$

and composing *BOTTOM* and *TOP* yields the space-map

$$(\text{(w:5) \& (x:2) \& (y:4) \& (z:6)})$$

Given such a composition operator over maps, it's easy to see how we can
build a program incrementally. The interpreter's current environment is
stored in a space-map called *CURRENT*. When a user types expression
e to the interpreter, we build a new map whose single region is (the
still unevaluated expression) *e*. We evaluate this map in the context of

CURRENT, and then simply layer the result on top of *CURRENT* and make this map the new *CURRENT*.

Couldn't we do the same thing in Lisp as well? Couldn't we remedy Lisp's lack of a structural model for incrementally built programs simply by introducing a `compose` operator or something similar? No: what would the Lisp version of `compose` manipulate? Lisp has no "environment" objects, and accordingly it's neither easy nor natural to introduce Lisp operators that manipulate environment objects.

The Meta-Circular Evaluator   In Chapter 1, we discussed the importance of self-describability a metric by which to judge the expressivity and clarity of a programming language. Fortran and Algol 60 are not very self-describing. For example, we referred in chapter 2 to the fact that in many languages, the order in which actual parameters are evaluated is unspecified, but there is no "evaluate these expressions in arbitrary order" construct in the language. Accordingly, we can't understand procedure invocation in terms of a pre-existing arbitrary-order evaluation rule; we must define it from the ground up, as a linguistic primitive. This holds both for Fortran and Algol 60. We've already noted an important limitation on the self-descriptiveness of Lisp: Lisp has no representation for what an incrementally constructed program *in toto* looks like. Still, Lisp is in general a highly self-descriptive language. We can define a small subset of Lisp and then describe the entire language in terms of this subset. As a result, we need only understand the small subset in order to develop a complete and accurate understanding of the entire language.

In his famous early paper on Lisp [91] McCarthy actually goes beyond this, though. He presents (in effect) a simple implementation of the small subset in terms of *itself*, a so-called *meta-circular interpreter* or evaluator. Now obviously if this interpreter merely stated "`car` means `car`, and `cdr` means `cdr`, and you can probably guess the rest," it would be somewhat unexciting. But the point is, rather, to express a *parser* for a set of symbols that *represents* a Lisp program by using Lisp. If we present the meta-circular evaluator with the expression

    (car *something*)

its role will be to dig out the "`car`" and the "*something*," and then figure out that it is supposed to apply its built-in **car** function to the result of evaluating *something*. The result is a nice demonstration of the flexibility and simplicity of Lisp (it would be far harder to write a Fortran parser in Fortran, or for that matter a Lisp parser in Fortran). The meta-circular implementation of the initial subset also forms the basis for an implementation of the entire language in terms of the subset.

Lisp's syntax is the key to understanding the structure of the meta-circular evaluator. Programs and data structures in Lisp have the same syntactic structure. To represent a Lisp program, we use a Lisp "list" structure. Thus the representation of the program

```
(defun fact (n)
   (cond (( = n 0) 1)
         (t (* n (fact (- n 1)))))))
```

is simply the list yielded by evaluation of the expression

```
(quote
  (defun fact (n)
     (cond (( = n 0) 1)
           (t (* n (fact (- n 1))))))))
```

Call this list L. Evaluating (**car** L) yields the symbol **defun**, evaluating (**caaddr** L) yields the symbol n, and so on.

In other words, we can manipulate the source text of a Lisp program by using the operations that manipulate lists. Does this mean that Lisp has torn down the "Algol wall" between programs and data structures? By no means; the reason why not is important.

A Lisp *program* is something that can be evaluated, something that has meaning. A Lisp *list* is merely a collection of atoms in some particular format. Certain Lisp lists can be *understood as* programs and can be evaluated—roughly in the same sense that if you arrange English words and punctuation marks randomly in a sequence, certain sequences will *make sense* as English sentences. Nonetheless, despite the fact that every English sentence happens to be represented by a sequence of English words and punctuation marks, "the English language" and "all random sequences of English words and punctuation marks" are clearly *not* the same thing; nor are "Lisp programs" and "Lisp lists" the same thing.

In more general terms, though, a Lisp "program," insofar as it can be captured syntactically in a list, is merely a series of function applications. The broader environment of which any particular function application is a part—the interpreter's incrementally constructed set of definitions and bindings—has no representation in Lisp. In discussing the unification or non-unification of program and data structures, however, it is this broader idea of a program structure—the kind of structure captured by the Algol 60 block or the ISM space-map—that is at issue.

Given a way of representing programs as lists, we can proceed to give definitions of some basic Lisp functions. The eval function (which is the name of the Lisp meta-circular evaluator) takes two arguments: the list representation of a Lisp expression and a list of variable bindings representing the evaluation environment within which its first argument is to be evaluated. This list isn't an environment, but is used by eval as though it were.

Eval examines the structure of its first argument and proceeds to evaluate it, based on the functions in its built-in definition of the basic Lisp subset and the binding-values for the identifiers given by the second argument.

To give a flavor of how the eval function is structured, we present a small fragment of its definition below. This definition isn't taken from McCarthy's paper, but it is the same in spirit as his original definitions.

```
(defun eval (exp env)
   (cond ((id? exp) (lookup exp env))
         ((constant? exp) exp)
         (t (cond ((quote? exp) (cadr exp))
                  ((car? exp)
                   (car (eval (cadr exp) env)))
                  ((cdr? exp)
                   (cdr (eval (cadr exp) env)))
                  ((cons? exp)
                   (cons (eval (cadr exp) env)
                         (eval (caddr exp) env)))
                  ((apply? exp)
                      (eval-apply exp env))
                  ... ))))
```

The predicates id?, constant?, *etc.* have the obvious meaning. If the
expression to be evaluated is an identifier, we look up its meaning using
the binding-values given by env. If the expression is a quoted object,
i.e., if it is of the form: (quote *exp*), we extract *exp* by using simple
list selection on this expression:

```
(cadr (quote exp))
```

which yields *exp*. If exp is of the form:

```
(car E)
```

we return the car of the list yielded by evaluating E, *i.e.*, we evaluate

```
(car (eval (cadr exp) env))
```

Similar rules apply for the other list operations. If the expression is an
application, *i.e.*, if it's of the form:

```
((lambda ( formals)  body)  actuals)
```

then we pass the expression along with the current environment as arguments to the function eval-apply. Its definition is given below:

```
(defun eval-apply (exp env)
   ((lambda (function evaled-actuals)
      (eval function
            (add-to-env env (cadar exp)
               evaled-actuals)))
     (caddar exp)
     (eval-actuals (cdr exp) env)
```

The expression (caddar evaled-exp) yields *body*, and the expression
cadar exp yields the list of (*formals*). Eval-actuals evaluates each
of the actual arguments in the current environment and returns a list
of the results. Add-to-env takes the current environment, the list of
formal parameters and the list of the evaluated actuals and returns a
new environment in which each formal is paired with the corresponding
actual value. Eval-actuals is a simple recursive function that builds
up its result using cons:

```
(defun eval-actuals (actual-list env)
   (cond ((null actual-list) nil)
         (t (cons (eval (car actual-list) env)
                  (eval-actuals (cdr actual-list)
                                env)))))
```

Note that `eval-actuals` doesn't really tell us the order in which the actuals are evaluated. We know that `eval-actuals` builds its result using `cons`, but since the order in which `cons` evaluates its arguments is unspecified (`cons` is, after all, defined in terms of itself), we can't infer a particular evaluation rule for the elements in `actual-list` based on this definition.

The complete evaluator in McCarthy's paper is short, fairly easy to understand, and well worth careful examination.

Lambdas and First-Class Procedures   It would be nice to have first-class procedures. Call-by-name gives us a bit of the power of first-class procedures, but it's only a fairly weak approximation. With `lambda` we confront the issue directly. Consider an expression E that evaluates to a procedure. What does E look like?

A hypothesis immediately leaps to mind: Classical Lisp's `lambda` phrase is a way to write an E. Just as (+ 3 4) evaluates to an integer,

  (lambda (x y) (+ x y))

evaluates to a procedure. But this hypothesis is wrong. The lambda phrase is *not* an evaluatable expression; the only expressions that can be evaluated in Lisp are atoms and function applications. If we type (+ 3 4) to the interpreter, the interpreter responds with 7, but if we type (lambda (x y) (+ x y)), the response is "I can't evaluate this."

So what good is lambda? Classical Lisp makes a distinction between *expressions* and *functions*. A *function* (unlike an expression) exists only to be applied to arguments; it can't be evaluated by itself. Similarly, we can ask the value of 4, or the value of $\sqrt{4}$, but not the value of $\sqrt{}$—the square-root sign is a *function* that exists only to be applied, and can't be evaluated in and of itself.

A `lambda`-phrase is a *function*. If we say that the "meaning" of some phrase in the language is given by the *behavior* of that phrase when it is evaluated, it's clear that `lambda` phrases have meaning only when applied to arguments; they have no meaning (can't be defined) independently. Here is a violation of an important design principle (one that is violated in fact again and again):

Definition 3.3 A language design is *orthogonal* to the extent that we can separate it into elements that can be defined independently.

Orthogonality (the term was introduced in this sense by Algol 68) is a relative thing, not an absolute attribute. The more orthogonal a language, the better: programmers have more freedom to combine things in ways that were not anticipated by the language designer, and the language is easier to define and to understand. Classical Lisp's treatment of lambdas is non-orthogonal: lambda phrases have meaning only in connection with function application expressions; they have no meaning on their own. Of course it might seem perfectly reasonable for lambda-phrases to be just like "$\sqrt{}$"—isn't this the obvious and natural thing? But suppose we want to include the square-root function in a data structure. We can't write

```
x := √
```

because we can't *evaluate* $\sqrt{}$. Nor can we write `f(`$\sqrt{}$`,...)`, nor can we return $\sqrt{}$ as the *value* of a function, and so on, for the same reason.

Like call-by-name, then, lambdas raise an interesting possibility but don't resolve it satisfactorily. On the other hand, lambda phrases give Classical Lisp a flexibility in dealing with functions far beyond what Fortran or Algol can offer. Classical Lisp *does* make it possible for functions to be passed as arguments, to be bound using ordinary assignment statements to variables, and to be stored in data structures—but lambda can't do this by itself; it must be propped up by a special gadget called the "function" expression, or through the explicit use of quotation.

Suppose I need a function whose argument is another function, the $h(E)$ case we discussed above—or in Lisp syntax, `(h E)` (apply function `h` to parameter E). I can't write `(h (lambda ...))`—can't use a lambda-phrase to represent E, because I must *evaluate* the argument to a function call, and lambda-phrases can't be evaluated. I *can* however write (h (function (lambda ...))): I wrap my lambda-phrase in a "(function ...)" wrapper. I can't evaluate lambdas, but I *can* evaluate (function ...), which yields an applicable version of the function descriptor passed as its argument.

As an alternative to using the (function ...) wrapper, we can prevent the interpreter from attempting (and failing) to evaluate a lambda phrase simply by quote-ing it: we can write

    (h (quote (lambda ...)))

A quoted lambda is in effect a *symbolic* (rather than a function-valued) constant. A quoted lambda doesn't represent a function in the same sense as the object yielded by evaluating a (function ...); it's simply a list. But it so happens that this list looks exactly like a function, and can therefore be applied to arguments by the interpreter.

The function wrapper produces a lexically bound function; quote results in a function that uses dynamic binding. We explain this distinction when we take up Scheme.

Classical Lisp gets many of the advantages of first-class functions by using "function," but there remain problems. We are left with a confusing distinction between (lambda ...) and (function ...), and a variety of both practical and conceptual problems. (For example, if lambda-phrases represent constant values of type "function," why can't we evaluate them, and why don't they simply yield themselves as values, the way 7—a constant value of type "integer"—yields 7?) We return to these issues in chapter 7.

Conclusions: Lambdas and First-Class Procedures   The central goal of programming linguistics is to find out what a program is, what distinguishes a program from assembly code on the one hand and a mathematical expression on the other. Classical Lisp's non-orthogonal treatment of lambda is interesting in part because of the light it sheds on precisely this issue. Lisp's treatment of lambdas—the fact that procedures almost but *don't quite* achieve first-class status in Classical Lisp— is evidence of a confusion between mathematical expressions and programs.

```
              3 + 4   =>    7

    (lambda (x) (* x x)) =>    ?

              ?     =>    (lambda (x) (* x x))
```

Figure 3.6
Expressions and values in Lisp. 3+4 is an expression that yields 7 as its value.
Question: is (lambda ...) an expression that yields a procedure as its value, in
the sense that 3+4 yields an integer? No: lambda phrases can't be evaluated.
Question: is there some *other* expression that yields (lambda ...) as its value, in
the sense that there is an expression that yields 7? Yes and no. We can understand
(quote (lambda ...)) as an expression that yields a (lambda ...) as its
value, but quote isn't a function-producing operator, and the result of evaluating
this quote is properly understood as a list that merely happens to have the form of
a lambda phrase. Furthermore, (lambda ...) isn't a constant value like 7; 7 can
itself be evaluated—its value is 7. (lambda ...), on the other hand, cannot be
evaluated. So lambda phrases don't precisely resemble either integer expressions like
3+4 *or* constant integer values like 7. (function ...) doesn't yield a lambda
phrase either because of the lexical binding protocol, discussed in chapter 7.

In mathematics, it's perfectly reasonable to write, for example,

$$f(x) = x^2$$

The phrase x^2 is an expression that behaves like a function; conceptually,
it's the same as $\sqrt{\ }$. It cannot in itself be evaluated (or is at any rate not
intended to be—the question never arises), but nobody cares. Classical
Lisp's lambda phrase is analogous: the phrase (lambda (x) (* x x))
is, like x^2, a phrase that defines a function, not an expression that can
be evaluated on its own. In mathematics we don't insist on knowing how
to evaluate each and every separate phrase; it doesn't bother us that we
don't know the "value" of x^2 or $\sqrt{\ }$. In programming languages we do
so insist, and when we can't evaluate some phrase, problems arise and
we need to add new constructs to the language (eg, (function ...)) in
order to fix them. Why?

Recall the idea of *recursive structure*: in order to understand complex
structures, it's desirable to be able to disassemble them into simpler
instances of *the same kind of structure*. In mathematics, the relevant
class of structure is the proof or derivation; in programming, we deal
not with proofs but with software machines. A proof is supposed to

be true; a machine is supposed to work according to some specification when you turn it on. We ask two basically different questions, then, in understanding a proof on the one hand and a program on the other. In mathematics, "is this true?"; in programming, "what happens when I turn this on?"

It's important in programming, then, that we know how to *evaluate* (how to "turn on") as many separate bits and pieces of our program as possible, because we will understand the workings of the large machine on the basis of the workings of the smaller, simpler machines of which it is composed. In mathematics, there is no similar need to understand what happens to an expression when you "turn it on"; this question is irrelevant to a proposition's truth or falsity. Hence it never bothers us in doing mathematics that x^2 can't be evaluated. Programming is another story.

3.3.3 ISM Comparison

Lisp's major restrictions compared to the ISM: Lisp has no complete version of the ISM's space-map—hence no general program structure, no general block structure, no records, modules or data systems; no parallelism.

Major additions: Lisp allows objects to be dynamically created and extended (using list structure) on a garbage-collected heap.

3.4 Fortran, Algol 60 and Lisp Finale: "Without the Errors"

Where did these three fundamental languages come from? What did they set out to do, and how well did they succeed? The answers are unusual and striking.

Fortran was developed at IBM by a group headed by John Backus; it was intended at first as an adjunct to the IBM 704 computer. The project began in 1954; the system was released for distribution in early 1957, and first described to the technical community at the 1957 Western Joint Computer Conference. It is amazing to note that in a survey of IBM 704 installations carried out in April of 1958, more than half reported using Fortran for more than half of their problems [114, p.177]. So Fortran was an immense success from the first. Late in 1958, Fortran was released for two other IBM computers; early in 1961 it became available on a UNIVAC machine; and thereafter, an immense number of implementations for IBM and non-IBM equipment followed. Original Fortran gave way to Fortran II in 1958; Fortran IV was first described in 1962 (Fortran III was described but never released as such). In 1966 a report by what was then called the American Standards Association (later to be ANSI, American National Standards Institute) was accepted as a standard definition for a language that was in effect Fortran IV.

What was the aim of the original Fortran project? The answer is extraordinary and worthy of careful contemplation: the goal was to *eliminate programming*. Sammet quotes as follows from the 1954 "Preliminary Report" on the Fortran project:

> The IBM Mathematical Formula Translation System or briefly, FORTRAN, will comprise a large set of programs to enable the IBM 704 to accept a concise formulation of a problem in terms of a mathematical notation and *to produce automatically a high-speed 704 program* for the solution of the problem [109, p.143]." (italics added.)

Backus *et al.* elaborate in their 1957 paper: "If it were possible for the 704 to code problems for itself and produce as good programs as human coders (but without the errors), it was clear that large benefits could be achieved [6, p.188]."

This is a remarkable statement—what does it mean? When the authors speak of automatic programming (programs written by machine and not by programmers) the programming they mean is, of course, assembly coding. In this sense, their goal was achieved. The success of Fortran meant that assembly coding within Fortran's domain—scientific computing—became the exception and not the rule. Fortran undertook an amazingly ambitious project *and succeeded*.

On the other hand ... But of course the complete story is not quite so simple; there is also a sense in which Fortran was a failure, but the failure is as illuminating as the success. The Fortran compiler was supposed to generate programs that ran as well as human-designed programs "(but without the errors)." Assembly coding is particularly difficult and error-prone because it is low-level, unstructured, designed to conform to a machine's and not a person's way of doing things. Under the circumstances it is understandable that Fortran's designers believed that, by eliminating assembly code, they could eliminate programming bugs. A Fortran program after all was *not* a program, but rather a series of mathematical formulas (hence *For*tran, formula translation). Now it is surely not the case that a physicist or chemist or engineer, in writing out a series of formulas to derive a useful equation or to prove some result, is bothered by what we think of as "programming bugs." Fortran eliminated assembly coding and substituted formulas of the type scientists use regularly; but needless to say, the programming errors did *not* go away. The same debugging problems familiar to assembly coders simply re-emerge, at a higher level, when we use a programming language like Fortran. Why?

Backus's own later view is that Fortran is too low-level a language. He writes in 1978 that languages like Fortran "constantly keep our noses pressed in the dirt of address computation and the separate computation of single words, whereas we should be focusing on the form and content of the overall result we are trying to produce. We have come to regard the DO, FOR, WHILE statement and the like as powerful tools, whereas they are in fact weak palliatives ... [114, p.178]." It is remarkable that a language's designer should come to renounce it in such colorful terms, and this renunciation itself forms a part of the Fortran story; we discuss Backus's current views later, when we take up declarative programming.

In considering this assessment of Fortran's weaknesses, note first that Backus's 1978 attack on Fortran-like languages calls to mind his 1957 criticism of assembly language. In 1978 Backus writes that "we should be focusing on the form and content of the overall result;" in 1957, Backus *et al.* wrote that "[i]n many cases the development of a general plan for solving a problem was a small job in comparison to the task of devising and coding machine procedures to carry out the plan [p.188]." What to do? The 1978 solution sounds again, at least in general intent, like 1957 all over again. At the risk of some oversimplification, the essence of Backus's later position is that programming must become more like mathematics. The languages among which he places Fortran "lack useful mathematical properties," he writes in 1978 [5]. But in 1957, Fortran was developed precisely "to enable the programmer to specify a numerical procedure using a concise language like that of mathematics [6, p.188]."

There are two ways to interpret this recrudescent interest in making things mathematical. Clearly we might argue that in 1957, the designers of Fortran had the right idea (programming should be as "mathematical" as possible), but did not go nearly far enough. Fortran's failure to deliver programming "without the errors" can be set right (if not fully, at least to a significant extent) if we carry through on Fortran's original interest in mathematical forms of expression. This position makes sense if the applications or structures of greatest interest to us are mathematical to begin with. APL, which we discuss in the next chapter, is a good case in point. It's hard to beat APL for conciseness or expressivity when it comes to dealing with arrays (the basic structure in mathematical programming); APL's mathematical syntax and built-in array manipulating operators go far beyond anything remotely similar in Algol, Fortran or Lisp. If we are interested in problems that are best expressed using arrays, it's probably a good bet that we can solve them more easily using APL than with any of these other languages. And if a program is easier to arrive at and more concise, it will probably have fewer errors than a lengthy, hard-to-write program would. (Of course, *efficiency* is another issue altogether; APL may be more concise and expressive than Fortran, but it's far less efficient. Efficiency is a vital factor in Fortran's continuing status as the language of choice in the scientific and engineering applications community.)

But there is another possible interpretation that sees Backus's later position not as an attempt to rectify a partial job, but as a kind of undaunted utopianism. If we look at the trend lines and not at the details, Backus is prescribing in 1978 another dose of exactly the same restorative (Distilled Essence of Mathematics, Extra-Concise) that was tried in 1957. Although Fortran on the whole worked beautifully, the 1957 allegation that making programming "more like mathematics" would eliminate programming errors *in general* is now known to be hopelessly naive.

There are those who would argue, then, that it is the analogy itself, not the way in which Fortran handled it, that is flawed. Programming after all is a kind of machine-building, not the derivation of formulas. No matter how great the superficial resemblance between a program and a mathematical derivation, the derivation has to be true, whereas the program has to work when you turn it on. It simply does not follow that by making a program look like a mathematical formula, programming takes on the characteristics of mathematics. True, certain programming tasks are highly "mathematical" in character, insofar as they center strictly on equation-solving; a more "math-like" language might conceivably be less error-prone than Fortran for these tasks. Other programming jobs have little or nothing to do with mathematics. If we are building a database, a text editor, an airplane controller, a bank-account manager, a yak-stampede simulator or any of a huge list of other programs, math-like languages *might* be a good idea, but there is surely no reason to suspect *a priori* that they should be.

Modest goals, part 2. The Fortran project set out to eliminate programming. Algol 60's designers were content merely to create a universal language. Thus Perlis and Samelson write in their 1958 report on Algol 60's predecessor, Algol 58, that "[a]mong other things, these conferees [in attendance at a major meeting of American computer users] felt that a single universal computer language would be very desirable [114, p.171]." The astute reader might regard the goal as strange: universal solutions are usually called for after periods of diversity and complexity, but we are now standing at the dawn of the programming-language era, and in 1958 Fortran is the only language with a broad following. Alan Perlis explains in a 1978 article [114]. True, "By the spring of 1958, ... Fortran's acceptance steadily grew." But on the other hand,

> Remington RAND was exploiting the MATH-MATIC and UNICODE languages for its UNIVAC I and 1101-03 computers, respectively. Several universities were developing programming languages and processors for their computers.... It almost seemed that each new computer, and even each programming group, was spawning its own algebraic language or cherished dialect of an existing one.... In 1957 computer users were already concerned about the difficulty of communicating programs, a difficulty caused by language and machine diversity and a lack of standards in almost every area relating to computer use [p.4].

In 1958, then, Fortran was doing well but had yet to achieve the enormously wide acceptance it was to establish by the early sixties; Furthermore, Europeans were wary of helping IBM to dominance in Europe, and Fortran was still an IBM product. Algol 58 was designed by an international committee representing the American and European computing communities. A second meeting early in 1960 produced the revised version that became Algol 60. The 1960 meeting involved seven Europeans and six Americans; among the Europeans were van Wijngaarden, later to lead the development of the radically different language Algol 68, and Peter Naur; among the Americans were Perlis, John McCarthy, whose seminal work on Lisp was already underway, and John Backus. Backus at this point had accomplished the development not only of Fortran but also of the notational device later called "Backus Normal Form"—a formal method for specifying programming-language syntax that was used for the first time in defining Algol 60. Backus Normal Form became the standard for syntax definition, and played a central role in the development of formal methods in specifying and studying programming languages. In 1964, it was agreed that the notation referred to as Backus Normal Form be changed to Backus-Naur Form in recognition of Naur's contribution as editor of the Algol 60 report.

Another success. Fortran did indeed (according to the applicable definition) eliminate programming. Did Algol become a universal language? Once again the answer is, in essence, yes. Algol 60 was at best a limited success as an implemented programming language: during the sixties it was widely used in Europe, but was never popular or widely available in the United States. The language nonetheless achieved phenomenal success as a *vehicle for communicating algorithms*. It is the *lingua franca* of computer science. Given in addition its huge influence on the subsequent evolution of programming languages, and the importance even of its defining document, Algol 60 emerges not only as a success in achieving its ambitious goal, but as a central design in the history of programming languages.

The dual origins of Lisp. Lisp was developed by John McCarthy during the same period that saw the genesis of Algol 60. One of the reasons that McCarthy's Lisp design is so interesting and important is the fact that it synthesizes two rather separate strands in language evolution, one theoretical and one pragmatic.

The 1960 paper [91] in which McCarthy first describes Lisp—a paper second only to the Algol 60 report in its importance to programming language evolution—is called "Recursive Functions of Symbolic Expressions." It describes a system which

> [i]n the course of its development went through several stages of simplification and eventually came to be based on a scheme for representing the partial recursive functions of a certain class of symbolic expressions. This representation is independent of the IBM 704 computer, or of any other electronic computer [p.175].

(Note that Lisp, like Fortran, was first developed for the redoubtable IBM 704!) The *partial recursive functions* are identical to the set of "all functions that a computer (or anything else) can compute."[4] There are many ways in which the partial recursive functions can be represented, but McCarthy's new scheme, as embodied in Lisp, was a particularly interesting one. Lisp functions operate over the domain of *symbolic expressions*—symbols organized into simple, recursive lists. It was therefore easy to define a scheme whereby Lisp programs could operate on other Lisp programs. A Fortran program operates (basically) on numbers; it isn't set up to manipulate other Fortran programs, which are expressed not as numbers but as a succession of *symbols* (like "FUNCTION," "COMMON" and so on). But Lisp programs operate precisely on lists of symbols, and if we can express a Lisp program as a list of symbols (as we discussed earlier), a Lisp program can operate conveniently on other Lisp programs in the same sense in which a Fortran program can operate conveniently on numerical data. It therefore became possible to express within Lisp itself the "universal function," the function that accepts any other function as an argument and *executes* that function, in a particularly concise and readable way.

Hence the theoretical impetus behind Lisp development. But Lisp was in fact originally developed with pragmatic goals in mind: "[t]he system was designed to facilitate experiments with a proposed system called

---

[4]These functions are "partial" insofar as they are defined, in general, over only a *part* of their domain: when they are invoked over an arbitrary set of arguments, they will sometimes compute the correct answer and will otherwise *diverge*—loop endlessly and never return a result.

the Advice Taker," McCarthy writes at the beginning of his 1960 paper;
"... [t]he main requirement was a programming system for manipulating
expressions representing formalized declarative and imperative sentences
so that the Advice Taker could make deductions [p.175]." Lisp's origins
and subsequent history are closely associated with research on artificial
intelligence, of which the Advice Taker project was an early example.
Research on artificial intelligence began during the late fifties, but, as we
noted earlier, Fortran was an inadequate tool for artificial intelligence
programming: it lacked the dynamic data structures that were essential.
In order to support this kind of programming, Fortran would have to
change.

Such a modified Fortran was first developed by H. L. Gelernter's group
at IBM. Gelernter's 1959 Geometry Theorem Prover, following Newell,
Shaw and Simon's "Logic Theorist" of 1956 and their "General Problem
Solver" of 1957, was among the first successful experiments in the new
field of artificial intelligence. The program was written in an extended
Fortran called FLPL ("Fortran List Processing Language") designed for
the purpose by Gelernter and his group.

FLPL departs from Fortran by including a series of operators for building and manipulating lists, including two that were designated `car` and
`cdr`—later to be among the most celebrated and obscure acronyms in
computer science.[5] These operations defined a simple recursive list
structure on which FLPL's dynamic data structures are based. Mc-
Carthy was a consultant at IBM while the Geometry Theorem Prover
and FLPL were under development, and contributed to the group's decision to develop a modified Fortran. Lisp is a radically different language
from FLPL (which after all was a species of Fortran), but its central
data-structuring construct is derived from FLPL's.

Fortran's success at serving the scientific programming community is
matched by Lisp's in serving artificial intelligence. Lisp and artificial intelligence have been almost inseparable since the early sixties.
Although other languages has enjoyed a modest vogue from time to
time, the vast majority of artificial intelligence programs continue to be

---

[5] `car` stands for "contents of the address register" and `cdr` for "contents of the
decrement register," in reference to particular architectural features of (you guessed
it) the IBM 704.

written in one kind of Lisp or another, and today Lisp's influence is (if anything) steadily expanding.

3.5 Readings

Basic Readings. The first widely read report on Fortran appeared in 1957 [6]. The definitive article on Algol 60 is the Algol 60 report published in 1963 in the *Communications of the ACM* [98]. Lisp was first described by McCarthy in 1960 [91]; the Lisp 1.5 reference manual was published soon thereafter [90].

Suggested Readings. The conference proceedings of the ACM SIG-PLAN 1978 Conference on the History of Programming Languages [114] provides fascinating reading on the design of many early programming languages (including those discussed in this chapter).

[66] is a comprehensive anthology of important programming language papers, several of which are discussed in this book. Among other things, the anthology includes the Algol 60 report and the Lisp 1.5 programmer's manual.

[7] and [76] give very readable summaries of the FORTRAN language. [44, 81, 101] are good introductions to the topic of vectorization and optimization of FORTRAN programs. [40, 78] give comprehensive treatment of both theoretical and implementation related issues involving dependency analysis.

Besides the Algol 60 report, Knuth's now famous 1967 article on the *Remaining Troublespots in Algol 60* [77] is a must for anyone interested in understanding the subtleties of the language. R.W. Bemer's paper on the history of Algol [12] is also interesting reading. For detailed discussion on the implementation of Algol 60-like constructs, see [4].

A good tutorial on Lisp can be found in [132]. Readers interested in Lisp's theoretical foundations should see [27, 75] or [82]. There are a number of dialects and extensions to Lisp; of these, we discuss Scheme in a later chapter. [96] describes MACLISP, the first widely used dialect of Lisp after McCarthy's Lisp 1.5; [124] discusses INTERLISP, a fully integrated Lisp system complete with compiler, programming environment

and debugger; [52] discusses the design and implementation of the Lisp
machine, a microprogrammable computer providing extensive hardware
and software support for Lisp. Common Lisp [116, 115], a relatively new
committee-designed dialect of Lisp is a descendant of MacLisp. Its main
goal was to serve as a common Lisp dialect that could be implemented
efficiently on a broad class of machines. Today it is arguably the most
widely used dialect of Lisp.

3.6   Exercises

1. "Despite the existence of subroutines and subroutines invocation,
   there is no template-instantiation in Fortran." Explain. What are
   the implications? "The idea of dynamic binding or lexical binding
   is meaningless in the context of Fortran." Yes or no? To what
   extent, and why?

2. Ignoring questions of syntax, what problems would be encountered in implementing an interpreter for Fortran in Algol 60? In
   Lisp? What conclusions can you draw about Fortran's programming method (vs. Algol 60's or Lisp's)?

3. To get the `swap` function to work correctly using call-by-name, we
   need somehow to bind the *l*- and *r*-values of the arguments simultaneously. (The *l*-value of a variable is the location of that variable
   in memory; the *r*-value is the value stored in that location.) Consider the following implementation of the `swap` procedure:

   ```
   PROCEDURE swap (x,y);
     INTEGER x,y;
     BEGIN
       INTEGER PROCEDURE w;
       BEGIN
         w := x;
         x := y
       END;
       y := w
   END;
   ```

Suppose we call **swap** with i and A[i] as arguments. The effect of this call is to evaluate the assignment A[i] := w, where w is a function call that executes the following piece of code:

```
w := i;
i := A[i]
```

The key to understanding why this version works lies in the assignment, A[i] := w. Before the function w is called, the *l*-value of the expression A[i] is computed; in other words, we fix the location into which the result of applying w is to be stored *before* we make the call. Things work as expected, although this solution is far more complicated than a comparable one under call-by-reference.

(a) Show that this solution does not work in the presence of side-effects by giving an example. (b) Can you come up with a solution that works using call-by-name? If not, give a precise explanation. (c) Can you sketch a translation scheme that takes a function implemented using a call-by-reference protocol and yields an equivalent function that uses only call-by-name? What are the limitations of your scheme, *i.e.*, for what class of applications will the translation fail to produce an equivalent program?

4. "It is for all practical purposes impossible to implement a dynamic data structure like a Lisp list in Fortran." True or false?

5. (a) What is the basic mechanism for associating names and values in Lisp 1? (b) How does this mechanism cope with or relate to interpreter-created environments? Algol-style blocks? (c) How is the answer to (b) reflected in the design of early Lisp?

6. What common function does the following Algol 60 procedure compute:

```
integer procedure f(n)
 integer n;
 integer procedure h (g,m);
  integer procedure g;
   integer m;
    h := if m = 0 then 1
                  else m * g (g, m-1);
 f := h(h,n)
```

Is f recursive? Is it tail-recursive? How about g? Can we write
such a function in Lisp 1? in Lisp 1.5?

7. Is it possible to write a Lisp 1.5 function **create-thunk** that takes
an expression as an argument and creates a *thunk*? (Recall that a
thunk is a procedure of no arguments constructed by a compiler to
defer the evaluation of an expression.) What does your answer tell
you about the suitability of Lisp for implementing a call-by-name
protocol?

8. Algol 60's call-by-name protocol is implemented using a copy rule
and not thunks. This was not merely a design decision but a practical necessity given the language's treatment of functions. True
or false? Explain your answer.

9. (a) What are the main applications of the **quote** operator? What
extensions or modifications to Lisp can you propose that would
make **quote** logically unnecessary? (b) If given the opportunity
to redesign Lisp, would you favor incorporating these changes?
Give technical justification for your answer. (c) "**quote** addresses
a question of syntax, not semantics." True or false? Explain.

10. What does the following Lisp expression evaluate to?

```
((lambda (x)
     (list x (list (quote quote) x)))
   (quote (lambda (x)
              (list x (list (quote quote) x)))))
```

((list l m) $\equiv$ (cons l (cons m nil)).)

What is the most important feature of Lisp that makes writing such an expression possible? Could we construct something similar in Algol 60?

11. Is it possible to get the behavior of Algol 60 own variables in Lisp 1? Lisp 1.5? Give justification.

4 APL and Cobol

On our most important issue, the **structure of programs and of data objects**, Cobol takes a significant if fairly tentative step forward: the *record* structure originates with Cobol. In Cobol, for the first time we can isolate a piece of the broader naming environment, enclose it in a wrapper, give it a name, and treat it as a single (compound) unit within the top-level environment. Unlike Algol 60 or Fortran, the structure of a Cobol data object mimics (albeit in a highly restricted way) the structure of the surrounding program; we get data objects that consist of heterogeneous typed fields identified by name.

Turning to data objects and their **first-classness** (or in other words, the degree of their power and versatility), APL's promotion of *arrays* to first-class status yields elegance and power (although APL gives up Lisp's gains with regard to the first-class status of functions). On the structure of **interpreter-built programs**, APL's solution (based on the *workspace*) is more elegant and workable than Lisp's—although the weaknesses in this scheme, particularly when compared to the same language's virtuoso treatment of arrays, make for a particularly vivid demonstration of the fact that naming environments have always been the Pandora's box of language design.

With these two languages we confront **type systems** as an important issue for the first time. Type systems differ along two major axes—we can have "passive types" or "active types"; typing can be relatively strong or weak. APL to some extent and Cobol even more markedly champion "active typing" versus passive typing, an approach that (in Cobol's sense at least) was destined for a quick spiral into the wastebasket of history. But that's not to say that active typing isn't interesting and valuable; we explain the issues involved. Cobol also presents our first occasion for discussing a distinction between **constructive** and **declarative** (or "descriptive") languages; this distinction gains importance as languages evolve.

APL development was begun by Kenneth Iverson in the late fifties, but at first the language was intended not for implementation but for the

description of algorithms and computer architectures. The language's
name is an acronym for the title of the book in which it was first completely described (in a somewhat different version from what was eventually implemented), Iverson's *A Programming Language* of 1962 [70].
Implementation began at IBM in 1964, and the completed system was
described and distributed in 1966 [42]. Cobol (for "Common Business-
Oriented Language") was designed by a committee that originated in
1959; the committee had representatives from the U.S. government and
from six computer manufacturers, all interested in a common language
for data processing. A design was finished and was implemented by several manufacturers in 1960; the revised version described in 1961 [32]
forms the core of all future versions and is the basis of our treatment
here.

4.1   APL

Our examination of APL focuses on the following proposition.

APL, like Lisp, faces the problem of defining the structure
of an incrementally constructed program; APL's answer in
terms of *workspaces* is far better developed than Lisp's. But
the strict boundary separating the computation from the
naming environment (or "workspace") portions of APL, and
the contrast between the organizational scheme on either side
of the boundary, are striking evidence of the continuing difficulties caused by naming environments. The computation
side is organized in terms of first-class objects (arrays) that
scale consistently and have uniform syntax. On the naming-
environment side there are no first-class objects, and no consistent scaling. Virtually the only place where the syntactic
consistency of the computational side breaks down is where
the issue of naming environments intrudes in the form of the
local variables of a procedure.

4.1.1   APL Profile

Program   Structure.   Conceptually,   a   non-trivial   APL   program
amounts to a series of transformations applied to arrays. While a generic
program might be conceived of as "do step 1, then step 2" and so on, an
APL program can be described as "starting with array A, apply transformation 1 to it, then apply transformation 2" and so on. Because each
transformation returns a value that can be treated as input by the next
transformation, such a program can be conceived as a single expression:

> *nth-transform* (
>   *n-1st-transform* (
>   ... *first-transform* (*original-array*) ...)

Not only can APL programs be conceived of in this way, they can often
be *written* in this way as well. In Algol or Lisp we might choose, in
particular instances, to regard a program as a series of transformations
to an initial data structure. But a program conceived of in this way
consists of necessity not only of the expression in which we apply the
transformations, but of the various procedure or function declarations
in which we *define* the transformations that we will use. Furthermore,
if we need to transform an *entire* data structure—an entire Algol array
or Lisp list, for example—we generally need to use a loop or a recursive
function to express the fact that "every member of this structure must
be transformed as follows." Neither of these two limitations apply in
quite the same way to APL.

APL includes an enormous repertoire of built-in array-creating and
array-transforming functions. To perform an operation such as, for example, "reverse the order of the components along the ith dimension of
the following array" in Algol, we would need to write the appropriate
procedure; in APL this operation and many others are built in. Furthermore, array-transforming operations in APL work on the entire array.
In this sense, iteration is implicit in their definitions. We needn't write
"do the following to *each element of* array A"; we write simply "do the
following to array A." The fact that we can omit *to each element* means
that in many cases, we can dispense with loops entirely.

An example will make APL's idiosyncratic structure clearer. Falkoff and
Iverson [43] give the following example: an APL program to compute

the prime numbers up to the integer N can be expressed as

(2=+/[1]0 = So .|S)/S← ι N)

Tracing the operation of this program won't make you an APL programmer, but should convey some feel for the language's unusual character to those unfamiliar with it.

This program is a single expression, and APL expressions associate to the right: we evaluate, first, the rightmost complete expression we can find. In this case the rightmost expression is

ι N

which yields a vector of integers from 1 through N. Thus ι5 yields

1 2 3 4 5

(Vectors are written without intervening commas, and parentheses are added only when they are needed to resolve ambiguity.) The next-rightmost expression is now

S ← ι N

which is an assignment expression. It assigns the 1-through-N vector to S, and yields this vector as its value.

To explain the next step, we begin by noting that an expression of the form

(*some bit vector*)/ *any vector of the same length*

returns as its value a new vector consisting of the elements of the right-side vector for which the corresponding element in the left-side is 1. For example,

(1 0 0 1 1)/1 2 3 4 5

yields the vector

1 4 5

We can now grasp in outline this approach to generating prime numbers. On the right side of the "/" symbol there will be a vector consisting of the integers from 1 to N; on the left side there will be a vector whose i^{th} element is 1 if i is prime, and 0 otherwise.

The role of the expression

$(2=+/[1]0=S\circ \:.|S)$

is to generate a bit-vector with a 1 corresponding to every prime. It works as follows. The expression

$S\circ \:.|S$

yields "the outer product of S with S using the operator '|' "—the modulo operator. A square array is returned; the entry in its ith row, j^{th} column is the value of the jth element of S (which happens to be equal to j) modulo the ith element of S (which is of course i). Thus the result is

```
1 mod 1   2 mod 1   3 mod 1 ...
1 mod 2   2 mod 2   3 mod 2 ...
1 mod 3   2 mod 3   3 mod 3 ...
1 mod 4   2 mod 4   ...
1 mod 5   ...
...
```

which is equal to

```
0 0 0 ...
2 0 1 ...
3 3 0 ...
4 4 ...
5 ...
...
```

The next expression we examine is

$0=S\circ \:.|S$

In APL, the comparison operations are functions that return values. If X and Y are single-element values rather than arrays, $X = Y$ returns 1 if X and Y are equal and 0 otherwise. If X and Y are arrays of the same size and shape, an array is returned whose i,j^{th} entry is 1 if the i,j^{th} entry of X equals the i,j^{th} entry of Y, and otherwise 0. Finally, we need

to know that a scalar such as 0 when compared against an array such
as the one returned by the outer-product operation will automatically
be converted to an array of the right size and shape to perform the
comparison. The result of the comparison expression, then, is an array
whose i,j^{th} element is 1 if the i,j^{th} element of the outer-product array
was 0, and otherwise 0. This array is

```
1 1 1 ...
0 1 0 ...
0 0 1 ...
0 0 ...
0 ...
...
```

Next we apply the "$+/[1]$" operation to the array, which has the effect
of summing each column of the array and returning a vector whose i^{th}
entry is the sum of the array's i^{th} column:

```
1 2 2 ...
```

In a final comparison operation, we compare this vector to a vector of
2's; the result, again, has a 1 for every 2 in the right-side vector, and a
0 for each non-2:

```
0 1 1 ...
```

We're done. We've generated a vector whose i^{th} entry is 1 if and only
if i is prime (because exactly under these circumstances, i was evenly
divisible twice, by itself and by 1, and this fact was recorded by the
presence of exactly two 0's in its column of the outer-product array).

This example is atypical in its cleverness, but it represents the goal to
which APL programmers aspire: to write programs of extraordinary
conciseness, in which conventional looping and control constructs are
superseded by operations over whole arrays at once.

Data Types. The array is APL's only data structure. Arrays are homogeneous; their elements may be either numbers or characters. APL
programmers needn't concern themselves with distinctions between integers, reals, floating-point numbers and so on; appropriate values are
stored and displayed by the system automatically. APL provides *type*

coercion between objects of different type: a scalar object passed as an argument to an array operator, for example, is automatically transformed into an array. We pursue this point further when we introduce the general question of active versus passive types, in the "Cobol Analysis" section.

Control Structure. APL's most important control device is the one we have been discussing, expressions that do away with the need for explicit iteration by operating on whole arrays at once. Other control structures are simple: conditionals and branches are used to organize loops when they are needed; recursive function definitions are also available.

Functions. APL functions may accept zero, one or two arguments. (The number of arguments to a function is referred to as the function's *arity* or *valence*.) Functions with arity 1 or 2 are written in the usual arithmetic style: -4 defines an application of the monadic (arity 1) operator "-" to argument 4; 2+3 defines an application of the dyadic operator "+" on arguments 2 and 3.

The invocation of a function f of more than two arguments, written

$$f(\ arg_1,\ arg_2,\dots,\ arg_n)$$

looks ordinary enough but has a non-standard interpretation. f is considered to be a *monadic* function applied to a *vector* whose elements are arg_1, arg_2, ..., arg_n. Since arrays must be homogeneous, the arguments to a function with arity greater than two must all be of the same type.

APL functions are not true first-class objects. There *are* primitive operators that take function-valued arguments. In the prime-finder example, the function "+" was an argument to "/." But programmers cannot write functions that yield other functions as results, nor can they embed functions within data structures.

Arguments in APL are passed by value only. Hence functions cannot alter their arguments (in the sense that the Algol 60 zero(k) procedure set k to zero, for example). APL uses a form of dynamic binding: free names are resolved in the environment of the applied function. The syntax and semantics of APL functions are discussed further in the **APL Analysis** section.

Naming Environments. An APL program consists of a series of function definitions and global variables. Functions may declare local variables, but there is no block structure; a variable that is not local to a function is global, and all function definitions are global.

APL is conceived as a tripartite structure: the APL interpreter, the "system" and the user. The three entities work in tandem and communicate with each other in well-defined ways. The setup allows users to give names to interpreter-created naming environments, and to store and retrieve them at will.

An APL naming environment is called a *workspace*. It is defined by a symbol table that gives definitions for a set of data objects and function definitions (and also, under some circumstances, *computations* that were suspended in the process of execution). Users can gather the named objects in their current interactively developed environments into a workspace, and save the workspace. Also, they can copy the contents of any previously saved workspace into the current working environment. For example, after defining two arrays called A and B, and a function called BAZBALL, the user can execute a "*)SAVE W1*" command; this causes a workspace called W1, whose contents are the two arrays and the function definition, to be saved. He might now execute "*)LOAD W2*," which activates some other previously saved workspace; $W1$'s definitions of A, B and BAZBALL disappear. At some later point, however, $W1$ may be reactivated, at which point its definitions become available again.

Within a workspace, definitions may be gathered into sub-workspaces (called *groups* instead of workspaces); a workspace may contain many groups and groups may contain nested groups. Workspaces may be gathered into super-workspaces (called *libraries* instead of workspaces or groups); libraries may contain only workspaces (no isolated variable or function definitions), and may not themselves be gathered into super-libraries.

The APL system contains a simple editor for text entry, sophisticated debugging capabilities that allow function-execution to be suspended at user-designated points, provisions for a public library, provision for communication between APL programs and system utilities and between two APL programs, and other constructs and operators that define a complete computing environment and not merely a language interpreter.

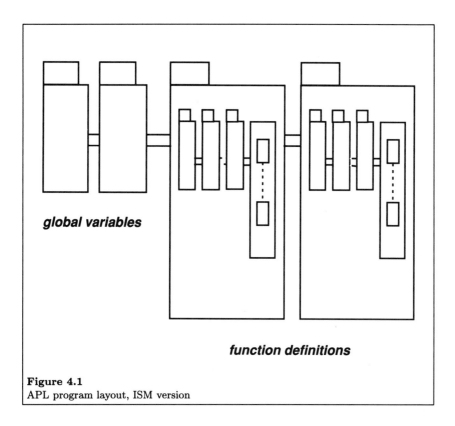

global variables

function definitions

Figure 4.1
APL program layout, ISM version

We illustrate APL's naming environment structure expressed in terms
of the ISM model in Figure 4.1.

4.1.2 APL Analysis

When a programmer builds a program incrementally by using an interpreter, what kind of structure is he building? Classical Lisp's only
answer is (in effect) "not a user-visible structure." APL has a better answer: an incrementally assembled program is a *workspace*. A
workspace is a well-defined object, and a well-developed set of operations is available for the manipulation of workspaces. Workspaces can
be given names, collected into named groups and divided into named
sub-collections. They can be saved, restored and erased, and elements

can be copied between them. Any APL programmer will vouch for the fact that this system is natural and convenient.

But there's a striking and instructive contrast between the way computation on the one hand and workspaces on the other are managed. Computation takes place over array-structured objects. There is remarkable uniformity, consistency and generality in the treatment of arrays: every data object that is not a primitive scalar is an array, and in addition much of an APL function definition or expression can *itself* be understood and manipulated as an array. For example, as we've described above, APL is one of the very few languages to store the arguments to a function in a well-defined structure—at least in cases when the function's valence is greater than two. Functions of zero, one and two arguments have their own special syntax, but a function F of (say) three arguments is invoked as

    F(A1, A2, A3)

This expression looks unremarkable—but then we recall that in APL, the comma is no mere separator; it represents the concatenate-vector operation. What the invocation statement does is

1. concatenate the values of A2 and A3, giving a two-element vector, then

2. concatenate the value of A1 to the front, giving a three-element vector, and then finally

3. pass this three-element vector as an argument to F.

The statements that constitute a function definition are themselves regarded as elements of a vector. When (for example) the APL system needs to refer to a particular line in a function definition (in identifying the location of an error, for example, or the point from which a function was invoked), the citation is a simple array reference. "BAZBALL[3]" might be the third integer in a numerical vector named BAZBALL, or the third line of a function definition named BAZBALL. The characters that *make up* the symbols that make up a function definition are *also* a vector—the ith element being the ith character of the source version of the function definition.

Now, consider the main naming-environment structure, the workspace. A higher-dimension array may be treated as an array of arrays, but a collection of workspaces is a library, not a workspace. The sub-groupings within a workspace are "groups," not workspaces. Arrays are first-class objects: for any array A in the language, there is an expression that yields A as its value. *Transparency* is a property that is closely related to first-classness.

Definition 4.1 A data type or data structure is *transparent* when values of that type can be represented within the language.

In APL, arrays are not only first-class, they are transparent: we can write down the value of any APL array using the syntax of APL. Workspaces on the other hand are not first-class, and they are not transparent. We can't write an expression that evaluates to a workspace; to create a workspace, we build it incrementally by typing definitions to the interpreter or by copying definitions from another workspace.

In other words, we can write an expression such as

   `ARRAY12` ←   *an expression that yields an array*

but not one such as

   `SPACE15` ←   *an expression that yields a workspace*

Like the result of a Lisp interpreter session, an APL workspace is not transparent: we can build, save and manipulate the workspace `BAZBALL`, but there is no way to express the value of `BAZBALL` (the collection of bindings and objects that make up `BAZBALL`) using the syntax of APL.

This omission is significant: in APL, we know what a program *is* (in effect it is a workspace), but we don't know what one *looks like*. Because we don't know what one looks like (a workspace is a black box with no discernible structure), we have no idea how a program structure relates to the other structures in the language.

What difference would it make if we did? Consider the fact that APL's remarkably precise and uniform syntax breaks down in the face of local naming environments, specifically the local variables within a function (these constitute the only local environments in the language, which has

no block structure). The following is the header for a function of two
arguments X and Y; variables I, J and K will be local to the definition:

> $\bigtriangledown$ X FUN Y; I; J; K
> ... *the definition of FUN*....

In other words, to declare local variables, we list their names in the
heading of a function definition, following the part of the heading that
gives the function's name and its formal parameters. It's striking that
the semicolon designates *no* operation in a language where virtually
every other symbol denotes an *operation* to be performed; in fact, most
symbols designate two different operations, one when used dyadically (A
symbol B) and a second when used monadically (*symbol A*). The semi-
colon is merely a delimiter. Where almost all other symbols have one
consistent dyadic meaning and another consistent monadic definition,
the semi-colon is a catch-all delimiter that performs several disparate
duties, including delimiting the names of local variables.

Suppose that workspaces *were* first-class and transparent—suppose that
a notation existed whereby we could indicate "the following variables
constitute a workspace." We could then use precisely this notation to
construct a *local workspace* for function FUN; the local workspace would
consist of the (unbound) variables I, J and K. After all, what are a
function's local variables but a kind of temporary workspace? Given
this understanding, functions execute within a "local workspace," and
name references are referred in the first instance to names within the
local workspace. Names that can't be resolved are referred to the local
workspace of the function that invoked this one, and so on, until we
reach the level of the "global" workspace. This name-resolution behavior
reflects APL's actual behavior, but not (of course) the way in which this
behavior is achieved.

How would we write down expressions that evaluate to workspaces? It's
striking that, just as the semi-colon denotes no operation, "stitch these
elements into a workspace" is *denoted by* no operation. Suppose we defined semi-colon to mean precisely "concatenate these two elements into
a workspace." We now have a consistent syntax for the local variables
in a function, and much more: we know what a program looks like.

Presumably a program looks something like

> $Name_1$: *First Definition* ;
> $Name_2$: *Second Definition* ;
> $\vdots$
> $Name_n$: n^{th} *Definition*.

Perhaps, now, we can define operations to manipulate workspaces by analogy with the operations that manipulate arrays, instead of providing two separate and disjoint sets of operations. Perhaps we have a notation for heterogeneous data objects, should we ever want them—these would simply be workspaces.

But in APL, workspaces are *not* first class and *not* transparent, and the semi-colon means nothing. APL draws no analogy between object structure (in particular, array structure) and program structure. We've been interested throughout in the distinction between programming and mathematics. APL is a powerful and original language closely modeled on mathematical forms of expression. But mathematics has nothing much to offer when it comes to understanding the structure of a program in general, and naming environments in particular. APL, therefore, inherits not only conciseness, power and flexibility from mathematical forms of expression, but the lack of any consistent model for naming environments.

> ? APL's version of the Algol Wall: arrays are a flexible and convenient structure for data organization, workspaces for the organization of incrementally built namespaces. APL arrays are first-class, transparent objects with uniform, recursively scaling structure; workspaces are non-first-class, opaque objects that are part of a heterogeneous hierarchy comprising groups at the sub-workspace and libraries at the super-workspace level.

A final point. We have suggested that there are two kinds of fundamental objects in APL, the array and the workspace, but why not one? Recall that in the ISM, there is no distinction between data objects and program structures or naming environments. Might it have been possible to define an APL workspace as a heterogeneous array with named

elements, thereby allowing us to operate on namespaces in the same
way we do on arrays? Perhaps, but now we really do have a different
language. Every thought-experiment must end somewhere.

4.1.3 ISM Comparison

APL's major restrictions compared to the ISM: There is no APL version
of an ISM space-map—hence no representation for a program as an
incrementally constructed group of definitions (workspaces are opaque,
non-representable). APL has no records, modules or data systems, and
no block structure; there is no parallelism.

Major additions compared to the ISM: APL provides a dynamic array structure and a coterie of special-purpose operations. The APL
workspace allows definitions to be added and removed. The language
supports a coordinated-system model.

4.2 Cobol

We focus on two points.

1. Cobol is close to assembly language in its lack of abstraction mechanisms. Particularly striking, there are no parameter-accepting
   subroutines in the language as it was originally defined. Cobol on
   the other hand is the first widely used language to propose the fundamental extension we've referred to as *heterogeneous data objects*
   or *records*, and in some ways its records are quite interesting. They
   can be operated upon as unit objects, and they also show the first
   signs of *recursive object structure*: they mirror the structure of the
   surrounding naming environment. On the other hand, the lack of
   abstraction or template mechanisms in the language sharply limits
   the generality of Cobol records.

2. Cobol's notion of types is based on the idea of pervasive *type coercion*. We define this term and discuss Cobol's approach.

4.2.1 Cobol Profile

Cobol is a language for business data-processing, not for computation *per se*. Businesses keep records of employees, customers, orders, merchandise, the status of accounts and so on *ad infinitum*. These records must be maintained, consulted, updated and used in the generation of new records. Cobol is designed, then, as a language for reading and writing large files.

Program Structure. A Cobol program is a well-defined structure: it consists of four divisions in a fixed order. The identification division names the program and may optionally give other descriptive information, for example, the program's author and installation. The environment division identifies the source and object computers and assigns symbolic names (for use within the program) to the files that will be manipulated. The data division holds a complete description of the files to be read and written and the variables to be used. The procedure division holds the executable statements that define the program's runtime operation.

In dealing with the structure of the data division we encounter Cobol's approach to names, values and types. The data division consists of the "file section" followed by the "working storage section." The file section describes each file to be manipulated; the heart of the description gives the structure of the *records* of which the file consists. Here is the debut of a significant structure. The term "record" had existed in computing since the earliest file-processing programs; it refers simply to one element of a file. The record's role in Cobol is to provide a model *within* the program for one piece of an *external* file; record declarations within the file section create, in effect, input or output buffers. To write data to a file F, you deposit the data in F's associated record structure. When you read data from file G, the data appears, again, in G's associated record structure. It follows that there is no idea of record *templates* in Cobol—the record idea is tied not to data objects within the program, but to files *outside* the program.

176 Chapter 4. APL and Cobol

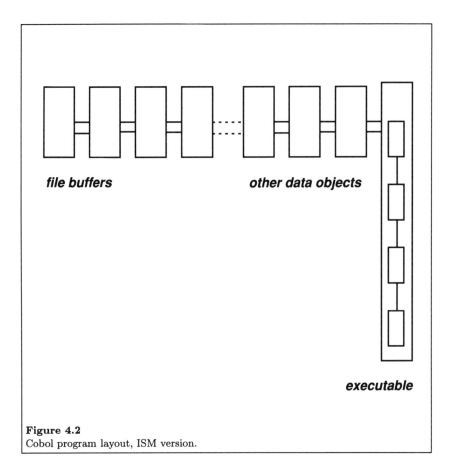

file buffers

other data objects

executable

Figure 4.2
Cobol program layout, ISM version.

Consider the excerpt

```
    FILE SECTION.
    FD   ELEPHANTS
         ...
    DATA RECORD IS ELEPH-CARD
01      ELEPH-CARD.
        02  EAR-SIZE      PICTURE 999V99.
        02  GRAYNESS      PICTURE 9(1).
        02  MOOD          PICTURE A(10).
        02  FILLER        PICTURE X(64).
    FD  ...
```

The program intends to deal with a file whose internal name is
ELEPHANTS. The ELEPHANTS file consists of a succession of records, each
one of which will be referred to as an ELEPH-CARD. There are three fields
in each record. The value of EAR-SIZE consists of three characters chosen from among "0," "1" and so on through "9," followed by a decimal
point that is to be understood although not stored explicitly, followed
by two more numeral characters. The value of GRAYNESS is a single
numeral character. The value of MOOD is ten alphanumeric characters.
The remainder of the record consists of 64 characters that are blank or
may be ignored. (A file record will often correspond to a single punched
card, which has room for 80 characters. Since this Cobol data structure
buffers one element of the file, enough room must be provided for the
entire record.)

ELEPHANTS might be an input or an output file. If it is an input
file, the program will execute "READ ELEPHANTS" operations: the next
ELEPHANTS record will be copied into the ELEPH-CARD data-structure.
If ELEPHANTS is an output file, the program will execute "WRITE
ELEPH-CARD" operations: data will be written into the ELEPH-CARD
structure and thence automatically into the ELEPHANTS file.

Data Types. The "working storage" section creates variables that are
not used directly as input or output buffers. Variables may be simple
variables, records or arrays. The basic data type is the *character*; all
variables are assumed by default to have character strings as their value.
But a declaration may also have the phrase "USAGE IS COMPUTATIONAL"

appended, in which case the value stored is a number (the binary encoding rather than the character representation of a numeric value). Arrays have at most three dimensions; they may occur within records, or contain records as elements. Although records declared in the working store section don't serve directly as file buffers, they are designed for use in direct conjunction with file operations, particularly as staging areas within which output records can be assembled for writing into a file buffer.

The names declared in the data division are global to the program; there are no nested scopes.

There are no procedures in basic Cobol—no subprograms that accept parameters—although a standard definition for a procedure construct exists, and it may be implemented "optionally" in extended versions of the language.[1]

Control Structures. The procedure division gives the sequence of actions to be taken at runtime. Unless the procedure division starts with an optional "declaratives" section (which may specify steps to be followed in the event that files of a given type are encountered, or file-handling errors occur, or a formatted report is to be generated), program execution begins with the procedure division's first statement. Control-organizing constructs are simple: there are conditional statements, GO TO's and a looping construct called the PERFORM statement that supports both bounded and unbounded (for-loop and while-loop style) iteration.

One part of Cobol's computational arsenal is, however, unexpectedly sophisticated and powerful. Cobol allows *implicit programming through type-coercion*—certain routines can be invoked implicitly and automatically simply by writing an assignment statement. We discuss this topic further in the next section.

Syntax. Cobol syntax is designed so that Cobol programs will be "English-like" or "self-documenting." Instead of being modeled on mathematical expressions, Cobol is modeled on simple English sentences. English as opposed to mathematical notation is less concise and more varied. Cobol reflects both these differences. The Algol statement

    c := a/b

---

[1]Procedures are part of the Cobol ANSI standard developed in 1974.

can appear in Cobol as

```
DIVIDE A BY B GIVING C
```

However, as in English, there is more than one choice in Cobol.

```
DIVIDE B INTO A GIVING C
```

is also permissible, as is

```
COMPUTE C = A/B
```

The last form represents Cobol's compromise with more conventional expression-style notation. Interestingly, the DIVIDE form can be expanded:

```
DIVIDE B INTO A GIVING C REMAINDER D
```

No such alternative exists given the COMPUTE form. Cobol includes not only varied phrasing but a collection of "optional words" that can be added to the source program to make it more readable. A variable can be initialized, for example, by appending a "VALUE *some value*" clause to the end of a declaration, but programmers can also write "VALUE IS *some value*" if they prefer.

To those unfamiliar with Cobol, all this may seem unusual and rather charming. It is fair to point out, though, that Cobol source programs are bulky and verbose, and Cobol programmers are required in many cases to generate far more text than they'd need to in other languages.

4.2.2 Cobol Analysis

Cobol, like Fortran, has no statement bracketing and no local variables *per se*. Unlike Fortran, Cobol is happy to dispense with subprograms altogether. The lack of procedures in the basic language, and the fact that procedure-based programming is cumbersome and unidiomatic, even in extended implementations, may strike readers as remarkable, and perhaps it is. It should however be remembered that the typical Cobol program merely hauls data out of a file, performing fairly simple computations or tabulations as it goes along. Cobol programs should in this sense be understood as simple fishing boats, not as floating factories.

Although Cobol's power is obviously limited, its design is prescient in several ways. One of the most important involves the idea of heterogeneous data objects, or *records*.

The languages we've discussed so far deal only with a limited world of data objects: the world of *homogeneous objects* with no internal names. (The Lisp list appears more heterogeneous than an array, but its elements, unlike a record's, don't have names.) The extension to heterogeneous structures with named components is crucial. As software machines make the conceptual transition from number-manipulators to arbitrarily intricate models of reality—from adding machines to "microcosms"—they must have a suitably rich and flexible world of data objects available to them. The Cobol record is a first step in this direction.

Cobol records don't make it to genuine first-classness, but they *can* be treated as units. For example: if X and Y are two records with different internal formats, the statement `MOVE CORRESPONDING X TO Y` will assign the value of X's field n to Y's field n for all names n that are shared between X and Y. Not only is this powerful operation not included in later and "more powerful" languages that use records (Pascal, for example), it tends to be impossible for programmers to express. Cobol also introduces (in a very limited way) the idea of *recursively structured heterogeneous objects*. Conceptually, Cobol variables *inside* a record are the same sort of object as variables declared at the top level, *outside* of any record. We explore these issues in greater detail when we move on to Pascal.

Cobol's non-interest in abstractions or templates weakens the importance of these innovations, of course. We can't specify a record template and use it to create many structurally identical objects; each record object must be hand-crafted.

Type Systems and Coercion. Cobol's approach to types is unusual and innovative. We begin by defining some important terms.

A type system may be based on what we will call "active types" or on "passive types". In an *active* type system, a type declaration serves a standing order to the system to maintain the value of some variable within the stated type. In a *passive* type system, a type declaration serves as a constraint: any use of a variable that is inconsistent with that variable's stated type should be flagged as an error. As in many other cases, active typing is a relative thing. In general, though, a "more active" view of typing is expressed in a relatively greater tendency to perform *type coercions*—to convert a value of one type into a "corresponding" value of some other type—when there is a potential mismatch.

Suppose that (in some generic language) c is declared to be a character-string and f is a function of one argument that returns an integer. Consider the assignment

```
c := f(x)
```

Under an active-typing system, the compiler treats this as an order: c is to be maintained as a variable whose value is a character string; therefore, the integer returned by f(x) must be converted to a character string and then assigned to c. Languages implemented using a passive type system, on the other hand, would treat this assignment as a programming error.

APL has an active typing system insofar as it performs automatic coercions between scalars and arrays. We gave an example in discussing the primes-finding program; in the expression

```
0=So.|S
```

a scalar (namely 0) is converted automatically into an array, for comparison with the array yielded by So.|S. A passive type system would probably have reported an error, along the lines of "type mismatch to the '=' operator." But APL deals only with numbers and characters, does not have typed variables (any name can be bound to a data object of any type), and performs coercions involving reshaping only. Cobol takes matters further.

In Cobol, variables do have types, and there are a variety of possibilities—character, numeric and "edited" types—to choose from (as we discuss further below). Cobol, then, needed to reach some understanding about the meaning and significance of types, and it chose the active-typing approach. PL/I, imitating Cobol, took the same position. This view of things was soon enough to be all-but-expunged by Pascal's contrary position. Cobol's choice is interesting, nonetheless, both intrinsically and because it holds an honorable place alongside core memory, *homo ne-anderthalensis* and the topless bathing suit in the endlessly fascinating Hall of Rejected Technologies at your local *Gedanken* museum.

Consider the following Cobol declarations:

```
77   FOOBAR PICTURE 9999, USAGE IS COMPUTATIONAL
77   BAZBALL PICTURE $$,$$9.99
```

FOOBAR is declared to be an integer between 0 and 9999 (that is, it can be represented using four decimal numerals with no decimal point). BAZBALL is an "edited" character string: its value will be a series of characters representing a price from "$0.00" through "$99,999.99." When we execute

```
MOVE FOOBAR TO BAZBALL
```

the integer value of FOOBAR is converted into an appropriate character string: zeros will be inserted to the right of the decimal point; if FOO-BAR's value is 1000 or greater, a comma will be inserted; a dollar sign will be inserted to the left.

(Cobol's use of an active type system as opposed to a passive one is in keeping with its "business data-processing" approach to the computer as less a fancy calculator than an electronic employee. English-like syntax is one manifestation of this viewpoint. Active typing is another and more fundamental one. A manager giving instructions does so not in hopes that they will be checked meticulously and any errors promptly reported, but rather with the intention that the employee do whatever is necessary to carry them out.)

It's interesting that Cobol's use of active typing and of "PICTURE" style declarations has a "declarative" feel.

Definition 4.2 A *constructive* program describes how a computation is to be performed. A *declarative* program merely describes the intended result, and leaves it up to the implementation to devise a method for achieving the result.[2]

---

[2]The phrase "procedural programming" is a reasonable and widely used alternative to "constructive programming"; "imperative programming" is a widely used, *un*reasonable alternative. The word "imperative" suggests urgency or peremptori-

Thus we might say that "Find a tub, place it under the oil pan, unscrew the stopper at the bottom of the oil pan, wait until everything has drained out, put the stopper back in, remove the oil cap on the upper part of the engine, add fresh oil" is a procedural or constructive program. "Let the oil be clean" is a declarative version.

Both "constructiveness" and "declarativeness" are, like "orthogonality," properties that programming languages exhibit not absolutely but to varying degrees. Cobol is basically a constructive language, but it includes elements with a highly declarative feel. Consider the PICTURE declaration above: the range of values "BAZBALL" can acquire is given implicitly by the "shape" of these values as specified by the PICTURE declaration. In most constructive languages, it's impossible to write type declarations of this sort. Cobol's active type system also has a declarative flavor. The single MOVE statement above causes a substantial amount of activity to occur implicitly. The programmer didn't need to invoke conversion or editing routines explicitly; he merely described the desired outcome.

All this is not to say that Cobol is a hero-language in disguise. Its limitations are obvious. But the design has interesting features that have been ignored, and shouldn't have been.

4.2.3   ISM Comparison

Cobol's major restrictions compared to the ISM: The Cobol program framework serves as a sharply restricted ISM space-map, but space-map nesting is allowed only in the form of record instances. Cobol has no modules or data systems, no block structure, no templates in the basic language, and no parallelism.

---

ness, or it describes the mood of a verb; neither sense is appropriate here. A verb or a course of action can be imperative. A language cannot be. The *intended* meaning of the phrase is also wrong. "Imperative programs" are supposedly lists of orders telling the computer exactly what to do, whereas declarative programs are not. (Clearly this makes "imperative programs" sound faintly nasty, as if they are given to barking out orders through bullhorns while their gentler declarative brethren strum lutes beneath the elm tree.) In fact, an "imperative program" may specify details that a "declarative program" omits (the precise order in which expressions are evaluated, for example), but what *is* specified in a declarative program is exactly as imperative as the corresponding material in an "imperative program." In both sorts of language, programmers "instruct" the computer to compute something, and in neither case is it welcome to compute anything else.

Major additions compared to the ISM: Cobol records have special buffering behavior. Cobol also has an active typing system, an extensive collection of file-handling and input-output operations.

4.3   Readings

Basic Readings. [43] is a good overview of the design of APL. [32] gives
a general overview of Cobol. It is one of a series of articles that appeared
in a special volume of the *Communications of the ACM* devoted to
various aspects of Cobol.

Suggested Readings. The definitive book on APL is Iverson's *A Programming Language* [70]. The APL programmer's manual [42] for the
IBM/360 gives information on implementation and System/360 specific
features of the language.

4.4   Exercises

1. What single most important feature of APL permitted us to construct a one-line prime-number finder? Could we have written such
   a program in Lisp? Why or why not?

2. What features of APL would hinder its implementation on a vector
   or parallel machine? What features of the language would help us
   in such an implementation?

3. "Loops are logically unnecessary in APL." True or False? Justify
   your answer.

4. Suppose that workspaces were first-class objects in APL, patterned
   as closely as possible on arrays. Write a brief description for this
   type of workspace construct. If you could perform indexing and
   comparison operations over workspaces, what might such operations mean?

5. "In syntactic terms, Cobol is a higher-level language than Lisp."
   Explain.

6. "On average, APL programs are too short and Cobol programs are too long." Explain. What does it (or might it) mean to say that a program is "too short" or "too long"? What concise metric can you propose for how long a program *should* be? (The metric will of course be abstract and qualitative.)

7. Suppose Cobol had chosen not to use an active typing system, deciding instead to raise an error if a variable of a stated type was used in a context not applicable for that type. What would have been the implications of such a decision? Would it have improved (or diminished) the expressivity of the language?

8. "Cobol's type system improves runtime efficiency." True or false? Give justification for your answer.

9. Cobol is not well-suited to be an interpreted language; APL is. Explain.

10. Discuss (a) a Lisp in which lists had the evaluation semantics of APL arrays, and (b) an APL in which arrays had the evaluation semantics of Lisp lists. Which of the two alterations is a greater departure from the language as it exists?

5 Pascal, with Notes on Algol 68 and PL/I

Pascal takes a major step forward on our most important issue, the **structure of programs and of data objects**. Pascal, like Cobol, allows sub-environments to be nested within top-level environments, giving a *record* construct; unlike Cobol, Pascal allows records to be instantiated from templates called "record types." Programmers can now specify and instantiate both program fragments (using procedures) and data objects (using types). But the Algol Wall itself is (if anything) reinforced by the distinction drawn between procedures on the one hand and types on the other—both are templates, but they are syntactically and semantically unrelated.

Pascal's view of **type systems** becomes normative for most subsequent Algol-based languages. Pascal's type system allows the programmer to place constraints on the use of variables, in the expectation that he will be notified before runtime of type violations. The type system can be extended with programmer-defined types, in the interests of expressivity or of better, more focused type-checking. Pascal is associated with an enormously significant contribution to **programming methodology**—Niklaus Wirth's idea of "stepwise refinement."

Finally, Pascal is a simple language that opposed a gathering trend towards complex designs. We discuss some associated questions about the aesthetics of language design in the appendix to this chapter.

Pascal's importance as a *simple* design won't be clear, though, unless we start by considering briefly two important languages designed before Pascal but after the languages we've considered thus far. In a 1977 paper [131] evaluating Pascal six years after it was first described, Welsh, Sneeringer and Hoare note that

> [a]t the time Pascal was first designed and developed, the most fashionable languages in the learned and practical world were ALGOL 68 and PL/I. The discovery that the advantages of a high-level language could be combined with high

efficiency in such a simple and elegant manner as in Pascal was a revelation that deserves the title of breakthrough [p.135].

Pascal must in fact be considered against a backdrop of Algol 68 and PL/I, two languages loosely based on Algol 60, Fortran and Cobol, but enormously more complicated than their predecessors. Their designers found numerous weaknesses (many of which we've discussed) in the earlier languages; the new languages gained power but gave up simplicity. It's *not* true, on the other hand, that PL/I and Algol 68 offer nothing beyond a certain brontosaurine appeal. PL/I, for one thing, is by no means extinct: it continues to be used within IBM, where it originated. More importantly, both PL/I and Algol 68 are powerful and original designs—and Algol 68 in some ways anticipates, in others goes far beyond, many of the introductions eventually to be popularized by Pascal. We discuss these languages briefly, then turn to Pascal.

PL/I development began in 1963; the language was designed by a committee with representatives from IBM and from an IBM user's group. Fortran had been designed for scientific computing and Cobol for business data-processing, but in 1963 the lines dividing these domains were less well-defined than they had been in the fifties. IBM accordingly decided that it would manufacture a new line of computers, "System/360," to serve both scientific and commercial purposes (hence "360," a machine with a full circle of applicability). PL/I ("Programming Language I") was an associated project: it would be a general purpose "full-circle" programming language, rightful successor both to Fortran and to Cobol. The design was completed in 1964 and implemented by IBM and, thereafter, by various other groups and companies.

Algol 68 was also designed by a committee but mainly reflects the influence of one man, van Wijngaarden. The original Algol 68 report made difficult reading ("one of the most unreadable documents which has ever been printed"[1]). Its celebrated incomprehensibility reflects in part the fact that Algol 68 was the first language to be described in terms of a formal operational semantics. The language is described using the *Vienna Definition Method*, a complicated formal language that was quickly displaced by denotational semantics and simpler operational models. A

---

[1] According to S.H. Valentine in a 1974 article [127].

revised version that appeared in 1975 [128] described a slightly modified and somewhat easier-to-implement language in a more comprehensible way. A number of Algol 68 implementations were built during the 1970s; the language was widely talked about but never widely used.

Pascal, the work of Niklaus Wirth, was first described in 1971 [137] (the design was based in part on Algol W [65], an Algol 60 dialect described in 1966); a revised Pascal report appeared in 1974 [72], and the language has been widely available ever since, Wirth himself having described the first compiler in 1971.

Readers will notice that Simula 67 is an earlier language than Pascal, but we examine it in a later chapter. The sequence reflects, in part, Pascal's greater continuity with earlier work: both Simula 67 and Pascal are based on Algol 60, but Simula 67 is the more "radical" design, as we'll see. It's also true, though, that Pascal and Simula 67 evolved over roughly the same period. Pascal is later than Simula 67, but Algol W is earlier, and to a certain extent the two languages draw inspiration from common sources—notably C.A.R. Hoare's work on the "record concept" (see *e.g.*, [64]).

5.1 The Foreground: PL/I and Algol 68

5.1.1 Pl/I

PL/I was intended for use both in scientific computing and in data processing, and for a third domain as well, the construction of operating systems. To PL/I's designers, this meant that the language must unite all the features of Fortran with all the features of Cobol and all the added features necessary for operating systems. The result was bound to be complicated. PL/I is closest to Fortran, although it has file handling and a type system modeled on Cobol's, and block structure like Algol 60; however, it also includes many features found in none of the earlier languages.

PL/I set out to provide programmers with more freedom than they had ever had to specify exactly the characteristics of each object and each computation in a program. The declaration of variables is a good example of the link between freedom and complexity in PL/I. Variables are

characterized by a collection of "attributes" that collectively constitute
a type definition for the associated object. Variables may be numbers,
strings of characters or bits, arrays or *structures* (structures resemble
Cobol-style records). We further discuss each of these possibilities below.

Consider a simple numerical variable. Numbers have four attributes:
"mode" (real or complex), "scale" (fixed- or floating-point), "base" (decimal or binary) and "precision" (number of digits on each side of the decimal point). Besides these number-specific attributes, *all* PL/I variables
are either EXTERNAL or INTERNAL to the subprogram in which they are
declared. Declaring a variable to be EXTERNAL makes it part of the global
environment: like a Fortran COMMON block, an EXTERNAL variable is declared *within* each subprogram (and only within those subprograms) that
make use of it. Each variable also comes equipped with a *storage class*,
which may be STATIC, AUTOMATIC, BASED or CONTROLLED. A STATIC local
variable acts like a Fortran local or an Algol "own" variable: its value is
retained between activations of the subprogram or block within which it
is defined. An AUTOMATIC local variable is allocated upon entry to and
deallocated upon exit from the surrounding subprogram or block. The
BASED storage class introduces an important innovation: the dynamic allocation of variables under programmer control. The object associated
with a BASED variable is allocated explicitly by the programmer, using
the ALLOCATE command; a dynamically-allocated variable must be freed
explicitly as well, using the "FREE" instruction—there is no automatic
garbage collector as there is in Lisp. The CONTROLLED storage class supports another (rather peculiar) approach to dynamic allocation: it sets
up a stack of objects, initially empty. The programmer can push new
objects on the stack (using ALLOCATE again) or pop them, using FREE.
Summing all these attributes gives us declarations like

```
DECLARE FOOBAR DECIMAL FIXED REAL (8,3)
              STATIC EXTERNAL
```

PL/I, to be fair, understood itself to be a highly complicated language,
and specified default values for omitted attributes. In the declaration
above, we can omit everything but "DECLARE FOOBAR." The compiler
will automatically supply values for the remaining attributes (although
these would *not* be the values we have specified in this example).

We briefly consider two aspects of PL/I that are particularly germane to broader issues in language development, PL/I's *structures* and its type system.

PL/I *structures* are modeled on Cobol's records. But in Cobol there is no record *template* or abstraction mechanism. PL/I provides such a template, albeit in a rather back-handed way. The BASED storage class supports dynamic allocation. Suppose variable S is a BASED structure: whenever we execute ALLOCATE S, a new S is allocated on the heap. ALLOCATE returns a pointer, which we can store and (if necessary) use in building linked data structures. We can execute ALLOCATE S any number of times, thus in effect using S as an object-generating template. This doesn't allow us to use S as a type designator—we can't declare new variables of type S the way we can declare REAL variables, say—but it's a step. Algol 68 and Pascal go further.

Pl/I's approach to *types* is a generalization (or apotheosis) of Cobol's. Because PL/I's repertoire of types and operations is larger than Cobol's, PL/I's version of active typing is more spectacular: a single innocent-looking assignment statement can cause an enormous amount of activity backstage. Suppose that CHARS is the name of a variable of type character-string. Consider the statement

CHARS = ('57' | |8) + 17

Executing this assignment has the following effects.

1. The "| |" sign means "string concatenation," and "57" denotes a character-string constant. However, "8" is a number, not a character string. It is coerced to a character string, and the result is the character string "578" (that is, a sequence of three characters, the first being the numeral "5," the second "7" and the third "8").

2. Addition is defined between numbers, not between character strings. To perform the addition, the character string "578" must be coerced into the number 578, which is added to 17, giving 595.

3. CHARS, though, is a character string, so the result of the addition must be coerced back into a character string; the string "595' is assigned to CHARS.

PL/I's type system is based squarely on the proposition that programmers know what they're doing. When this proposition breaks down,
active typing causes serious trouble: the PL/I compiler will go to any
lengths to avoid diagnosing a type-mismatch error. In fact, though, programmers frequently make such errors, and bugs can be avoided if they
are diagnosed at compile-time. In Pascal's view, languages should be
based on the sterner but perhaps more realistic proposition that programmers often don't know what they're doing, and can use all the help
they can get. This view has replaced PL/I's almost universally. We
explore it further in the next section.[2]

5.1.2   Algol 68

Algol 68, like PL/I, is a large and complicated language; it bears little
direct resemblance to Algol 60. One measure of its size and complexity
is the freedom it offers programmers to write their own ticket without
worrying about the kind of conventional constraints that virtually all
previous languages had imposed. For example, Algol 68 identifiers may
be arbitrarily long and may include embedded blanks. For example,

```
this is an acceptable name for a variable of type integer
```

is an acceptable name for a variable of type integer. Operator symbols
may be re-defined: we might (for example) define a procedure whose
name is the symbol "+." This new "+" might be defined in such a way
that it takes a character string and an integer and concatenates them
to form a new string. Whenever the addition sign appears between
arguments of type character string and integer respectively, this new
version of "+" is assumed; otherwise the standard definition still holds.

The redefinition of operators makes for a complicated language, but most
programmers can imagine situations in which it might come in handy;
other constructs seem to be included mainly for their shock value. Programmers may, for example, redefine the *priority* (or "operator precedence level") of operators like "+" and "*." Thus you may write an

---

[2] A final historical note on PL/I: it is the last language to be examined here in
whose development IBM researchers played a major role. IBM had been an out-
standingly creative force in programming languages: Fortran, APL and PL/I were
directly associated with IBM, and Lisp indirectly, via FLPL and IBM's early (and
also largely abandoned) interest in artificial intelligence. *Sic transit....*

Algol 68 program in which 2*3+2*4 evaluates to 40, if the mood is upon you, simply by resetting the priority of "+" to be greater than "*." Extensive input and output constructs are provided, including a large and complicated set of patterns for the formatting of output.

Four aspects of this complex but intriguing design are particularly germane: the consistent use of first-class objects, an extensible type structure using pointers and variant types, the treatment of heterogeneous objects and the "collateral clause."

In one sense, Algol 68 is the most advanced and consistent language we will examine. Data structures are more useful if they can be treated as units; *first-class* objects are more flexible than non-first-class; and *transparent* first-class objects are best of all. In Algol 68, almost every type describes a first-class transparent object, and *procedures* in particular are included; procedures are first-class transparent objects. The only exceptions to universal first-classness are dynamic linked structures like trees and lists that are hooked together at runtime, and a few special-purpose objects like files and semaphores. First-class objects include the basic numeric, character and logical types, arrays, heterogeneous objects called *structures*, and procedures.

Consider the following three assignments:

```
[1:3,1:2] int A := ((1,2), (0,0), (3,4))
struct (string mood, weight,
        int pounds,
        bool pet) S := ("benign", "heavy", 16.0, true)
P := (int bazball):
        (table[bazball*2] :=   bazball;
        print("done"));
```

The right sides in all three cases are constant expressions; they evaluate to a 3-by-2 array, a four-element structure and a procedure, respectively. The procedure specifies a single formal, called bazball. If we invoke, say, P(4), 4 is assigned to table[8] and a message is printed. Array objects, structure objects and procedure objects may be passed as parameters and returned by functions.

Besides array and structure types, Algol 68 provides a union type that is a forerunner to Pascal's variant record. If color is a variable whose value is drawn from a union type:

union (string,bool) `color`

we can legally assign to it either string or Boolean values. The type of value currently bound to a union type can be determined using a special **case** construct:

```
case color  in
        ( int i) :  print (("integer", i)),
        ( string j) :  print (("string", j))
   esac;
```

If `color` happens to be an integer at the time the above statement is executed, the integer value is bound to variable i which is then printed along with the string "`integer`." A similar result occurs if `color` happens to be bound to a value of type **string**.

Algol 68 supports pointers to objects of any type. We can declare variables whose values are pointers to numerical values, structures, unions, arrays, procedures, or even other pointer objects. In the following program fragment, i's value is an integer; j's is a pointer to an integer (in Algol 68 terms, a "**ref int**," a reference to an integer).

```
begin
    int i;   ref int j;
    i := 3;  j := i
end
```

Assigning 3 to i causes the integer 3 to be bound to the name i; assigning i to j causes the *address* of i to be bound to j, because the declaration states that j's value is a *reference* to an integer, not an integer.

Pointer types are a powerful programming tool, but their significance in Algol 68 goes far beyond their roles in other languages. Objects of type **ref** T serve as pointers, but they can also be used to achieve a call-by-reference parameter-passing rule in an unusually flexible and uniform way. The application rule in Algol 68 directly supports call-by-value only: a copy is made of every actual value, and the copy is bound to the corresponding formal parameter. But **ref** types and the simple rules that govern their behavior allow us to use call-by-value to achieve call-by-reference: when a formal is declared to be a **ref**, the value to which it is bound upon application is the *address* of the corresponding actual, not the value stored at that address. For example, consider a procedure with the following header:

proc f (**int** a, **ref int** b)

Suppose x is a variable of type integer, and we execute the invocation $f(x, x)$. The first x corresponds to a formal of type integer, and so we pass the value of the integer that is currently bound to x. The second x corresponds to a formal of type reference-to-integer, and so we pass the *address* of x. This means in effect that the second x is passed by reference. Assignments to b within the body of f cause changes to the x that is visible in the caller's environment.

First-class transparent data-objects and pervasive use of pointer types are significant breakthroughs. What Algol 68 did *not* achieve, though, is the unification between the structure of programs and data objects that we've discussed previously and to which we return in describing Pascal. We discuss two aspects of this "non-unification" which involve, at the same time, two of the language's most interesting innovations.

As noted above, Algol 68 introduces a heterogeneous data object and associated template; the object is called a *structure* and the associated template mechanism is a *structured mode declaration*. Algol 68's construct is more general than Cobol's or PL/I's, and in certain ways more powerful than Pascal's. Pascal's was to become far better known and more influential, but only because Pascal as a whole proved a more attractive (because it was much simpler) design.

One resemblance between Algol 68 and Pascal is the fact that in both languages, heterogeneous data objects are patterned not on heterogeneous *program* structures, but on *homogeneous* data objects. An Algol 68 structure isn't a small program nested within a big one; it's a funny kind of array. We explain when we take up Pascal. But consider the following Algol 68 fragment. Ordinarily we've cited program fragments in a uniform typeface, but in this case we use (approximately) the typefaces of the Algol 68 report, which are significant:

```
int n;
mode elephant = struct
                (string mood, weight,
                 real age,
                 bool big ears;
elephant boris;
proc succ = (int j) int: j + 1;
```

The first declaration creates an integer called n. The second defines a
template for a structure. The template is called "**elephant**"; we can
instantiate new elephants by writing declarations such as "**elephant**
boris."

Compare the ways in which **elephant** and *succ* are printed. These are
both templates—but **elephant** is printed in boldface because the user,
when he defines a new mode, is considered to be *extending the language*,
adding a new mode designation that will henceforth be treated just
like the language's native modes, for example, **int**. Procedure *succ* on
the other hand is not an extension to the language; it's a new object,
like *boris*. Why the difference in approach? If *procedure* templates and
mode templates were structurally the same, then (presumably) mode
definitions (*i.e.*, user-defined type definitions such as "**elephant**") would
be first-class, just like procedures. We would be able to pass mode
definitions as parameters, return them as function results and so on. We
would also, presumably, have *parameterized* mode templates just as we
have parameterized function templates. However, we don't have these
things, and the fact that we don't is a consequence of the conceptual
wall that still separates data objects from program structures.

Algol 68's *collateral clauses* are another path-breaking idea. Among
the languages discussed in this book, Algol 68 comes closest by far to
a major aspect of the ISM: the observation that the arguments to a
procedure and the elements of an array or of a heterogeneous object can
all be stored in the same kind of structure, which can be a *concurrent
evaluation* structure. A "collateral clause" is a series of statements or
expressions that are evaluated either concurrently or in some unspecified
order, at the implementation's option. For example,

$$(i := f(x), \ j := f(y), \ k := f(z))$$

is a collateral clause; so is

(x, y, z)

This last form is particularly significant, because we've seen it in the language before. This is how the value of an array is represented, and likewise the value of a structure; it is also the form in which we pass parameters to a function. No other language we'll examine achieves this degree of conceptual unification among these superficially-diverse ideas.

Once again, the lack of unification between program and object structure intrudes to some extent. Algol 68 is a block-structured language like Algol 60. A block consists of some declarations separated by semicolons from the block-statement and from each other, as in Algol 60. If programs and objects had been the same thing, blocks *per se* would have been unnecessary; declarations would have been introduced as elements of collateral clauses. A block would have been identical to the description of a new mode.

□ Algol 68 is the first language to achieve structural unification between complex *data objects* (like arrays and structures), the *arguments to a function* and a *concurrent evaluation structure*.

? Algol 68 does not abolish the Algol Wall: it draws a firm distinction between *data-object templates* (which are new types) and *program-fragment templates* (procedures). Nor does it allow the powerful new collateral clause to subsume the functionality of an Algol 60 block.

Algol 68 is, in sum, responsible for a succession of breakthroughs. But Algol 68 is not a hero language; it is more nearly a tragic-hero language. The breakthroughs and simplifications of this design are swamped by a mass of complex and forbidding minutiae. Their import has never been clearly recognized, and the language has never been influential to the extent it should have been. Humbler and more comprehensible languages were left in charge. Pascal is the prime example.

5.2   Pascal

We concentrate on three propositions.

1. Pascal originated during a period of increasing interest in user-extensible type systems and a richer set of data objects. Pascal's approach—its strong typing, its heterogeneous objects modeled not on program structures but on data structures like arrays—was more influential than any other, and its influence remains important through the present day.

2. Pascal's synthesis of flexible templates (procedures and user-defined types) with Cobol's idea of the program as a well-ordered, pre-arranged structure made it ideally suited to the practice of *top-down programming*. The Pascal design is strongly linked to the top-down program-development method called "program development by stepwise refinement" and to the related techniques of "structured programming." These methods proved enormously useful and influential.

3. Pascal was modeled on Algol 60, but on balance it is both simpler and more powerful. This fact reversed a major trend towards complicated languages—at least for awhile.

5.2.1   Pascal Profile

Program Structure. A Pascal program is by definition an instance of a "program" structure. A program structure has a series of well-defined slots; it begins with label declarations followed by constant definitions, proceeds with type definitions, variable declarations, procedure definitions and the main body of the program. Algol 60's structure was based on two quasi-orthogonal structures, the block and the compound statement. Pascal has no such basis; it retains the compound statement only. Variable declarations may occur in the opening section of a program (these are global variables) or of a procedure definition (variables local to the procedure), but there is no block *per se*, and block-structure in Algol 60's sense doesn't occur in Pascal. We can't introduce local variables at *any* point, as in Algol 60; local variables occur only at the head of procedures.

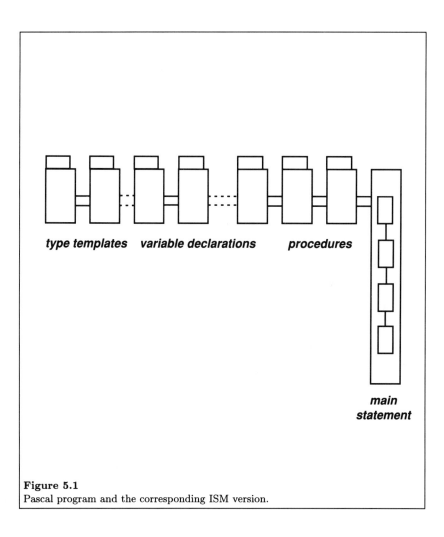

type templates   variable declarations   procedures

**main
statement**

Figure 5.1
Pascal program and the corresponding ISM version.

Control Structures. Pascal's control structures are similar to Algol
60's but generally simpler. Pascal's **for** statement, for example, is a
stripped-down version of Algol 60's. A **repeat** statement allows iteration to be conditional on a check performed at the end of the sequence
rather than (as in **while** loops) at the beginning. Algol's rather complicated "switch" mechanism, which allows branching to one of a series of
destinations, is superseded by a **case** form that allows for the selection
of one of a series of statement-sequences based on the outcome of a test
expression. Thus,

```
CASE < expression> OF
    condition₁  :   action₁
                ⋮
    conditionₙ  :   actionₙ
END
```

Pascal vs. Algol 60: Pascal simplifies and restricts Algol constructs in
a series of small ways. Algol allows dynamic arrays (arrays whose size is
determined not at compile-time, but when execution enters the block to
which the array is local) as local variables and parameters; in Pascal, the
size of every array must be known at compile-time. Requiring that array
bounds be known at compile-time improves runtime efficiency, but there
is a cost in terms of flexibility and expressiveness. Suppose, for example,
that we need a procedure to sort arrays of integers. In Algol 60 we can
write a procedure that accepts an array of any size, but in Pascal we
must commit ourselves to some fixed size. On the other hand, allowing
fixed-size arrays makes it possible for the compiler to determine exactly
how much storage each variable in a program will require. Runtime data
management becomes easier: an Algol 60 implementation of dynamic
arrays must rely on extensive use of indirect addressing, but Pascal can
assign a relative address to each variable at compile-time.

Algol includes conditional expressions and conditional statements; Pascal makes do with conditional statements only. Thus the Algol 60 statement

```
z := if x>0 then 3 else 4
```

must be replaced by the slightly more verbose statement

```
if x>0 then z := 3 else z := 4
```

In Algol 60, operators fall into nine precedence levels, to avoid forcing the use of parentheses where they would be unnecessary in standard mathematical usage; Pascal makes do with four precedence levels.[3] Where Algol 60 provides the fancy call-by-name mechanism, Pascal makes do with call-by-reference. There are many similar examples.

There are also a few cases (including some important ones) where Pascal is more powerful than Algol 60. Pascal provides a heap and supports the dynamic allocation of variables; user-extensible types are the most dramatic example in this category.

Types. In Algol 60, programmers have no way to extend the language's type system by adding types of their own definition. In Pascal, user-defined types are enshrined as a central language principle. Pascal programmers may extend the type system in two ways. They may give new names and identities to existing types, or they may *combine* variables of existing types into a heterogeneous collection. Thus the Pascal definition

```
Type SmallRealArray = array[1..3] of real;
```

introduces a new type to refer to 3-element real array. The definition

```
Type Color = (mauve, indigo, puce)
```

in effect allows counting over natural numbers whose names are "mauve," "indigo" and "puce" instead of 1, 2 and 3.

Given the variable declarations

```
A: SmallRealArray; C: color;
```

the value of A will always be a 3-element real array, and the value of C will always be "mauve," "indigo" or "puce."

---

[3]Of Algol's nine precedence levels, exponentiation is highest, then multiplication and division, addition and subtraction, comparison operations, logical negation, logical "and," logical "or," logical "implies" and, bringing up the rear, logical "equivalence."

User-introduced compound types relate strongly to the issue of named
sub-environments. A "record" in Pascal is a named sub-environment
of a very restricted sort: the environment within a record variable may
contain only variable declarations, no procedure definitions or type definitions or executable statements. Thus,

```
x: record re, im: real end
```

makes variable x the name of an environment; within environment x
are two variables, named re and im respectively; both are of type real.
We can access the variables within environment x by writing x.re or
by using a "with x" statement, which opens the scope of environment
(*i.e.*, record) x.

A record *type* is a template that stamps out records. If we want many
environments with the same internal structures as x, we can write

```
type complex = record re, im: real end
```

We can now declare variables to be of type "complex"; each such variable
is a two-element environment.

5.2.2   Pascal Analysis

Strong Typing   Of the languages we've taken up in detail, Fortran,
Lisp and APL aren't much interested in the types of variables. There
are no variable declarations in Lisp or APL; the programmer can bind
any series of data objects he chooses to any name he likes. Fortran's
type system is easily bypassed. Algol 60 introduces the idea of *strong
typing* in a preliminary way:

Definition 5.1   In a *strongly-typed* language, it must be possible to
determine the type of every expression before runtime, and every data
object must be used only in the ways prescribed for its type.

This statement correctly describes Algol 60; but Algol 60's type system
is so limited (it is restricted to numerical and logical values, and can't be
extended) that typing, strong or otherwise, becomes a fairly minor issue.
Cobol has a more complicated type system, and typing in Cobol might be
described as fairly strong—but biased by the presence of active typing.

If we try to assign a number to a character-type Cobol variable `charvar`, `charvar`'s type doesn't change (as it would, in effect, in Lisp or APL), but the operation isn't forbidden either. Type coercion violates the spirit if not the letter of strong typing. PL/1's typing resembles Cobol's; Algol 68's typing generally anticipates Pascal's, but is more complicated and less influential. Pascal's typing is the first highly-influential, fully-developed strong typing system.

The advantages of active typing are obvious: power and conciseness. Why would a language choose strong, passive typing instead? For *security*: from Pascal onward, security becomes an ever more dominant concern. Programs, it seems, are not easy to get right. Debugging is a major part of program development. Given a sufficiently large program, it's difficult to be certain that it is *ever* completely correct. Hence the growing conviction that error prevention is a major part of a programming language's duties.

How can a programming language help prevent bugs? Strong typing is one way. In a Pascal-style strongly typed language, the programmer makes a series of assertions about his program in the form of variable declarations. The assertions say "variable x is of type t, and I will operate on x only in ways that are consistent with t." What we'd like is for the compiler to be able to check these assertions; if it finds a violation, it reports back to the user. A violation means, presumably, a programming error, and any error that can be found and fixed at compile-time is a squashed bug.

(A strongly-typed language can also be built *without* type declarations. It's possible to construct type systems that can *infer* the types of variables based on their use in the program. We'll investigate this topic when we take up declarative languages.)

To be strongly typed, a language needs several things. Variables must have types that describe and constrain the use to which the associated data objects may be put.[4] There must be limited uses of automatic type-coercion. It should be possible to detect type violations at compile-time.

---

[4]It's possible to construct strongly-typed languages that allow a variable to be associated with several different types that are related in a well-defined way. For example, a language with record types may allow a record object containing fields a, b and c to be passed as an argument to a procedure that expects a record object containing fields a and b only. Such a language may still be strongly typed, since the presence of field "c" in the actual parameter cannot affect the behavior of the

Finally, the programmer needs a certain amount of freedom to add new types to the type system. Without such freedom, programmers will be forced to use the built-in types in a wide variety of ways. Better to allow them to use types that are, as far as possible, specific to the purpose at hand. The more "special-purpose" a type—the narrower the circumstances under which it *should* be used—the more likely that the compiler will notice when it is used where it should not be.

Pascal is quite strongly typed. (Again, strong typing is relative.) All variables must be declared, and there are few circumstances in which type coercions are performed automatically. Almost all type violations can be detected at compile-time. There is one notable exception: Pascal's *variant record* makes it possible to declare a variable whose type is merely one of a series of possibilities. The variant record comes in two flavors.

In a variant record with a *tag field*, one designated element of the record serves as a tag. If the tag has value *v1*, we know that this is a *t1* type record; if the value is *v2*, we have a *t2* type record and so on. Such a variant record can't be type checked at compile-time: the compiler will notice that (say) we are treating record *R* as if its current type were *t1*— is this right or not? If the value of the tag field is *v1*, fine; otherwise we're making a mistake. But at compile-time we can't tell what the value of the tag field will be when the program reaches this point at runtime. In theory we can detect this kind of type error at runtime, but Pascal is rarely implemented with runtime type-checking (which slows program execution), so these errors go undetected.

It is the variant record *without* a tag field that really gives strong-typing proponents fits. Such a record has one of a stated series of types, but does *not* have a field whose value distinguishes among the types. At any point in his program, the programmer can treat such a record as if its

---

procedure application. This notion of *subtyping* or *inheritance* is important to object-oriented languages; we'll examine this issue when we investigate Simula and Smalltalk in chapter 6. Another example: a variable that is a formal parameter in a procedure may take on several different types, provided that its use in the body of the procedure is consistent with the operations allowed on these types. Thus, a procedure to sort the elements of an array may be applied to arrays of any type, so long as each type provides a well-defined ordering relation on its elements. A strongly-typed language that allows procedures to operate on arguments of different types is said to be *polymorphic*. We'll investigate polymorphism in chapter 8.

type were any one of the types on the list. If he makes an error, there's
no way to detect it, either at compile-time or at runtime.

Why did Pascal allow this substantial shortcut around strong typing?
When he designed Pascal, Wirth believed in strong typing, but not fa-
natically. Other things mattered too, and among these *efficiency* was
near the top of the list. To eliminate the untagged variant record would
have required programmers, in some cases, to waste substantial storage
space on tag fields they didn't need. Wirth was adamant on this point
even in the face of withering criticism from the strong-typing set.

We have yet to discuss the last point on the strong-typers list of demands:
a user-extensible type system. Pascal provided this also, and the way it
did so is our next topic. It should of course be borne in mind that user-
defined types serve the ends of strong typing, but strong typing is not
their only (or even their main) reason for being. Wirth saw clearly what
the Algol 68 designers also saw, that user-defined types add expressivity
and power to the language.

User-Defined Types Pascal's user-extensible type system encompasses two separate features. First, users are allowed to rename, for
their own purposes, types that already exist in the language, or subsets
of those types. Second, users can concoct new types out of pre-existing
ones. This second feature involves heterogeneous data objects, specifically the Pascal record, and the Pascal record is a crucial design for
programming language evolution.

Fortran, Algol 60 and Lisp offered, in essence, numbers and arrays of
numbers, symbols and lists of symbols as data objects. This wasn't
enough: Cobol needed to manipulate objects that modeled the structure of data files, and data files are not ordinarily arrays of numbers
or lists of symbols. Cobol introduced the record specifically to model
the structure of data files, and Pascal's record preserves much of this
original "file modeling" flavor, down to the term "record" itself. But,
as we've mentioned several times, the need for heterogeneous objects involves much more than file handling. Computers began life as glorified
adding machines; nowadays their mission includes the simulation, analysis and monitoring of arbitrary chunks of external reality. An interesting
chunk of reality can sometimes be modeled by a system of equations,
in which case we're back to numbers. But oftentimes it can't, in which

case we build software machines that represent, in essence, microcosmic models of the chunks that interest us. A graphics program might deal not with numbers but with polygons, a medical expert system not with numbers but with lab tests and patients, and so on through innumerable examples. To build these software microcosms, we need heterogeneous data objects.

How to add heterogeneous objects to Pascal? There were two fundamentally different possibilities. Pascal made a fateful choice. Consider a typical Pascal record definition:

```
Type patient = record
                name: Alpha;
                birthdate: DateType;
                Sex: (M, F);
                Diagnosis: DiseaseType
              end
```

(Figure 5.2 gives definitions for the types referred to by the "patient" template.) What kind of object is this?

Here are two possible answers.

(1) We understand "patient" by analogy with the surrounding program in which it is embedded. The definition of "patient" resembles, structurally, the variable-declaration part of the big program in which it appears: it's a list of variable names and associated types. Unlike the big program in which it's embedded, the program named "patient" includes no executable statements; it's merely a set of variable declarations. But, given that the structure of "patient" reproduces on a smaller scale one part of the big program in which it's embedded, we can describe "patient" as a *little program*—it's an instance of a *limited* kind of program (it can't contain any executable statements), but it is recognizably a program-like structure nonetheless.

(2) We understand "patient" by analogy with arrays. An array is a data object that contains many homogeneous sub-objects that are identified by position. A record is a different version of the same thing: it contains many *heterogeneous* sub-objects that are identified by *name*.

Pascal chose the second answer. As Wirth writes in his 1971 paper, "In an *array structure*, all components are of the same type.... In a *record*

```
Program DiagnosePatients(input, output);
   ...
Type Alpha = packed array[1..25] of char;
     DateType = array[1..3] of integer;
     Diagnosis = (FootDisease, HeartDisease,
                  HeadDisease)
     patient = record ... end;
   ...
Var (* create some "patient" type variables *)
     P1, P2, P3 : patient;
Begin
   .
   .
   .
End.
```

Figure 5.2
A framework for the "patient" record definition. "Alpha" is declared to be a
character array of a variety ("packed") appropriate to efficient character storage;
"DateType" is an array with slots for a month, day and year.

structure, the components (called *fields*) are not necessarily of the same type [137, p.37]." This choice follows the lead of Algol 68, and of Hoare's pre-Pascal paper on the "record concept."

What difference does it make? Pascal's choice is to be understood in the context of increased interest in data types. Consider an object of type integer. We don't know anything about what's "inside" an integer; the computer we are using represents integers using some bitstring coding mechanism, but we don't know or care what it is. All we know about an integer is that we can add it to other numbers, subtract it and so on. For our purposes, an integer is defined by the way it behaves when we manipulate it, not by its "internal structure."

Pascal's understanding of records is analogous. All we know about a variable P of type "patient" is that references to P.name, P.sex and so on are meaningful, and that P can be assigned to other variables of type "patient." The internal structure of type "patient" (*i.e.*, the layout and representation of its fields) and the rules for assembling its instantiations are as irrelevant to patient-type variables as the rules of integer representation are to integer-type variables. Integers and patients are alike *black boxes*; their identities are defined strictly by their *behavior* (*i.e.*, the operations allowed upon them), not by their internal structure. Internally they may look like "little programs," but this resemblance is accidental and irrelevant.

This view is sensible if our main concern is strong typing. It makes clear that users are *not* free to manipulate variables in arbitrary ways; they are allowed to operate on them only under a restricted and pre-arranged set of rules. Programmers *ought* to regard data objects as black boxes. In Pascal this issue is mainly one of style and emphasis, but it develops (as we'll see) into the *abstract typing* strategies that followed Pascal and generalized this aspect of its design.

On the other hand, Pascal's strategy entails major sacrifices. By removing the wall between programs and data objects, Wirth could have simplified the structure of the language (leaving it with only one set of structure-building rules instead of two separate sets). He could have made a more powerful language capable of handling data systems in a clean and consistent way. We pursue these points in the next chapter.

? Pascal views records not as nested naming environments but as specialized arrays. Hence, records templates are equated with array types, not with procedures, and Pascal's records do *not* generalize into modules or data systems. The Algol Wall remains intact.

Pascal and its Programming Method   More than any language that preceded it (with the possible, partial exception of Simula 67), Pascal was designed with a particular programming method in mind and played a central part in the further development of that method. What does "programming method" mean? Clearly the designers of any language have a mental model of what programs in their language should look like—how programmers should use the constructs they are given. The designers of Algol 60 did not envision Algol programs in which for and while loops were completely bypassed in favor of recursive definitions; the designers of Fortran did not envision Fortran programs revolving around a large COMMON array that is managed at runtime as though it were a heap. A "programming method" deals not only with how finished programs should look, but with how they got that way: it deals with the *development* of programs.

The programming method associated with Pascal revolves around "structured programming" and "stepwise refinement," and it is by far the most influential and important of any method in programming history. The stepwise refinement method calls for the programmer to begin by specifying the entire program at a coarse level of detail, in the sense of identifying a short sequence of major steps by which the task will be accomplished. If the task is (for example) to simulate and analyze the performance of a computer network, the coarse steps involved might be to

1. initialize the simulation and read any values specific to this run from the user or a file,

2. run the simulation,

3. analyze and print the results.

The stepwise refinement method is then to be followed recursively over each of the steps in the sequence: they are in turn to be broken down into sub-steps and so on, until each sub-step is simple enough to be represented in a small number of statements in the target language. It is a concomitant of the method that each stage results in a valid (although, until the last step, incomplete) source program. Thus at the end of the first step described above, we can write a program that consists of calls to three procedures in succession. We don't yet know how to define these procedures, but in the second step we make a first pass at doing so. At each stage in the process, we know *where* each procedure is called and *what* it is supposed to do before we get around to figuring out *how* it will work.

Stepwise refinement is reminiscent of synthesis or analysis by layered abstraction, a general technique we described in chapter 3. However, the two approaches are not equivalent. "Stepwise refinement" is a well-defined, top-down technique; "layered abstraction" is merely a way of thinking. A programmer who likes to think in layered abstractions but has never heard of stepwise refinement might do perfectly well by roughing out his entire design from the top down using layered abstraction, then proceeding to implement the code from bottom up. The "roughing out" process might be informal or even subliminal. "Stepwise refinement" is a highly specified version of the general technique.

"Structured programming" represents (in a sense) the continuation of this technique at the "micro" level. When it comes time to write the code that defines step P, how should we proceed? In 1968, E.W. Dijkstra had published a soon-to-be-famous letter that denounced "goto" statements [37]. He argued that goto statements made programs hard to understand; programs should be written in such a way that step i is guaranteed to be followed by step $i + 1$. The resulting programs are more easily debugged and understood because their flow of control is transparent. Dijkstra's note was influential in the rise of "structured programming," which refers to the technique of assembling programs out of a series of statement groups such that execution always proceeds from statement-group i to statement-group $i + 1$. Note the strong methodological resemblance to stepwise refinement: structured programming also calls for a program to be constructed as a sequence of big steps, each defined as a sequence of smaller steps and so on. In structured programming, though, the level of detail is finer. The enemy is a goto statement that sends execution careening off in unexpected directions, thereby disrupting a smoothly and predictably sequential flow of control.

Wirth originated stepwise refinement and was an early proponent of structured programming. Pascal is well suited to these methods. Structured programming makes modest demands on a language: it calls for a battery of loops and conditionals sufficient to avoid situations in which programmers feel compelled to use branches. Algol 60 already provided a fairly complete set of these, in addition to a "goto" statement; Pascal also provides a fairly complete set and a "goto" statement. What is new is mainly the fact that "goto" is now frowned upon, and accordingly is made less pleasant to use. (Algol 60 allowed identifiers as statement labels for goto's to jump to; Pascal allows only integers as statement labels, indicating its displeasure with branch statements by making them even harder to follow.)

Stepwise refinement can be used with many languages, but the extent to which it is in harmony with Pascal is interesting. Languages offer a spectrum of possibilities regarding the rigidity with which a program structure is defined. On one end, programs in Lisp or APL are merely collections of definitions with no concrete structure. In the center, Algol 60 programs are well-defined structures, but if we choose to structure our program as a block (rather than as a compound statement), the order in which program elements appear is largely unconstrained. So long as a statement comes last, variable declarations and procedure definitions may be arbitrarily intermingled in the rest of the block. At the other end, Cobol and Pascal specify not only the nature of a program structure, but the order in which elements appear.

A Pascal program, then, is a fill-in-the blanks sort of structure in which the programmer knows exactly what he is called upon to supply. This kind of framework is philosophically in keeping with stepwise refinement. In stepwise refinement, you begin by planning the program in its entirety, and proceed to fill in the blanks at increasingly finer levels of detail.

To some extent, the good and the bad things about stepwise refinement are mirrored in the good and bad things about the Pascal program construct. The program construct makes it easy (up to a point) to grasp the totality of a program; you know where to look for each relevant part of the grand design. You know that the type definitions will always follow the constant definitions, you know that once you get to the variable

declarations you have seen all global type definitions, and so on. The
structure is also a useful guide for beginning and inexpert programmers.

On the other hand, however, some applications, particularly larger ones,
are difficult to develop in a single pass and to store in a single structure.
Large applications may grow and change; their structures may be impossible to predict with complete accuracy beforehand. They may also
consist of many fairly independent pieces. Stepwise refinement asks that
an entire structure be planned out beforehand and then maintained in
effect unchanged. The **program** structure supports this requirement, and
makes it impossible to disperse a program physically into a collection of
separate modules or files. (Dispersion is important—especially in a large
program—not only because a single structure is simply too bulky to deal
with as a unit, but because it is essential to allow separate components
to be compiled separately.) When Pascal is used in the construction of
large programs, the language used in practice is almost always a super-
set of Pascal that overrides the requirement that the entire program be
defined in a single **program** structure. But these supersets are necessarily *ad hoc* extensions; Pascal itself has no conceptual mechanism for
dealing with such cases.

Pascal's type system also supports stepwise refinement. In the stepwise
method, when you need something, you assume that you have it. Later
on you worry about how to get it. In Pascal, if you need a type that
isn't part of the language, you can program as if you had that type, and
then write a type definition that augments the language with your new
type.

We close this section by noting that Pascal itself, for all its design choices
that in retrospect appear rather ominous, ought to be recognized as the
hero-language it is. It stood against a mounting flood-tide of complexity and turned back to simplicity. We pursue the point further in the
appendix to this chapter.

5.2.3 ISM Comparison

Pascal's Major restrictions compared to the ISM: A named space-map
may occupy one region of an encompassing space-map, but the nested
space-map may contain named data-objects only. Record templates exist

in the form of type definitions, but they can't be parameterized. Pascal has no modules, block structure or parallelism.

5.3 Readings

Basic Readings. An early paper on NPL (the precursor to PL/I) describing the goals of the PL/I development project first appeared in 1965 [105]. Tanenbaum's tutorial on Algol 68 is an indispensable introduction to the language. The original Pascal description is given by Wirth in [137].

Suggested Readings. Lawson gives a short introduction to PL/I in [83]; Valentine presents a comparative analysis of PL/I and Algol 68 in [127]. A comprehensive, informal description of Algol 68 is given in [84]; implementation of the language is also discussed. Cooper and Clancy's *Oh! Pascal!* [30] is an enjoyable, easy-to-read programming textbook based on Pascal.

Habermann [53], in contrast to the relatively mild critique given by Welsh *et al.* [131], presents a scathing attack on Pascal and questions its utility as a good teaching tool for introductory programming. [136] gives Wirth's assessment of the language four years after the original report was released. The stepwise refinement method itself is described by Wirth in [133].

5.4 Exercises

1. When pointers were added to PL/1, a single pointer type was provided and all pointers are of the same type. In what ways does this give programmers more flexibility than they have in Algol 68? In what ways is Algol 68 more flexible than a language which combines Algol 60 with the capacity to declare variables of types "pointer" and "integer (or any other type) referenced by pointer"?

2. (a) Relate Algol 68's collateral clauses to APL vectors. In what sense are they similar? In what sense are they different? (b) "Algol 68's design is closer in spirit to APL than to Pascal." Yes or no?

3. Because of Algol 68's pervasive use of pointer types, the language requires that in an assignment statement, the lifetime of the object denoted by the left-hand side must be *less than or equal to* the lifetime of the object yielded by evaluation of the right-hand side. Why? Is it possible to detect whether such a condition holds at compile-time?

4. Besides efficiency, are there other reasons for having the type-loophole for variant records in Pascal?

5. (a) Can you give technical justification for Pascal's omission of own variables? Was its omission a significant one? (b) Consider the addition of a new construct to Pascal: if *D1* and *D2* are declarations, then the declaration "*D1* within *D2*" allows *D2* to be available in the surrounding scope while *D1* is used locally in defining *D2*. Thus, a procedure to maintain a counter could be written:

```
var n = 0 within
  procedure count;
    begin
      n := n + 1
    end;
```

What are the merits of such a construct compared with Algol 60's own variables?

6. "Simple languages are more influential than complicated ones." Agree or disagree? Explain, cite as much concrete historical data as possible.

7. We say that a variable x is an *alias* of a variable y if x and y denote the same location. List at least four ways in which aliasing can be introduced in Pascal.

8. (a) How would you compare the stepwise refinement method in Pascal with APL's idiomatic programming style? With Lisp's? (b) In what sense is Pascal's treatment of functions similar to Lisp's? In what sense is it different?

9. Is it possible to transform any Pascal program into another Pascal program with the same meaning but with every non-recursive procedure call replaced by an in-line expansion? Justify your answer

either by providing a sketch of a transformation or by providing an example for which the transformation cannot be performed. Make sure to consider the interaction of such a transformation with a call-by-reference protocol.

10. "Insofar as the Pascal statement 'with R do *expr*' causes *expr* to be evaluated in the environment defined by record R, and R's identity isn't known until runtime, Pascal supports a form of dynamic binding." True or false? Explain.

Appendix: The Aesthetics of Simplicity

> Beginning with Telford's [the noted engineer] 1812 es-
> say on bridges, modern structural artists have been
> conscious of, and have written about, the aesthetic ide-
> als that guided their works.... The elements of the
> new art form were, then, efficiency (minimum mate-
> rials), economy (minimum cost), and elegance (max-
> imum aesthetic expression). These elements underlie
> modern civilized life. (D. Billington, *The Tower and
> the Bridge* [13, p.6])

> A work of engineering such as a Maillart bridge or a
> bridge by Christian Menn can outdo some other works
> of art, because it is not only a gift to the imagina-
> tion but also structural in the matrix of the world.
> (J. McPhee, *The Control of Nature* [92, p.52])

We've discussed the fact that Pascal is remarkable for its simplicity, and
also that it represents merely one point in a series of oscillations between
simple and complicated designs that recur throughout the history of
programming languages. Pascal was simple, but its predecessors were
complicated; some of its most important successors were also highly
complex. Here we turn briefly aside from languages *per se* to glance at
an important, fairly obvious but largely neglected issue:

> The design of programming languages draws on the science
> of computation but also on *the art of design*. The strug-
> gle between complexity and simplicity, and the oscillation
> in taste between these two, is widespread and typical in the
> history of design.

The obvious question: who cares? Why should a student of programming languages direct his attention in such an unscientific direction?
There are several good reasons.

First, we can learn something interesting about the general nature of
simple designs as opposed to complicated ones by studying resemblances
of this sort.

Second, resemblances between programming-language design and other kinds of design remind us of the enormous significance of aesthetics in the design of languages, indeed of software in general. And if aesthetic factors are indeed important, we're right to be skeptical of any claim that some language is destined to be the "ultimate" one, or is demonstrably superior purely on technical grounds. In the nature of things, aesthetic issues can't be decided on objective grounds alone.

Finally, as improbable as it may sometimes seem, computer science and its history are in fact a sub-topic within a broader syllabus: intellectual life and *its* history. We can't aspire to understand this one bit without some appreciation for the pattern of which it is a part.

In discussing the opposition between "simple" and "complicated" styles, we're obviously abstracting and simplifying. In designating some design "simple" we're hardly giving a full and sufficient description of it. Nonetheless, relative complexity is clearly one of the (many) axes that define "design space," and for present purposes, we're interested in the projection of points in design space onto this particular axis.

A more important misunderstanding to avoid: in emphasizing the importance of aesthetics, we don't mean to suggest that language design is *dominated* by aesthetics, to the exclusion of the obvious first concern—to provide efficient working tools for program-building. Here David Billington's reflections on the art of structural engineering are particularly useful. If you're designing a bridge, your first responsibility is to make sure that the bridge stands up. Next, you consider implementation: a bridge that can't be built efficiently won't be built at all. Efficiency for a bridge is very different from computational efficiency, but what's crucial in both cases is that practical engineering imperatives don't mean that aesthetics are unimportant. To the contrary. "Economy has always been a prerequisite to creativity in structural art. Again and again we shall find that the best designers matured under the discipline of extreme economy." [13, p.6] It's a subtle but vital point that art flourishes in the presence of constraints and dies in their absence. (If you let go of a kite's string, the kite falls.) McPhee [92] alludes to the same effect in praising the aesthetic quality of the best bridges.

Let's consider some instances. We've argued that simplicity is a good thing in language design, but this point isn't self-evident; many distinguished computer scientists implicitly dispute it. The designers of languages like PL/I or Algol 68 (in the first generation of complicated designs) or, as we discuss later, of CLU and Ada (in the second generation) needn't have argued that simplicity is bad—merely that other things are better. We need to be aware of this disagreement, and to realize that it is a fixture in the history of design. Consider the facade of Chartres cathedral, which captures and confronts us with this stylistic antithesis as boldly as any object anywhere (figure 5.3). It has two unlike spires. The simple south spire dates from the mid-twelfth century. When the elaborate north spire was planned, early in the sixteenth century, it was clear that (so to speak) the earlier spire lacked many important features, and the new spire would accordingly need to be considerably more complicated. Henry Adams writes memorably in his famous treatise *Mont-Saint-Michel and Chartres*:

> The first glimpse that is caught, and the first that was meant to be caught, is that of the two spires ... nine persons out of ten—perhaps ninety-nine in a hundred—who come within sight of the two spires of Chartres will think it a jest if they are told that the smaller of the two, the simpler, the one that impresses them least, is the one that they are expected to recognize as the most perfect piece of architecture in the world. [2, p.67]

But it's true. The north spire is a distinguished example of late gothic building, but it is the "noble south spire" that has for centuries moved and inspired by its profound and perfect simplicity, by its "restraint and discipline," its "quality of integration" (G. Henderson, *Chartres* [56, p.34]), by the "beauty and grandeur of composition ... where all the effects are obtained, not by ornaments, but by the just and skillful proportion of the different parts" (Viollet-le-Duc, cited by Adams [2, p.69-70]).

Now obviously the perfection of the south spire at Chartres doesn't prove that Pascal is a good programming language and PL/I isn't. The point is rather that Chartres presents two solutions to a hard problem in design. Simplicity and economy are dominant characteristics of one solution and not the other. Both are good solutions. The simpler is decisively the

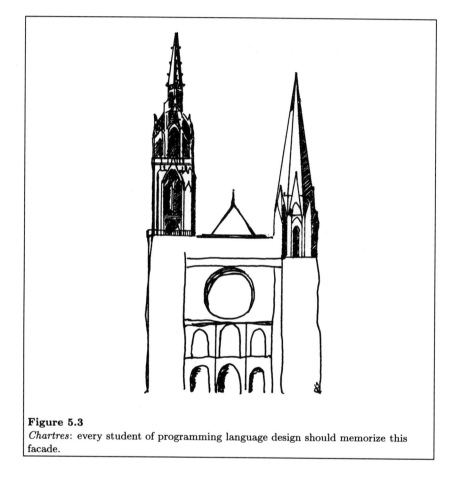

Figure 5.3
Chartres: every student of programming language design should memorize this facade.

greater achievement. And when Alan Perlis describes the simple and harmonious design of Algol 60 as "an object of stunning beauty ... a rounded work of art" [114, p.12], we may be reminded of Viollet-le-Duc on Chartres.

The stylistic dispute between simple and complex is a given in the history of design. So is the oscillation in taste between simple and complicated. This is strikingly clear in the history of architecture—at the cost of some drastic simplification and editing perhaps, but no fundamental distortion. The relative simplicity of early gothic gives way to the flamboyance of the late middle ages. Neo-classical renaissance simplicity gives way to the baroque. The classical revival of the early nineteenth century is replaced by high-Victorian exuberance, which is eventually replaced in turn by the austere international style, which is supplanted by the fancy post-modern puffery that prevails today.

For another example of an oscillation whose period is more nearly in keeping with what we are accustomed to in the programming language world, consider the Chevrolet. During the golden age of Detroit Iron, from 1955 through the early seventies, the big Chevy started with a strikingly simple design that has become an American classic (1955), developed big fins and major glitz (1959), struggled back to a cool simplicity that epitomizes early sixties class (1963) and then—although Chevrolet never participated wholeheartedly in the pig wallow of late-sixties design (as General Motor's cheap car a certain demure was expected of it)—deteriorated by 1968 into a slackness from which it never recovered. (The "downsized" Chevy of 1977 was again a clean design, but in spirit it was a different car.)

The history of programming language style is fully a part of the history of style generally. A solid grasp of programming language design must be based on the understanding that this topic is merely one instance of something larger. Such a grasp also presupposes some inkling, at least, of the intimate connection between good engineering and aesthetic insight.

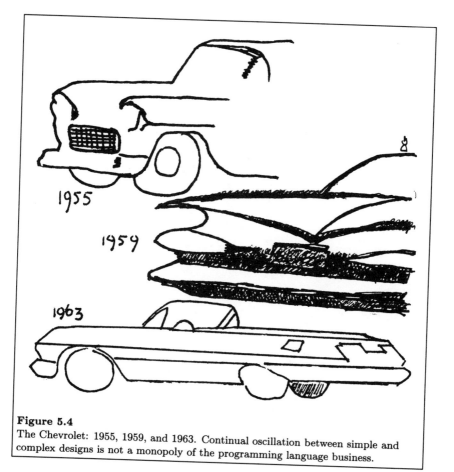

Figure 5.4
The Chevrolet: 1955, 1959, and 1963. Continual oscillation between simple and complex designs is not a monopoly of the programming language business.

6 The Class in Simula 67 and Smalltalk, with Notes on Specification, Abstract Typing and Ada

The **Algol Wall** falls at last: the designers of Simula 67 discovered that the same template used to create program fragments—namely the procedure—can *also* be used to create data systems and heterogeneous data objects. In Simula 67, procedures that are intended to create data objects rather than program fragments are referred to as *classes*, and a data object instantiated from a *class* is called an *object*. From this comes the term **object-oriented programming**, a highly significant programming methodology created by Simula 67 and generalized, extended and "universalized" by Smalltalk. The "objects" that are instantiated from classes are full-fledged data systems, and thus significantly more powerful than the record structures we've encountered previously. "Factoring" and "inheritance" (based on the idea of sub- and super-classes) are important concomittants of the object-oriented method. Smalltalk's contribution to **interpreter-based user interfaces** is original and significant.

In a postlude, we return to the issue of **type systems** and their character: languages based on the idea of "abstract types" and inspired by formal specification techniques represent (in a sense) the natural continuation of Pascal's type-centered approach to data objects. These languages also go beyond the record and achieve the full-fledged data system—but they do so in a way that leaves the Algol Wall intact, and as a consequence tends to entail greater complexity in language structure.

Simula 67 is an extension of the Simula I language developed in the early 1960s by Kristen Nygaard and O.J. Dahl of the Norwegian Computing Center. Simula I was intended initially to be a language "... which could serve the dual purpose of system description and simulation programming ... " [114, p.246]. The original design (documented in early 1963) modeled programs as networks of communicating stations whose behavior varied over time. The language was well received, but it had shortcomings that prompted Nygaard and Dahl to begin work on Simula 67. The idea of stations and queues is discarded in Simula 67 in favor of a more general model. In developing this revolutionary new model,

Nygaard and Dahl were strongly influenced by the contemporary work
of Hoare on a general record concept [64].

Smalltalk was developed at Xerox Corporation's Palo Alto Research
Center during the mid 1970s in a group headed by Alan Kay. Flex,
Smalltalk 72, Smalltalk 74 and Smalltalk 76 were successive refinements of a programming *system* encompassing a language and a powerful program-development environment based on the object-oriented
programming model. Our discussion is based on Smalltalk 80 [51].

6.1 Simula 67 Profile

Simula 67 is derived from and in most ways strongly resembles Algol 60.
We focus here on the aspect of the design that is most strikingly different,
the introduction of *classes* and *objects*.

What is a class? The following significant thought appears in an early
paper about Simula 67:

> In Algol 60 a sharp distinction is made between a block,
> which is a piece of program text, and a dynamic block in-
> stance, which is (a component of) the computing process.
> An immediate and useful consequence is that a block may
> be identified with the *class* of its potential activations. (em-
> phasis added) [34]

What, then, is the meaning of the word *class*? Clearly, according to this
definition, a *class* is the set of all activations of some block or procedure.

In the context of programming languages this is an unusual concept:
it means that a class exists at runtime only. It's not an entity whose
existence can be manifest explicitly in a program text. By this definition,
class is to *block* or *procedure* as "the set of all star-shaped cookies" is to
"the star-shaped cookie cutter."

We can focus without loss of generality on a class as a set of procedure
invocations (ignoring classes generated by independent lexical blocks).
We'll refer to the procedure that generates a particular class as the "class
procedure." Each thing in a class, then, consists of the execution of a

procedure within a naming context that includes the parameters of the
class procedure and the local objects created by the class procedure.

In short, each entity in the class encompasses an *environment*—whatever
kind of environment the class procedure creates for its own local use. A
Simula 67 procedure follows basically the same rules as an Algol 60
procedure; recall that an Algol 60 procedure may declare local variables *and* local procedures. Hence, the environments encompassed by
each member of a class may contain both *variables* and *procedures*. In
other words, each member of a class may contain what we have called a
data system. Each class member may encompass a heterogeneous set of
variables (the local variables declared by the class procedure), a set of
procedures designed to manipulate the variables (the local procedures
declared by the class procedure) and an executable statement (the initialization statement evaluated when the class procedure is invoked).
The class procedure itself is the template that is used to create data
systems.

In some sense, then, the relationship between the *class procedure* and
the *class* resembles the relationship in Pascal between a *record type* and
the set of all records instantiated from the type. But there are several
crucial distinctions. The members of the class are more general than
Pascal records (insofar as a data system may contain procedure-valued
fields whereas a Pascal record cannot). Further, the *class procedures* we
have been discussing are merely procedures—they aren't special-purpose
data-object-generating templates. A class procedure is structurally analogous to a Pascal *procedure*, not to a Pascal record type definition. Finally, *many records may co-exist*, but at any one time *only one member
a class is accessible*—at least, given the definitions we've assumed so
far. It can never be the case that at time *t*, six different versions of procedure **foobar**'s local variables are all accessible simultaneously. Nor,
by the same token, can six different members of a class be accessible
simultaneously—if a class procedure is really *identical* to a procedure.

So we can think of procedures as a generalized kind of environment
template—except that they aren't very useful templates, because only
one instance of the objects they are designed to create can be accessible
at any one time. (If a cookie-cutter worked according to these principles,
cookie #1 would necessarily have vanished by the time you start on #2.)
A procedure works this way because, when it is invoked, it creates a new

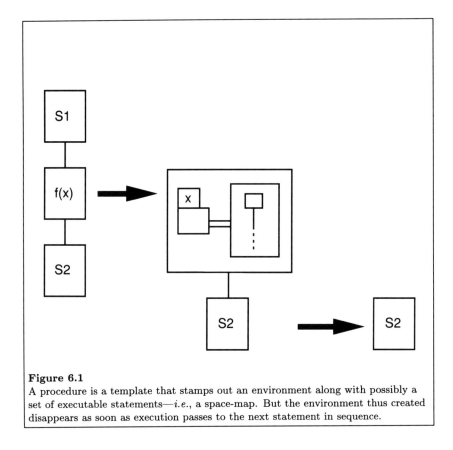

Figure 6.1
A procedure is a template that stamps out an environment along with possibly a
set of executable statements—*i.e.*, a space-map. But the environment thus created
disappears as soon as execution passes to the next statement in sequence.

space-map inside whatever region it has been allotted. When execution
of the procedure is complete, control passes to the statement following
next in the sequence. The next statement takes over the region that had
been occupied by the procedure, and the new environment created by
the procedure activation disappears (see figure 6.1).

Suppose, instead, that we could invoke a procedure in such a way that
a brand new map region is created and tacked on to the end of the
top-level space-map. The procedure activation executes within this new
map region. When execution moves forward to the statement following
the procedure invocation, the new environment is *not* overwritten, because it occupies its own purpose-built region off to the side someplace
(figure 6.2). Once the procedure has been invoked, in other words, its

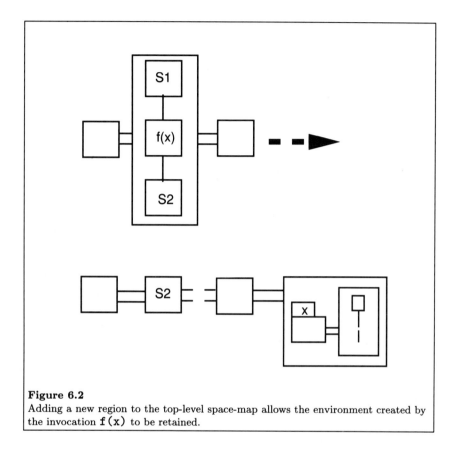

Figure 6.2
Adding a new region to the top-level space-map allows the environment created by
the invocation **f(x)** to be retained.

local environment persists; it is accessible throughout the remainder of
the program's lifetime. Executing n of these new-style procedure invocations results in n new regions being tacked onto the top-level program
space-map, and n new data systems becoming accessible.

This new-style invocation is the heart of what is new in Simula 67. A
statement such as

    f(x)

is an ordinary procedure invocation, as in Algol 60. But the statement

    new g(y)

causes a new region to be added to the top-level space-map; the invocation of **g** executes within this region, and the local environment created by **g** remains accessible throughout the remaining lifetime of the program.

We now have something that (first) subsumes most of the functionality of Pascal's record type. Consider the Pascal fragment

```
type Three  = record
                 x,y : integer;
                 z : real
              end;
   ...
var ThreeInstance:   Three;
   ...
```

Execution of this program results in the creation of a space-map region corresponding to the variable **ThreeInstance**. The region is divided into three sub-regions, two for **x** and **y**, the third for **z**. Now consider the following fragment in pseudo-Simula. (We can't give Simula code that is correct in all details until several other points have been discussed.)

```
Procedure Three;
   begin integer x,y;
          real z
   end
   ...
   new Three;
```

These statements have essentially the same effect as the Pascal fragment. First we declare a template which, upon instantiation, will create a three-variable environment. Then we instantiate the template—by declaring a variable in Pascal, by invoking a procedure using **new** in Simula.

There is an important distinction between the two examples, however. The Pascal record instance is merely a variable like any other; in Simula, we create a record-like object by executing a "**new**" statement. It follows that the Pascal record instance can be given a name in the usual way (precisely as we would give a name to an integer); but the "new" statement in Simula is *not* part of a declaration section *per se*, and we need

some other mechanism to attach a name to the object created by "new."
The solution in Simula is for new to return a *pointer* to the new object
it creates. This pointer can be assigned to a variable of type "pointer to
objects created by new invocations of procedure Three." We can move
our pseudo-Simula example one step closer to the real thing by writing

```
Procedure Three;
   begin integer x,y;
         real z
   end
   ...
ref (Three) ThreeInstance;
ThreeInstance :- new Three.
```

The ":-" symbol is the special assignment operator for cases in which a
pointer rather than a value is being assigned. Executing this fragment
makes ThreeInstance a pointer to the object created by new. We can
now write

```
ThreeInstance.x
```

to refer to the variable x within this new object, and so on.

Only one more detail need be added to our pseudo-Simula examples in
order to make them real Simula: a procedure that is to be invoked using
new is designated a *class*, not a procedure; the keyword class replaces
the keyword procedure in the definition. Thus we have

```
class Three;
   begin integer x,y;
         real z
   end
   ...
ref (Three) ThreeInstance;
ThreeInstance :- new Three;
```

In some ways, this new piece of nomenclature is unfortunate and confusing. Having presented one definition for the term "class," we must
now present a second one, this time the official definition:

Definition 6.1 A *class* is a procedure that can and must be invoked
within a new region that is added dynamically to the top-level space-

map; in other words, a *class* is a procedure that is invoked (only) by
using **new**.

From now on, when we use the term *class* we will have this second
definition in mind.

Simula makes no structural distinction between classes and ordinary
procedures; there is no reason in principle why we are not allowed to
invoke *any* procedure using either **new** or an ordinary procedure invocation. In other words it is the **new** operation, not the **class** structure,
that represents the essence of Simula's innovation.

Simula refers to the data systems created by **class** invocations simply
as *objects*. To avoid confusion in the remainder of this chapter, we will
write **object** when we mean specifically "the entity instantiated from a
class."

We know (in essential outline) how to use Simula's **new** to get the behavior of a Pascal record, but we can go beyond this as well, at no added cost
in new machinery or complexity. We can use exactly the same mechanism to create a data system. Consider the following simple example:
a **bank account** is a data system that implements two functions over
a local variable called **balance**. **DEPOSIT(sum)** adds **sum** to **balance**,
and **WITHDRAW(sum)** subtracts **sum** from **balance**. When we create the
account, we specify an initial balance. The Simula implementation looks
like this:

```
class ACCOUNT(balance); real balance;
 begin
   procedure DEPOSIT(DepositAmt); real DepositAmt;
     balance := balance + DepositAmt;
   procedure WITHDRAW(WithdrawAmt); real WithdrawAmt;
     balance := balance - WithdrawAmt;
 end;
```

To create an account:

```
ref (ACCOUNT) MyAcct;
...
MyAcct :- new ACCOUNT(1200);
```

To use the account,

```
MyAcct.DEPOSIT(900);
```

Any object instantiated from a class may contain an executable statement that is evaluated when the object is created. Thus, we can include
a statement to initialize the local environment in a class definition; this
statement will be executed when we execute "**new**." The following example (taken from [33]) creates a **histogram**. When the histogram is
created, we supply an array that divides the real line into a set of disjoint
partitions. Each histogram supplies a **tabulate(x)** procedure, which in-
crements a table entry corresponding to the total number of values that
fall into the same partition as **x**, and a **frequency(y)** function, which
returns the relative frequency of tabulated values that fall into the yth
partition.

```
class histogram (X,n);
  array X; integer n;
  begin
    integer N; integer array T[0:n];
    procedure tabulate (Y); real Y;
      begin
        integer i; i := 0;
        while
          (if i < n then Y < X[i+1]
                    else false) do
          i := i + 1;
        T[i] := t[+1]; N := N + 1;
      end of tabulate
    real procedure frequency (i); integer i;
      frequency := T[i]/N;
    integer i;
    for i := 0 step 1 until n do
      T[i] := 0;
    N := 0
  end of histogram;
```

Concatenation. One more language feature is crucial to Simula 67,
the idea of *class concatenation* or *inheritance*. We need first to define

factoring as it applies to software:

Definition 6.2 *Factoring* means (1) recognizing a set of program elements that occurs repeatedly in some program text, (2) encapsulating those elements and then (3) referring to the encapsulated version in lieu of verbatim repetition of the common elements.

Concretely: in the most common case, we notice that the same sequence of statements is executed repeatedly, or the same complex expression repeatedly evaluated. We define a procedure to execute the statements or evaluate the expression, and we replace verbatim repetition of the statements with invocations of the procedure.

Factoring is useful because it makes the source program more compact, hence easier to write and to read, but it plays a conceptual role as well. Factoring lends itself to a program development method that resembles Wirth's stepwise refinement as seen from the bottom up instead of top-down. Under Wirth's method we start with the grand design, then refine it. Using factoring, we start with a mess of details and then notice patterns. Generally speaking, the more "factored" a program, the more transparent its structure: one good way to understand a complex structure is to notice repeated patterns. Factoring highlights repeated patterns.

In most languages, factoring can only be "time-wise factoring": given a sequence of evaluation steps, we remove a sub-sequence and replace it by a procedure call. But we can define "space-wise factoring" as well. We notice that a series of space-map regions—a series of variable declarations or function definitions—recurs verbatim in many contexts. We remove these declarations, encapsulate them somehow and then invoke this encapsulation whenever we needed the declarations (see figure 6.3). For example, consider the Pascal fragment

```
type elephant = record
                    weight, height, age: real;
                    name: NameString;
                    grayness: integer;
                    BigEars: Boolean
                end;
```

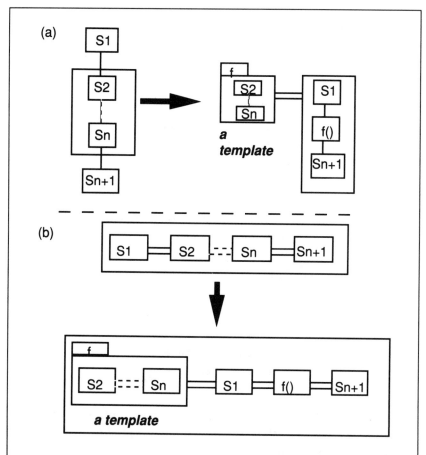

Figure 6.3
In time-wise factoring (*a*) we encapsulate a fragment of a time-map; in space-wise factoring (*b*), a fragment of a space-map.

```
whoopingCrane = record
            weight, height, age: real;
            name: NameString;
            FeatherCount: integer;
            end;
marmoset = record
            weight, height, age: real;
            name: NameString;
            ...
        end
```

Why repeat the first segment verbatim every time? We might encapsulate the shared elements in a new record definition, giving something
like this:

```
type animal = record
            weight, height, age: real
            name: NameString
        end
```

An elephant would look like this:

```
type elephant = record
            BaseFields: animal;
            grayness: integer;
            BigEars: Boolean
        end
```

But this is a poor solution. The name of some **elephant** fields will be
two-part and the rest will be three-part, for no logical reason. If **Edmund**
is an elephant, we write

```
Edmund.grayness
```

to find Edmund's "grayness," and

```
Edmund.BaseFields.height
```

to find his height.

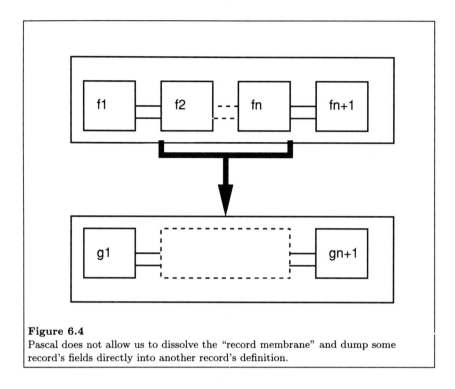

Figure 6.4
Pascal does not allow us to dissolve the "record membrane" and dump some
record's fields directly into another record's definition.

The more factoring we do, the more complicated the scheme gets, and
the more arbitrary the names (such as "**Basefields**") we are forced to
invent. We might have references such as

```
Henry.Basefields.weight
Henry.Birdfields.FeatherCount
```

and so on.

The immediate problem is that Pascal won't allow us to dissolve the
shell that envelops a record's fields and dump those fields directly into
some other record definition (figure 6.4). There is another rather subtle
problem as well, having to with the relationship between space-wise
factoring on the one hand and Pascal's strong typing on the other.

Suppose we need a linked list of animals; every animal must now include a pointer field, so that we can link each animal to the next on
the list. But despite the fact that the pointer field is shared by all ani-

mals, we can't factor it out and include it within type **animal**, because
a pointer in Pascal must point to an object of *a single type*. We can't
declare a pointer of type elephant *or* marmoset *or* whooping crane. We
might use Pascal's variant record to encompass elephants, marmosets
and whooping cranes within a single *variant* type; still, we are permanently restricted in our use of these pointers to the types that are
included explicitly in the variant record declaration. We can define a
function without any knowledge of where it will be used, but we can't
define a pointer without stating *a priori* the full range of object types
to which it will point. Hence a function definition can be maintained as
is, even if the surrounding program grows much more complicated than
at first, and the same function can be reused in many programs in new
and unanticipated contexts. It is exactly this degree of flexibility with
respect to space-wise factoring that Pascal cannot support, but Simula
can.

Simula 67 recognizes space-wise factoring as a fundamental method, and
supports it strongly. By writing

```
ANIMAL class ELEPHANT ...
```

we can make **elephant**s include (or "inherit") all the fields defined by
class **ANIMAL**. Class **ELEPHANT** is said to be a *sub-class* of **ANIMAL**—in
other words, an elephant is a specialized kind of animal. If some field is
defined in **ANIMAL** and redefined in **ELEPHANT**, the definition in **ELEPHANT**
takes precedence.

The concepts of sub- and super-class are sufficiently important to deserve
special emphasis:

Definition 6.3   When a class Q inherits fields from class R, in the
process adding new fields and possibly overriding some of R's definitions
with new ones, we say that Q is a *sub-class* of R; R is a *super-class* of
Q. Thus **ELEPHANT** is a sub-class of **ANIMAL** or, equivalently, **ANIMAL** is a
super-class of **ELEPHANT**.

From the ISM's point of view, inheritance is map concatenation. We
defined a **layer** operation over space-maps in chapter 3, in describing the
structure of an interpreter environment. We can use the same operation
to model inheritance. **Objects** are maps; classes are map templates.

To build an "ISM object," we start with a space-map instantiated from the super-class template, then overlay it with maps instantiated from the sub-classes (see figure 6.5). The order in which maps are overlayed determines the inheritance hierarchy: names in lower-level maps are superseded by names in higher-level maps; thus, super-class maps must be overlayed with sub-class maps.

□ In the ISM, *building an "object" out of a hierarchy of classes* and *extending an interpreter-built environment incrementally* are instances of the same operation. In both cases, a pre-existing environment is augmented (and some of its definitions selectively superseded) by new definitions.

Class concatenation is carefully integrated with Simula's type system. A pointer of type "`ref (BAZ)`" may point to BAZs *or* to objects instantiated from any immediate sub-class of BAZ. Thus if `AnimalRef` is declared to be a `ref (ANIMAL)`, it may point to ELEPHANTs as well as to ANIMALs—that is, to objects instantiated from class ELEPHANT, not only to those instantiated from class ANIMAL. However, while `AnimalRef` may be used to get access to any field declared within class ANIMAL, it may *not* be used to access the internal fields of ELEPHANT. `AnimalRef.weight` is acceptable, but `AnimalRef.grayness` is not. In order to look at a **grayness** field (at a field that is peculiar to elephants, in other words), you need an explicit ELEPHANT pointer. This particular type discipline is known as *subtyping*. ELEPHANT is said to be a *subtype* of ANIMAL because objects instantiated from ELEPHANT can be used in any context where ANIMAL objects are allowed; ELEPHANT is a special *type* of ANIMAL. In particular, any procedure that operates on ANIMALS can operate over ELEPHANTS as well.

Class concatenation makes it easy and convenient to support structures such as linked lists in Simula 67. If we declare link fields within a class LINK, the pointers within LINK may point to objects of any class that is a sub-class of LINK. If a linked list is to hold objects within classes A, B, C and D, we simply write

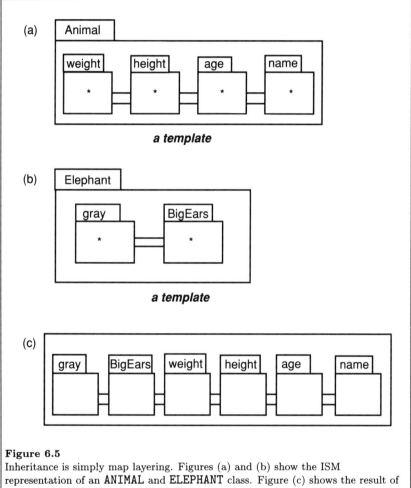

Figure 6.5
Inheritance is simply map layering. Figures (a) and (b) show the ISM representation of an **ANIMAL** and **ELEPHANT** class. Figure (c) shows the result of layering **ELEPHANT** on top of **ANIMAL**.

```
LINK class A
LINK class B
    ...
```

Simula 67's concept of inheritance (in our terms, of space-wise factoring) amounts to more than a small convenience in a few special cases. There is a methodology underlying these tools that is as significant as Wirth's stepwise refinement. This methodology came to be known as *object-oriented programming*. We discuss this term, and Simula's contributions in general, in the discussion following the Smalltalk profile.

6.2 Smalltalk Profile

Smalltalk was derived from Simula 67; it represents either the carrying-to-their-logical-conclusions or the *reductio ad absurdum* of the ideas in Simula, depending on your point of view.

In Simula 67 there are two kinds of data object: the **objects** that are constructed using classes, and the built-in, primitive data objects that are part of the language. Thus if you want objects of type "histogram," and wish the operations "tabulate" and "frequency" to be defined over objects of this type, you define a class called "histogram" and include the necessary data fields and their associated operations. If you need objects of type "integer," on the other hand, you rely on the fact that this type of data object is intrinsic to the language. You merely declare objects to be of type "integer"; you don't need to create a class "integer," including all the necessary operations (plus, minus and so on) defined over this type.

In Smalltalk, on the other hand, the distinction between data systems (*e.g.*, histograms) and objects of primitive type (*e.g.*, integers) is, in principle, abolished. *Every* data object is assumed to represent the instantiation of some class. In other words, the only kind of data object is an **object**. *Every* operation—whether it is something simple and primitive such as integer addition, or something more complicated (such as the "tabulate" operation defined over histograms, for example)—is

assumed to be a procedure defined inside a class. Furthermore, classes
are *themselves* **objects**. The **object** corresponding to a class is responsible for creating new **objects** of its class. It follows that classes can be
created from other classes. A *meta-class* specifies a special set of methods that are responsible primarily for initializing class variables and new
instances.

How do we refer to the elements of an **object**? In Simula 67, we use the
familiar dot notation: if `foobar` is an **object** of type `histogram`, then
`foobar.tabulate(x)` invokes `foobar`'s version of the `tabulate` procedure. In Smalltalk the same thing takes place in effect, but it's described
in a different way. In Smalltalk we "send messages" to **objects**: in order
to invoke procedure `f` within **object** Z, we "send a message" to Z. The
message says "invoke procedure `f`"—or, in Smalltalk nomenclature, "invoke *method* `f`." Instead of `foobar.tabulate(x)`, we use a statement
that translates as "send the message 'tabulate value `x`' to the **object**
named `foobar`."

Certain classes are built in: programmers don't need to implement a
class "integer," for example. But *every* Smalltalk operation is defined
within some class. In Smalltalk, then, performing *any* operation on *any*
data object requires, in principle, that we dispatch a message to the
appropriate **object**. We can picture a Smalltalk program as a set of
disjoint, self-contained **objects**, communicating via messages that are
constantly zipping back and forth among them.

Bear in mind, however, that message sending in Smalltalk is essentially
the same operation as procedure invocation in Simula. When I send
a message to some histogram **object** asking it to "invoke *frequency* on
category *q*," the value yielded by the *frequency* function is returned to me
as an integral part of the message-sending transaction. In other words,
my "send a message" operation is incomplete until the *answer* to my
message has arrived. Smalltalk's use of the phrase "message sending"
is misleading: intuitively, the act of *sending a message* does not imply
the act of *receiving an answer to the message*. The action of dropping
a letter into a mailbox does not mean that a reply will materialize in
my hand automatically, as part of this very message-sending act. If I *do*
get an answer to my letter, I must assume that my correspondent has
done exactly as I did—that he strolled over to *his* mailbox and mailed
a letter to *me*. But in Smalltalk, again, "sending a message" is merely a

different way of describing what Simula (and most other languages) call "invoking a procedure."

The premise underlying Smalltalk is simple: every entity is an **object**. But Smalltalk's syntax is the most peculiar of any language in this book, and requires special attention. The basic idea is that in order to send the message f to object Z, we write:

```
Z f
```

A message may entail "arguments," in the same way that a Simula procedure invocation may involve arguments; the arguments associated with a message follow the message. If f is a message of one argument, we write:

```
Z f x
```

(The equivalent form in Simula would be "Z.f(x).")

This sounds simple, but things rapidly get more complicated. We'll consider an example taken from an early paper about Smalltalk [68]. Suppose we are writing a program to display images on a terminal screen. One kind of image we'll want to display is a simple point. To manage the display of points, we will define a class called "Point"; each point in the display will represent one instance of this class. What operations will class "Point" include? (In Smalltalk terminology, what *methods* will be defined within class "Point"?) For one, we will want to *add* one point to another—that is, assuming we represent each point as a set of Cartesian coordinates, we will want to add the x and y values of some new point to those of a pre-existing point. Hence, class "Point" will include the operation *plus*. Point itself will be an instance of a meta-class that defines operations and constants particular to Point, *e.g.*, operations that create new points or that initialize various fields in new instantiations.

In Smalltalk, the definition of *plus* within class "Point" looks like this:

```
+pt [↑ Point new x: x+pt x y: y+pt y]
```

The initial + character is, in effect, *the name of the procedure we are defining*. The pt immediately following is the (single) *argument* to this procedure. The equivalent in Simula notation would be:

```
class +(pt); ref (Point) pt;
  begin ... end;
```

except that Simula does not allow us to use symbols like + as names; we would write plus(pt) instead.

Another distinction between Simula and Smalltalk: in Simula we get new points by instantiating classes, in Smalltalk by sending messages to **objects** which *represent* classes, and are (in turn) instances of meta-classes. We comment further on this distinction below.

The phrase within the square brackets constitutes the definition of method + as defined within class Point. The phrase ↑*some expression* means "return the result of *some expression* as the value of this procedure." So we must decode the phrase following the up-arrow; this phrase will tell us how the + procedure works.

In principle this should be easy. Whenever we see Z f, we know that we are to send message f to object Z. But we need to understand a few more rules before we can make sense of this example. We need to know that

1. A phrase of the form id: value is a *keyword message*. It doesn't mean "send value to the object named id:." Instead,

   id: value

   constitutes a *single* message to be sent as is to some object. When the message is received, value will become the value of an argument called id within the method definition. Furthermore,

2. (to quote directly from the above-mentioned paper), "if several keyword messages appear at a given level, they combine to provide a message with multiple arguments." Thus in the example above, the new message entails two keyword arguments, an x: argument and a y: argument. We combine them, giving an aggregate message of the form x: *Something* y: *SomethingElse*. Furthermore,

3. Given a series of send-message operations, we execute the message sends neither strictly right-to-left nor left-to-right. Instead,

messages of *fewer* arguments are sent before messages with *more* arguments. Thus in the example above, the **new** message will be sent last, because it involves two arguments; the remaining messages all entail only one argument. Furthermore,

4. "Arithmetic messages"—for example, the message "**+**"—are sent before keyword messages.

We can now interpret the definition of class "Point."

1. Messages of no arguments are dispatched first: in this case, we execute the send-message operations **pt x** and **pt y**. The object **pt** responds to the **x** message by returning its *x*-coordinate, and to the **y** message by returning its *y*-coordinate. An object can examine its state using a special variable called "**self**": evaluating ↑ **self x** within **pt** causes the current value of **x** to be returned.

2. We now dispatch the "arithmetic" messages—we execute **x + pt x** and **y + pt y**. The result is a new **x** and a new **y**, representing the original **x** plus **pt**'s *x*-coordinate, and similarly for **y**.

3. We can now send the two-argument keyword message—we send the message

   new x: *new-value-of-x* **y:** *new-value-of-y*

   to **Point**. The definition of **new** is found in **Point**'s meta-class. The object **Point** implements the *class* **Point**: object **Point** responds to a **new** message by creating a new **Point** object initialized with the **x** and **y** values that are sent as keyword arguments.

4. Finally, we return this new **Point** object as the value of the method invocation.

The Smalltalk programming environment.   No description of Smalltalk would be complete without some mention of the Smalltalk programming environment. Smalltalk's integrated programming environment was the first fully successful attempt to build an entire computing system around a single language. The Smalltalk-80 system subsumes not only the language proper, but an editor, a window manager, a debugger, an **object**-display routine and an interpreter, all of them implemented in Smalltalk. Users can edit a program, compile, debug and execute it without ever having to leave the Smalltalk environment.

Smalltalk's uniformity and self-describability have a great deal to do with the success of the Smalltalk system. Remember that everything in Smalltalk is an object; every object remembers its own state and can receive messages from and send messages to any other object. In particular, an executing Smalltalk *process* can itself be represented as an object. If a process encounters a runtime error, it can send a message to a debugger which can then proceed to inspect the process' state. In fact, the *entire* Smalltalk-system environment (method definitions, data objects, processes, windows, etc.) is represented as a large object that can be saved, examined and resumed by the user. The editor is an object as well. To insert a character into a text buffer, for example, the user in effect sends an "insert" message to the editor object. The user is free to extend or customize any part of the Smalltalk system using the factoring techniques described earlier.

The Smalltalk system has prompted a number of innovations in programming environment technology: integrated text editors, overlapping windows, object inspectors and interactive debuggers, to name just a few. Almost all modern programming environments developed subsequently incorporate some of these features in one form or another.

6.3   Discussion: Object-Oriented Programming

Simula in part and Smalltalk *in toto* demolished the Algol Wall. Simula draws no distinction between the templates used to instantiate a histogram on the one hand and the function "frequency" defined *within* the histogram on the other. A histogram **object** is structurally the same as a block. Smalltalk goes further: *every* data object (whether complex and heterogeneous like a histogram, complex and homogeneous like an array, or simple like an integer) represents the instantiation of a *class* template, and is in concept identical to an Algol 60 block.

Thus in Smalltalk, the two worlds of program structure and data-object structure flow together and become indistinguishable. No longer are program structures governed by simple, flexible, recursively interlocking and hierarchical rules, while data objects languish under an *ad hoc* regimen inherited from traditional mathematical notation, poorly integrated with program structure and incapable of expressing general-purpose data systems. The full panoply of expressiveness inherent in the idea of data systems and of simple, uniform, well-integrated language structure follows—we pursue these points below. *But*—the Wall's abolition was accomplished by these two languages in a fateful way that had problematic consequences.

Simula and Smalltalk summoned the wrecking crews to the scene, but then a decision was necessary: there were two basically different ways in which to demolish the Algol Wall. The Wall divides program structure on the one hand from data-object structure on the other. It can be demolished by making everything look like a program structure (in effect eliminating the data-object category), or by making everything look like a data object (eliminating the program structure category).

Simula tentatively and Smalltalk wholeheartedly chose the former route. The Wall is demolished by (in effect) replacing data objects with program structures. A Pascal record is a data object of a certain type. A Simula histogram is the instantiation of a class, just as the program fragment that evaluates "frequency" is the instantiation of a procedure; conceptually, a histogram instance is a newly minted piece of program structure. Smalltalk goes all the way: even an *integer* is a newly minted piece of program structure. This represents an intriguing but (in some ways) questionable choice, for two reasons.

1. Under this view of things, particularly under Smalltalk's approach, there are no passive objects to be acted *upon*. Every entity is an *active* agent, a little program in itself. This can lead to counter-intuitive interpretations of simple operations, and can be destructive to a natural sense of hierarchy.

2. Algol 60 gives us a representation for procedures, but no direct representation for a procedure *activation*. Simula and Smalltalk inherit this same limitation: they give us representations for *classes*,

but no direct representation for the **objects** that are instantiated
from classes. Our ability to create single **objects** and to specify
(constant) **object** "values" is compromised.

We'll consider each of these issues in turn.

Every data object in Smalltalk results from the instantiation of a class (in
effect, keeping the Simula model in mind, from the invocation of a procedure). There are no mere integers or vectors or Booleans; instead, there
are a series of local environments created by class instantiation. This
means that instead of having procedures that operate over **objects**, we
have only the **objects**. All procedures are absorbed into the **objects**—
performed by the **objects** upon themselves. As a consequence, we can
never write "do this or that to the following passive entities"; **objects**
are never merely passively acted upon; some **object** or other must always be in charge. This is fine when the entities we are dealing with are
large or complex or multi-part (like histograms), but it is conceptually
awkward when they are small and homogeneous (like integers). It also
leads to complications when we consider how **objects** are created.

For most people, it is natural to think of arithmetic in terms of expressions that state "do something to the following numbers." It is less
natural to think of arithmetic as being performed by one number (the
big boss number?) upon the rest. But in Smalltalk, the expression 4 + 5
is to be understood *not* as "apply the *plus* operation to 4 and 5," but
instead as "send a message to the object 4 asking it to add the value of
the object 5 to its own value." If we write 5 + 4 instead, the answer is
the same but the sequence of events is altered. Now 5 is the boss and
performs the addition. This will strike many people as a strange and
artificial way to think about arithmetic and about integers. When we
look at an arithmetic expression and try to understand it, the "plain
sense" for most observers entails an *active* operation applied to *passive*
objects—but there are no passive objects in Smalltalk.

A similar effect holds when we consider **object** creation. "Creating
something from a template" is a simple and intuitive process that "naturally" entails an *active* agent performing an operation (instantiation,
stamping-out) upon a *passive* object (the template). But in Smalltalk,
the template must itself become an active agent. Hence a *class* is no

longer simply a template with which we instantiate **objects**; instantiation must be performed by an **object** standing in for the class. But where did *this* **object** come from? It was created by an **object** standing in for the meta-class, and so on. This complicates the intuitively simple distinction between classes and **objects**.

These (admittedly fairly subtle and subjective) objections hold only for Smalltalk, but there is a more basic point that applies both to Smalltalk and to Simula.

Representability. Because the idea of "**object**" is derived from the idea of "procedure invocation," **objects** are inappropriate where procedure invocations are inappropriate—even in cases where, in the abstract, "**objects**" *should* be just the idea we are looking for.

An **object** consists of some definitions (a local environment) and an executable statement; so does a Simula program *in toto*. But a Simula program *itself* is *not* an **object**. Nor can we structure a large Simula program as (let's say) ten **objects**, each serving as a module. In other words, we can't write a Simula program that looks like this:

```
object Program
    ⋮
  object Module1
      ⋮
  object Modula2
      ⋮
```

even though the entities that go inside an **object** (variable declarations, procedure definitions and an executable statement) are *exactly the same* as the entities that go inside a program. Furthermore, suppose we want only a *single* **object** of some type. In Pascal we can declare some variable to be a single record, bypassing record *types* altogether—e.g., in Pascal,

```
(* there's only one of these *)
var OneOff: record
             x, y : integer
           end;
```

We can't do this in Simula; we must *first* define the class, and *then* (at runtime) instantiate it:

```
class OneOff;
        begin
           integer x,y
        end;
ref (OneOff) OneOffInstance;
   ...
OneOffInstance :- Oneoff;
```

The same holds for Smalltalk. A Smalltalk program is a collection of **objects**, but a collection of **objects** *itself* is not an **object**.

To explain these related phenomena, we note again that the Simula **object** is derived from the Algol procedure invocation. Hence you can *represent* (write down as part of your source program) the *definition* of an Algol 60 procedure, or of a Simula or Smalltalk class. But a procedure *invocation* is something that happens at runtime. You can't represent the *invocation* of an Algol 60 procedure, *nor* can you represent a Simula or Smalltalk **object**. In other words, we know what the *template* for an **object** looks like, but we don't know what the **object** *itself* looks like. Hence we can never build an **object** directly, simply by writing it down as part of the source program (we can't because we don't know what one looks like). We can only get **objects** indirectly, by instantiating templates. Hence, again, we can't declare a single **object** by itself, nor can we explicitly structure a program as a single large **object** that includes smaller **objects**, and so on.

There's another related reason why a Smalltalk program (a collection of **objects**) can't itself be an **object**. As we noted in discussing Lisp, the environment created by a procedure invocation is *static*—a collection of entities (parameters and local variables) that are created together and eliminated together. Such an environment is a bad model for the collection of all **objects** in a Smalltalk program—the collection of Smalltalk **objects** grows and shrinks dynamically as the program runs.

Suppose Simula had taken the other tack, and achieved uniformity by treating everything as data, rather than by treating everything as a procedure. A class would have been a generalized record template, and procedure invocation would have been derived from the idea of **object** rather than *vice versa*. We'd know exactly what an **object** looked like (and also, for that matter, what a procedure invocation looked like). We would have eliminated the bipartite nature of program structure—but not at the cost of turning integers into objects. (What we have described is, in essence, the ISM itself.)

6.3.1 Object-Oriented Programming

The programming method induced by Simula, by Smalltalk, and by a large collection of subsequent languages inspired by these originals, is called "object-oriented" programming. This tacky-sounding phrase[1] alludes to the fact that the definition and instantiation of **objects** is the basis of the method.

Object-oriented programming implies both a general vision of what programs are and a set of language constructs. This view of programming represents an interesting and significant departure from previous approaches. represents an interesting and significant departure. In all other languages we've considered, a program consists of passive data-objects on the one hand and the executable program that manipulates these passive objects on the other. Object-oriented programs replace this bipartite structure with a homogeneous one: they consist (partially in Simula, exclusively in Smalltalk) of a set of *data systems*, each of which is capable of operating *on itself*. For example, to remove one element from a linked list in Pascal (or in most other languages), we would invoke a `Remove-element` procedure and supply the *element to be removed* as an argument. The argument is a passive object; it is operated upon by the procedure. In the Simula or Smalltalk world view, we would locate the element to be removed and, rather than passing it as the argument to a procedure, we would *instruct it to remove itself* from the list. As noted, Simula permits this approach but does not enforce it across the boards; Smalltalk makes this method uniform and absolute.

---

[1]The word "orient," after all, means to point in some direction, to align, especially with respect to the points of the compass. The phrase "object-oriented" is supposed to mean "object-based" or "having to do with objects," "based on the use of objects." Perhaps, after a hectic afternoon of phrasemaking, the exhausted wordsmiths adjourned to a local movie theater to take in "Life with Smalltalk—Oriented towards a True Story."

What do we gain by programming with **objects**? Most importantly, *expressivity*. A language is expressive to the extent that it allows program structure to mirror the programmer's way of thinking. Data systems allow us to bundle the passive data fields of some object together with the procedures that will operate on them. Without data systems, the passive fields must be in one place (in a Pascal record definition, for example) and the procedures someplace else. But insofar as programmers *think* of the passive fields and the active operations together, an expressive programming language will allow them to *program* in this way also. What is a histogram? "An entity that supports the operations *frequency* and *tabulate*" is a natural answer. What is a bank account? "Something that you can *withdraw* from and make *deposits* into." As Hoare wrote presciently in an influential early paper on "the record concept,"

> A fundamental feature of our understanding of the world is
> that we organize our experience as a number of distinct *ob-
> jects* (tables and chairs, bank loans and algebraic expressions
> ...).... When we wish to solve a problem on a computer, we
> often need to construct within the computer a *model* of that
> aspect of the real or conceptual world to which the solution
> of the problem will be applied.... [64, p.294]

The point is crucial. Software isn't merely a medium for building fancy adding machines; it can be used to model arbitrary pieces of reality. Object-oriented programming offers programmers a model that in a wide variety of cases, naturally mirrors the way they think. It represents in this sense an immensely significant advance in language design and programming methodology.

Several related but more specific points: object-oriented programming promotes *modularity* insofar as (again) it tends to concentrate conceptually related program elements in a single place (the class definition), rather than scattering them among variable declarations on the one hand and procedure definitions on the other. *Class concatenation* promotes modularity as well, in the obvious way: it allows us to concentrate a set of related definitions within a single class, and then to make use of this one class repeatedly in many contexts. To change or update this set of related definitions, we need look in *one* place only (the class definition);

we don't need to comb the program text for every occurrence of some particular functionality.

6.3.2 Name Overloading

A final advantage of this method may seem like a minor detail, and in a sense it is, but it's often promoted to a position of central importance by the proponents of the method, and it raises some thought-provoking issues. This final advantage is *name overloading*—the ability to use *one* name to mean several *different* (though presumably related) things.

Every class defines a local environment of its own; every class may accordingly apply whatever names it wishes to the object it defines. If each and every class chooses to define procedures named `foo`, `bar` and `baz`, so be it. By the same token, every procedure within an Algol 60 program may choose to define a local variable named `x`.

For example—and this is precisely the case most frequently cited in this context—every Simula or Smalltalk class may define a procedure called `print`. As a result, we can tell any **object** in the system "print yourself!" and each **object** will respond by doing exactly what's called for. A table-object might format itself in columns, a rectangle-object might draw the appropriate lines on the display, an integer will simply print the required digits and so on. In short, we've succeeded in using one name ("`print`") to designate many different (though obviously related) procedures.

To achieve this effect in the absence of the object-oriented method, we'd have had to define a single complicated `print` routine, which would have examined its argument (the thing to be printed) and then branched to the correct alternative. Adding new kinds of **objects** to the system requires alterations to this central routine. Under the object-oriented method, on the other hand, no central `print` routine is required; each new **object** is fitted out with its own print routine as necessary. (**Objects** with no special printing requirements will inherit ready-made print routines from their super-classes.)

In pragmatic terms, it's probably fair to describe name overloading as a useful but fairly minor gain. But in broader terms we confront, again, the issue of expressivity. Name overloading is so ubiquitous in natural language that it's easy to suspect that there is something basic about this phenomenon. People tend naturally to use a single name in a variety of related contexts. English itself has many definitions for the word "print." Name overloading conserves names (prevents the number of entries in your mental dictionary from growing unnecessarily), and also makes explicit the relationship among superficially different but conceptually similar entities. In terms of expressivity, then, strong support for name overloading may be another significant advantage of the object-oriented method.

6.3.3   Conclusion: Simula the Hero Language

We've said several critical things about the Simula design. We close by emphasizing, however, that Simula is a Hero Language in the best sense of the term. It achieved a crucial advance in programming language expressivity, and it did so *by simplifying rather than complicating*, by discovering new power in language constructs that were already part of its starting language, rather than by inventing new constructs. In short both *what* Simula achieved and *how* it did so are exceptional. After Fortran, Lisp and Algol 60, Simula 67 is the most important language in this book.

Smalltalk is a fascinating and highly influential language, but hero status eludes it for several reasons. Object-oriented programming properly originates with Simula, not with Smalltalk. Smalltalk's radically uniform application of this technique is interesting but not necessarily persuasive. Smalltalk's syntax has struck more than one observer as difficult and peculiar.

Smalltalk differs radically from Simula in the nature of the programming environment it offers—in being an interpreted language, with a highly sophisticated, novel and influential display format. But it takes nothing away from the significance of Smalltalk's achievements in this area to note that these are programming-environment, not language-design accomplishments.

6.4 Specification, Abstract Typing and Ada

The remarkable contributions of both Simula and Smalltalk were achieved in the name of *expressivity*. Their purpose was to bring programming languages closer to the programmer's way of thinking, close enough to achieve a self-sustaining interaction between the programmer's mental landscape and the model's potential. The programmer approaches the language with certain structures in mind, the language accommodates these and suggests new angles or refinements, and the programmer responds in turn. Here the language plays the kind of role that the equal-tempered keyboard played for Bach, that reinforced concrete played for Robert Maillart—it accommodates, challenges and inspires.

We now consider some design contributions aimed in another direction, intended to improve the *security* rather than the expressivity of programming languages. As we've said, a secure language is intended not so much to inspire programmers as to protect them from their own not inconsiderable frailties. Programs can be complicated machines, particularly when they are large. When many programmers cooperate in building a single program, the probability is high that some mistakes will creep in. Accordingly, designing languages in a way that minimizes programming errors is a reasonable goal. (The only *unreasonable* stance is to insist that security is *necessarily* more important than every other desirable language attribute, in every circumstance.)

The security-based topics we discuss in this section relate to modularity; they belong here because in some cases, they result in constructs that strongly resemble data systems, or the **objects** of Simula and Smalltalk. This is a striking and thought-provoking coincidence. It is as if a White Knight seeking the Rose of Expressivity and a Black Knight searching for the Sword of Security both took off from the same city, only to discover that both of their goals lay halfway around the world in the same small village—albeit in somewhat different parts of town.

6.4.1 Parnas's Specification Technique

In 1972 David Parnas published an important paper on program specification [102]. Parnas notes that complicated programs should be designed

as a collection of modules, not as monolithic entities. He then claims
that it is important for programmers to have a mechanism for describing
the *behavior* of each module without revealing its implementation—that
is, without explaining how this behavior is achieved. He describes such a
mechanism, a "specification language" designed for exactly this purpose.
But his goal, he notes, isn't to promote this particular specification language, but to insist on the principle—that it is desirable for modules to
be described in *some* such language.

Parnas assumes a cooperative programming environment in which a
module may be developed by one programmer and used by many others. A module is said to consist in general of "a number of subroutines
or functions which can cause changes in state, and other functions or
procedures which can give to a user program the values of the variables
making up that state [102, p. 331]." We might describe a data system
or a Simula **object** in more or less the same terms: the **object** consists
of a "state" made up of some variables (that is, the parameters and local
variables of the class), and some functions or procedures that manipulate
the state. Parnas's intention is not to capture the expressive power of a
Simula class: there is no discussion of templates being used to instantiate these modules, still less of class concatenation or other **object**-based
stylistic issues. The point is rather to characterize in a generic way what
a typical "module" probably contains: Parnas assumes that it includes
some variables and some procedures.

He gives several examples, one of which became a ubiquitous standard.
A pushdown stack, Parnas notes, could be specified in such a way that
users of the stack understand exactly what to expect when a value is
pushed on the stack or popped off, but are given no clue as to how this
behavior is achieved. The stack elements might be stored as an array or
a linked list or in some other fashion, and *push* and *pop* might be implemented in any convenient way; nothing about the actual implementation
is revealed to the user of the stack.

One goal is obvious: in line with Wirth's top-down approach to program
engineering, a systematic method for writing specifications is clearly
desirable. Programming can't be orderly and systematic in the absence
of initial agreement about the goals of the project.

Is it fair to describe Parnas's method as an initial step designed to precede stepwise refinement? That is, you write systematic specifications, and then develop a program top-down on the basis of the specs? Not altogether. Parnas's modules tend to embody, again, what we have called data systems. When Parnas thinks about specifying the components of a program, he thinks naturally in terms of a *type* called "stack" which makes operations *push* and *pop* available. There's no way to embody such a specification directly in Pascal or in other conventional Algol-based languages, and this fact drives some further linguistic developments we discuss below.

The Parnas technique has another, more specific goal, which is important but fairly subtle. His technique revolves around "information hiding," based on the notion that users of a module should understand its specifications, but know nothing about its implementation. The point is not to suppress information merely for the sake of suppressing it; instead, since the stack's users don't actually *need* to know how the stack is implemented, they are better off not cluttering their brains with this information. The points are rather that (1) the specification shouldn't bias the implementor in the direction of any particular implementation strategy, and (2) programmers can't depend on knowledge they don't have. Writers of other modules who don't know how the stack is implemented can't *rely* on any particular implementation in the course of writing their own code. This means in turn that the stack's implementor is free to change the implementation as need be (to correct, improve or expand it) without damage to the rest of the program. So long as the stack module remains true to its specification, the implementor can tinker with the interior machinery as much and as frequently as he wants to.

Here, the presupposed program-development model is not merely subtly but markedly different from the top-down model of stepwise refinement. The implicit base assumption is that program development is an iterative process in which revisions, refinements and alterations are to be expected—rather than an orderly, top-down process of filling in the blanks. Under this view, it's important to allow any module to be changed without affecting the rest. Most programmers would agree that this is a fair assumption.

Parnas doesn't insist on the importance of the particular specification language he proposes; the only thing he does insist on is that natural

languages are unacceptable. He excludes natural language because he
wants to machine-test specifications for consistency and comprehensive-
ness.

Without dwelling on the details of the Parnas specification language, it
is useful nonetheless to consider the most famous example in the paper,
the specification for a stack module, given in fig 6.6. The specification
may seem puzzling in its abstractness: how can we tell what the stack
does? The stack's behavior is specified, in effect, by the phrase that
occurs in the definition of POP: "the sequence "PUSH(a); POP" has no
net effect if no error call occurs."

It's important to note that this puzzling abstractness was a positive goal
of Parnas's work. Elsewhere he notes that *obscure* function names might
be more useful than mnemonics in these specifications. Readers aren't
supposed to make surmises about the specification on the basis of their
(possibly erroneous) preconceptions; instead, they are intended to derive
any and all knowledge they possess from the language of the specification
itself. The point is to ensure that the specifications are used rigorously,
not treated merely as informal comments or annotations.

The stack example also points to an interesting side effect of Parnas's
technique. The intuitive model that underlies our notion of a pushdown
stack—the pile of physical objects, with new ones removed from or added
to the top—is completely missing in the specification. From the specification's standpoint, this is fine: users should rely on the specification
alone, not on a preconceived mental model. But there's another important message here that's so obvious it is sometimes overlooked: the
intuitive, quasi-physical idea of a pushdown stack is *simple*; the Parnas
specification is *complicated*! Imagine defining "pushdown stack" for a
beginning programming class in terms of this specification; for that matter, imagine eradicating your own mental picture of a pushdown stack
and substituting the Parnas specification instead.

Specification languages are fine in their place, but they can't and
shouldn't be called upon to replace the simple (often quasi-physical)
intuitions that in many cases underlie a programmer's way of thinking. A programming language should strive to accommodate the programmer's way of thinking as far as possible. Suppressing these simple
quasi-physical models leads to the replacement of simple things (like the

Function PUSH(a)
possible values: none
integer:a
effect: call ERR1 if a > p2 ∨ a < 0 ∨ 'DEPTH' = p1
    else [VAL = a; DEPTH = 'DEPTH'+1;]

Function POP
possible value: none
parameters: none
effect: call ERR2 if 'DEPTH' = 0
    the sequence "PUSH(a); POP" has no effect if
    no error calls occur

Function VAL
possible values: integer initial; value undefined
parameters: none
effect: error call if 'DEPTH' = 0

Function DEPTH
possible values: integer; initial value 0
parameters: none
effect: none

p1 and p2 are parameters.
p1 is intended to represent the maximum depth of the stack,
and p2 the maximum width or maximum size for each item.

Figure 6.6
The pushdown stack. Names enclosed in single quotes refer to the "old" value of
some function—its value before we call it.

intuitive idea of a stack) with complicated ones (like the Parnas specification). Again, this isn't a criticism of the Parnas technique; it's a
suggestion that the Parnas message not be misconstrued. We'll return
to these issues later.

6.4.2 Abstract Types

What does all this have to do with language design? We noted that the
modules Parnas describes tend naturally to define the sort of objects
we've referred to as data systems. The "conventional" languages of
1972 don't support data systems; a Parnas style specification *cannot* be
reduced directly to code using a language like Pascal.

What linguistic changes are required in order to support this kind of
specification? We already know of one good approach, the Simula 67
class. Here we discuss a different technique.

The "security-based" approach to data systems centers conceptually on
the idea of *types* and strong-typing systems, and it follows naturally from
the issues raised by Parnas. Simula looks at histograms as objects, in
the sense that a histogram is a data system; the security-based approach
looks at histograms as *types* with enforcable characteristics, in the sense
that a histogram encapsulates a set of variables that are intended to be
manipulated *only* by the procedures local to the class. This approach
is conceptually more in keeping than Simula's with the goals of Parnas-
style specification. The Parnas technique aims to promote orderly and
secure program development with as much automatic checking as possible, not to enhance the *expressivity* of a programming language. This
security-based approach to data systems was captured in the linguistic
idea of *abstract types*, described by Liskov and Zilles in 1975 [87]. These
abstract types were incorporated in a language called CLU, described
by Liskov, Snyder, Atkinson and Schaffert in 1977 [86]. CLU itself was
not widely used, but the "abstract type" idea has been influential, and
CLU was a significant influence on Ada—a language of great practical
importance.

Abstractions. An "abstraction" is said to be the description of a kind
of behavior; it is distinguished from an *implementation*, which captures
in working code the behavior specified by the abstraction. This distinction is the same one drawn by Parnas between the specification and the

program text. An ordinary "non-abstract" type (a type specification in Pascal, for example) merely describes the passive data-objects that constitute the type, but an *abstract* type specifies the *behavior* of those objects. Thus a "non-abstract" pushdown stack is merely an array and a top-of-stack pointer (say), but an *abstract* stack is something whose *behavior* we understand—not an array, in other words, but something that can be pushed and popped. CLU's main contribution is to provide language support for the idea of abstract types.

Why bother providing such language support? After all, it's simple enough to write a class "stack" in Simula 67 that combines the stack's behavior and its state in one neat package. We might describe class "histogram" as an abstract type in which the behavior of histogram-type objects is captured. The problem is that although Simula's class *allows* this point of view, it doesn't *require* it, and as far as CLU is concerned, good intentions are not enough.

The Simula class is "insecure" in the sense that it allows direct access not only to the procedures within an object but to the state values also. If `foobar` is a histogram, `foobar.tabulate(x)` is a legal reference, and so is `foobar.n`. (n is the internal variable that records the total number of values tabulated.) Simula provides the frequency and tabulate functions for use with histograms, but doesn't restrict programmers to these functions: if they want to perform some other operation over a histogram's internal state, they are welcome to. For example: a user of histogram objects might want to reset some histogram for re-use; he might accordingly write a procedure that accepts a histogram's tabulating array, the array's length and the counter variable n, zeroes the array and resets n to 1.

From CLU's viewpoint, however, references like `foobar.n` should be forbidden. They are inconsistent with the Parnas specification approach *and* with the security implicit in strong typing. When a program refers to the internal variables of a histogram, we are *not* free to reimplement the histogram class. We are committed to maintaining a particular implementation—or, if we change the implementation, we run the risk of breaking the rest of the program. Furthermore, we can't guard against the accidental application of an inappropriate operation to the histogram's internal variables.

A fairly trivial change to Simula 67 might have provided this kind of security: merely forbid external references to class variables. But Simula's designers weren't thinking in these terms. CLU's designers were.

It should be noted that in introducing abstract types and the necessary support mechanisms, Liskov *et al.* don't speak of security exclusively. Some of their goals resemble Simula's: to support a smooth reduction to working code of the programmer's mental model of a problem. But CLU is substantially later than Simula 67; why was it necessary? On design terms, the two languages differ mainly in CLU's persistent emphasis on types and security. "The benefits arising from the use of data abstractions are based on the constraint, inherent in CLU and enforced by the compiler, that only the operations of the abstraction may access the representations of the object [86, p.237]."

Instead of a class, CLU has something called a "cluster". Figure 6.7 is a small example from [86]. The idea is to provide a data abstraction called "wordbag"; a wordbag is something that other modules can insert words into and can print. The wordbag is realized in terms of another cluster (unspecified here) called a "wordtree"—the bag chooses to store its words in a tree, and makes use of the "wordtree" cluster for this purpose. We've usually avoided reproducing published typeface-styles, but here once again the form of the original is interesting.

The special "**cvt**" notation designates an object that can be manipulated only from within the cluster. Objects of this type might be assigned to local variables, and can be passed as arguments to routines defined inside clusters, but can't be inspected directly (in the sense that we can inspect a Simula **object** directly, via references like **foobar.n**). The special **rep** notation defines the representation type of the cluster—in other words, the way in the programmer has chosen to implement the cluster's structure.

To create a new wordbag, we use a declaration such as

```
wb: wordbag := wordbag$create()
```

To make use of the wordbag, we write such invocations as

```
wordbag$insert(wb, w)
```

where **wb** is a wordbag and **w** is the word to be inserted.

```
wordbag = cluster is
   create,        %  create an empty bag
   insert,        %  insert an element
   print,         %  print contents of bag

   rep = record [contents: wordtree, total: int];

   create = proc () returns (cvt);
                  return (rep${contents:
                               wordtree$create(),
                               total: ()};
                  end create

   insert = proc (x: cvt, v: string));
                  x.contents :=
                     wordtree$insert(x.contents,v);
                  x.total := x.total + 1;
                  end insert;

   print = proc (x: cvt, o:outstream);
                  wordtree$print(x.contents,x.total,o);
                  end print;

   end wordbag;
```

Figure 6.7
A simple CLU cluster.

It's valuable to compare this cluster with a comparable Simula class. In the class, `contents` and `total` would be local variables; if `wb` were an instance, we'd be able to refer to these fields directly—`wb.contents`, `wb.total`. The whole idea in CLU is that such direct references should be disallowed. Tampering with the "implementation" can lead to errors. Type checking in CLU prevents these errors: the **cvt** form ensures that the wordbag's state can be manipulated by the `insert`, `create` and `print` functions only.

The cluster versus the class. On the other hand, the cluster is more complicated than a comparable Simula class in several ways. CLU, like Pascal, has record types. A record type is a template for a heterogeneous data object, and in essence a cluster is too. But the cluster isn't a generalized record; it's a new structure that CLU has acquired *in addition* to records. In contrast, Simula discovered classes by generalizing the existing idea of a procedure. It was natural in Simula to allow the variables of a class to be initialized by an executable statement playing the same role, syntactically and semantically, as a procedure's executable statement; in CLU, each cluster must be provided with a "`create`" procedure, which must be invoked explicitly.

(CLU provides a special phrase for the initialization of *record-type* objects—it's used in the expression

   `(rep${contents: wordtree$create(), total: ()};`

However, this initialization form won't work for clusters.)

In Simula, the procedures defined within a class are treated as constituents of the **objects** instantiated from the class. If `wb` were an instance of a wordbag class, we would invoke the `insert` procedure by writing `wb.insert(w)`. In CLU, we must invoke the generic procedures of the cluster, and pass a cluster instance *explicitly* as a parameter, using another special piece of syntax: `wordbag$insert(wb, w)`.

CLU's rather complex world view is reflected in the syntax of the brief example we presented—in the special words and phrases (**ref**, **cvt**, *type*`${...}`), the three kinds of bracket symbols, and the generous supply of keywords (which appear in boldface). The rest of the language shows similar tendencies. CLU is clearly one point along the counter-swing of the complexity pendulum. This particular oscillation tops out with Ada, which we discuss below.

It's important to emphasize that the whole apparatus is motivated by *security*:

> □ The linguistic embodiment of an *abstract type* is in essence a restricted form of *class*.
>
> ? In Simula 67, procedures, classes and "record types" are structurally and conceptually the same thing. In CLU, procedures, clusters and record types are three *different* things, structurally and conceptually.

A programmer *could* build cluster-like structures in Simula. He could in fact accept the Parnas technique enthusiastically, and construct a complete and detailed specification. He could then implement his specification in Simula in a "safe" or "abstract type-style" way, by avoiding any direct reference to the state variables of an **object** (in the same way he might avoid other stylistic lapses or bad coding practices). The main innovation in CLU is not to make this programming style possible but to make it mandatory.

Why would a language design aim to *restrict* rather than to expand a programmer's stylistic freedom? One possible answer is as follows. Even if a programmer has accepted the wisdom of some particular style, the compiler can't help him live within its bounds unless the style is incorporated into the language. Suppose a programmer decides that he should never refer directly to a Simula **object**'s internal state. If he makes a mistake (due to a typo, or the passing weakness of a moment), the compiler can't point this out to him. The compiler knows nothing of the programmer's stylistic or methodological choices.

But in fact the answer must lie deeper or elsewhere, because this objection fails to sustain serious scrutiny. A "style checker" is a program separate from the compiler but similar to it; a style checker examines a source program according to whatever stylistic criteria seem appropriate. Programmers who use the language C, for example, often make use of a style checker called "lint" for information about program elements that are legal but questionable. Clearly the same approach would have been possible in our context.

So we're left with an interesting question, to which we return in the chapter dealing with declarative languages.

One other aspect of CLU is relevant here: the CLU *library*, which stores descriptions of "abstractions" together with the modules used to implement them. When reference is made to some abstraction within the library, the reference is type-checked against an *interface specification*, which describes the interface presented by the abstraction to the rest of the program. For example, the **wordbag** abstraction defines a procedure **insert** of two arguments, types **cvt** and **string**; this information (but not the code itself) is stored in the interface specification. Any invocations to the **wordbag**'s **insert** routine can be type-checked by consulting this specification. Interface specifications may be added to the library before the corresponding implementations, thus allowing a Parnas-style programming style in which rigorous specification-writing is the first step.

6.4.3   Ada

Ada is a large and complicated language with an interesting history. In the mid-1970s, the U.S. Department of Defense was increasingly worried about the rising costs of developing and maintaining application software, particularly software for "embedded systems." Embedded software is built into and generally plays a part in controlling some machine—a missile, an airplane, a communications device and so on. The Defense Department decided that a good way to control software costs would be to standardize on a single programming language; it furthermore concluded that no existing language filled the bill. A new language was needed. Ada was the result. (See especially [11] for a good, brief summary of Ada's origins.)

Ada was based on and inspired by Pascal, but differs in significant ways, and has many noteworthy features. We focus here on aspects of Ada that have to do with modularity and the related issues of live data systems and abstract types. Ada's treatment of modularity and data systems arguably constitutes its most important difference from Pascal, and the most important part of the language. The Ada design represents the current status of the modularity techniques associated with Parnas specifications and with abstract types, as opposed to Simula's **object-based** direction.

The Package. A package consists of some state variables and some procedures—in other words, it's a data system. Unlike a class or a cluster, however, the package is the *instance*, not the template, a point we'll discuss further below.

A package comes in two parts, the specification (referred to as simply the "package") and the implementation (called the "package body"). Figure 6.8 gives an example, from [11, p.870], of the famous pushdown stack. The distinction between packages and package bodies is an important feature in Ada; it directly mirrors Parnas's distinction between the specification and the implementation, and CLU's between the abstraction (in particular the *interface description* that captures an abstraction) and the code modules in which an abstraction is realized. Thus the "package" (like the interface specification in CLU) describes the externally accessible parts of the module, in this case procedure **push** and function **pop**. These subroutine headers in effect constitute a limited kind of specification for the module. (They don't fully describe the intended behavior of the subroutines, the way a Parnas specification would, but they do describe what arguments are expected and what results are returned by each accessible subroutine in the module.) The package body gives the associated "implementation" for this specification.

The entities described in a package body needn't all appear in the specification. Those that are intended for internal use only don't appear in the specification, and as a consequence they are inaccessible outside of the package body itself. (Users of the stack module can invoke **push** and **pop**, but they can't reference **max** or **ptr**.) This represents, again, the clear influence of Parnas specifications and abstract types: "implementation-specific" parts of a module's state should be unavailable outside of the module. (A specification may also describe *types* that are "private" to the package body. Users of the package may create objects of these private types, but only for purposes of passing arguments or receiving results when dealing with the package's procedures. Outside of the package body, access is forbidden to the internal structure of private-type variables. A private type is, in effect, the same as a CLU **rep**-type; both forms create a type whose internal structure is accessible

```
package stack is          --- the specification part
   procedure push(x:real);
   function  pop return real;
end;

package body stack is      --- the implementation part
   max : constant := 100;
   s : array(1..max) of real;
   ptr: integer range 0 .. max;

   procedure push (x:real) is
     ptr := ptr+1;
     s(ptr) := x;
   end push;

   function pop return real is
     ptr := ptr-1;
     return s(ptr+1);
   end pop

   begin
     ptr := 0
   end stack
```

Figure 6.8
A pushdown stack package in Ada.

only to the procedures implementing some abstraction, never to mere *users* of the abstraction.)

Once again we've discovered a construct that amounts in essence to a data system. Again, it's useful to compare Ada's approach to Simula's. It's easy to define a class that creates a pushdown stack. But here we run into an interesting and significant difference: the stack defined by the Ada package is an *instance*, not a template. It provides us with exactly one stack. It follows that, unlike Simula and Smalltalk and CLU, Ada actually provides a *representation* within the language for data systems. We know exactly what a data system looks like: it's simply a package body. This means in turn that we can define single-instance packages without the overhead of building a template first. It leads also to an important simplification in viewpoint. Simula failed to support the observation that in principle, the program *itself*, *in toto* is an **object** (or, if the code is structured as a series of separate modules instead of a single monolithic unit, the program is then a *collection* of **objects**).

We've discussed instances; how do we create templates? Ada's package-template mechanism is rather strange. It's called the "generic unit." We can preface the declaration of a package with a special "generic" notation that turns it into a template: figure 6.9 gives an example of a generic stack (again from [11, p.884], slightly simplified). We instantiate the template by writing a declaration of the form

package my_stack **is new** stack(100, **real**)

The template in figure 6.9 has two parameters. The first determines the size of the array used to implement the stack; we've seen analogous usages in Simula (the array that implements the histogram's table is parameterized by length, for example). The second parameter is a simplification of a facility first introduced in CLU. In CLU, we can *parameterize* the type of a user-defined data abstraction. For example, to specify a cluster that implements a *sorted-bag* (a bag whose elements can be ordered), we can write

```
sorted_bag = cluster [t: type] is ...
    where t has
        lt,equal : proctype (t,t) returns bool;
```

```
generic
  max : integer;
  type elem is private;

package stack is
  < same specification as above >
end;

package body stack is
  s : array (1 .. max) of elem;
    ⋮

end stack;
```

Figure 6.9
An Ada generic package.

This specification allows us to create sorted bags of any type, so long as objects of the type we choose may be compared using the operations lt and equal. The type "elem" in the above Ada code is similar to the type t in the CLU description, in the sense it permits the user to specify the *type* of the items to be stored in the stack. (Exercise: How would Simula handle this situation?) Thus, the declaration above creates a new stack which is capable of storing 100 reals.

So what's so strange? We turn to the interesting question of how Ada's "package" templates relate to the rest of the language.

6.4.4   The Context

The ISM's space-map is a collection of objects, definitions and executable statements (in other words, a collection of map regions). Instances of what would be space-maps in the ISM model occur in Ada in a variety of forms. Ada has *records* that in most ways are similar to Pascal's records. It has *packages*, as we've discussed. Both records and packages are in essence collections of named, heterogeneous fields: both translate into ISM space-maps. Ada has a third kind of space-map instance as well, called a *task*. A task is a special kind of package, a package that includes an executable statement. Creating a package merely creates a set of passive objects and procedures along with some initialization code; creating a task creates some objects and procedures, and also a new thread of control, which executes the statement in the task. A program that creates five tasks creates five new threads of control, all of which execute concurrently with the original program. (The details aren't important here; we discuss language issues relating to concurrency in a later chapter.) A task, too, translates into an ISM space-map.

It's logical that every space-map *instance* should have a *template*. The ISM has one kind of instance (the space-map) and a single kind of template. In other words, in the ISM, Ada's records, packages and tasks are all instances of the same kind of structure, and they can all be stamped out using the same kind of template.

Ada (following Pascal) has no blocks, in the Algol 60 sense. In the ISM, an Algol-60-style block is again a space-map; "blocks" can also be stamped out by using ISM templates.

Consider, now, the way in which templates relate to instances in Simula 67. Simula has two kinds of templates, the procedure and the class. Procedures and classes are identical in structure. It has two corresponding kinds of instances, the block and the **object**. Invoking a procedure creates (in essence) a block. Invoking a class creates an **object**, which is a structure that Simula recognizes but can't represent.

Now, let's consider the corresponding relationships in Ada. Ada has procedures, which again create blocks (although it has no independent idea of a block in the stand-alone Algol 60 sense). Then, Ada has *record types*, which are used to create records. Ada, unlike Pascal, provides no representation for a *single* record: the only way to create a record is to define a record type first, and then instantiate it. Further, Ada has *generic packages*, which are used to create packages. Finally, Ada has *task types*, which are used to create tasks. To sum up, procedures, record types, generic packages and task types are all *templates*; blocks, records, packages and tasks are the corresponding *instances*. The first two kinds of instance can't be represented in the language; the latter two can be.

The multiplicity of templates in Ada is somewhat disturbing. Procedures, record types, generic packages and task types are all designed to create collections of heterogeneous named objects—it's not immediately clear why we should need four separate variants on this one theme. What's more disturbing, though, is that each template follows its own rules. There is no commonality either in form or in meaning among these obviously related structures. To define a procedure, we write:

procedure foobar(*params*) **is**
 procedure body

A record type looks like this:

type foobar **is record**
 record body

We can also have parameterized record types:

type foobar(*params*) **is record**
 record body

except that the *params* here follow different rules (are restricted to a different class of possibilities) than the *params* in the procedure definition.[2] A generic package is a package template, and we now have two different template forms to choose from. Will the correct choice be

generic package foobar(*params*) **is,**

as per a procedure header, or will it be

type foobar **is package,**

as in record types? The correct choice is *neither*; we write

generic *params* **package** foobar **is**
 package description

Once again, the *params* are governed by their own rules; there is a broader range of possibilities than in the case of records or procedures[3].

---

[2] The arguments to a procedure template may be an element of any structure or scalar type. The *params* in a parameterized record type, on the other hand, are restricted to be either scalars or elements of an enumerated type.

[3] A generic package may include type and procedure declarations; procedure and record templates may not.

---

procedure foobar (*params*) **is**

type foobar (*params*) **is record**

generic *params* **package** foobar **is**

task type foobar **is**

Figure 6.10
Syntactic uniformity among a series of structures, all variations of *environment templates*, was not in the cards for Ada.

Finally, consider task templates. We now have *three* alternative template structures, but the creativity of the Ada syntax- and structure-designers is inexhaustible; a task template takes the form

   task type foobar **is**
     task description

No parameters are allowed.

> **?** Ada's procedure, record type, generic package and task type are all *environment templates* of one kind or another, but the Ada design makes them structurally and conceptually *unrelated*.

Suppose we now made the obvious claim to the Ada designers:

> "You've provided four variants on one structure, introducing a degree of complexity which is unnecessary on abstract, conceptual grounds—but even accepting that four separate forms are necessary, you've chosen to *obscure* rather than to reveal their interrelationships under irregular syntax and varying semantics."

Ada's designers were distinguished, knowledgable computer scientists; obviously they'd have a rejoinder, perhaps along the following lines.

"Granted, there is some deep structural similarity among the forms under discussion, but in practice all four are *used* in different ways, under different circumstances. We use packages when we're thinking of fairly large modules that include procedures. The record type may look and act like a template, but we think of it as analogous to other *types* (like 'integer'), and not as a template. A task is a separate locus of computation, and in practical terms is governed by different constraints from the others—and so on."

How can we evaluate this position? A Pascal programmer might have made an analogous argument in a different domain.

"Consider the following three 'for' loops:

```
for i:= 1 to n do print('*');
for i:= 1 to n do A[i] := k;
prod := 1; for i:= 1 to n do
                prod := prod * i;
```

"In fact, these three loops are performing three very different kinds of function. We could improve Pascal by eliminating the 'for' loop and substituting three appropriate *specialized* constructs, each tailor-made for a given set of circumstances:

```
do n times: print('*');
A[i=>n] := k;
prod := */1::n
```

"The specialized forms are more concise and cleaner. A clear step forward!"

Unfortunately it's hard to accept this kind of argument. First, although we've made each statement more concise, we've made the language as a whole more complicated: we've added new *constructs*, but we haven't added any functionality. Furthermore, our fancy new constructs will do us no good at all when we're faced with a statement that (for example) *would* have been expressed as follows:

```
for i := 1 to n do
  if A[i] = i then A[i] := 0
```

When we are confronted with a complicated language design based on a large collection of special cases instead of a few general forms, the right conclusion is usually not "This design is clearly out to lunch—the designers must have been crazy!" We must not lose sight of the fact that the issue under discussion is fairly subtle. There *are* good reasons to treat records and packages differently, to disallow parameters in task types and so on. There might also have been good reasons to introduce special looping forms instead of a general-purpose `for` loop. The point is *not* that no such good reasons exist. The point is rather that there are *also* good reasons for simplicity and uniformity.

A simpler and more uniform language won't merely be simpler to learn and to use; in many cases it will be more flexible as well. A language design based on patchwork is more than likely to have some cracks. It was easy to build a `for` loop that wasn't covered by our three special cases; if we were to add a new special form to accommodate this new `for` loop, it would be easy enough to synthesize yet another special case. There are a variety of cracks in Ada's complicated worldview—things that make perfect sense in the abstract, but which (for one good reason or another) you can't do in Ada. Ada makes it easy to build a single package, but not a single record; I can parameterize procedures, records and packages, but not tasks. Thus if I have a package that, as my program evolves, looks like it should become a task instead (after all, a task is merely an "active" version of a package), the transformation isn't necessarily simple.

Once again we've asked the obvious question about a language design (why does it have to be so complicated?), proposed an answer, hesitated to accept the answer, and are left with an interesting question ...

6.5 Readings

Basic Readings. A good introduction to Simula 67 can be found in [33]. An early and influential paper on Smalltalk was published in

1976 by Ingalls [68]. [86] is the standard reference for CLU. The Ada
survey by Barnes in [11] is a good introduction to the language.

Suggested Readings. A good discussion of the motivation underlying the Simula design can be found in [114]; [15] gives a comprehensive
description of Simula 67 and presents several non-trivial program examples.

The definitive book on Smalltalk is the one by Goldberg and Robson [51].
Not surprisingly, efficient Smalltalk implementations require sophisticated compiler analysis and runtime support. [123] and [36] give two
different approaches to the problem; [25] presents the design of an optimizing compiler for a Smalltalk-like language currently under development. [3, 58] suggest a new model of parallel computing based on the
object-oriented paradigm.

[130] gives a detailed discussion on the data abstraction mechanisms
found in Ada; the CLU reference manual [85] gives detailed examples
of non-trivial CLU programs and discusses aspects of the language not
described in the original article. Modula-2[134] is a relatively recent language that also provides support for data abstraction and concurrency.

Cardelli and Wegner [19] give a comprehensive introduction to abstract
data types and subtyping. [35] is a good introduction to the formal
theory underlying object-oriented systems.

6.6   Exercises

1. Give a concise comparison of the ISM and (a) Simula and (b)
   Smalltalk.

2. Can you think of a reasonable example where a nested class (*i.e.*,
   a class that contains other classes) would be useful?

3. "The structure of the Lisp meta-circular evaluator is similar to the
   structure of a Simula class hierarchy." Explain.

4. How does Smalltalk's "everything is an object" programming
   method affect its view of types? How is this view related to PL/1's
   type-system? To Pascal's?

5. In what ways are Simula classes more expressive than the "own" variable mechanism in Algol 60? In what ways are they more expressive than Pascal-style records?

6. (a) Describe a minimal extension to Pascal that results in Pascal's becoming an "object-oriented" language (in the Simula sense). ("Minimal extension" means "introduce as few new constructs and operations as possible.") (b) In what sense is Algol 68 an object-oriented language? In what sense is it not?

7. In a "multiple-inheritance" system, it is permissible for a class to be a sub-class of two classes which are themselves incompatible. (For example, a car may be regarded as a sub-class of "moving-thing" and also of "machine," but not all moving-things are machines, and not all machines are moving-things.) What problems might arise in adding multiple inheritance to Simula and to Smalltalk? Suggest extensions or modifications to both languages that address these problems.

8. "The inheritance of methods in Simula and Smalltalk can be understood in terms of dynamic binding." True or false? Explain your answer.

9. "Message passing is an inept metaphor for the way Smalltalk objects communicate." Explain. What changes to the language would make the metaphor less inept?

10. How would you achieve the behavior of CLU's parameterized clusters or Ada's generic package in Simula?

11. Smalltalk and Simula provide for abstraction hierarchies by means of the super-class mechanism. (a) Show how we might implement an abstraction hierarchy in CLU with *no* linguistic extensions. Sketch an example. (b) What does your answer in part (a) tell you about the impact of *security* on *modularity*? (c) Extend CLU with a linguistic mechanism to support abstraction hierarchies. Compare your mechanism with the method described in part (a). Be specific.

12. Outside of the environment in which they are defined, objects of a **private** type in Ada may be created, passed as procedure argu-

ments or tested for equality, and variables of such types may be assigned. Variables of **limited private type** cannot be assigned or compared for equality. (a) Give an example where **limited private types** are useful, and explain why assignment and equality tests should not be permitted. (b) What difficulties do you see in the use of limited private types? (c) If t is a type, then Ada permits variables of type **access** t: their values are pointers to dynamically allocated objects of type t. Variables of type **access** t can be assigned-to and tested for equality even if t itself is **limited private**. (1) Compare the meaning of assignment and equality testing for **access** t objects with their meaning for type t objects. (2) To what extent does the ability to assign-to and compare **access** t objects compromise the restrictions on **limited private** type t?

7 The Closure in Scheme

Scheme is a Lisp-derived language that presents another approach to the demolition of the **Algol Wall**. We revisit the issue of **dynamic vs. lexical binding**; the programming methodology that is characteristic of Scheme, based on a pervasive use of lexical binding, results in a system under which *exactly the same* template can be used to create program fragments and data objects. Although the Scheme *closure* is superficially very different in concept from the Simula class, there are (as we will see) strong similarities as well as some differences between these approaches.

Scheme represents the end of the road for the principal evolutionary thread we are following in this book. Our final two chapters deal with languages that are focused on special problems or programming models, and are not yet part of the linguistic mainstream.

The design and implementation of Scheme were presented in a series of influential papers [119, 120, 117] in the mid-1970s by Guy Steele Jr. and Gerry Sussman. An optimizing compiler for the language was described by Steele in 1975 [118]. Our description of Scheme in this chapter is based on [28].

Scheme is a variant of Lisp rather than a completely new language. We therefore concentrate both in the profile and in the discussion not on Scheme as a whole, but on the aspect of Scheme that most clearly distinguishes it from Lisp (and is most important to us in language design terms)—namely Scheme's idea of the closure. Less central to our discussion, but important nonetheless, is the role of the *continuation* (a powerful control abstraction mechanism we define below) both as a control device and as an implementation mechanism.

7.1 Profile: Closures in Scheme

We return to a previous question addressed in our investigation of Lisp: what does it mean to evaluate a `lambda` phrase? The question may sound narrow and esoteric, but recall that this issue lay at the heart of Lisp's failure to disentangle programming from mathematics. Recall also that this question—what *is* programming (as opposed to mathematics, assembly coding and everything else)—is the central one for this book. Specifically: mathematical expressions are mere descriptions, but a *program* is a machine—it's something that you can turn on, or in other words *evaluate*. Lisp took the "mathematical" view of function definitions: they merely sit there, like sonnets. You can *apply* a function, but it doesn't make sense to ask "what do we get when we evaluate this object?"

By the principle of recursive structure, however, we'd like to understand the result of evaluating a *whole* expression by understanding, first, what it means to evaluate each *part* of the expression. Similarly, if we are trying to understand how a car works, we'd like to be able to understand how the engine and the transmission work *individually* before we study the system as a whole. In other words, when we try to understand the Lisp function invocation

```
(SomeFunction ARG1 ARG2 ARG3)
```

we'd like to understand what it means to evaluate each argument *and also* SomeFunction *itself* individually. But Lisp provided no rule for evaluating function definitions: lambdas are not expressions, and cannot be evaluated. Scheme provides a lambda-evaluation rule; in so doing, it also provides a tool that can underlie a wide-ranging approach to data systems and to modularity.

Scheme's rule is called *lexical binding*. There are two significant moments in every function's life: function-*definition* time and function-*application* time. We'll refer to these as define-time and apply-time for short. Apply-time obviously refers to the time at which a function is applied; a single function will usually be applied many times, and so has many apply-times. Each function has only a single define-time, however. Define-time refers to the point at which the definition of the function is processed—the point at which it becomes accessible by name to the rest of the program.

The lexical binding rule addresses the following question: "Suppose free names occur in a function's definition; how do we figure out what these names mean?" There are two possible answers. Free names may be bound once and for all at define-time; or they may be re-bound every time we invoke the function. The latter case is dynamic binding: "dynamic" because the free names in function definitions are never bound permanently; they take on the coloration of the surrounding environment every time the function is invoked. The former is lexical binding, which means that the free names in a function definition will be bound permanently at define-time. ("Lexical" refers to the fact that we can determine the meaning of a function's free names simply by looking at the program text itself.)

Lexical binding in Scheme, then, works like this: defining a function will cause the current environment to be stashed inside the function definition. When the function is applied, this stashed-away environment will be consulted whenever definitions for free names are required. (Classical Lisp's (function ...) wrapper works in the same way: it yields a function whose free names are bound permanently in the define-time environment.)

What does this have to do with our initial question: "How does one evaluate a lambda expression?" The connection is simple and direct. To *define a function* will require that we *evaluate a lambda expression*. Concretely, we will define a function by binding *the result yielded by a lambda expression* to some name. Hence *function definition* entails lambda-*expression evaluation*. To make function definition behave in the way we want, we need only make lambda evaluation behave in the right way.

Now, to the details of Scheme's lambda-evaluation rule. The rule stipulates that to evaluate a lambda expression, we *enclose the definition within the naming environment that applies when and where the* lambda *is evaluated. The result is a two-part object called a "closure": the first part points to an environment, the second part to the text of the* lambda *expression.*

In order to apply a function, we must first evaluate the function definition. The result will be a two-part object of the sort described, in other words, a *closure*. What do we do with this closure? We know how to apply a function to a list of arguments, but how do we apply a closure to a list of arguments? The answer: bind the formal parameter names to the actual parameter values, as always, and then evaluate the function

body. While evaluating the body, to find the meaning of any name that
is not defined by the function itself, look it up in environment that the
closure points to.

Let's consider some examples. Suppose we define a function scale to
multiply each element of a vector by some constant. The vector will be
stored in a list. (The example is taken from [117].)

```
(define scale
   (lambda (V c)
      (mapcar (lambda (x) (* x c)) V)))
(define mapcar
   (lambda (f l)
      (cond ((null l) nil)
            (t (cons (f (car l)) (mapcar f (cdr l)))))))
```

The first definition binds scale to a function of two arguments, a vector
V and the scaling factor c. The body of the function is an application
of a function called mapcar to two arguments. The first argument is the
lambda expression

```
(lambda (x) (* x c))
```

The second is V. Mapcar is a type of *higher-order function*, one that
accepts a function as its argument; it applies its function argument to
each element of some list, and returns a list of the results. Applying
mapcar to the lambda expression above results in a list whose i^{th} element
is the result of multiplying the ith element of V by c.

When we evaluate the lambda expression bound to scale, the result is
a two-part object; the first part is a pointer to the current environment,
and the second is the text of the lambda expression. We'll refer to this
object as CLOSURE#1. Note that the name mapcar is free in this lambda
expression, since it is not provided explicitly as an argument to the
function.

We evaluate the lambda expression bound to mapcar in the same way
as the one bound to scale. The result is again a two-part object, containing first a pointer to the current environment, second the text of
the lambda expression. We'll refer to this object as CLOSURE#2. Note

that the body of this `lambda` expression also has `mapcar` as its only free name.

To evaluate the invocation

```
(scale '(1 2 3) 4)
```

we first evaluate the arguments (they yield the list (1 2 3) and the constant 4 respectively) and the identifier `scale`. Evaluating `scale` yields `CLOSURE#1` (because `CLOSURE#1` is the object to which `scale` was bound in the preceding binding statement). Now we apply `CLOSURE#1` to arguments (1 2 3) and 4. First we create the appropriate environment, which includes the environment to which `CLOSURE#1` points and new bindings for the formals `V` and `c`.

Then we evaluate the function body

```
(mapcar (lambda (x) (* x c)) V)
```

in the context of the bindings defined by this new environment. This expression is also an application, and it's evaluated in the same way. We first evaluate the arguments

```
(lambda (x) (* x c))
```

and `V`. Evaluating the `lambda` expression yields (as usual) a two-part object. The first part points to the current environment (the one containing bindings for `V` and `c`). The second part points to the body of this `lambda` expression. We'll call this object `CLOSURE#3`. Note that the body of this `lambda` expression contains a free reference to identifier `c`. Evaluating `V` yields list (1 2 3). Evaluating the reference to `mapcar` yields `CLOSURE#2`.

To evaluate the application of `mapcar`, we first create a new environment (as we did before) that binds the formals in the `lambda` expression to the actuals. This new environment contains, in addition to bindings for `V` and `c`, a binding for `f` to `CLOSURE#3` and for `l` to the list (1 2 3). Once this environment has been created, we are ready to evaluate the body of the `mapcar` function.

The most interesting part of the `mapcar` body is the application of `f` to an element of the list `l`. F is bound to `CLOSURE#3`. The `lambda` expression

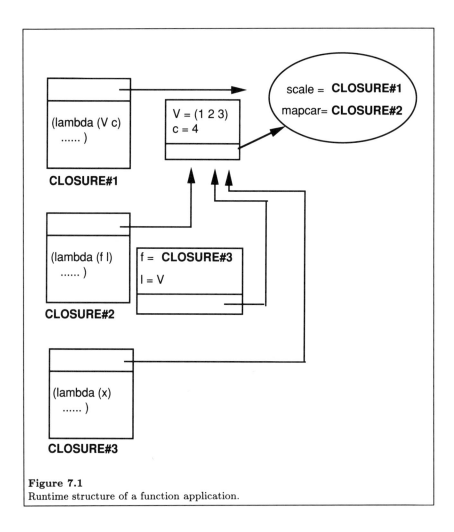

Figure 7.1
Runtime structure of a function application.

associated with CLOSURE#3 contains a free reference to identifier c. When
this closure is applied, the value of c is determined by looking at its
binding in the environment pointed to by CLOSURE#3. The value of c
in this environment is 4. After the recursion completes, the application
yields as its result a pointer to the list (4 8 12). We illustrate the
runtime structure of this application in figure 7.1.

Suppose we'd used dynamic instead of lexical binding in this example.
No closures are created. Lambda evaluation takes place in the apply-time

environment, augmented with bindings for the formals. In this case, the
end result is the same.

Let's now consider a slight twist to the example. Suppose, instead of
defining the mapcar function the way we did above, we defined it as
follows:

```
(define mapcar
   (lambda (f c)
      (cond ((null c) nil)
            (t (cons (f (car c)) (mapcar f (cdr c)))))))
```

The code is structurally the same, but we've chosen to name one of the
formals c instead of l. This minor change doesn't affect anything under
a lexical-binding policy, but yields a very different result under dynamic
binding. Recall that f is bound to a function whose body is

```
(lambda (x) (* x c)).
```

The free occurrence of c is intended to refer to the value of scale's
formal. Using dynamic binding, however, the value of c is determined
in the apply-time environment; here, c's value happens to be the second
argument to mapcar, the list (1 2 3). We'll get an error when we
attempt to multiply a list by a number. It's a quirky feature of dynamic
binding that the choice of names for a function's formals is crucial in
determining what the function does.

We now consider another type of higher-order function, one that returns
a function as its result.

```
(define (ADDx)
   (lambda (x)
      (lambda (y) (+ x y))))
```

This expression binds the name ADDx to a function: when we invoke
ADDx, the result is another function. So let's invoke ADDx and consider
the result:

```
(define ADD3 (ADDx 3))
```

To evaluate the ADDx application (more precisely, to evaluate the application of the closure that is bound to ADDx), we must first bind formal

to actual parameters in a new environment. The result is that x (ADDx's formal) is bound to 3. Next, we evaluate the body; ADDx's body is the lambda expression

```
(lambda (y) (+ x y))
```

Evaluating this lambda will (as always) yield a closure; we'll call it CLOSURE#4.

CLOSURE#4 will include a pointer to the environment in force at lambda-evaluation time. We are evaluating this lambda in the context of an environment in which the name x is bound to 3. (Recall that we are still in the process of evaluating ADDx, and the first step in evaluating ADDx was to bind x to 3.) The environment to which CLOSURE#4 points will (in the abstract) include bindings for many names—for all the names visible in the program at this point (including all accessible function definitions, variables and so on). But whatever else this environment includes, it must *also* include an entry in which x is bound to 3.

Evaluating (define ADD3 ...) results, then, in the symbol ADD3 getting bound to CLOSURE#4. Now let's consider what happens when we apply ADD3 in the following context:

```
(let ((x 4))
  (ADD3 5))
```

The let-form defines a set of local bindings. Here, it binds x to 4; it then evaluates the application (ADD3 5) in the context of this new binding.

ADD3 is bound to CLOSURE#4. The first step in applying CLOSURE#4 is to bind actuals to formals: formal y is bound to actual 5 in a new environment. Next we evaluate the body of the lambda, namely the expression (+ x y). The value of y is 5. What is the value of x? Recall the closure application rule: when we encounter a name that is not defined within the function itself (*i.e.*, a free name), we look up that name in the environment which is pointed to by the closure. Here x is a free name; we look up the value of x in CLOSURE#4's environment, and discover that its value is 3. The fact that x is bound to 4 in the *application*-time environment is irrelevant to evaluation of the application. The result is 8.

In short, the closure rule amounts to the following: whenever we evaluate a `lambda`, we trap and preserve the environment that was in force at `lambda`-evaluation time, and we revisit this environment every time we apply the `lambda`. A closure is a kind of time capsule. If we evaluate the assignment (`define (foobar) (lambda ...)`) in 1931 and apply `foobar` in 1963, 1989 and 1992, every time we apply it, we revisit the environment that was defined at `lambda`-evaluation time in 1931. (Note that the *values* of some of the names within this environment may have changed—we may have altered them via assignment statement—but the names themselves are the same, and unless we explicitly alter them, the values are too.)

This time-capsule effect should be contrasted with the ahistorical, go-with-the-flow approach that is characteristic of dynamic binding. When we apply a function under dynamic binding, we use whatever environment is in force at function application-time to resolve the meaning of any free names within the function body. The function's *definition*-time environment has been forgotten.

7.1.1 What Can We Do With Closures?

So what good is all this? We have succeed in formulating a `lambda`-evaluation rule, and this in itself is a significant step, as we've discussed. But we might have defined a far simpler rule than this lexical-binding rule. A dynamic-binding semantics might have simplified the `lambda`-evaluation rule considerably: "a `lambda` expression is a constant: it evaluates to itself." (Bear in mind that although Lisp uses dynamic binding, it does *not* use this or any other `lambda`-evaluation rule. It treats `lambda`s not as constant expressions but as *non*-expressions. The point is, however, that we can easily formulate a `lambda`-evaluation rule that is consistent with dynamic rather than lexical binding.)

The complexity of the lexical-binding rule is justified by the fact that lexical binding makes it easy to support higher-order functions; *i.e.*, closures can be used to implement functions that accept function arguments or return function results. Higher-order functions can in turn be used to achieve the same effects that Simula and Smalltalk classes are capable of achieving.

In general, higher-order functions can be used to create customized, special-purpose functions. `Mapcar` and `ADDx` are two examples. If we find ourselves constantly needing to apply a function uniformly across a list or incrementing numbers by 3, it may be convenient to construct a special-purpose function specifically for these purposes. This is another example of the *factoring* we discussed in the previous chapter: if we can recognize a repeated pattern, it's often desirable to encapsulate the pattern and use the encapsulated version rather than repeating the whole pattern *verbatim*. In so doing we usually make the text more concise, and almost always make the structure of the program more transparent. Two ways to accomplish this kind of factoring are:

- Use a template whose behavior depends upon an argument template; the rules for determining the value produced by this template come from the outside. `Mapcar` is an example of this style of template.

- Use a template that can stamp out customized functions—a higher-order function can be used in this way, and `ADDx` is an example of such a function.

Then, we need to use our custom-function-stamping template to create exactly the function we need. To do this, we apply `ADDx` to 3, and the result is our customized increment-by-three function, namely `ADD3`.

(To emphasize the nomenclature: a *higher-order function* is either (a) a function-accepting template: it accepts a function as its argument, or (b) a function-stamping template: it yields a function as its result. The *customized function* is the function yielded by an invocation of this latter style of higher-order function.)

The `ADDx` example happens to be trivial. In fact it's as easy to write

    (+ 3 Number)

as it is to write

    (ADD3 Number)

so we gain nothing in conciseness or performance, although factoring of this kind *does* make the program's structure more transparent. But there are cases in which function-yielding functions can be a more substantial convenience. For example, if (FOOBAR W X Y Z) is a function of four arguments, and it is frequently used in such a way that the first three are held constant while the last varies, we can define a (FOOBAR-PRIME Z) function. Constant values for the first three arguments are captured in the definition of the special-purpose function FOOBAR-PRIME, and consequently don't need to be repeated every time it is invoked.

Of course, it's easy enough (in some cases) to build customized functions explicitly, without higher-order functions and closures. Let's say that Foobar is a Pascal function of four arguments, and we want a FoobarPrime in which the first three arguments are set permanently to 3, 4 and 5. We write

```
function FoobarPrime(z: integer):integer;
  FoobarPrime := Foobar(3, 4, 5, z)
```

Similarly for a Pascal version of ADD3:

```
function ADD3(x: integer):integer;
  ADD3 := 3 + x;
```

Higher-order functions automate this process. The saving in space may be minor in this case (these Pascal definitions are clear and concise), but automating the process does allow us to generate customized functions at runtime, rather than forcing us to build them statically. It becomes easy to build a customized function whose "customization" depends on values that aren't known until runtime.

7.1.2   Data Systems

Closures can also be used to implement data systems, along the lines of Simula objects. Consider a simple example we've discussed before: we want an object that implements a bank account. It supplies two functions, DEPOSIT and WITHDRAW. We create the account with some initial balance.

Our strategy will be the following: we create a higher-order function ACCOUNT; invoking ACCOUNT yields a customized function. This customized function (we'll refer to it as CUSTOM-ACCOUNT) *also* returns a

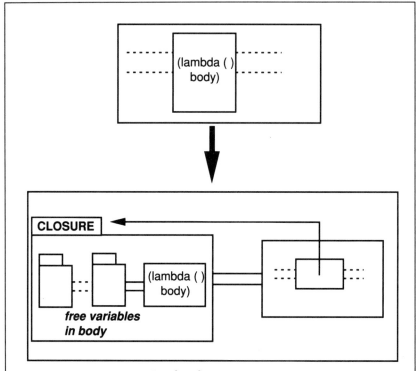

Figure 7.2
The ISM structure of a Scheme program is rather strange. When we evaluate a
`lambda`, the result is a closure that includes a pointer to the define-time
environment. If the `lambda` is returned by a higher-order function, this define-time
environment includes the local environment prevailing inside the body of the
higher-order function. Ordinarily, this environment would have disappeared once
evaluation of the function body was complete; but the existence of the closure
requires us to *save* this environment somewhere, rather than allowing it to
disappear. In effect, then, we tack a new region onto the top-level space-map, and
store the local environment inside this new region. This results, in effect, in the
same kind of map-extension that Simula's `new` operation brings about—but there
is a twist. The environment inside the new region is accessible *only* when we apply
the closures on whose behalf it was created. Pointers to the new region are stored
inside these closures.

function when it is invoked. CUSTOM-ACCOUNT accepts an "operation selector" argument; if the operation selector is DEPOSIT, it yields the customized DEPOSIT function, and similarly for a WITHDRAW selector. These DEPOSIT and WITHDRAW functions manipulate a free variable called balance, and this balance will be precisely the balance with which ACCOUNT was initialized: the balance parameter to ACCOUNT is trapped inside a closure.

The code looks like this:

```
(define ACCOUNT (lambda (balance)
  (lambda (operation)
    (cond
      ((equal operation 'DEPOSIT)
        (lambda (deposit-amt)
          (set! balance
                (+ balance deposit-amt))))
      ((equal operation 'WITHDRAW)
        (lambda (withdraw-amt)
          (set! balance
                (- balance withdraw-amt)))))))))
```

The expression

```
(define my-acct (ACCOUNT 1500))
```

binds my-acct to a higher-order function that serves as a customized bank account.

To invoke the deposit function (with a deposit of $100, say) we evaluate

```
((my-acct 'DEPOSIT) 100)
```

In conclusion: we've accomplished the trick we set out to accomplish. Using Scheme's closures, we've implemented a data system similar to what we might have achieved using Simula's class mechanism.

It's important to understand that we *can't* do this under Lisp's dynamic binding. Consider the higher-order function ACCOUNT. Under dynamic binding, this function yields a function that references the free variable balance. When we apply this function, we'll need to find a definition for this name; we'll find it by consulting the apply-time environment. The name **balance** may or may not occur within the apply-time environment; there's no guarantee that it will. Five different invocations may yield five different bindings for the name **balance**. We'll never find the **balance** that occurred as a formal parameter within the original invocation of **ACCOUNT**—that variable (since we never trapped it in a closure) has disappeared.

7.2   Continuations

Scheme provides control mechanisms—devices to control the sequence in which the program executes—that go well beyond those of any other language we have examined so far. A Scheme *continuation* is a function that represents the computation remaining from the point at which the continuation is created: to invoke this function means (in effect) "go on and execute the rest of the program." Thus, in the Scheme fragment

```
(define (f x)
   (begin      ;; begin is Scheme's version of progn
      e₁
      e₂
      ...
      eₙ))
```

the continuation associated with e_1 is a function that computes e_2, ..., e_n, and then proceeds to evaluate whatever expressions follow the invocation of **f** in the program as a whole.

Why include continuations in a language design? First, they allow the programmer great freedom in managing the way his program executes: we give an example below. Continuations are also valuable to the compiler; we discuss this point in a later section.

The basic operator used to manipulate control is **call/cc**.[1] **Call/cc** accepts a single procedure **proc** as its argument; **proc** also accepts a single argument. **Call/cc** captures the current control point and passes it as an argument to **proc**. This control point is manifested as a procedure

---

[1]**call/cc** is an abbreviation for **call-with-current-continuation**.

of a single argument that, when applied, will ignore the current control state and will instead pass its value to the control point active at the time `call/cc` was invoked.

Consider a function that accepts a binary tree of numbers and returns either their sum (if there is no zero in the tree) or zero (if a zero value does occur in the tree). We assume that a tree is either empty or a node containing a number and two sub-trees.

We could write such a function in Scheme making no use of continuations. We assume the following operations over trees: `empty-tree?` returns true if its argument is an empty tree and false otherwise; `num-tree` returns the integer value found at the root of its argument tree; `left` and `right` return the left and right subtrees of their argument trees respectively.

```
(define zero-in-tree nil)
(define (sum-tree tree)
   (cond ((empty-tree? tree) 0)
         (t (begin
               (if (zerop? (num-tree tree))
                     (set! zero-in-tree t))
               (if (not (zero-in-tree))
                   (+ (num-tree tree)
                      (+ (sum-tree (left tree))
                         (sum-tree (right tree))))
                   0)))))
(sum-tree <a tree>)
```

We need to define an auxiliary variable `zero-in-tree` that is true if a zero has been seen during the traversal and false otherwise. Note that in this solution, a zero encountered in one branch will still not prevent a recursive call to traverse the other branch. The same program written using continuations is given below:

```
(define (sum-tree tree)
   (call/cc
     (lambda (k)
       (letrec
         ((sum (lambda (tree)
           (cond ((empty-tree tree) 0)
                 ((zerop? (num-tree tree))
                   (k 0))
                 (t (+ (num-tree tree)
                       (+ (sum-tree (left tree))
                          (sum-tree (right tree)))))))))
         (sum tree)))))
(sum-tree < a tree>)
```

(**letrec** defines a set of mutually recursive definitions and returns the result of evaluating an expression in the context of these definitions; in this example, we define a recursive function **sum** and apply it to **tree**.)

When this continuation-based function is applied, the **call/cc** operator grabs the current continuation (which happens to be the control point immediately following the application) and binds this continuation to **k**; the traversal of the tree begins with the invocation of **sum**. If a zero is encountered during the traversal, the continuation is applied to 0 and control jumps out of the application to the expression waiting for the result of the application. No auxiliary variables are required.

Continuations, then, are a general mechanism for implementing "non-blind" backtracking. Consider a chess program that works by generating a complex game-tree whose nodes contain possible board positions that may result from a given move. Our program must be capable of examining and pruning different portions of the tree dynamically. Continuations make structuring such a program easy: we simply associate a continuation with each control point responsible for computing a particular node in the tree.

7.3   Discussion

It's clear that support for data systems is important, and we've now seen two competing ways to achieve it: Simula's classes and Scheme's closures. How do we compare the two? Which is better, under what circumstances?

We've seen Scheme's version of the bank account. Let's consider the Simula version once again:

```
class ACCOUNT(balance); real balance;
 begin
   procedure DEPOSIT(DepositAmt); real DepositAmt;
     balance := balance + DepositAmt;
   procedure WITHDRAW(WithdrawAmt); real WithdrawAmt;
     balance := balance - WithdrawAmt;
 end;
```

To create an account,

```
ref (ACCOUNT) MyAcct;
  ...
MyAcct :- new ACCOUNT(1200);
```

To use the account,

```
MyAcct.DEPOSIT(900);
```

The Simula version is slightly more concise, and most readers will agree that it is simpler and clearer than the Scheme version. There are two reasons for this difference in clarity.

The main one is that higher-order functions return either *functions* or *ordinary data structures* in which functions are embedded; they do *not* return environments. In other words, when we invoke the Scheme function ACCOUNT, the thing we get back is merely a function. It is *not* an environment in which the names DEPOSIT and WITHDRAW are bound to customized versions of these functions. When we invoke the Simula class we get an **object** (*i.e.*, a kind of environment) back, and we can write "look inside this environment and invoke the function named DEPOSIT."

We *can't* do this with the entity yielded by Scheme's `ACCOUNT`: we can't write "invoke the `DEPOSIT` function that is defined inside this thing," because "this thing" is not an environment, and doesn't define any names.

Hence we are forced, in Scheme, to provide a dispatch function that translates calls on the customized account into invocations of the appropriate routine. Note that because the Scheme version doesn't define an environment, we can't apply a factoring technique to the `ACCOUNT` object in the way we might have in the Simula version. The Simula environment might have been included in an elaborate tree of objects. We might have defined `ACCOUNT` as a super-class of two classes, say, `CHECKING` and `SAVINGS`, which incorporate the `DEPOSIT` and `WITHDRAW` routines in addition to their own procedures. To accomplish the same thing in Scheme, the checking account would have to provide a dispatch function that in addition to dispatching on names specific to a checking account, also recognizes that `DEPOSIT` and `WITHDRAW` requests need to be dispatched to `ACCOUNT`. Because objects themselves are not environments, the Scheme compiler can't optimize calls to a super-class in the same way that the Simula compiler can: `DEPOSIT` requests made to the checking account entail two function calls before the deposit operation is actually invoked. The first is the call to the checking account and the second is the dispatch made by this object to `ACCOUNT`. The more complex the inheritance tree, the more expensive super-class requests become.

The second reason for Simula's greater clarity is strongly related to the first: the **object** yielded by a class invocation is explicitly an environment, and accordingly it *looks* like an environment. By glancing at the definition of class `ACCOUNT`, we can see that it defines the two functions `DEPOSIT` and `WITHDRAW`. The entity yielded by the invocation of a Scheme higher-order function is *not* an environment, and doesn't look like one. It does not consist (as does the class) of an orderly series of names, each associated with a definition.

Simula wins this match. But consider a more "traditional" use of higher-order functions—the sort of example in which a higher-order function is employed to create and return a single customized function. `ADDx` is an example of this kind of function. Consider the Simula version of `ADDx`:

```
class ADDx(x); real x;
  begin
    real procedure add(y); real y;
        add := x + y
  end
```

To build an ADD3, we execute

```
ref (ADDx) ADD3;
  ...
ADD3 :- new ADDx(3);
```

To use the customized function, we evaluate

```
ADD3.add(14)
```

Here, the Scheme version is more convenient. Scheme's ADDx returned
a function as its value; we simply apply the function as needed. But
a Simula class *always* yields an environment (never a single function).
There may be only a single entity in the environment, hence no choice
in the matter of *which* definition I want (there being only one). Even so,
we need to make up a name for this entity, and cite the name explicitly
whenever we make use of it. In general, a Scheme function of the form

```
(lambda (x)
  (lambda (y)
      ...
        (lambda (z)  body) ...))
```

must be implemented in Simula by building a nested series of class definitions. The ith class in this series corresponds to the ith-level higher-order
function definition. The last class in this series defines the procedure implementing *body*.

Scheme wins this round—but this example is interesting and significant
for a more general reason. Higher-order functions are generally taken to
be an innovation of Scheme and related languages (*e.g.*, the functional
languages we discuss in Chapter 8). As we've noted, Algol 60 allows
functions to be passed to other functions as arguments, but does *not* allow functions to be yielded as results. Hence it's not possible in Algol 60

to write a higher-order, function-generating function. Speaking literally, Simula 67 takes over this same restriction—a function may be passed as an argument, but may not be yielded as a result. But the example above should make it clear that Simula *overcomes* this limitation by providing the class mechanism. In short,

□ a class definition *is* a higher order function,

in the sense that a class invocation *yields an environment in which customized functions are embedded.* In other words, one definition of a Simula (or a Smalltalk) class is "a higher-order function returning an environment in which a series of functions customized to some particular set of data objects are embedded."

Concretely: we can think of the Simula class ADDx as yielding the customized function ADDx.add. In fact, the mechanism whereby customized functions are created in Simula is in essence identical to Scheme's method. The function returned by the Scheme ADDx function *and* the function defined by the Simula ADDx class are *both* defined in terms of the free variable x. Lexical binding is a central design feature in Scheme because dynamic binding was a recognized choice. But lexical binding is also a feature of Simula: the free names within the procedure definitions of a class are bound when the class is invoked (*i.e.*, when the procedures themselves are defined). In both cases, lexical binding means that when we invoke the Scheme higher-order function or the Simula class, any free variables are bound permanently to the appropriate "custom" values. A function with free variables plus permanent bindings for those free variable equals a customized function.

We noted in the previous chapter a major shortcoming of the Simula class: we can represent the class, but not the **objects** that they create. Scheme closures suffer from exactly the same problem. Scheme provides no representation for closures, and (generally speaking) where **objects** won't work, closures won't work either. We can't structure a Scheme program as a single explicit closure made up of sub-closures; we can't specify a one-off environment as a single explicit closure.

Despite their radical differences on a superficial level, then, the Simula class and the Scheme higher-order function are two versions of exactly the same thing. We return to our initial question: which mechanism is better? Scheme's version is preferable when our generating template is intended to return exactly *one* entity. We don't need to make up an extraneous name for this entity; we can make use of it simply by applying the closure in which it is embedded. But Simula's version seems preferable whenever we need to provide more than one entity within our active data object. Simula allows us to bind names to these multiple entities, so that we can specify them clearly and distinguish them readily; Scheme forces us to define a logically irrelevant dispatch framework in order to dig out the (unnamed) entity we need. Is it better, in this case, to optimize for $n = 1$ or for $n > 1$?

This is a subjective and stylistic question. It's important, though, to keep the following in mind. We might be tempted to phrase the "which is better?" question as follows:

> Consider two programming devices, the "traditional" higher-order function that returns a single customized function, and the object-oriented programming style in which objects define, in general, many procedures. Which is more useful? Which will the "average programmer" tend to depend on more?

In fact, this reduction isn't quite legitimate. Let's set aside the higher-order-function vs. object-oriented question for a moment. It's widely agreed that the Pascal-style record is important to all sorts of programs. Whether we are higher-order-function fans or object-oriented programmers, we will need Pascal-style records. Given the Simula class, we already have them: it's trivial to build a Pascal-style record using the class mechanism. We can build Pascal-style records using closures too, but this is just another example of that same daunting assignment—use a higher-order function to create an environment with lots of things in it. To build records using higher-order functions, we need the same general kind of dispatch apparatus we discussed above.

In theory, any and all modularity requirements can be satisfied by using Scheme's closures. On balance, the Simula class would appear to be the slightly better optimization.

7.3.1 Efficiency

(*This section deals with implementation questions, and may be skipped without loss of continuity.*)

Scheme's success owes as much to the efficiency of its implementation as to the elegance of its design. Of the large number of Lisp variants and Lisp-based languages available, Scheme is the most efficiently implemented. In many cases, Scheme implementations compare favorably in efficiency to implementations of Pascal and other Algol-based languages. This represents an interesting and thought-provoking achievement: Scheme, unlike the Algol-based languages, encourages liberal use of higher-order functions and dynamic data structures, and this kind of language was believed to be difficult or impossible to implement efficiently until the advent of optimizing Scheme compilers.

The two Scheme features that contribute most to the language's efficient implementation—lexical binding and first-class continuations—are precisely its two most important points of departure from earlier Lisps. When identifiers must be resolved dynamically, the runtime system is forced to spend time tracing down chains of environments in search of the current value. Lexical scoping means that if we choose to compile a program, the compiler can do this work instead. (A Scheme program can of course be executed interpretively as well, but if we are interested in efficiency, we will certainly make use of the compiler.) Identifier references can be translated into offsets within closure-generated environments. Creating closures can also be expensive, but the full mechanism isn't always needed in effect; good Scheme compilers minimize the overhead of closure creation by using a number of different optimization techniques. Elimination of tail recursions (discussed in chapter 3) is an important instance of this class of optimizations.

Another kind of closure-related optimization allows functions defined at the same lexical level to share common pieces of the environment. Thus, if f and g are two functions that share references to free variables x, y and z, the compiler can generate a customized environment containing the bindings for these variables, to be shared by the closures for f and g.

Continuations make it possible for the compiler to minimize the cost of function application. Recall that the continuation of an expression represents the "rest of the program" following the expression. A function application can be understood in terms of a series of control branches: when we apply a function, jump to the body; when the function completes, jump back to the point of call.

The runtime costs of packaging function-return information are potentially significant in languages like Scheme which make heavy and continual use of function application. The runtime expense can be eliminated by using a source-to-source transformation technique known as *continuation-passing*. The basic idea is to package the address to which the function value should be sent inside a continuation before executing a jump to the body of the function. The code is transformed in such a way that every function application passes its continuation as the first argument to the invoked function. Every function is made to apply this continuation as its final operation.

The result of this continuation-passing transformation is another Scheme program (hence a "source-to-source" transformation) that can be examined, optimized and evaluated. The Scheme runtime system never needs to build a control stack or an activation record; the transformation makes explicit in the source program (and hence available to the compiler) the information that *would* have been captured by these runtime control structures.

To illustrate, consider the following simple program:

```
(lambda (x y)
   (begin
      (write x)
      y))
```

After this program is transformed using continuation-passing, it looks something like this:

```
(lambda (k1 x y)
   (write (lambda (v1)
             (k1 y))
          x))
```

The transformed function applies function **write** to two arguments. The first is the continuation that supplies y to the continuation passed as the

first argument to the outer `lambda`; the second is **x**. After **write** prints
x, it invokes its continuation argument, transferring control to the point
immediately following the call to the outer `lambda`. No activation frame
is created and no function return operation is executed. We continue
in this way, applying functions but never returning, until we reach the
top-level continuation.

7.3.2   Scheme the Hero Language

On what grounds does Scheme qualify for this select company? True,
the closure appears to be, on balance, a slightly less powerful innovation
than the Simula class. But Scheme, like Simula and Pascal, has the
heroic virtue of simplicity; and like Simula, the Scheme design achieves
a great deal of expressive power by generalizing constructs inherited
from its base language rather than by inventing new constructs. Furthermore, Scheme bases its expressive power on functions alone; Simula
relies on classes in addition to ordinary procedures. (Of course Simula
by the same token might have abolished ordinary procedures and relied
on classes alone, but this would have entailed some further changes and
adjustments: see exercise 3.)

Scheme's simplicity derives not merely from the wide-ranging consequences of the (fairly) simple lexical-binding protocol; it extends to other
language aspects as well. Previous Lisps, for example, had incorporated
a peculiar device that allowed any name to be bound to a function and
also, simultaneously, to a non-function. For example, the name **foobar**
might simultaneously refer to the function *square-root*, say, and to the
integer 5. Scheme does away with this bipartite namespace. The mere
fact that Scheme *does* allow **lambdas** to be evaluated, irrespective of
the lexical-binding rule *per se*, permits functions to be bound to names
using simple binding operations, and eliminates the logically irrelevant
clutter associated with **quote**-ing function definitions or wrapping them
in **function** envelopes.

Readers should keep in mind, of course, that Scheme's approach to de-
molishing the Algol Wall is in concept exactly the same as Simula 67's.
Both languages realize that heterogeneous data objects such as records
don't need to be understood merely as funny arrays; they are more
naturally understood in terms of the blocks, or local naming environ-

ments, created whenever a procedure is applied. Hence a procedure (or procedure-like entity) becomes the template to be used in creating heterogeneous objects. Hence, too, heterogeneous data objects don't need to be restricted to variables only, as per Pascal's record; they may contain procedures and an executable statement for initialization; they may be full-fledged data systems. *On the other hand,* this approach restricts us to unrepresentable heterogeneous objects, hence doesn't constitute a fully general modularity structure. And, unless the approach is carried to Smalltalk-like extremes (which it is not in Scheme), we are left with a distinction between data objects that are program-like (closures, data systems) and data objects that are data-object-like (for example, lists).

In sum, Scheme is a powerful and elegant language that falls just short of realizing the simplicity, power and elegance (interlocking recursive structures for every program *and* every data object) that lurked beneath the surface of Algol 60. That sword may remain trapped in its stone forever.

7.4 Readings

Basic Readings. The original papers on Scheme appeared in a series of reports [119, 120, 117] by Guy Steele Jr. and Gerry Sussman of MIT.

Suggested Readings. An excellent textbook on Scheme and its programming method is Abelson and Sussman's *Structure and Interpretation of Computer Programs* [1]. It has detailed chapters devoted to the design of data systems, complex data structures and their applications, meta-circular evaluators and compilation. [41] is an expository textbook focusing exclusively on the Scheme language. Steele describes an optimizing compiler for Scheme in [118]; [80] discusses the implementation of an optimizing compiler for T [106], an extended dialect of Scheme.

The idea of a continuation was known in the programming semantics community well before the advent of Scheme. Continuations play an important role in the denotational description of programming languages, for example. [93, 110, 122] are good introductions to the subject. The idea that continuations could be incorporated directly into a programming language was first suggested by Friedman *et al.* in [48, 47].

7.5   Exercises

1. Give a concise comparison of the ISM and Scheme.

2. Consider the Pascal record type

   ```
   foobar = record
               franz, felix, robert: integer;
               clara: real
            end
   ```

   Write a comparable template in Scheme (ignoring the types of
   variables) using higher-order functions; include the code necessary
   to access fields.

3. Inspired by Scheme, the Simula 67 designers decided to abolish
   procedures and rely on classes alone. In what sense have they
   made Simula more like Scheme? In what other ways must (or
   should) the Simula design change?

4. (a) "lambda forms as described in McCarthy's original paper are
   not merely a programming convenience, they are necessary to the
   language described, which couldn't have existed without them."
   Explain. (b) "Scheme's treatment of lambda forms results in a
   more orthogonal language than McCarthy's original Lisp." Explain.

5. Consider   the   following   top-level   Scheme   interpreter
   session:

   ```
   ==> (define a 2)
   2
   ==> (define b1 (+ a 1))
   3
   ==> (define b2 (lambda () (+ a 1)))
   B2
   ==> (+ b1 (b2))
   6
   ==> (define a 3)
   3
   ```

```
==> b1
3
==> (+ b1 (b2))
7
```

Explain the interpreter's strategy. What does your answer tell you about the way top-level **defines** are realized?

6. (a) How does lexical-binding affect the structure of the Scheme interpreter? In particular, consider how the Scheme interpreter handles free variables found in a function bound at the top-level. (Note that in the example above, the value of the free variable **a** in **b2** is determined at the point where **b2** is applied.) (b) Would it be easier to build an interpreter using lexical or dynamic binding? What would be the ramifications?

7. (a) "Scheme is more self-describing than Lisp." True or false? (b) Can think you think of a Scheme-based representation of a closure? Is this representation a "reasonable" implementation?

8. (a) Give a high-level semantic description of a continuation mechanism (similar to **call/cc**) in the ISM. Be sure to consider the interaction of continuations with the parallel evaluation semantics of space-maps. (b) Based on your answer to part (a), to what extent are continuations a reasonable construct to incorporate in a parallel language?

9. Give a Scheme implementation using continuations of the operators **delay** and **force**. The definitions given below are taken from the Scheme report [28]:

> (**delay** < expression >) returns an object called a promise which at some point in the future may be asked (by the **force** procedure) to evaluate < expression > and to deliver the resulting value. [p.10]

> (**force** < *promise* >) forces the value of *promise*. If no value has been computed for the promise, then a value is computed and returned. The value of the promise is cached (or "memoized") so that if it is forced a second time, the previously computed value is returned without any computation. [p.26]

[28] gives an example of how these operators can be used:

```
(define count 0)
(define p (delay
            (begin
              (set! count (+ count 1))
              (* x 3))))

(define x 5)
```

count	$\Longrightarrow$ 0
p	$\Longrightarrow$ a promise
(force p)	$\Longrightarrow$ 15
p	$\Longrightarrow$ a promise, still
count	$\Longrightarrow$ 1
(force p)	$\Longrightarrow$ 15
count	$\Longrightarrow$ 1

Your solution should rely primarily on continuations to capture the intended semantics of these operators. Contrast your solution to a solution that relies primarily on higher-order functions. What does your answer tell you about the relationship between continuations and closures?

10. Smalltalk supports name-overloading by allowing sub-classes to define methods found in their super-class. (a) Would a Scheme-based inheritance system also share this property? (Consider the structure of the bank account example.) (b) Sketch a design of an inheritance system of the kind supported by Simula in Scheme and show how it can be used by giving some examples. How does the Scheme version of inheritance compare with Simula's? What are the reasons for the differences?

11. Unlike Lisp, Scheme does not provide an **eval** operator as a primitive. Why do think **eval** was omitted from the language? Was this a significant omission? Is the expressive power of **quote** reduced by not providing **eval**?

12. In what ways is Scheme more similar to Pascal than to APL? In what ways is it more similar to APL?

8 Declarative Languages

Software machines can do many things. Sometimes, they behave as if they were finding the solutions to a set of equations. Under these circumstances, we can think of the equations to be solved as constituting the program in and of themselves. In this chapter, we discuss the use of equations as a programming language. We will consider two different kinds—the recursion equations depending on function application that underlie *functional languages*, and equations within the simple logic known as the first-order predicate calculus that underlie *logic languages*.

Both functional and logic languages are said to be *declarative*. Declarative languages allow the programmer merely to state what should hold true with respect to a computation, without bothering to say precisely how the computation should be done. In their pure form, declarative languages of the sort we describe here have one immediate and dramatic difference from the languages we've discussed previously: they exclude the idea of modifiable-state objects, in other words, of variables whose values can be reassigned as the program executes. The first value that a variable gets stuck with, it keeps; these languages maintain no implicit state and thus there are no assignment statements for changing a variable's value.

The equation-solving languages we describe in this chapter share the properties of *referential transparency* and *determinacy*. A language is *referentially transparent* if (a) every subexpression can be replaced by any other that's equal to it in value and (b) all occurrences of an expression within a given context yield the same value. A language is *determinate* if the value of an expression is independent of the order in which its subexpressions are evaluated. This chapter focuses on the ramifications of these two properties.

All functional languages are based on the pioneering work of Alonzo Church in the early 1940s on the lambda calculus. The goal of this work was the development of a sound logic for reasoning about functions as computational entities. McCarthy used the lambda calculus as the semantic basis for `lambda`s in Lisp 1.5, but he used a dynamic instead of a lexical scoping rule for functions, a deviation from the model that was subsequently corrected in Scheme. Landin's ISWIM, a contemporary of Lisp 1.5, was grounded more firmly in the lambda calculus. Unlike Lisp it had no assignment operator, hence (like subsequent functional languages) no modifiable state objects. ISWIM had many of the features found in modern functional languages: mutually recursive definition-blocks, lexically scoped higher-order functions, and the use of infix (as opposed to Lisp's prefix) notation for expressions.

It wasn't until Backus' Turing Award lecture of 1978 [5], however, that functional languages drew widespread interest in the computer science community. Backus's lecture dealt with a new functional language called FP. FP, stylistically closer to APL than to ISWIM or Lisp, was important less as a language than as a symbol. In the FP design, Backus—chief designer of Fortran and co-designer of Algol 60—emphatically renounced this whole style of language in favor of the radically different functional-language style. Needless to say, this dramatic public conversion drew widespread attention.

The late 1970s and early 1980s also produced the first efficient implementations of full-fledged general-purpose functional languages. ML, originally conceived at Edinburgh as a meta-language for an interactive proof system, developed into an almost-functional language (ML does have assignment statements). ML extends earlier work of Landin by supporting strong typing, algebraic and abstract data types, polymorphic functions and a powerful type-inference facility. Miranda, developed by Turner at the University of Kent, is similar to ML in its type discipline, has no assignment statement, and is based on a lazy (rather than eager) evaluation mechanism. We'll use Miranda as our main case study for functional languages in this chapter.

Logic languages trace their origin to the development of the predicate calculus by Frege in the late 1800s. The general predicate calculus is a symbol-manipulation system that allows formulas of the propositional calculus to be quantified using universal and existential operators. Despite early interest in using the predicate calculus as a semantic basis for the design of a programming language, it was not until Robinson proposed the use of *resolution* and *unification* as pragmatic algorithmic techniques for generating satisfiable instantiations of predicate calculus formulae that it first became possible to implement a substantial subset of first-order logic efficiently. Kowalski subsequently refined the resolution process, and Colmerauer and Warren soon after developed the language Prolog in the early 1970s. For efficiency reasons, current implementations of Prolog often support some form of assignment; for present purposes, we'll consider the purely declarative subset.

8.1 Miranda

8.1.1 Miranda Profile

Program Structure. A Miranda program is a sequence of mutually recursive *equations*. The following set of definitions, for example, constitutes a legal program fragment:

```
n = 3
f x = g y h
        where
            y = h n
            h x = (sq x) - 1
m = n * f n
```

Identifiers n and m are bound to integer-yielding expressions; f denotes a function of one argument. The notation for function application uses juxtaposition; the expression g y h denotes an application of function g to arguments y and h.

Miranda has no special terminating symbols (no terminating semicolons, for example). Expressions are distinguished on the basis of their relative position on the page: if e_1 is to be a subexpression of e_2, then e_2 must be written to the right of e_1. The definitions of y and h are considered to be a single "equation group"; the definitions of n, f and m define another group.

The **where** clause introduces a local binding environment similar to an Algol block or a Lisp **let** structure.

In a sense, we can think of a Miranda program (or for that matter of any functional language program) as the specification for a restricted ISM in which there are no time-maps, no empty regions and no assignment

statements. Every named region holds, upon creation, either a value or
an expression that will yield the value that it will contain throughout its
lifetime. We say "in a sense" because conceptually, the ISM version of
a functional language program is an *implementation* rather than a *representation* of the comparable functional program. Functional language
(and logic language) programs (unlike the ISM) have no model for time;
they are mere sets of equations. Where the ISM program says "these
entities have concurrent or disjoint lifetimes," the functional program
merely shrugs its shoulders—says, in effect, "just solve the equations"
(see exercise 1).

Besides the **where** clause, there are two other main program structure
forms in the language: guarded equations and pattern-matching-based
function definitions. The guarded form allows an equation to have several alternative right-hand sides, each distinguished by a predicate expression called a *guard*. Using guarded equations, the definition for
factorial can be written as follows:

```
fact n = 1, n = 0
       = n * fact (n - 1), n > 0
```

The particular expression evaluated when **fact** is applied depends upon
the value of the actual. Consider the application **fact 10**. To evaluate
this expression, we bind **n** to **10** and then proceed to find the first guard
(starting from the topmost guarded equation and proceeding down) that
is satisfied based on the current binding for **n**. Since **n** is greater than
but not equal to 0, the expression associated with the second guard is
evaluated. The value of this expression is the result of the application.
The order in which a series of guarded equations appears is important—
evaluation always starts from the top and proceeds downward.

Guarded equations are a special form of a more general notational mechanism called *pattern matching*. We say that the *pattern*—an expression
e_l—*matches* an expression e_r if there exists a consistent set of bindings
for the formals in e_l that makes e_l and e_r structurally identical. The
pattern expression e_l may contain literals, constants—possibly complex
structures such as lists—and formals; but expression e_r may contain
only literals and constants. For example, we can rewrite the factorial

function using pattern matching as follows:

```
fact 0       = 1
fact (n + 1) = (n + 1) * fact n
```

The application `fact 10` doesn't match the first pattern definition for `fact`—`fact 0` is not structurally identical to `fact 10`. On the other hand, the pattern `fact (n + 1)` does match `fact 10` if the formal n is bound to 9. Once a pattern match succeeds, the right side of the equation associated with the matched left side pattern is evaluated based on the bindings used to satisfy the pattern. The expression

```
(n + 1) * fact n
```

would be evaluated with n bound to 9.

Functions. Functional languages rely heavily on higher-order functions and powerful abstraction and composition operators to regain some of the expressive power lost by the absence of modifiable state objects. Closures are arguably their most important state-capturing device. By allowing local bindings to be established and then released to the outside via a closure, functional languages can support common applications (*e.g.*, simple iterations over an index variable) typically implemented through the use of assignment.

To illustrate, consider the following definition of a reduction operator, `reduce(f,x,a)`. f is a binary function,

$$x = (x_1, x_2, \ldots, x_n)$$

is a list, and a is a constant. `reduce` yields

```
f(x₁, f(x₂, ..., f(xₙ,a) ...))
```

We can write such a function in Miranda as follows:

```
reduce f i []     = i
reduce f i (a:x)  = f a (reduce f i x)
```

`[]` denotes an empty list; the pattern `(a:x)` signifies a list whose first element is bound to a and whose tail is bound to x.

reduce is easily written in other languages that support higher-order
functions, such as Scheme, but Miranda provides an extra degree of
flexibility by allowing functions to be *partially* applied. Most languages
require that a function of n arguments always be applied to n actuals;
Miranda drops this restriction. A function of n arguments applied to m
actuals (where $m \leq n$) returns as its result a function of $n-m$ arguments.
If this function is subsequently applied to $n-m$ actuals, the result is the
same as if the original were applied to all n actuals. Given a function
f of arguments x_1, x_2, ..., x_n, there exists an equivalent function f' of
x_1 that yields another function f'' of x_2 that yields another function,
...and so on. f' is said to be the *curried* version of f.

As a simple example of currying, consider the following definition for
plus:

```
plus x y  = x + y
```

We can define a plus1 function by writing

```
plus1 = plus 1
```

plus1 is a curried version of plus parameterized on the second argument; *e.g.*, plus1 3 yields 4.

Going back to our reduce function, it's easy to see that with the help of
currying, we could use reduce to define basic list reduction operations:

```
sum-list      = reduce (+) 0
product-list  = reduce (*) 1
   ...
```

Control Structures. Miranda uses three main techniques to express
control flow: (a) recursion, (b) ZF-expressions and (c) lazy evaluation.
We've seen recursion elsewhere; here we'll concentrate on ZF-expressions
and lazy evaluation.[1]

Generators. A ZF-expression expresses iterations over lists *without*
requiring updateable index variables.

---

[1] "ZF" is an acronym for Zermelo-Frankel. Zermelo and Frankel were two promi-
nent set theorists in the early 1900s.

x	a	y	perms x
[1,2,3]	1	perms [2,3]	[1 : perms [2,3]]
	2	perms [1,3]	[2 : perms [1,3]]
	3	perms [1,2]	[3 : perms [1,2]]
[2,3]	2	perms [3]	[2 : perms [3]]
[1,3]	1	perms [3]	[1 : perms [3]]
[1,2]	1	perms [2]	[1 : perms [2]]
[3]	3	perms []	[3]
[2]	2	perms []	[2]

Figure 8.1
Expanding the ZF-expression that computes the permutation of a list on the input [1,2,3] yields the list [[1,2,3],[1,3,2],[3,2,1]]. The list notation [a,b] is shorthand for [a : [b]].

As an example of a ZF-expression, the following definition generates all permutations of a given list:

```
perms []   = [ [] ]
perms  x   = [ a : y | a <- x; y <- perms (x---[a]) ]
```

The expression a : y in the above definition constitutes the body of the ZF-expression; it is evaluated for each binding defined by the *generators* occurring on the right-hand side of the "|." The generator

```
a <- x
```

returns a list of environments; the ith environment in this list binds a to the ith element in x. For each environment in this list, the generator

```
y <- perms (x---[a])
```

is evaluated; this generator also returns a list of environments binding y to all permutations of x not including the element bound to a. The body is evaluated once in each of these environments. We illustrate this process in Figure 8.1.

Besides generators, the right-hand side of a ZF-expression may include filters that remove certain environments from the environment list returned by a previously defined generator. For example, the following expression to compute all factors of some number uses filters to remove any multiple of a previously recorded factor:

```
factors n = [ i | i <- [1..n div 2] ; n mod i = 0 ]
```

Lazy Evaluation. All the languages we've seen so far (with the partial exception of Algol 60) are based on a so-called "eager evaluation" strategy, meaning that the actual arguments to a procedure are evaluated *before* control enters the procedure body. Algol 60's call-by-name protocol delayed the evaluation of call-by-name actuals until their use within the body of the procedure. Miranda's version of call-by-name (referred to as *lazy evaluation*) is the only argument-passing protocol in the language. Miranda's lazy evaluation strategy is widely accepted as the strategy of choice in other modern functional languages as well.

In the lazy evaluation strategy, the arguments to a function application are not evaluated unless and until their values are required within the function body. For example, we can define a conditional function as follows:

```
If True  x y  = x
If False x y  = y
```

The application If True 0 (1 div 0) returns 0; the uncomputable expression 1 div 0 is never evaluated, because its value isn't needed in order for the application to yield an answer.

A lazy evaluation strategy makes it possible to express functions that generate and operate upon data structures of unspecified length, sometimes called "infinite data structures" (although of course, strictly speaking, they are nothing of the sort). These structures are yielded by functions that would never terminate under ordinary "eager" evaluation.

For example, the Miranda definition

```
primes = sieve [ 2 .. ]
          where
              sieve (p : x) = p : sieve [ n | n <- x ;
                                            n mod p > 0]
```

generates all the prime numbers. The notation [2 ..] generates an unending list of positive integers starting from 2; the sieve function filters out all integers that are not prime. The result of evaluating **primes** is, in the abstract, an infinite list of primes. Because of lazy evaluation, however, what is actually returned is a two-element list whose first element is 2 and whose second is a closure that computes

```
sieve [ n | n <- [ 3. .] ; n mod 2 > 0 ]
```

Only if and when we access the tail of this list is the closure applied and another two-element list returned, containing 3 as its first element and a closure for an expression computing all primes starting from 5 as its second. The computation unravels in this fashion, one element at a time, whenever the last element of the primes list is accessed.

To understand structures of this kind, note that we might have described the random-number generators discussed earlier as "infinite data structures" consisting of unbounded sequences of random numbers. The difference between the random number generators and the "primes" example above is mostly a matter of presentation: to get the next random number, we invoke a function; to get the next prime, we reference an element of a data structure. We should keep in mind, however, that the implementation of the random number generator given earlier depends upon assignment; the implementation of the prime number generator doesn't. In other words, the prime number program is referentially transparent; the random number program isn't. (See exercise 2.)

The Type System. Miranda, like most functional languages, has a rich type system. In addition to primitive types such as integers, Booleans and characters, Miranda supports function types and two structure types: lists (ordered sets of homogeneous elements, similar to Pascal arrays) and tuples. A tuple is a set of heterogeneous elements, analogous to a Pascal-style record. For example, a person-tuple could be defined as

```
person = ("Jones",32,Male,Married)
```

The elements of a tuple are unnamed. To access tuple elements, we use pattern-matching. Thus, a function to return the age of a person may be written as

```
person-age (name,age,sex,martial-status) = age
```

Evaluating (person-age person) yields 32.

Miranda allows users to introduce new types. A user-defined type is known as an *algebraic type*. Consider the following specification of a binary tree of integers:

```
tree  ::=  Leaf  num | Root tree tree
```

This specification introduces three new identifiers: **tree** (the name of the new type), **Leaf** (a constructor that serves as a label for the leaf nodes in a tree), and **Root** (a constructor that serves as a label for non-leaf nodes).

An instance of this tree may be written as

```
my-tree = Root (Root (Leaf 1) (Leaf 2))
              (Root (Leaf 3) (Leaf 4))
```

Pattern matching is used, again, to extract the elements of an algebraic type. For example, the following function definition sums the leaf elements of a tree:

```
sum-tree (Leaf leaf) = leaf
sum-tree (Root t1 t2) = (sum-tree t1) + (sum-tree t2)
```

Miranda also supports abstract data type definitions, roughly similar to the kind found in languages like Ada.

Polymorphism. In the strongly typed languages we've seen so far, every expression is associated with at most one type; in particular, functions are allowed to operate only on arguments of a specific base type. Some languages like APL, Algol-68 or PL/I relax this restriction slightly either by allowing operator symbols to be overloaded or by coercing data objects from one type to another.

Overloading is a syntactic transformation that allows the same name to be used for different objects. Thus, in Fortran, we could write "2.5 + 3.2" or "2 + 3." Even though the symbol "+" is used in both instances, the code generated is quite different. In the first case, the "+" refers to a real number addition; in the second, it refers to a scalar addition. Thus, even in languages that allow operators to be overloaded, it is never the case that an expression can be associated with more than one type. Of course, in languages like Lisp that perform no compile-time type-checking, we could write expressions that operate on many different types, but it is the programmer's responsibility to make sure that the expression has a meaningful interpretation for each object it manipulates.

Miranda's type system is based on the foundational work of Hindley; its type-checking algorithm is similar to the one developed by Milner for ML. Like Lisp expressions, a Miranda expression may be associated with more than one type. Unlike Lisp, however, Miranda programs are strongly typed; thus, a well-typed Miranda program is guaranteed not to generate type-errors at runtime.

The Hindley-Milner type system allows functions to be defined that operate on arguments of many different types. In such a type system, a type may be either a primitive (*e.g.*, integer, boolean, real), a constructor or a *type variable*. A constructor maps types to other types; thus $Int \rightarrow Bool$ is the type of a function that takes an integer argument and returns a boolean result). A type variable (usually denoted by a lower-case greek letter) is a placeholder that stands for an arbitrary type. A type containing type variables is said to be *polymorphic*.

For example, consider the definition of a function that returns the number of elements in a list:

```
count []      = 0
count [a : x] = 1 + (count x)
```

This function can operate on lists whose elements may be of any type, but there is only a single piece of code associated with count. Its type is

List [α] → num

A polymorphic type definition in effect defines a type *scheme*; an application of a polymorphic type is well-defined if there exists a consistent instantiation of the type variables that yields a monomorphic type, *i.e.*, a type with no type variables. If a polymorphic type is applied to an argument for which no such instantiation is possible, the application is ill-typed. For example, if count is applied to an integer rather than a list, the type-checker would be unable to instantiate α to a type t such that the equation List[t] = num is satisfied. The type-checking process is based on a *unification* algorithm similar to the algorithm underlying the pattern-matching analysis used elsewhere. The unification algorithm is guaranteed to produce a "well-typing"—it never infers a type for an expression that is inconsistent with the way that expression is used in the program. The algorithm is also guaranteed to compute a *principal* or most-general type for every expression. For example, given the definition of count, each of the following is a legal type for the function:

1. List[Num] → num

2. List[Int → Bool] → num

3. List[α] → num

The third type is the most general, subsuming the previous two; this is the type inferred by the type-checker.

To type-check an expression, we establish a set of type constraints and solve this system with respect to the type variables. For example, the set of type constraints for the count procedure is shown in figure 8.2.

Solving this constraint system results in the following bindings being established:

$$\gamma \; = \; \text{List}[\alpha] \; = \; \text{List}[\beta] \; = \; \text{List}[\delta]$$
$$\psi \; = \; \text{num}$$

Expression	*Type*
[ ]	**List**$[\alpha]$
0	**num**
1	**num**
a	β
x	**List**$[\delta]$
[a : x]	**List**$[\beta]$
+	**num** $\rightarrow$ **num**
count	$\gamma \rightarrow \psi$
count x	ψ
(1+ count x)	**num**

Figure 8.2
The type constraints for the count function.

The resulting type is **List**$[\alpha] \rightarrow$ **num**.

In a Hindley-Milner type system, all occurrences of a bound variable within the body of a polymorphic function must have the same type. Since functions are polymorphic, this type may vary for different applications, but in order to ensure type correctness, the same bound variable cannot be associated with two different monomorphic types within the body of a function. For example, the expression

```
f g = ( (g 2), (g true) )
```

would be considered ill-typed. The argument to f is a function g whose type would be given as

$$\alpha \;\rightarrow\; \beta$$

In type-checking the body of the function, we are confronted with the task of unifying α to both **num** and **Bool**. Since we can't unify distinct monomorphic types, a type-error must be raised.

This restriction on the use of polymorphism can be relaxed when local variables introduced within a where-clause are used in different type contexts within the clause's body. For example, consider the expression

```
f = ( (g 2), (g true) )
    where g x = x
```

This function should certainly be considered well-typed. If a type-checker is unable to type-check **f**, it's clear that polymorphism becomes quite useless since no polymorphic function could be applied to distinct types within the same context.

A Hindley-Milner type-checker will infer that **g** is simply the identity function with type

$$\alpha \;\rightarrow\; \alpha$$

Even though **g** is used in two different type contexts within the tuple expression, the type-checker need not raise a type-error since it knows precisely what **g**'s type happens to be. It can use this information to provide a separate monomorphic type for each occurrence of **g** within the tuple. The type of **g** when applied to 2 can be given as

num $\rightarrow$ **num**

and its type when applied to **true** can be inferred to be

Bool $\rightarrow$ **Bool**

In effect, a "copy" of **g**'s type is made for each occurrence of **g** in the function body. The type-checker unifies the type variable in the separate copies to the type of the corresponding argument.

8.2   Prolog

Prolog is an acronym for *Programming in Logic*. It is based on a model in which an *algorithm* is said to consist of two disjoint components: a logical component that specifies *what* has to be solved and a control component that describes *how* the solution is to be be carried out. We begin with a digression intended to provide some background on the relationship between Prolog and formal logic.

(*The following two sections may be skipped without loss of continuity, particularly by readers familiar with the predicate calculus and the unification process.*)

8.2.1 The Predicate Calculus

A Prolog program is a statement in a subset of the first-order predicate calculus defined as follows:

Definition 8.1 The *theory* of the first-order predicate calculus is a quadruple, $< \Sigma, \mathcal{L}, \mathcal{A}, \mathcal{I} >$, where:

1. Σ is an alphabet consisting of variables, constants, function symbols, predicates, connectives and quantifiers.

2. $\mathcal{L}$ is a first-order language (see below).

3. $\mathcal{A}$ is a set of axioms.

4. $\mathcal{I}$ is a set of inference rules.

Definition 8.2 A *term* is a statement of the predicate calculus defined inductively:

1. A variable is a term.

2. A constant is a term.

3. If f is an n-ary function and $t_1, t_2, \ldots, t_n$ is a term, then

$$f(t_1, t_2, \ldots, t_n)$$

is a term.

Definition 8.3 A *well-formed formula* (wff) is defined inductively as follows:

1. If p is a predicate and $t_1, t_2, \ldots, t_n$ are terms, then $p(t_1, t_2, \ldots, t_n)$ is a well-formed formula. Such a formula is known as an atom. p is referred to as a *functor* and the t_i are known as the *components* of the formula.

2. If F and G are wffs, then so are $F \vee G$, $F \wedge G$, $\neg F$, and $F \rightarrow G$.

3. If F is a wff and x is a variable, then $\forall x F$ and $\exists x F$ are wffs.

An important point to note here is the restriction that terms may be either variables or function symbols. $\mathcal{L}$ is a first-order language as a result of this restriction.

For the sake of efficient implementation, Prolog programs are drawn from a subset of the first-order predicate calculus referred to as the class of *Horn clauses*. First we need to define a general clause:

Definition 8.4 A *clause* is a formula of the form

$$\forall x_1, x_2, \ldots, x_k(L_1 \vee L_2 \vee \ldots \vee L_m)$$

where each L_i is an atom or the negation of one and $x_1, x_2, \ldots, x_k$ are the variables occurring in $L_1 \vee L_2 \vee \ldots \vee L_m$.

Any wff can be translated into clausal form as follows:

1. Eliminate all implication symbols ($\rightarrow$) using the substitution $\neg X \vee Y$ for $X \rightarrow Y$.

2. Reduce the scope of negation symbols to at most one atomic formula.

3. Rename variables to ensure that each quantifier has a unique quantified variable.

4. Eliminate all existential quantifiers by Skolemization. A Skolem function is a function symbol that names the individual element specified by an existential quantifier. Thus, Skolemizing the clause

$$\forall x \exists y P(x, y)$$

   yields

$$\forall x P(x, g(x))$$

   where g maps x onto that element y known to exist.

5. Put the resulting clause into *conjunctive normal form*, replacing all expressions of the form $X \vee (Y \wedge Z)$ by $(X \vee Y) \wedge (X \vee Z)$.

6. Remove all universal quantifiers.

7. Eliminate all $\land$ symbols by replacing terms of the form $X \land Y$ by the set of clauses $\{X, Y\}$. Each wff in this set is a clause consisting only of disjunctions of literals.

A *Horn clause* is simply a clause with at most one unnegated literal. A Prolog program consists of a series of Horn clauses, each written as

$$A \leftarrow B_1, B_2, \ldots, B_n$$

or

$$A : - B_1, B_2, \ldots, B_n$$

This expression denotes the clause

$$A \lor \neg B_1 \lor \neg B_2 \lor \ldots \lor \neg B_n$$

8.2.2   Procedural Semantics

Despite outward appearances, a Horn clause has a simple procedural interpretation. Instead of regarding the clause

$$A \leftarrow B_1, B_2, \ldots, B_n$$

as defining a predicate on A and the B_i, we can view this statement as a procedure definition that reads "To solve A, solve $B_1, B_2, \ldots, B_n$." Each of the B_i can be viewed as a procedure invocation.

The idea of a *refutation* is central to our understanding of how Horn clauses can be viewed as programs. A problem to be solved is couched as its denial; if a refutation for this denial can be established given the specification provided, the values of the variables yielded during the refutation process represent a solution to the problem being solved. For example,

$$C_1, C_2, \ldots, C_n$$

represents the denial of the formula

$$C_1 \land C_2 \ldots \land C_n$$

If it can be established that this formula is satisfiable, then the solution
to the original clause consists of the binding values of the variables at
the completion of the refutation process.

Refutation is a process whose behavior is captured in the inference rule
known as *resolution*. Resolution is similar to the *modus ponens* rule;
given two ground clauses (clauses not containing variables)

$$X_1 \vee X_2 \vee \ldots \vee X_n$$

and

$$\neg X_1 \vee Y_1 \vee \ldots \vee Y_m$$

we can infer a new clause (the *resolvent*) computed by taking the dis-
junction of the two clauses, eliminating the complementary pair.

Resolution is the logic-programming analog of function application. The
power of resolution becomes evident when we try to compute the resolvent of clauses that have quantified variables. In this case, computing
the resolvent may require *matching* terms of the clause, performing substitutions to determine if the two clauses can be made identical (disregarding the outermost negation). Determining the substitutions needed
to compute the resolvent is a process known as *unification*; the substitutions yielded by the unification procedure are referred to as the *unifier*
of the two clauses.

Definition 8.5 A *unifier* is a finite set of the form $\{v_i/t_i\}$ where each
v_i is a variable and t_i is a term distinct from v_i.

An example is computing the resolvent of the clause

$$\neg p(f(x, y), g(z), a)$$

with

$$p(f(y, x), g(u), a)$$

It is necessary to find appropriate substitutions for the variables x, y,
and z that would make the two clauses identical (disregarding the outer
negation). (Note that f and g are functional constants.) One such
unifier would be $\{x/y, z/u\}$—the substitution of y for x and u for z.

8.2.3   Prolog Profile

Program Structure. A Prolog program consists of three components: (1) a set of *facts*, (2) a set of *rules* or *relations*, and (3) a query. The Prolog interpreter attempts to answer or "solve" the query by using the facts and rules provided. A fact is a statement that expresses a relation between objects; a rule relates groups of facts. In the language of Horn clauses, a rule is simply a Horn clause, and a fact is an atom.

For example, we could write the following program:

```
female(annette).
female(marilyn).
female(audrey).
parents(annette, fred, marilyn).
parents(audrey, fred, marilyn).
parents(marilyn, john, liz).
sister(X,Y) :- female(X), parents(X,M,F),
               parents(Y,M,F).
```

The following query—which means "Are **annette** and **audrey** sisters?"— returns **yes**.

```
? :- sister(annette, audrey).
```

However, this next query returns **no**.

```
? :- sister(annette, marilyn).
```

(Prolog is supplied with an interpreter as well as a compiler. Hence we can type queries to the interpreter and expect answers to be returned directly.) The program contains a number of facts indicating the sex and parentage of different objects. It also contains a single rule relating these facts that reads, "X is a sister of Y if X is a female and if the parents of X are M and F, and the parents of Y are M and F." The term **sister** (X,Y) is called the *head* of the rule; the terms on the right of the ":-" constitute the rule's *body*. Capital letters denote variables (commonly referred to as *logical variables* because they obtain a value only via the unification process).

The interpreter returned **yes** to the first query because there exists a consistent instantiation of variables X and Y in the **sister** rule based on the facts provided; it returned **no** to the second query because no such instantiation was possible.

A query can itself contain logical variables. The answer returned by the interpreter to a query containing variables are the bindings associated with the variables. Thus, the interpreter returns the answer **X = annette** in response to the query

   ?   :- sister(X, audrey).

It's also possible to leave a component of a term unnamed. For example, if we're interested merely in *whether* **audrey** has a sister (we don't care what her name is), we could express the query as

   ? :- sister(_ , audrey).

The "_" stands for an anonymous variable.

Data Types. The only primitive types in Prolog are integers, characters and strings. There is no explicit Boolean type although certain Boolean operations can be simulated. Note that pure Prolog cannot express logical negation. A rule written as

$$A \leftarrow \neg B_1, B_2, \ldots, B_n$$

is equivalent to the clause

$$A \vee B_1 \vee \neg B_2 \vee \ldots \vee \neg B_n$$

This clause is not a Horn clause since it has two unnegated literals. Typical implementations of Prolog must provide an interpretation of negation that doesn't depend on the refutation procedure.

Prolog supports the standard set of relational operators, best understood as rules that succeed if the necessary relation holds, and that fail otherwise.

The main structured type in Prolog is the list. A list is an ordered sequence of terms (it may include nested lists) written within square brackets. Consider the following program to determine whether a given element is a member of a list:

```
member(X, [X | _]).
member(X, [_ | Y ]) :- member(X,Y).
```

(The "|" symbol is used to partition a list into a head and a tail.) We can read this program as the following specification: "X is a member of a list whose head is X. X is also a member of list whose tail is Y, provided that X is a member of Y."

Given this definition, the query

```
? :- member(foo, [bar, bam, zoom, foo, blat]).
```

returns **yes**.

As another example, the following definition of an **append** operation illustrates how we can use the consistent substitution (or *unification*) process to write an "ordinary" procedure (as opposed to a Boolean-valued function that can naturally be interpreted as a query):

```
append([] , L, L).
append([X|L1], L2, [X|L3]) :- append(L1,L2,L3).
```

The first fact can be interpreted to state that appending an empty list to another list L yields L. The rule can be read as follows: "If the **append** of a list whose head is X and whose tail is L1 with the list L2 is a list whose head is X and whose tail is L3, then the **append** of L1 and L2 is L3."

The "query" (or procedure invocation)

```
? :- append([a,b,c],[d,e,f],X).
```

returns the binding X = [a,b,c,d,e,f]. It's interesting that we can use **append** to solve the inverse problem as well: "Given a list L1 and a list L2, return the list L3 such that L2 is the append of L1 and L3." We pose the following query:

```
? :- append([a,b,c],X,[a,b,c,d,e,f]).
```

The result of this query is the binding X = [d,e,f]. The unification process is insensitive to the position of the variables in a query; it simply attempts to find a consistent substitution based on the facts and rules provided.

Control Structures. Each of the component clauses in a query is known as a *goal*. The Prolog interpreter attempts to *satisfy* each goal found in the query by using the facts and rules provided. A *goal* is satisfied if

- there exists a fact that unifies with it, or

- there exists a rule whose head unifies with the goal such that each clause in the rule's body is satisfied (based on the current set of variable bindings).

If a particular goal cannot be satisfied, the interpreter *backtracks* and attempts to find an alternative means by which to satisfy the goal.

As an example, consider the behavior of the interpreter as it attempts to solve the query

```
? :- prince(Y).
```

given the following program:

```
male(edward).
male(henry).
mother(edward, victoria).
mother(henry,liz).
queen(liz).
prince(X) :- male(X), mother(X,Z), queen(Z).
```

To solve this query, the interpreter unifies the head of the rule defining what it means to be a prince with the single goal in the query. The effect of this unification is a binding of Y to X. It then attempts to satisfy each clause in the body of the rule. The first clause, `male(X)` is satisfied by unifying X to `edward`. Given this binding for X, the second clause, `mother(X,Z)` unifies with the third fact; Z gets instantiated to `victoria` in the process. However, based on these bindings, there is no corresponding fact or rule that unifies with the clause `queen(Z)`; `victoria`, alas, is not a queen.

The interpreter now backtracks to the second clause to find a new instantiation for Z; since victoria is the only mother for edward, the interpreter has no other choice but to backtrack further to the first clause to find a new instantiation for X. It thus reattempts to satisfy the three clauses in the body based on a new binding of X to henry. The second clause is unified with the fourth fact, instantiating the binding of Z to liz. The third clause is satisfied since it matches the fifth fact. The interpreter at this point returns, with the binding X = henry.

The evaluation strategy of the interpreter is based on a top-down, depth-first search; the interpreter attempts to satisfy each clause in a goal from left-to-right by searching the relevant facts and rules given in the program top-to-bottom. In the above program, for example, no backtracking would have occurred had we interchanged the first and second facts. It is a "feature" of Prolog that, although the elements of a program are supposed to be mere declarations of facts and rules, the order in which these declarations appear is highly significant to the program's behavior. For example, given the program

```
q(foo).
p(X) :- p(X).
p(X) :- q(X).
```

the query ? :- p(z) would not terminate—the second clause would be chosen perpetually. On the other hand, if clauses (3) and (2) were interchanged, the query would yield a proper solution, namely the substitution of foo for z.

Prolog does allow a limited form of control over how backtracking is performed via the cut operator. A rule of the form

```
r(X) :- f(X), !, g(X).
```

indicates that once f(X) is satisfied, no further backtracking should be performed on X; the binding for X derived from satisfying the first clause in the body cannot be revoked even if the clause g(X) fails. Thus, for example, we can use cut to define a simple conditional expression

```
f(x) = if p(x) then g(x) else h(x)
```

as follows:

```
f(X,Y) :- p(X), !, g(X,Y).
f(X,Y) :- h(X,Y).
```

Y holds the result of the conditional. If the predicate p (X) yields true, it is impossible for the false branch of the conditional to be evaluated. Incorporating cut into the program makes this assertion explicit. The cut operator plays an important role in Prolog because it constrains the search process and eliminates generation of unwanted results.

8.3   Analysis

8.3.1   The Nature of the Model

What sorts of computations can be conveniently described in terms of equation solving? It's clear that whenever a computer is acting like a glorified calculator—accepting input values, performing some kind of transformation and producing output values—its behavior can be conveniently described in these terms. Of course, we can write this kind of program in Fortran too; we don't need an equation-based language for this purpose. But most readers will agree that declarative languages are conceptually at a "higher level" than ordinary languages like Fortran. The higher a language's level, the closer it is to the user's own way of thinking—and also, presumably, the more concise the program.

Furthermore, the declarative languages we've discussed have the properties of *referential transparency* and *determinacy*, as we noted above. These properties, it is asserted, make programs easier to understand, to develop, and to execute on parallel computers. Referential transparency is attractive insofar as it implies that every expression has a unique value within a given environment. A declarative language compiler can take advantage of referential transparency to perform program optimizations and transformations that would not be otherwise possible. Determinacy implies that the meaning of a program does not depend on the underlying machine implementing it; the same program will exhibit the same behavior regardless of whether it is executed on a sequential or a parallel machine.

The implications of the model will be clearer if we consider how it approaches problems that we might not ordinarily conceive in equation-solving terms. A simple example: suppose your program reads a file of election results, tallying "yes" and "no" votes. It's easy to think of the program in terms of a "yes" counter and a "no" counter, each initialized to 0 and incremented as appropriate. But this solution is not acceptable in an equation-solving model: we can't repeatedly change the value of a "yes" counter by solving an equation. Changing the value of a variable, or altering a pre-existing data-object, are activities that fall strictly outside of this model. There are no assignment statements in functional languages or pure logic languages. Whatever value a variable gets, it keeps forever.

Should we infer that we can't write vote-tallying programs using a functional or logic language? Not at all. True, we can't program with mutable objects—but we can achieve the same effect by other means (or in other words, we can fake it). The strategy is fairly simple: instead of incrementing the value of an object, we create a new object whose value is the old object's value plus one. We can write our vote-tallying program as a function that accepts two arguments, `total-yes-votes` and `total-no-votes`; upon reading a new "no" vote, this function reinvokes itself, passing `total-yes-votes` and `total-no-votes + 1` as arguments.

By using this strategy we can always turn a state-based program into an equation-language program, unless the state-based program involves time or indeterminacy—circumstances we discuss below. Whether it is *reasonable* to perform this transformation depends on the nature of the problem to be solved and your point of view.

In some problems, mutable objects play a minor role or none, and equation-solving accordingly becomes a natural programming model. Certain problems in signal processing and numerical analysis (for example) fall into this category; certain problems in logical inferencing and simulated reasoning fall (not surprisingly) into the category of problems that are naturally modeled by using logic equations.

There are other problems in which mutable objects are obvious and natural, even though they aren't conceptually fundamental. Consider the data systems we've discussed extensively—for example, *bank accounts.* Although degree of "naturalness" is a subjective issue, most people would agree that it's natural to associate a variable called `balance` with a `bank account`, and to imagine this `balance` as a mutable object whose value is incremented by `deposit` and decremented by `withdraw`. It's true that when using a declarative language, we might design an implementation of `bank account` in which `balance` is an immutable object, recreated whenever it should change. Some programmers will be delighted with such an implementation. Others will regard it as counter-intuitive and "unnatural."

A declarative language advocate might respond as follows:

> "Some programmers might call our solution 'unnatural,' but that's only because they were brought up on languages like Pascal. A programmer who is brought up right, trained from the start in the declarative language way of thinking, won't have these problems. The benefits of referential transparency and determinacy far outweigh any presumed loss in expressivity."

Bear in mind, however, that the allegation that `balance` is "naturally" conceived as a mutable object is grounded ultimately not on Pascal or Simula but on a simple physical model. There is a pile of money somewhere, and money is added to or removed from the pile. It is *not* the case that the pile is destroyed and recreated whenever something is added or removed. Whether the underlying physical model is accurate or realistic is irrelevant; the relevant questions are: "Do people think in quasi-physical terms like this, or not? Do they find it helpful to think in these terms?" Exactly the same type of question arises when we consider "abstract" data systems, for example, a pushdown stack. Is it useful (or desirable) to have in mind a quasi-physical model of something like a stack, or not? Different people will answer in different ways. But in any case, the most expressive, most "natural" language is the one that allows us to walk the shortest path from our mental model to a working program.

To be clear, there is no question that declarative languages *can* express data systems of the kind we've discussed. There is a final category of problem, however, in which mutable objects are conceptually fundamental, and declarative languages seem inappropriate. An operating system, for example, is a program that must control the physical devices that constitute the computer. A computer's memory and the mapping tables that control it are mutable objects; the buffers that are used for communication between the processor and the i/o devices are mutable objects; the registers that the processor uses to control the i/o devices are mutable objects, and so on. These are physical facts; they are non-negotiable. Similar arguments apply to a database system, which alters records as needed without recopying the entire database. There is a wide variety of related instances.

In dealing with problems like operating systems or databases, these languages experience an important difficulty we haven't yet touched on: the fact that they provide no model for time or for non-determinism—where "non-determinism" refers, in essence, to program behavior that can't be predicted from the source text alone, but depends on circumstances at runtime. Non-determinism is important in many systems and database applications. Consider an airline reservation system in which two ticket agents both enter a request for the last seat on some flight. The agent whose request is received first should get the seat. Without even considering how the program is implemented, we have already stepped outside the bounds of the equation-solving model. To see why, remember that under this model, a function must always yield the same result when applied to the same argument. But the function "Get-me-seat(x)" yields different results depending on circumstances. (We might include the time at which the request is entered as an argument, but it's the time at which the request is *received* that is important.) The fundamental point is that the system's response to a seat request depends on the state of the system as a whole, not merely on the contents of the request. In other words: the word *function* has a simple mathematical definition, and the functions that occur in declarative languages adhere precisely to the requirements of the mathematical definition. Under this definition, "Get-me-seat(x)" is *not* a function; hence it is impermissible in these languages.

(To put these criticisms in proper perspective, we should keep in mind that these languages were never seriously intended to support applications involving non-determinism. Declarative language advocates rarely argue that non-determinism is a "good" thing and are more than willing, in general, to forget about applications that require it. This position shouldn't be very surprising given the emphasis the equation-solving model places on determinism and referential transparency, both of which are obviously compromised in the presence of non-determinism.)

In sum: equation-solving is an abstract process designed to convert values into other values. The creation and manipulation of mutable objects plays no role in the equation-solving model. But the world at large—the world of computers, programmers and other things—consists of mutable objects. Sometimes it's natural to structure a problem as a set of recursion or logic equations, but it's hardly surprising that at other times, structuring a program in terms of operations performed over mutable objects seems more natural. Programs often need to model or even to encompass pieces of external reality—they need to simulate a yak stampede, manage a database or fly an airplane. Yaks, databases and airplanes are mutable objects, and it's not surprising that the software to deal with these entities will often be most naturally expressed in terms of some software version of mutable state.

We should note in conclusion that these comments don't apply to functional and to logic languages in quite the same way. Pure logic languages impose the same kind of restrictions with respect to mutable state that are found in functional languages, but they compensate in another area, by supporting the powerful idea of unification and automatic theorem-proving. Furthermore, pure logic languages are easily extended in such a way that they encompass a (mutable) database model. Prolog has attracted a committed, if still rather small, user community among programmers interested in logic-based expert systems, database query systems and other related areas. Functional languages, on the other hand, have by and large remained research tools in the hands of computer scientists (ML is a notable exception). This may be due in part to the lingering unfamiliarity of these languages, and in part to the fact that functional languages are still inefficient in some cases. Both problems should grow less pronounced with time. We comment on these questions further in the appendix to this chapter.

8.3.2 Specifications vs. Programs

It's instructive to observe that our descriptions of Miranda and Prolog had little to say on the issue of *control*. None of the structures we've seen in either of these languages have the semantics of a Lisp progn or an Algol compound statement. Although Prolog's cut operation and Miranda's top-down evaluation of pattern-based function definitions are mechanisms by which the evaluation of expressions can be controlled to some extent, both mechanisms are weak compared to control structures we've seen in other languages and, more important, both are completely foreign to the programming model upon which the associated language is based.

Declarative programs are best thought of as *specifications*. They present a set of equations that describe the constraints to be satisfied by the solution to some problem, but they don't give any *control strategy* (or at most, they sketch only a partial control strategy) for carrying out the solution.

By abstracting state information into closures or logical variables, declarative programs avoid the need for a vocabulary to describe control mechanisms for the manipulation of implicit state; in writing a declarative program, the programmer is, in essence, free to ignore all operational concerns regarding the ultimate implementation of this specification. The compiler for a declarative language is responsible for transforming a specification into a software machine: compiling a declarative program results in a software machine that manifests the state and control strategies latent in the specification.

There are some clear advantages to this approach. For example, consider the prime-finder problem described on page 312. The Miranda program that solves this problem is three lines long. A Prolog version wouldn't be much longer. Figure 8.3 is a Pascal implementation of this problem, given in [72].

The Pascal program is bulkier than the Miranda specification, and it's certainly less clear as well. To understand the Pascal program, the reader will find himself mimicking the underlying Pascal machine: only by tracing the execution of this program for a number of iterations does its behavior become clear. The Miranda version, on the other hand, isn't

```
program sieve (output);

const n = < upper bound>
var sieve,primes : set of 2 .. n;
    next,j : integer;

begin
  sieve := [2..n]; primes := []; next := 2;
  repeat
    while not (next in sieve) do next := succ (next);
    primes := primes + [next];
    j := next;
    while j <= n do
       begin
          sieve := sieve - [j]; j := j + next;
       end
  until sieve = []
end.
```

Figure 8.3
A Pascal implementation of the Sieve of Erasthosenes prime-finding algorithm.

cluttered with the kind of operational detail found in the Pascal program; understanding the Miranda program doesn't involve keeping track of temporary variables (*e.g.*, j or **next**), loops or assignment statements.

(Readers will remember, of course, that the APL implementation of a slightly simplified version of this problem was even more concise than the Miranda specification. But although the APL version was also declarative, it was certainly *not* easy to understand—not transparent and self-explanatory.)

The Miranda programmer depends on the compiler to do a good job of translating his specification into an efficient executable program. In applications that are naturally realized in terms of simple function composition and application, or make little use of state (as in the above example), this is not a problem; the executable realization of the Miranda specification would probably not be too much different from the compiled Pascal program. On the other hand, for applications that are naturally expressed in terms of state and state change, a declarative language compiler must often go to great lengths to produce a reasonably efficient implementation.

8.3.3 Parallelism

Declarative languages have a number of interesting properties as a consequence of their prohibition on general assignment. For functional languages, the most important of these properties is captured in the Church-Rosser theorems. Central to these theorems is the notion of *reduction*. In a purely functional program, the effect of a function application can be described in terms of substitution: each occurrence of a formal in the body of the function being applied is replaced with the value of the actual. Each application is "reduced" to an evaluation of the body of the function being applied; when there are no more applications to be performed, evaluation stops. If e is some expression, then we say e reduces to e_1 (abbreviated $e \Longrightarrow e_1$) if e_1 is the result of reducing some application within e. (We'll use the notation $e \overset{*}{\Longrightarrow} e_1$ to stand for the reflexive, transitive closure of $\Longrightarrow$—to mean that we can get from e to e_1 via 0 or more $\Longrightarrow$'s.)

There may in general be many reducible applications within an expression. The first Church-Rosser theorem says that the order in which these applications are reduced doesn't affect the final value of the expression:

THEOREM 1 (Church-Rosser I) If $e \overset{*}{\Longrightarrow} e_1$ and $e \overset{*}{\Longrightarrow} e_2$, then there exists an e_3 such that $e_1 \overset{*}{\Longrightarrow} e_3$ and $e_2 \overset{*}{\Longrightarrow} e_3$.

We've seen a number of different application strategies in this book: call-by-name, call-by-value, call-by-reference and so on. Each comes with its own set of advantages and disadvantages, but a program that uses call-by-name or lazy evaluation exclusively has the special property that it may terminate with a value in some cases where evaluation of the same program under another protocol diverges (that is, never terminates). On the other hand, a program that terminates under some other protocol is guaranteed to terminate with the same value under a call-by-name or lazy evaluation strategy. This property is stated in the following theorem; a "non-strict evaluation strategy" means, in general, a call-by-name or lazy evaluation strategy.

THEOREM 2 (Church-Rosser II) If $e \overset{*}{\Longrightarrow} e_1$ and e_1 is a value, then e_1 can be derived from e under a non-strict evaluation strategy.

The first Church-Rosser rule is pertinent to the issue of parallelism. It states that the subexpressions of a declarative program can be evaluated in any order, or in parallel. Of course, the character of the algorithm may constrain the extent to which parallel evaluation can actually take place. If our program computes the n values of a vector in such a way that the jth value is defined in terms of the $j-1^{st}$, we may start work on all n computations simultaneously (or in any order), but computation of the jth value will be unable to proceed until computation of the $j-1^{st}$ is complete. This kind of constraint is known as a "data dependency"; we discussed the same phenomenon in another context in the Fortran chapter. Except for the constraints imposed by data dependencies, all sub-expressions in a functional program may evaluate simultaneously.

Consider the following specification to compute the Fibonacci numbers written in Miranda:

```
fib 0      = 1
fib 1      = 1
fib (n+2)  = fib (n+1) + fib n
```

The application fib 10 is reduced to the applications fib 9 and fib 8; these two applications can be evaluated in parallel. Each of these applications in turn spawns two sub-applications; these applications evaluate in parallel with each other as well.

The effect is to build a tree of processes—the nodes in the tree represent the addition operators, and the leaves are either 0 or 1. The number of nodes in the tree is exponential in the Fibonacci number being computed, but all addition operators at a given level can evaluate in parallel. Note that parallelism occurs because the "+" operator is "strict" in its arguments: that is, it is known to require the value of both its arguments in order to yield a result. If a Miranda compiler can determine that an operator is strict in some argument, it can bypass the default lazy evaluation rule by having the argument and the body evaluate simultaneously.

The second Church-Rosser rule is in a sense, then, an impediment to parallelism. It states that if we are to be assured that a program's non-termination reflects its semantics and not merely the operational characteristics of the underlying interpreter, the interpreter should perform a minimal amount of work. Implementations of lazy-evaluation languages must work around this rule by trying to find expressions that are strict in their arguments; such expressions are candidates for parallelization. Naive implementations of lazy-evaluation languages often can't exploit much parallelism, precisely because of lazy evaluation.

Pure logic languages are also determinate (provided that the order of evaluation of clauses is fixed by the underlying interpreter). We could suitably rephrase the first Church-Rosser rule in terms of unification (rather than reduction) and thereby make it applicable to pure logic languages.

For example, given the clause

```
head :- t₁,t₂,...,tₙ.
```

written in pure Prolog, all of the t_i can be evaluated in parallel. This kind of parallelism is referred to as AND-parallelism—logically, the terms in the clause body are connected by "AND." Implementing AND-parallelism requires more than the simple creation of n processes: bindings established during the course of evaluating a term must be propagated to other terms in the body that may require it, and care must be taken to ensure that concurrently executing processes don't attempt simultaneously to bind a shared logical variable. If such constraints are obeyed, the final bindings yielded under an AND-parallel evaluation strategy are the same as they would be had the terms in the body been evaluated left-to-right.

Declarative languages are sometimes described as the ultimate parallel programming languages. In the same way that Fortran's restricted language model lends itself to the production of highly efficient vectorized object code, the prohibition of assignment and the absence of mutable objects in declarative programs should be conducive to effective implementation on parallel machines. A declarative program with n reducible applications is in effect a program with n parallel processes.

In practice, however, very little of the enormous progress in parallelism to date has involved these languages. The reasons are in part technical and in part conceptual. The goal in parallel programming is to run programs fast (by executing them on many processors at once). But declarative programs can be expensive in computing time, because (a) data structures often need to be copied to preserve referential transparency, (b) strictness analysis in lazy functional languages is a conservative optimization technique that often can't detect concurrently executable subexpressions, and (c) in the case of logic languages, the resolution process and the overhead introduced to synchronize access to shared variables can entail significant runtime cost.

These problems may well be overcome by continued research. The conceptual problem is more fundamental: there exists a large and growing body of explicitly parallel algorithms—algorithms conceived in terms of statements like "do the following n steps simultaneously." To make use of explicitly parallel algorithms, programmers need a way to express parallelism explicitly in their programs. The declarative languages discussed in this chapter are "implicitly parallel"—they may be executed on a parallel machine—but they don't allow programmers to state *explicitly* how parallelism is to be created and controlled. In the next chapter we turn to explicitly parallel languages.

8.4   Readings

Basic Readings. [125] is an introduction to Miranda. [79, 129] are good introductions to logic programming and Prolog.

Suggested Readings. Church's text on the lambda-calculus [27] is the foundational work for all functional languages. [10] is an encyclo-pedic reference to the topic. Landin's article on ISWIM [82] is an early reference that introduces many of the ideas found in modern functional languages. [14, 57] are introductory textbooks on functional program-ming.

The ML language is discussed in [94]; the classic paper on polymorphic type-inference is by Milner [95]. [19, 18] are very readable and compre-hensive introductions to polymorphic type-systems.

[73] gives a detailed survey of current implementations for lazy functional languages. [17] is a more concise alternative.

Functional languages need not necessarily be implemented using lazy evaluation. An alternative approach is to have all arguments to a func-tion be evaluated in parallel. Such an "eager evaluation" strategy leads to a programming model that is non-strict but not lazy. This model is best embodied in dataflow-based programming languages. [31] is a sur-vey of dataflow architectures; [99] describes Id, a programming language intended to be implemented on dataflow machines.

A good translation of Frege's original treatise on the predicate calculus can be found in [46]. Resolution as an operational semantics for a pro-gramming language was first described by Robinson in [108]. [88] is an introduction to the foundational issues in logic programming. [29] is an easy-to-read introduction to Prolog programming; [121] is a more com-prehensive text. [111, 112] discuss Concurrent Prolog, a Prolog-based parallel language.

8.5   Exercises

1. A declarative language program specifies a set of equations; an ISM program specifies a structure in computational space and time. There may be efficiency advantages in giving the programmer control over the space-time layout of his software machine—but are there any conceptual advantages? Is so, what are they?

2. Write a Simula 67 version of the "infinite data structure" that holds prime numbers discussed in the lazy-evaluation section. (Define a function that returns the next prime every time it's invoked.)

3. A curried boolean function of n arguments is called a tautology if it returns **true** for every one of its 2^n possible combinations of boolean arguments. Write a Miranda program called **taut** which takes as arguments a boolean function **f** and **f**'s arity n, and determines whether **f** is a tautology.

   ```
   yep a b c  = a or (not a);
   nope a b   = b
   taut yep 3   ===> true
   taut nope 2  ===> false
   ```

   What problems would you encounter in writing the same program in Prolog? In Scheme?

4. Consider adding a new ISM operation **fill** defined as follows: **fill(id,<some exp>)** drops the value yielded by evaluating **exp** into the region labeled **id**. **fill** differs from the assignment operator in requiring that **id** designate an empty region. (a) Is an ISM program containing **fill** (but no assignment statements) referentially transparent? Determinate? (b) Describe an alternative semantics for the ISM in which evaluation is based on resolution and unification. (Use the **fill** operator as a first step.) How does this new ISM semantics differ from Prolog's?

5. What does the following Prolog program do?

```
foo([],L,L).
foo(L,[],L).
foo([X|L1],[Y|L2],[X|L3]) :- X < Y, !,
                             foo(L1,[Y|L2],L3).
foo([X|L1],[Y|L2],[X,Y|L3]) :- X = Y, !,
                             foo(L1,L2,L3).
foo([X|L1],[Y|L2],[Y|L3]) :- Y < X, !,
                             foo([X|L1],L2,L3).
```

(a) Can you think of a more appropriate name than `foo`? (b) What role does the cut operator serve in the program?

6. Prolog's control strategy is based on depth-first search. But as we've seen, this strategy makes the order of appearance of facts and rules significant. Can you suggest another evaluation strategy that would avoid this problem? If yes, compare your strategy with Prolog's; if no, why not?

7. Recall the Miranda function to compute the Fibonacci numbers:

```
fib 0     = 1
fib 1     = 1
fib (n+2) = fib (n+1) + fib n
```

This solution is inefficient: its running time is exponential in the Fibonacci number being computed. (To compute `fib(n)` (n > 2), we'll need to compute `fib(n-2)` twice.) Can you suggest a way to make this program more efficient? (Hint: Consider using a table that stores previously computed results. The problem is to construct this table without using assignment statements.) Can you characterize the situations in which such a transformation is useful?

8. In Chapter 6 we discussed a Simula "histogram" class. Can you sketch a solution to the same problem in Miranda? In Prolog? What conclusions can you draw from this example about the expressivity of these languages?

9. (a) "Resolution is more expressive than reduction." True or false? (b) Consider the following syllogism:

- functions are a restricted kind of relation,

- functional languages use only functions, logic languages use only relations,

- Therefore, functional languages are a restricted (and less expressive) form of logic languages.

Is this conclusion a valid one? Explain. (c) Can you think of a class of applications for which Miranda would be better suited than Prolog? Explain.

10. On page 8.1.4, we gave a definition of a logic program to concatenate two lists:

```
append([], L, L).
append([X | L1], L2, [X | L3]) :-
                append(L1,L2,L3).
```

It's easy to write a similar function in Miranda:

```
append-M [] x  = x
append-M [a:x] y = [a:(append-M x y)]
```

The two solutions look similar, but note that in the Prolog program, we can evaluate

```
? :- append(L, M, [1,2,3]).
```

to compute all possible splits of the list [1,2,3]; we can't do the same in the Miranda version. (a) What is the fundamental reason for this difference? (b) Can you write a Miranda program to support this functionality? How does it compare with the Prolog version? What conclusions can you draw based on this example?

11. (a) Consider the following ISM program (assume that templates are treated as closures as described in Chapter 7)):

```
(f : template ()
       <   (x : *) &
           & (g : return(template (a, b)
                         <if a
                           then x := b
                           else x)) >
    & h : f ())
```

Assuming a Hindley-Milner polymorphic type-system, what should h's type be? (b) Based on the type you derived in part (a), would a compile-time type-error be raised for the following time-map expression?

```
(h(true & true);  h(false & 5) + 6)
```

(c) Would any runtime type-errors arise in this example? (d) Based on your answers to parts (b) and (c), what conclusions can you draw about the interaction of assignment statements and polymorphism?

12. (a) Why is the following Miranda expression *not* well-typed under a Hindley-Milner type system:

```
Y f = g g
      where g x = f (x x)
```

(Note: this function computes the least fixed-point of a function f.[2]) (b) Does this function have a meaningful well-defined type under another type discipline?

---

[2]A fixed-point of a function f is an element x such that $fx = x$; the least fixed-point is the "least" element for which this property holds on f where "least" is used in a domain-theoretic sense. Readers are referred to [110, 122] for details.

Appendix: Ideology and Engineering

Occasionally the student of programming languages stumbles upon positions that he can't fully account for under his ordinary assumptions.
For example, we discussed the design of CLU. We noted that the sort
of style it advocates is available within a less restrictive framework; a
language needn't *compel* some style in order to support it. The CLU
designers understand this. But it is their belief that

> ... Conventions are no substitute for enforced constraints [86,
> p.576].

This isn't a mere statement of fact, like "interpreters are no substitute
for compilers." It reads instead like the assertion of a strongly held
belief. Of course, there is nothing in the least wrong with basing a
language design on strong beliefs. Many brilliant designs originate in
mere intuition. It's not that we've uncovered a defect in the design of
CLU. But we have isolated an interesting and neglected facet of language
design. The CLU designers are willing to "weaken" their language, in the
sense of restricting or eliminating some aspect of earlier, related designs,
in the belief that this sacrifice will lead to something better down the
road. Our goal here is to understand in broader context the world-view
in which it is allowable (even desirable) to trade what *is* valuable for
what might *ultimately* be.

Declarative programming languages are a striking example of this phenomenon. These languages abolish modifiable state objects as conceptual entities. Now there is no doubt that such objects are obviously,
blatantly useful *sometimes*, at least; nor is there much disagreement
that in strictly practical (philistine, if you prefer) terms, the gains to
date from this abolition have been modest. It is an obvious fact, un-
contested even by declarative language purists, that you cannot make
a language more powerful simply by leaving features *out* (no matter
how displeasing those features may be). But the declarative programming community is ready to sacrifice what *is* valuable for what might
ultimately prove more valuable. Thus John Hughes [67], in describing
how functional languages are viewed by the outside community, writes
strikingly that

The functional programmer sounds rather like a medieval
monk, denying himself the pleasures of life in the hope that
it will make him virtuous.

There's nothing wrong with this kind of behavior, and it may even be
admirable and inspired. But this particular approach to problem solving
hardly originates with computer science, and we need to consider its
position in the wider context.

A final example: In 1978 the distinguished computer scientist Per Brinch
Hansen described a language called "Distributed Processes"—a parallel programming language of the sort we discuss in the next chapter.
In reflecting on the implications of his design and its future course of
development, Brinch Hansen remarks that

It may also be necessary to eliminate recursion in order to
simplify verification and implementation. [54, p.935]

Program verification is concerned with demonstrating by means of mathematical logic that a program's behavior is correctly described by some
set of "predicates." The predicates are designed to capture precisely
what a program is supposed to do. For example, if the program is designed to find the square root r of some number x within a tolerance of
ϵ, one predicate might state that

$$(r - \epsilon)^2 \leq x \leq (r + \epsilon)^2$$

Now, "implementation" is one thing—recursive languages are indeed
harder to implement than languages in which recursion is not allowed
(although the relevant techniques are well understood). "Verification" is
a different matter. At the time when Brinch Hansen wrote this sentence,
verification had achieved little in the way of worldly success. A negli-
gible proportion of working programs had been formally "verified"—a
fact that still holds true. *Recursion* on the other hand was a firmly
established programming technique of undisputed value.

In understanding the viewpoint that underlies these related approaches
to language design, a 1982 paper by James Morris is of great help. In a

volume of essays dedicated to the proposition that functional programming is a good idea, James Morris writes, not as a functional language
insider but as a sympathetic observer,

> Functional languages as a minority doctrine in the field of
> programming languages bear a certain resemblance to social-
> ism in its relation to conventional, capitalist doctrine. Their
> proponents are often brilliant intellectuals perceived to be
> radical and rather unrealistic by the mainstream, but little
> by little, changes are made in conventional languages and
> economies to incorporate features of the radical proposals.
> Of course this never satisfies the radicals, but it represents
> progress of a sort. [97, p.173]

Morris's view of history at large may or may not be sound, but the quotation's great value is the light it sheds on a central fact about functional
programming, and by extension on the assembly of related approaches
referred to above. Functional programming, it clearly suggests, is an
ideology. Like Marxism and innumerable other clever notions of the
intelligentsia over the years, it is an integrated, internally consistent
system of assertions and expectations. It's not intended to stand or fall
in the short term, on the basis of a few experiments or a couple of logical
objections. It is a prescription for radical development and change over
the long haul. So we must be patient with it.

To refer to these approaches as *ideologies* is neither to praise nor to
condemn them. The point is, once again, to make connections between
this narrow sub-field and its broader context. There's a great deal to
be said about ideologies and ideologues; they have been decisively important in modern intellectual history. Thus on the one hand, as Morris
points out, some ideologues have been brilliant. Ideas at first denounced
have sometimes proven visionary in retrospect. Undoubtedly we make a
mistake to dismiss these systems unthinkingly or too fast. But we make
an equally serious mistake to ignore the darker side of this intellectual
tendency. The philosopher Robert Nisbet notes that "[t]he single most
revealing and frightening thing about an ideology is its immunity, once
it has begun to grow on its own psychological nutrients, to the voice of
experience and concrete reality. [100, p.183]"

In pursuing the attempt to place programming languages in context, there's one more significant datum we should mention. We've discussed a number of approaches that seem to partake of the ideological. It's particularly interesting that—furthermore—all these ideologies seem to lean in roughly the same direction.

The researchers we've mentioned tend to agree that it's important for the field to become more formal, more rigorous, to rely as fully as possible on mathematics. CLU was designed in part as a vehicle for the exploration of various formal program-specification techniques or "specification logics." (CLU was contemporary with several other languages also designed primarily with formal specification techniques in mind— Alphard [113] and Euclid [104] are two good examples.) Program verification consists of the application to software development of simple proof techniques from mathematical logic. From within the functional programming community, David Turner writes sternly of "conventional programming languages" that "they have broken the basic ground rules of mathematical notation. [126]" This mathematics tendency isn't limited to the few instances we've cited; C.A.R. Hoare, one of the most influential of all language designers, asserts with several colleagues in a paper on the *Laws of Programming* that "programs, as well as their specifications, are mathematical expressions. . . . [60, p.686]"

Many students of programming languages are unaware that this impulse —to reject intuitive strategies based on physical models, to go forward on the basis of rigorous theory instead—has been important *and* controversial in other technical fields as well. Billington discusses the long-standing disagreement among structural engineers on a related issue— should bridge designers be constrained by the limits of available mathematical analysis techniques, or should they view their field in terms of a harder-to-define mixture of analysis, experience and a sense of form? He writes that the emphasis placed by the Germans on analysis in the late nineteenth century "drew them away from forms for which they had no calculations, and thus narrowed the range of structural possibilities. [13, p.157]" He notes that in the U.S. of the 1930s, engineers were "led away from the possibilities for new forms" involving deck-stiffened arches by the complexity of their analytic models; "The result was an arrested growth in structural art for American concrete bridges. . . . [13, p.163]" He writes that "The fact that these works need not—indeed, in some cases should not—be based on general theories is apparent from concrete studies in the history of technology. [13, p.10]" Feynman and his co-authors write as follows in the celebrated *Feynman Lectures on Physics*: "Anyone who wants to analyze the properties of matter in a real problem might want to start by writing down the fundamental equations and then try to solve them mathematically...." But this is not Feynman's approach; "the real successes come to those who start from a *physical* point of view.... [45, Vol.1, 39.2]"

The analogies here are loose, but that doesn't make them uninteresting. Whether mathematical techniques are a guiding light or merely one useful tool is a question that has surfaced repeatedly in the history of science and engineering. Students of programming languages are right to resist drawing conclusions about their own field based on approximate analogies, but naive to assume (as they so often do) that computer science exists in an intellectual vacuum.

9 Parallel Languages

9.1 The Problem

The task of writing parallel programs—programs that do many things simultaneously—imposes new language requirements: we need to *create* and to *coordinate* multiple processes. What does this mean? A process represents a thread of control, an independent program counter. For the most part, the languages we have examined have been intended for creating single-process programs, programs in which there is no concurrent execution. A language for parallel programming must give users some way to create multiple processes: broadly speaking, to write statements like "do the following n things simultaneously: $Thing_1$, $Thing_2$, ..., $Thing_n$."

Merely to create many simultaneous activities isn't sufficient, though. A useful parallel language must allow simultaneous processes to *coordinate* their activities: specifically, it must allow them to *communicate* data among themselves, and to *synchronize* with each other. One process may develop a result that some other process needs (hence the two must communicate). An algorithm may require that all processes in some group complete step n before any one of them proceeds to step $n + 1$ (hence the need to synchronize). Communication and synchronization are required in a wide variety of other circumstances as well, as we will discuss.

Of the languages we've described, PL/I, Algol 68 and Ada support the creation of multiple processes. Ada alone supplies a complete, general-purpose strategy for *coordination* among processes. The ISM model is highly concurrent—it calls for simultaneous evaluation in a wide variety of cases. But the ISM model doesn't provide the mechanisms we need for *coordination*: we must provide coordination as an "added feature" when we use the ISM to model parallel programs. In this chapter, we focus on two new and different languages, Occam and Linda. But before we introduce these two, we need to address several general questions.

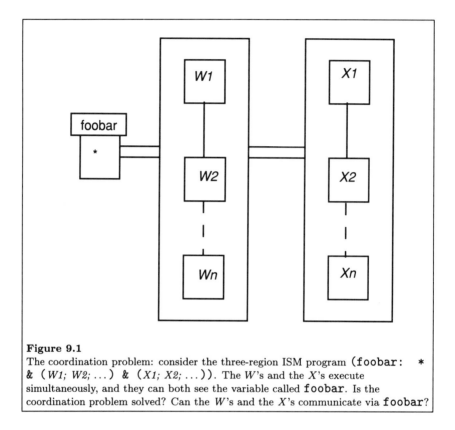

Figure 9.1
The coordination problem: consider the three-region ISM program (foobar: *
& (W1; W2; ...) & (X1; X2; ...)). The W's and the X's execute
simultaneously, and they can both see the variable called foobar. Is the
coordination problem solved? Can the W's and the X's communicate via foobar?

9.1.1   Coordination

We've said that the ISM doesn't support coordination. But clearly the
concurrent threads of an ISM program can communicate with each other
if they choose—if they share access to the same variable, one process can
assign a value to the variable, and the second can read the variable.

Such shared access constitutes communication between processes; does
it solve the coordination problem?

The answer is no: communication via shared variable is not a safe,
effective approach to coordination. The reason why is implicit in a
slightly more complete definition of the key term:

Coordination entails communication and synchronization between *asynchronous* processes.

Two processes are *asynchronous* when each executes at its own rate (in
effect, under the control of its own program counter). It follows—and
this is the key point—that two concurrent, asynchronous processes can't
make predictions about each other's current state.

To expand on the simple example: suppose that the *W*'s and the *X*'s
use `foobar` as a mail-drop for communicating values back and forth.
They both compute for a while, and then the *W*'s need to send a value
to the *X*'s. Accordingly, a *W*-statement assigns a value to `foobar`, and
the *X*'s simply look at `foobar` when they need to know what the value
is. Another computational phase follows, and at the end of this phase
the *X*'s need to send a value to the *W*'s; an *X*-statement simply assigns
the value to `foobar`. Then the whole process repeats. In short,

phase 1

W's compute   *X*'s compute
`foobar := `*something*;

phase 2

W's compute   *X*'s compute
                                     `foobar := `*something*;

phase 1′

W's compute   *X*'s compute
`foobar := `*something*;
...

Will this work? Clearly not. Suppose the *W*'s are faster than the *X*'s.
They assign a value to `foobar` at the end of phase 1, then race through
phase 2 and check `foobar` again: they expect to see a new value put
there by the *X*'s. But if the *X*'s are still slogging through phase 2, the
W's simply re-read their *own* `foobar` value. Suppose this happens, and
that the *W*'s then proceed erroneously onward, repeating phase 1. If
the *X*'s finish their own first swing through phase 2 when the *W*'s finish

their repetition of phase 1, both the W's and the X's try to write a new value to foobar simultaneously, with unpredictable results. (This unpredictability is significant especially if foobar is a complex structure like an array. At the end of this dual assignment, some entries of foobar might reflect X's values while some reflect W's.)

The result is a mess, and the problem isn't simple to fix. We could use two versions of foobar, one to be written only by the W's and the other only by the X's, but this doesn't solve the problem. The W's can't write a new value until such time as the previous one has been read by the X's—but how can they tell when that time has been reached?

We could continue to contemplate problems and fixes, but the message should be clear. Safe and convenient coordination will probably require a mechanism above and beyond ordinary variables. Dijkstra supplied such a mechanism when he invented the *semaphore* in the late sixties; semaphores are a type of "protection variable" that can be used in combination with ordinary foobar-type shared variables in order to get safe coordination. Many contemporary approaches to coordination derive from Dijkstra's semaphores. Other approaches do things differently: they abolish shared variables like foobar, and allow concurrent processes to communicate only by sending each other messages. Message-passing can be used when two processes are running on separate computers that don't share memory, but semaphores cannot. Shared variables, on the other hand, whether or not they are protected by semaphores, can only be used by two processes that do share access to one slice of memory. (We explain the significance of this distinction in the next section.) Tuple spaces are another coordination strategy we'll discuss in this chapter; they combine aspects of shared variables and of messages. The point, at any rate, is that we can't solve the parallel programming problem merely by introducing concurrency; we will need special mechanisms for coordination as well.

9.1.2 Concurrent, Distributed, Parallel

The phenomenon of one program composed of many coordinated processes—we'll refer to the topic in general as *coordinated programming*—occurs in a variety of settings.

Multi-process programs may be designed for conventional single-processor machines: a process scheduler takes charge of sharing the single processor among waiting processes, and all processes proceed together (one process running for a while, then the next process and so on), as in any time-shared or multi-programmed operating system. coordinated programming for single-processor machines arises mainly in the context of systems programming: many operating systems depend on a collection of concurrent processes. In fact, coordination came to the fore as a language design issue specifically in the context of *languages designed for building operating systems*: if you intend to build an operating system entirely within a high-level language model, and your operating system is conceived in terms of multiple processes, your programming language must support multiple processes. PL/I was an early example; Hoare's work on monitors [63], Brinch Hansen's on Concurrent Pascal [55] and Wirth's on Modula [135] emerged during a period in which considerable attention was devoted to this issue.

Languages for concurrent operating system programming must fulfill, in essence, exactly the criteria discussed above: they must support the creation and coordination of multiple processes. But these requirements can be addressed within a fairly narrow framework. Since all processes execute on one machine, they can be assumed to have access to the same set of addresses (*i.e.*, to the same address space); some kind of shared-variable communication scheme will be adequate. Furthermore, the fact that no two processes would ever be active simultaneously was sometimes relied on as a simplifying assumption in handling certain synchronization questions.

Nomenclature is somewhat confused at present, but we'll use terms in such a way as to reflect at least a modicum of consensus. We refer to this first kind of coordinated programming as *concurrent* programming, reflecting the widespread use of this term in the relevant papers (and in languages like "Concurrent Pascal").

(Today, most operating systems in fact use high-level languages rather than assembly code—but they don't use concurrent languages of the sort we've described. Instead, the operating system designers themselves define a set of process-creation and coordination operators, and then implement these operators using a standard, non-concurrent language and—probably—some assembly code. The operating system can draw on these operations in the same way it relies on other programmer-implemented routines.)

Coordinated programs may also be designed to solve compute-intensive problems quickly by executing on many processors simultaneously; we refer to these as *parallel programs*. Parallel programs can execute on multi-computers or on networks. A multi-computer is a single machine incorporating many sub-computers; a network is a collection of wired-together autonomous machines.

Networks aren't ordinarily designed for parallel computing; machines are inter-connected so that they can exchange files and mail, share devices like printers and file-storage facilities, and give their users remote log-in access to computers beyond their home base. But once we have gone to the trouble of inter-connecting a bunch of computers, it's clear that (in principle) we might focus the entire collection on one hard problem. Today few networks are routinely used in this way. In future many or most will be. Typically, parallel programs executed on networks run at night, when relatively few nodes are in use, or they run during normal hours on nodes that happen to be idle or computationally under-employed.

Multi-computers have been around since the mid-1960s; they were intended originally to improve turnaround and response time in large multi-user settings, by allowing several user jobs to execute at once on several different processors. Since the early 1980s, a new generation of multi-computer has been designed specifically to support parallel programs. These computers typically encompass on the order of ten sub-computers, although a fair number incorporate on the order of a hundred, and commercial machines exist that encompass more than a thousand general-purpose sub-processors. These machines fall into two sub-categories: in *shared memory machines*, processors share access to a common memory; *distributed memory machines* resemble networks: computers are wired together without sharing any memory in common.

Languages for parallelism face a basic choice. If they provide a coordination model based on ordinary shared variables, they'll be appropriate for one kind of parallel machine only (namely for shared-memory machines), and they won't work on networks. But "message passing," which is the obvious approach to communication in the absence of shared memory, has been criticized as a difficult and non-intuitive programming technique. We pursue these questions further in the discussions following.

Finally, *distributed programs* are coordinated programs that are intended to cope with a physically dispersed environment. In writing systems-level software for networks—file systems, distributed database systems, mailers—we might want a programming language that supports (again) the creation and coordination of multiple processes. The language requirements here are similar to those for parallelism—but communication *must* be suited to a non-shared-memory environment, and issues like reliability and security may be particularly important in designing (or at any rate, implementing) appropriate language constructs.

Our focus here is on *parallel programming*, but many of the issues we discuss will apply equally to concurrent and to distributed programming.

9.1.3 Is This a Language Design Problem?

Are coordination and process-creation proper topics for programming language design? In fact, we can support parallel programming without addressing language design issues at all: we simply provide *operating system routines* to handle process creation and coordination. Users program in any conventional language; they create and coordinate processes by invoking external procedures supplied in utility libraries or the operating system. For example, the Unix[1] operating system supplies a routine called *fork*. *Fork* creates new processes by cloning the process that invokes it—reproducing it identically, leaving two processes where there used to be one. *Fork* isn't part of a programming language; it's an operating system service that any program can draw upon. Unix (and most other operating systems) provide routines that allow processes to coordinate with each other as well. So why bother with parallel *languages*?

It's generally agreed that the process-creation and coordination services supplied by operating systems are too crude to be a good basis for parallel programming. These system calls are ordinarily *terra incognita* to the compiler or interpreter that handles the user's program. Hence their syntax may be messy and poorly integrated with the rest of the program, they can't be checked for errors in a uniform way, debugging and

---

[1] "Unix" is a registered trademark of AT&T Bell Laboratories.

tracing information can't be gathered at compile-time, and no compile-time optimizations are possible. The lack of assistance from the compiler implies not only syntactic crudeness but, to a certain degree, semantic crudeness as well. The lack of compiler optimization makes it harder to provide operations that perform complex or sophisticated functions efficiently.

For all these reasons, the necessity for language-level parallelism is now generally—if still not universally—conceded.

9.1.4   The Two Basic Approaches: Programming Languages vs. Coordination Languages

Once we've accepted the importance of language-level support for parallelism, the next step seems obvious: design new programming languages to provide this kind of support. We will examine one language that embodies this approach.

However, there is another radically different possibility as well. We can embody our process-creation and coordination tools in a separate language of their own, a language we'll call a *coordination language*. If we combine a standard *non*-parallel language with a coordination language, the result is a hybrid that can be used to write parallel programs. (We refer to the standard, non-parallel language as the *computing language*. In other words, we get a complete parallel language by combining a computing language with a coordination language.) We use the computing language to specify the activities to be carried out by each process; we use the coordination language to write the "stage directions" that create an ensemble of concurrent processes and glue them together into an integrated program.

The advantages of the first approach are clear. We get a single integrated language; we don't need to worry about choosing tools from two separate toolboxes. This integrated-language approach has dominated research on parallel languages.

Interest in parallel languages reaches back at least to the era of PL/I and Algol 68; the "modern era," however, begins with a 1978 paper by C.A.R. Hoare called *"Communicating Sequential Processes"* [62]. (The modern era corresponds roughly to the maturity of the semiconductor revolution. By 1978 it was clear that large-scale integration spelled the end of the expensive central processor. Henceforth there would be no practical impediment to parallel computers incorporating large numbers of sub-processors.) Hoare's paper didn't present a complete language design, but it seemed like a good basis for a complete parallel language. Occam[2] [89], designed by David May and his colleagues at the English company Inmos, represents the embodiment of Hoare's ideas in an integrated parallel language. Many other integrated designs followed, but Occam remains one of the most influential.

The second approach, centering on the use of coordination languages, also has advantages. Some of these are pragmatic; others are conceptual, and rather subtle. The pragmatic points center on the fact that coordination languages enhance existing languages instead of replacing them. Many significant, related advantages follow. Programmers aren't required to learn entirely new languages. Furthermore, existing serial (*i.e.*, *non*-parallel) programs can be converted for use in parallel environments with a minimum of gratuitous rewriting. Experience to date suggests that many compute-intensive serial applications can be converted for parallelism at relatively low cost in terms of new code. The parallel version winds up looking mostly the same as the serial version; only the top-level superstructure changes. Use of a coordination language means that we can preserve as much as possible of the old program (assuming, of course, that if the old program is written in language X, we use $X +$ *some coordination language* as our new parallel programming vehicle). If we'd switched to an entirely new parallel language, we'd have had to toss out every line of every existing serial application in the transition to parallelism.

In principle, a single coordination language can be combined with many different serial languages, allowing us to recoup our investment in coordination-language implementation and tool-building within many different environments. Also, the fact that one coordination language can be combined with many serial computing languages suggests that *heterogeneous* applications—programs whose components are written in many computing languages—should be convenient to build. The coordination language is glue that binds the whole thing into an integrated whole.

---

[2] "Occam" is a registered trademark of Inmos Ltd.

There are conceptual advantages to the coordination-language idea as well. These languages promote "coordination" to the same status as the older, simpler and seemingly more fundamental idea of "computation." The promotion is long overdue.

We might be tempted to believe that computation languages are useful by themselves, while coordination languages can only be useful when they are combined with computation languages—making computation the more "fundamental" member of the pair. But it becomes clear upon reflection that computation languages are useful "by themselves" only in a special and limited sense. We need to get data into and out of a program; most programs read and write files. Both activities are examples of coordination as opposed to computation: they require a rendezvous between two separate, asynchronous activities. (One of these "activities" may be a person.) To pass data back and forth from outside the computer to inside requires, in the simplest possible case, a mechanism whereby users can load values into a register or memory; meanwhile, the computer will be spinning, awaiting a signal to proceed. This transaction itself relies on a primitive, minimal coordination language (whose operators might be "type a character at the terminal," "spin awaiting keyboard buffer full" and so on).

In effect, an operating system defines a coordination language for the use of the processes it supports. The operating system supports coordination of applications programs with the external user, with the devices that implement the file system, with system-level utility processes that may implement a scheduling or memory management policy or provide a mail service, with other user processes executing concurrently. This "language" is realized as an *ad hoc* collection of services—buffered device interfaces, data exchange through semaphore-protected system tables and so on. There's nothing wrong with this shaggy collection in practice, but *conceptually*, it adds up to a coordination language, and all these lifelines that tie a user process to its environment could in principle be implemented using a single integrated coordination language.

Linda[3] is a coordination language. There are other coordination languages as well; Dongarra and Sorensen's Schedule [39] is a particularly significant example. However, integrated parallel languages are

---

[3] "Linda" is a registered trademark of Scientific Computing Associates.

considerably more widespread than coordination languages in the research literature.

9.2   Occam and Linda

Occam is an unusual language insofar as it was designed in tandem with a particular computer, and remains closely associated with that computer. The Inmos *Transputer* is a family of processors designed specifically as building blocks for parallel machines. Each Transputer comes equipped with four link-ports; using these ports, we can assemble Transputers into multi-computer ensembles. The only constraint on network design is the obvious one: each Transputer in the ensemble can have only four neighbors. Beyond that, we can build an ensemble of any size and shape we choose.

Although in principle Occam should be an easy language to implement on almost any multi-computer, few implementations exist for other machines. Occam has been a widely used language nonetheless, because the Transputer itself has been a popular machine, especially in Europe. Transputers have been fast processors; and the Inmos approach to multi-computer architecture—buy as many processors as you want, and hook them together—has an obvious and appealing simplicity.

Linda was first described by Gelernter in 1982 [50]; the first successful implementation was reported by Carriero and Gelernter in 1985 [21]. The language has since been implemented on a wide range of shared- and distributed-memory multi-computers, and on several types of network. Linda is a focus for a wide range of research projects at many sites, and for commercial development both at software and at hardware companies.

9.3   CSP and Occam Profile

9.3.1   CSP

Hoare's 1978 language fragment came to be known as CSP. Occam was derived from and strongly resembles it, but the basic ideas in Occam show up in their simplest and "purest" form in CSP. (CSP represents the design studio's glossy concept car, Occam the slightly less daring production version, so to speak.) Accordingly, we start with a discussion of CSP, then turn to Occam and consider the ways in which the CSP approach was altered in the process of defining a complete language.

Process creation. Processes are created by listing process specifications as elements of a single "execute in parallel" statement, a so-called "parallel command." We write

$$[\quad Process_1 \quad || \quad Process_2 \quad || \quad ... \quad || \quad Process_n \quad]$$

Hoare develops the solution to the following simple problem as an example: "Read a sequence of cards of 80 characters each, and print the characters on a lineprinter at 125 characters per line. Every card should be followed by an extra space, and the last line should be completed with extra spaces if necessary. [62, p.670]" (The quaint references to old-time devices like punched cards and lineprinters date the passage to some extent.) Hoare gives the following CSP solution:

```
[west:: DISASSEMBLE || X:: COPY || east:: ASSEMBLE]
```

The uppercase names refer to code fragments that must be substituted in place. This is merely a sketch of the complete solution; the general intent is as follows. Three processes are created, named west, X and east; the three run simultaneously. The process named west reads the images of punched cards and disassembles each image into a stream of characters. Process X reads these characters and sends them onward, one by one, to the process named east. East formats the characters into 125-character lines, and sends them to the lineprinter.

Coordination. CSP supports process coordination with two basic operations, the *input* and the *output* commands. These commands implement a special form of message-exchange.

First, let's consider the general idea of message passing as a programming concept. Suppose two processes need to exchange information, but they don't have access to shared memory—hence, they can't rely on shared variables to mediate data exchange. What they can do instead is send messages back and forth. A *message* is a collection of data values lobbed from one memory or address space into another.

A message transaction involves two separate activities. When process Q has some data for process R, Q executes a *send message* operation of some kind. (The details depend on the version of message passing we're using.) When process R needs to receive data from some other process, it executes a *receive message* operation. In principle, these two operations are independent and unsynchronized: if Q *sends* a message before R chooses to *receive* one, R will find a message waiting for it (in its mailbox, so to speak) when it executes its *receive message*. R may also attempt to *receive* a message before one has been sent. It will find its "mailbox" empty. It might wander off to resume what it had been doing, and check the mailbox again later; or it might be obliged, either by the programming language (as in Ada) or by the logic of the algorithm, to wait hopefully at the mailbox (to suspend execution for the time being) until a message arrives.

An aside: note that regardless of the details, the operation we've described is markedly different from the "message passing" that occurs in Smalltalk. The operation we've described is *symmetric* and *asynchronous*. Sending a message does not (as in Smalltalk) imply receiving a response; hence two communicating processes must *each* send and receive messages. In Smalltalk, the object serving as the message "recipient" gets the message automatically. In "true" message passing, the recipient must explicitly choose to receive a message, because it is an independently executing entity.

Having described the mechanism in general, we turn to CSP's version— which happens to be a highly idiosyncratic one. Suppose Q needs to send R a message consisting of the current value of the variable `foobar`. Q must execute the "output command"

> `R ! foobar`

R executes the matching "input command"

> `Q ? bazball`

Bazball is a variable of the same type as `foobar`; after the message exchange is complete, `bazball` is bound to the value in the message (*i.e.*, to the value of R's variable `foobar`). Message exchange in CSP is *synchronous*: when Q reaches its output command, it can't merely send the message and proceed; *it must wait until R reaches its matching input command.* If R reaches the input command first, R likewise stops and waits until Q has reached its matching output command. When Q and R have *both* paused at the appropriate command, the message containing foobar's value is transferred from Q to R, whereupon both processes can proceed.

Thus, the *copy* process referred to in the example above repeatedly executes the operation

    west ? c

followed by the operation

    east ! c

where c is a local variable of type *character*. The first operation results in the transfer of a message *from* the process named west (the value received is bound to the variable c); the second operation transfers a message *to* the process named east (the message consists of the current value of c).

Guards. To complete the picture of CSP-style coordination, we need to reexamine the guarded command, a topic introduced in our discussion of Miranda.

Guards were introduced by Dijkstra [38] in a context unconnected with parallelism; they form the basis for a kind of "symmetrical, non-deterministic" conditional statement. A guarded statement consists of a series of guarded commands, each of the form

> *Guard* → *Command List*

The *Guard* is an expression that must yield a truth value; the *Command List* is eligible for execution if and only if the *Guard* yields *true*. Given a collection of guarded commands, *some* command list whose guard yields *true* will be executed. If many guards yield *true*, the choice of which command list to execute is arbitrary, or in other words *non-deterministic*. A choice is said to be *non-deterministic* when the programmer can't determine which choice will be made—the implementation, not the programmer, makes the decision. (Recall that guarded equations in Miranda have roughly the same definition, *except* that there is no non-determinism involved: the set of related guarded equations in Miranda program are evaluated top-down.)

Dijkstra's guards have seen their most widespread use in precisely the role to which Hoare adapted them in his CSP design—as a kind of stoplight for message traffic in parallel programs. The basic problem is the following: some process in a coordinated program might be capable of performing a variety of services. In a typical and often-discussed case, a process may provide a buffering service; it's capable of accepting two kinds of requests, "put something in the buffer" and "get something from the buffer."[4] Now: although a process may *in general* be capable of responding to different sorts of request (*i.e.*, both to *put* and to *get* requests in the case of the buffer), there are *particular times* when it *can't* do something or other. If the buffer is full, a buffering process can't respond to a *put* request; if the buffer is empty, it can't respond to a *get*. CSP uses guards to ensure that messages don't arrive at awkward times. Using guards, a process can guarantee that it only gets the messages it's capable of responding to at any particular time.

CSP's input guards are most important in the context of the "repetitive command." A repetitive command takes the form

$$
\begin{aligned}
*[G_1 &\rightarrow CL_1 \; [] \\
G_2 &\rightarrow CL_2 \; [] \\
&\vdots \\
G_n &\rightarrow CL_n \;]
\end{aligned}
$$

The G's are guards and the CL's are matching command lists. The repetitive command executes as a series of iterations. On each iteration, we execute some command list whose guard is *true*. "*Some* command" means any eligible command, where the choice again is non-deterministic. However, non-determinism should be implemented in a

---

[4]This example points to the underlying reason for the existence of such multiple-service processes: a data structure like a buffer may be manipulable in many ways. Message-passing models don't ordinarily allow many processes to share access to a single structure, because they assume that processes run in separate address spaces. Hence, every operation that can be performed on some data structure must be performed by a *single* process; hence one process is called upon to respond to a variety of different request types. The analogy to data systems and abstract data types should be clear.

reasonable or "fair" way, meaning that no eligible command should be repeatedly passed over. When an iteration is reached at which all guards prove to be *false*, the repetitive command terminates (and execution proceeds to the next statement following).

One final important detail: a guard may consist of a series of separate expressions (they are evaluated left to right, and the guard is *true* only if every constituent expression is *true*); the last element in the series may be an input command. If a matching output command happens to be outstanding when the guard is evaluated, the input command is considered to yield *true*. Should this guard's command list be chosen for execution, the first action to take place will be a message transfer to the input command in the guard. If (on the other hand) the process named by the input command in the guard has terminated, the input command yields *false*. If neither condition holds—there is no message waiting, but the process responsible for generating the message hasn't terminated, and accordingly might still generate one in future—we can't determine the truth or falsity of the guard as a whole.

This sounds complicated, but it's fairly simple in practice. Consider CSP's version of the buffer process we discussed above, from [62]:

```
X:: buffer:(0..9) portion;
    in,out:integer;
    in := 0; out := 0;
    *[in < out + 10;  producer ? buffer(in mod 10) →
          in := in + 1 []
       out < in; consumer ? more() →
          consumer ! buffer(out mod 10);
          out := out + 1 ]
```

The buffer process is named X. It communicates with two other processes, named producer and consumer. The buffer is a 10-element array whose components are of type portion (which is defined elsewhere). The first command list in the repetitive statement is eligible for execution if (1) in < out + 10, meaning that there is room in the 10-element buffer, *and* (2) the process named producer is waiting with a message, consisting of a new portion to be buffered. The second command list is eligible if (1) the buffer is non-empty, and (2) the consumer process has sent a request for data. The input command

```
consumer ? more()
```

expects to receive not a data value but merely a "signal"—in effect an empty message, indicating a "more data" request.

Note the roles played by the guards. If there are no empty slots in the buffer, the buffer process refuses to receive *put* requests (which it can't act on anyway); if there are no full slots, it refuses *get* requests.

What is the point of non-determinism? Why allow the implementation to make a choice, instead of telling it what to do? The intent should be clear from this buffering example. If one guard but not the other yields *true*, the right course of action is clear. If they *both* yield *true*, that's because (1) the producer and consumer are both asking for service, and (2) there's no reason why either request can't be satisfied. Non-determinism in this case means "do whatever you want—either course of action is correct; don't bother me with the details."

9.3.2 Occam

Occam differs substantially from CSP in detail, but its basic approach to coordination—to creating processes and to inter-process communication—is largely the same. Our description is based on Occam 2 [69], the latest revision of the original language [89].

The most significant difference between CSP and Occam centers on the use of *channels* rather than process names for communication. A channel corresponds to a one-way stream of data connecting two processes. Occam output commands send values along some channel; input commands receive values from a channel. Suppose process Q must send a value to process R. In CSP, Q executes R ! value and R executes Q ? var.

In Occam, we declare a *channel* which Q and R *both* cite: if the channel is named foobar, Q can execute

```
foobar ! value
```

and R executes

```
foobar ? var
```

This difference in approach is important. In CSP, message operations designate *particular processes*. Thus, it is impossible to write a library routine whose mission is to receive input from whichever sending process is appropriate; the identity of the sending process must be *part of the routine's code*—must appear in every receive-message operation. In Occam, the corresponding routine receives messages from a channel rather than a particular process, and channels may be parameters in process-describing templates. Thus, we can write a utility routine in the form of a process template that receives requests along a channel called foobar; we bind foobar to the appropriate *actual* channel when we build some particular application. (Note that it remains impossible in Occam, as it was in CSP, to write a utility routine that is capable of receiving a request from *any* process that chooses to make contact; the Occam routine we've discussed must designate some particular channel, and for the life of any program that channel's other end will be tied to *one* particular process.)

Channels are governed by *protocols*, which specify the types of messages that may be conveyed over the channel. Protocols may be fairly complicated: a channel may transmit unit objects of some base type (integers or bytes, for example), or it may transmit fixed or varying-length arrays, or sequences of values (each message consisting of a real followed by an integer, for example), or it may choose one format from a pre-defined collection of possibilities.

Occam retains CSP's guards, and provides versions of CSP's message-based control structures. In most cases, CSP's unusually elegant and concise syntax is replaced by more conventional, keyword-based forms: thus, PAR to introduce a list of statements to be executed in parallel, WHILE to build loops, and so on. Occam adds a series of constructs adapted to the new protocol-based communication style. It's possible, for example, to choose a statement for execution based on the type of the message just received over a channel governed by a choose-one-from-the-collection protocol.

After building and debugging a program, Occam programmers face an interesting and rather idiosyncratic last step in the program-development process: they must write a *configuration description* that specifies the correspondence between the processes and channels in a *program* and the processors and links of the *multi-computer* (specifically, the Transputer ensemble) on which the program will execute. In a special language provided for this purpose (see [69]), the configuration description specifies the location of every process in the program (*i.e.*, which processor it will run on) and the location of every channel (*i.e.*, which physical inter-process link it will correspond to). Many processes may share a single processor, but the Transputer architecture imposes a limitation on the shape of Occam programs: the processes assigned to any given processor must share no more than four channels to the rest of the program among them.

9.4   Linda

As we've noted, Linda is a model of coordination that is independent of base "computing language." It includes exactly what's necessary to create and to coordinate multiple processes, and no more; the manner in which these processes go about their work is irrelevant from Linda's point of view. Clearly, Linda must be used in conjunction with some computing language; it's not a self-sufficient programming model in itself. Most Linda development has taken place in the context of C as a base computing language, and we will assume this particular hybrid ("C.Linda," so-called) in the discussion. Linda itself has been added to a variety of other base languages, however.

9.4.1   C

C [74] itself is a language that in most respects resembles Pascal. It's a larger and more complicated language than Pascal, and richer in the range of choices it offers the programmer. It qualifies nonetheless as a fairly small and simple language. C was developed by Dennis Ritchie and his colleagues at AT&T Bell Labs in the course of their work on the celebrated Unix operating system. It was based on an earlier language called (you guessed it) *B*, which was based in turn on a curious but powerful language called BCPL [107]. BCPL had been developed by Martin Richards as a language for compiler writing and systems programming.

C is today an immensely popular and widespread language. Although such things are difficult to gauge, the chances are that it had surpassed

Pascal in popularity by the early 1980s, and that it is today the most popular, most widely used and (in the United States, at least) most widely taught derivative of Algol 60 extant. Its popularity is based on its simplicity and power, and on the wide availability of efficient and portable implementations.

If C is such a marvelous and highly esteemed programming language, why isn't there a chapter about C in this book? Although C is a graceful and effective synthesis of available language ideas, it isn't an innovative or path-breaking design and didn't intend to be. A C programmer who reads this book will be able to trace most of C's features back to their sources in the language designs of the 1960s.

9.4.2   Tuple Spaces

Linda's coordination mechanism is based on an idiosyncratic kind of memory called a "tuple space". To *create* multiple processes, a Linda program adds so-called "live tuples" to tuple space: a Linda program encompassing fifty simultaneously active processes consists of fifty live tuples floating in tuple space. Processes *coordinate* with each other by adding "passive tuples" to tuple space, which can then be examined or removed by other processes. We explain below.

Note first, though, that a tuple space is a different kind of computational landscape from the others we've discussed in this book. When we use the ISM to model a program in some language, we assume that the machine we are building is created at a certain time on behalf of a certain user, that it performs its computation and then disappears. A tuple space is, in concept, a more inclusive and longer-lasting structure. A tuple space is assumed to contain many independent computations. These separate computations communicate with each other, because collectively they are assumed to define a single coordinated application. But in principle these computations might have been created by many separate users; the tuple space itself may have existed before the creation of any process it now contains, and may persist after all of its current inhabitants have terminated. In short, the relationship between the tuple space idea and the ISM model is shown in figure 9.2: we can think of a tuple space as containing many simultaneously executing, independent ISMs floating around inside.

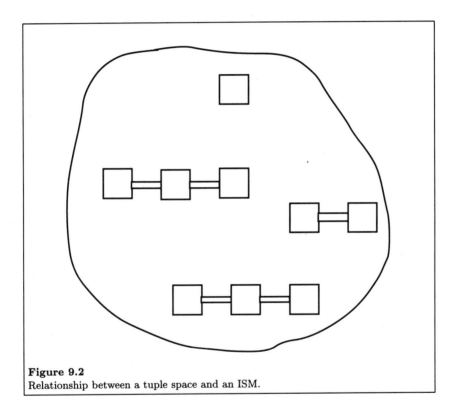

Figure 9.2
Relationship between a tuple space and an ISM.

Tuple Space Operations. There are four basic tuple space operations
(out, in, rd and eval) and two variant forms (inp and rdp). These
operations are defined over "tuples" and "anti-tuples." A tuple is a
series of typed fields, for example,

("a string", 15.01, 17, "another string")

or (0, 1). The field types allowed in a tuple depend on the base language; in C.Linda the values in a tuple may be numbers (within C's
basic numerical types), characters, arrays (including character strings)
or structs. (A C "struct" is like a Pascal record.) An anti-tuple
is the same, except that zero or more of its fields may be "formal
parameters"—typed variables whose significance is explained below.[5]

out(t) causes tuple t to be added to tuple space; the executing process
continues immediately. in(s) causes some tuple t that matches anti-
tuple s to be withdrawn from tuple space; the values of the actuals in t
are assigned to the formals in s, and the executing process continues. A
tuple t matches an anti-tuple s when t and s have the same number of
elements, all corresponding elements have the same type, a value in one
is matched by an identical value or by a type-consonant formal in the
other, and a formal in one is matched by a type-consonant value in the
other. If no matching t is available when in(s) executes, the executing
process suspends until one is available, then proceeds as before. If many
matching t's are available, one is chosen arbitrarily.

rd(s) is the same as in(s), with actuals assigned to formals as before,
except that the matched tuple remains in tuple space.

Predicate versions of in and rd, namely inp and rdp, attempt to locate
a matching tuple and return 0 if they fail; otherwise they return 1, and
perform actual-to-formal assignment as described above.

eval(t) is the same as out(t), except that t is evaluated after rather
than before it enters tuple space; eval implicitly creates a new process to
perform the evaluation. When computation of t is complete, t becomes
an ordinary passive tuple, which may be in'ed or read like any other
tuple.

---

[5]Actually, tuples may *also* include formal parameters. Tuples and anti-tuples are
in fact structurally the same, although they play different roles. But we can ignore
formals in tuples for present purposes.

A tuple exists independently of the process that created it, and in fact
many tuples may exist independently of many creators, and may collectively form a data structure in tuple space. It's convenient to build
data structures out of tuples because tuples are referenced associatively,
somewhat like the tuples in a relational database.

For example: executing the out statements

```
out("a string", 15.01, 17, "another string")
```

causes the tuple

```
("a string", 15.01, 17, "another string")
```

to be added to tuple space. (The process executing out continues once
the tuple is added.) An in or rd statement specifies a template for
matching. Consider the statement

```
in("a string", ? f, ? i, "another string")
```

Executing this statement causes a search of tuple space for tuples of four
elements: first element "a string", last element "another string",
and middle two elements of the same types as variables f and i respectively. When a matching tuple is found, it is removed, the value of its
second field is assigned to f and its third field to i. The read statement,
for example

```
rd("a string", ? f, ? i, "another string")
```

works in the same way, except that the matched tuple is not removed.
The values of its middle two fields are assigned to f and i as before, but
the tuple remains in tuple space.

A tuple created using eval resolves into an ordinary data tuple. Consider the statement

```
eval("root", 7, sqrt(7))
```

It creates a three-element "live tuple," and continues immediately; the
live tuple sets to work computing the values of the string "root", the
integer 7 and the function call sqrt(7). The first two computations are
trivial (they yield "root" and 7); the third ultimately yields the square
root of 7.

Expressions that appear as arguments to **eval** inherit bindings from
the environment of the **eval**-executing process for whatever names they
cite explicitly. Thus, executing **eval("Q", f(x,y))** implicitly creates a
new process, and it evaluates **"Q"** and **f(x,y)** in a context in which the
names **f**, **y** and **x** have the same values they had in the environment of
the process that executed **eval**. The statement

```
rd("root", 7, sqrt(7))
```

might be used to read the tuple generated by this **eval**, once the live
tuple has resolved to a passive data tuple—*i.e.*, once the necessary computing has been accomplished. (If executed before this point, it blocks
until the active computation has resolved into a passive tuple.)

To write parallel programs, programmers must be able to *create* and to
coordinate multiple processes. Linda processes are created using **eval**,
and coordinated using **out**, **in** and **rd**. Note that in Linda, process
creation and process coordination are intertwined: a process is a live
tuple, and it turns into an ordinary passive tuple when it has finished
computing. Why this intertwining? Linda might in theory have included
a "create process" operation that had nothing to do with tuples. But
identifying a process with a "live tuple" has several advantages. We
discuss these in the next section.

Linda's tuple space is a form of shared memory, albeit an unusual form.
The elements of this memory are tuples (live or passive) instead of bytes
or words, and they are immutable. A tuple can't be altered; if its contents must be changed, the tuple is **in**'ed (that is, removed) and then
out'ed (regenerated) in some new form. The basic operations over a
conventional memory are "read" and "write"; over a Linda memory, the
basic operations are "generate object," "read object" and "remove object." The elements of a conventional memory are accessed by address;
elements in a tuple space are accessed via associative matching. One
other crucial implementation detail distinguishes a tuple space from a
conventional memory: many processors may share access to a Linda
tuple space even if they *don't* share access to a conventional shared
memory. Linda has been implemented not only on shared-memory
but on distributed-memory multi-computers, and even on networks of
autonomous computers.

Distributed data structures. In Linda a parallel program consists of a collection of simultaneously executing live tuples, which communicate by generating and consuming passive tuples. But it's important to note that Linda programs don't ordinarily deal with tuples as isolated objects. A Linda tuple space is a form of memory; tuples can be assembled into arbitrary kinds of data structures. A data structure built out of tuples is called a "distributed data structure." A *distributed data structure* is a data structure which can be accessed directly by many processes simultaneously.

Consider a simple example. Suppose a Linda program needs to deal with an n-element vector called V. The vector may be an input datum to the program, or it may be a table in which intermediate results are stored, or it may be the program's final result. Assuming that many separate processes will need access to it, the vector will be stored in tuple space, where it is directly accessible to any process that needs it. One simple way to store such a vector is in the form of n tuples:

```
("V", 1, FirstElt)
("V", 2, SecondElt)
    ⋮
("V", n, NthElt)
```

To read the jth element of the vector and assign it to x, processes use

```
rd("V", j, ? x)
```

To change the ith element, they use

```
in("V", i, ? OldVal)
out("V", i, NewVal)
```

9.5 Analysis

Occam and Linda are radically different, but they do have some similarities, and we will start with those.

Most important, both languages are designed to the same aesthetic standard: they are both as simple as their designers could make them.

Their other important shared characteristics are that both languages have been implemented efficiently, and both have been used in a wide variety of applications. The point is worth stressing particularly in the context of parallel programming languages, which is a rather odd field. An enormous number of parallel languages have been proposed—but not all have been implemented. Of those that have, relatively few have been implemented efficiently, and of these, even fewer have seen any significant use outside of the research group directly responsible for their creation.

There are marked differences in the hardware environments which support these two languages, and in crucial aspects of the languages' implementation. We'll turn to these after discussing more basic issues.

9.5.1   What is a Parallel Program? Two Views

The fundamental question addressed by any programming language is: *What is a program?* A parallel programming language must address a particular variant of this general question: What is a *parallel* program? What activities should proceed in parallel, and how should these activities relate to each other?

The View in CSP and Occam   According to CSP and Occam, a parallel program is in essence a kind of network. We can think of a parallel program in terms of a set of nodes connected by links, where each node corresponds to a process, and the links indicate communication paths among processes. We'll consider several examples.

Any activity that can be understood in terms of a *pipeline* fits neatly into this model. Generally speaking, a "pipelined activity" is an activity that

1. accepts or produces an ordered series of values, and

2. carries out an ordered series of operations over these values, in such a way that

3. the nth operation can be carried out over the kth value while the $n + 1^{st}$ is being applied to the $k - 1^{st}$.

An assembly line is the classic non-computing example: The fifteenth step can be applied to the millionth car at the same time the fourteenth is applied to the million-plus-first. Certain computations can be structured this way as well: an image-processing system, for example, might apply each of a series of transformations to each of a series of image regions. A software pipeline is a kind of network. Each node in the network corresponds to a step in the pipeline. All processes (*i.e.*, all network nodes) execute simultaneously, corresponding to the simultaneity of activity along the pipeline. We give a more detailed example below.

Any activity that can be understood in terms of a physical network can (unsurprisingly) be handily modeled by a software network as well. Consider a program to simulate the behavior of electronic circuits. We can build a network-shaped program in which each node corresponds to an element or a region of the circuit, and communication among nodes in the network corresponds to physical connections in the circuit.

Let's consider one example in greater detail. Hoare [62, p.674] presents an interesting CSP program to compute all prime numbers within some interval, structured as a pipeline.

The Sieve of Eratosthenes is a simple prime-finding algorithm in which we imagine passing a stream of integers through a series of sieves: a 2-sieve removes multiples of 2, a 3-sieve likewise, then a 5-sieve and so forth. An integer that has emerged successfully from the last sieve in the series is a new prime. It can be ensconced in its own sieve at the end of the line. (We've already discussed related algorithms in APL, Pascal and Miranda.)

Hoare presents a parallel program based on this algorithm (figure 9.3). We imagine the program as a pipeline that lengthens as it executes. Each pipe segment implements one sieve. The first pipe segment inputs a stream of integers and passes the residue (a stream of integers not divisible by 2) onto the next segment, which checks for multiples of 3 and so on. When the segment at the end of the pipeline finds a new prime, it extends the sieve by attaching a new segment to the end of the program.

It's important to note that CSP and Occam don't allow processes to be created while a program executes; all process must be accounted for at compile-time. It follows that the CSP program can't literally embody the description above—it can't implement a pipeline that lengthens, in the sense of adding new processes, as the program runs. Instead,

```
[SIEVE(i:1..100)::
   p,mp: integer;
   SIEVE(i-1)?p;
   print!p;
   mp := p;        comment mp is a multiple of p;

 *[m :integer; SIEVE(i-1)?m →
    *[m > mp → mp := mp + 1];
    [m = mp → skip
    [] m < mp → SIEVE(i+1)!m
    ] ]

 || SIEVE(0):: print!2; n: integer; n:=3;
          *[n < 10000 → SIEVE(1)!n; n:= n+2]

 || SIEVE(101)::*[n:integer; SIEVE(100)?n → print!n]

 || print::*[(i:0..101) n:integer, SIEVE(i)?n → ...]
 ]
```

Figure 9.3
The Sieve of Erasthosenes algorithm in CSP.

the CSP solution uses an *array* of processes. The following expression creates such an array:

```
SIEVE(i:1..100):: ...
```

Each element in the array is a process created from the template following the array declaration. The template has a parameter named i. In the first process i will be 1, in the second 2, and so on through 100. (Occam supports this process-array feature also.) Instead of *adding* new processes to the end of the pipeline, we simply *inform* the next process (which has been waiting around idly from the start) that it is to *start acting* like a new process at the end of the sieve. Of course, we must ensure when we write the program that the process array is long enough to hold the entire pipeline that will ultimately be created.

CSP and Occam capture the "network" model of parallel programming simply and directly—up to a point. The CSP or Occam programmer starts out by envisioning a network that represents the logical structure of his application. To embody this network in a CSP or Occam program, he simply creates one process for every node in the network, and then uses the appropriate input and output statements to ensure the proper network connections. (In other words, if processes P and Q represent connected network nodes, P will send output to or receive input from Q, or both.) The *up to a point* is important, however: Occam (the implemented language, that is, as against the design study) imposes a restriction on the kinds of networks the programmer can represent. Because Occam's channels correspond directly to the physical links in a Transputer array, the processes located on any one Transputer can't have more than four links to the rest of the network.

Parallel Programming in Linda   Linda's answer to our fundamental question (*what is a program?*) is very different. In Linda, a parallel program is merely a swarm of active tuples surrounded by a haze of passive tuples. If this doesn't help much, the fact that it doesn't is significant: Linda imposes very little in the way of pre-arranged structural assumptions on the programmer, who is consequently free to build a broad range of program structures.

In the Linda world-view there are three main types of asynchronous parallel programs, called *specialist*, *agenda* and *result* parallelism. Linda supports all three types.

The terms refer to ways in which a programmer might answer the inevitable first question in designing a parallel application: where do I put the parallelism? Which activities should proceed simultaneously? We can envision parallelism in terms of a program's *result*, its *agenda of activities* or the *ensemble of specialists* that collectively constitute the program.

Specialist parallelism is in essence identical to the network-style parallelism discussed above. In this kind of program, a collection of "specialist agents" solve problems by working cooperatively. Each node in the networks discussed above represents a process which specializes in some portion of the job to be accomplished: in simulating some particular portion of a circuit, for example, or in removing the multiples of some particular prime number. Agenda parallelism focuses on the list of tasks that constitute the job as a whole. The tasks on the agenda are executed one by one, but at each stage many processes work simultaneously, the point being to finish each agenda item as quickly as possible. Result parallelism centers on parallel computation of all elements in a data structure. For example, if the result of some program is a complex data structure (such as a two-dimensional array), we create one process for each element of the resulting data structure, and set them all to work simultaneously. Each process computes and then turns into one element of the data structure yielded as result. Some processes may suspend temporarily while awaiting the value yielded by others, but eventually all processes terminate and the result is complete.

We'll outline Linda's strategy for dealing with these three approaches in the context of the simple problem raised above, the computation of all primes within some interval. We've already outlined a specialist-parallel approach; the Linda solution resembles the CSP program above. We use the `eval` operator to generate each new pipe segment as needed; successive values are transmitted from one segment to the next by using `out`, and are received using `in` and `rd`.

Even where CSP and Linda program strategies are basically the same, however, there are fundamental differences in approach. The Linda version starts with a single process. New processes are generated as needed; there is no pre-allocated process array. Communication in CSP and in

Occam is (as noted) *synchronous*: a pipe segment with a new value
to hand forward down the pipe must *wait* until the next pipe segment
is ready to receive it. Thus when process 9 executes the CSP output
command

    SIEVE(i+1)!m

it must wait until process 10 executes the corresponding input command:

    SIEVE(i-1)?m

Linda's out statement, on the other hand, is *asynchronous*. When a
process executes an out, a tuple is generated and dumped into tuple
space, and the executing process continues immediately, without waiting
for the tuple to be retrieved. (The tuple may in fact be retrieved long
after the executing process has terminated and disappeared, or it may
never be retrieved.) In Linda, then, pipe segments dump successive
values into tuple space and then continue immediately. To communicate
each value, pipe segments execute a statement such as

    out("PipeSegment", next, OutIndex, num)

When process 10 executes this statement, the value of next is 11: the
first two fields of the tuple *collectively* designate the next process downstream. The variable num is bound to the number actually being transmitted. These tuples should be arranged in an ordered stream—pipe
segment 11 should read values in the same order in which segment 10
generates them. To accomplish this, we include an index field in each tuple (here, OutIndex). The transmitter and the receiver each increment
this field every time a tuple is out'ed or in'ed.

A final difference between the Linda and Occam version of the CSP
program is that the Occam version needs a last development step: being
hand-configured to suit a particular Transputer array. Linda programs
configure themselves automatically.

Agenda-parallel and master-worker programs. An agenda-
parallel approach to finding primes in Linda is very different from the
specialist-parallel version. Here is one possible strategy. The trivial

agenda has only a single item: find all primes within the designated interval. We must now break this item into sub-tasks, so that many processes can work on it simultaneously. "Find all primes within a fixed-length sub-interval" is a reasonable task. We'll neglect algorithmic details that are vital to the program but irrelevant to the topic at hand. The Linda program takes the following form: there is a "master process" and a collection of identical "worker processes." The master process creates a queue of task-descriptors in tuple space; each worker process removes the head task from the queue, performs the task, and then repeats. When the task queue is empty, the job is done. Here, each task assignment on the queue is "search the interval from x to y for primes." As the program runs, worker processes build a table of primes in tuple space; they consult this table in the course of searching for new primes.

This program structure is representative of an extremely important class, usually called master-worker programs (and occasionally "processor farm" programs). These programs center on a collection of identical worker processes, each prepared to perform whatever sub-task is assigned. The tasks may be intended for execution in some fixed order (as in the example above), or in arbitrary order. Because they are handed out *dynamically*—rather than pre-assigning tasks to workers, we let each worker grab a fresh task whenever the previous one is complete—these programs accomplish an important goal called *load balancing*. A parallel program can't be effective unless the work is spread uniformly among the available processes. Master-worker programs *automatically* tend to have good load balances (tend to have fairly even distribution of work to processes), because of the dynamic distribution of tasks to workers.

In practice most Linda programs are, in fact, master-worker programs. Tasks are stored in tuples; workers grab them using in. Input values, intermediate results (the growing table of primes, for example) and final results are often stored in tuple space as well.

It's not impossible to build master-worker programs in CSP or Occam, but these languages were clearly not designed for this kind of program structure. They don't support global data structures of the sort that Linda's master-worker programs rely on. Instead, we must store all of these data structures (including the list of outstanding task assignments) locally within some process, and use message passing to forward requests to this process.

Result-parallel programs. Finally, we consider result-parallel programs, beginning with a generic example of this type of program structure. Consider a program that yields an nxn matrix whose j^{th} counter-diagonal depends (only) on the preceding counter-diagonal. The computation can proceed in wavefront fashion: as soon as we know one counter-diagonal, we can compute in parallel all elements of the next counter-diagonal. To express such a program in Linda, we use eval statements of the form

```
eval("M", i, j, compute(i,j))
```

to create one process for each element of the result. The function compute(i,j) uses rd to examine the values of the preceding counter-diagonal. For example,

```
rd("M", i-1, j, ? value)
```

As soon as the processes along the kth counter-diagonal are done computing, they turn into passive tuples and become visible to the processes along the $(k+1)^{st}$ counter-diagonal. Thus the computation proceeds in stages, as active processes turn into passive tuples along a wavefront from upper left to lower right.

The general strategy, then, is the following: use eval to create one process for each element in the data structure to be returned. Use rd to find what values other processes have yielded.

A result-parallel Linda program for finding primes is shown in figure 9.4. This is an *atypical* Linda program: the result-parallel style often yields concise and elegant programs that are relatively *fine-grained*. The *grain size* of a parallel program is an informal measure of the ratio of time spent computing *versus* time spent coordinating. Coordination—message sending, tuple manipulation, or any other comparable operation—takes time to accomplish. A process that does only a little computing but a great deal of coordinating is in danger of being overwhelmed by the costs of coordination. A program whose granularity is too fine (*i.e.*, does too little computing relative to coordination) is in danger of *slowing down* rather than speeding up as we run it on more processors. The gain in faster computing can be overwhelmed by the loss in coordination costs.

```
lmain()
{
  int i, ok;

  for(i = 2; i < LIMIT; ++i) {
    eval("primes", i, is_prime(i));
  }

  for(i = 2; i <= LIMIT; ++i) {
    rd("primes", i, ?~ok);
    if (ok) printf("%d\n", i);
  }
}

is_prime(me)
     int        me;
{
  int          i, limit, ok;
  double       sqrt();

  limit = sqrt((double) me) + 1;

  for (i = 2; i < limit; ++i) {
    rd("primes", i, ?~ok);
    if (ok && (me%i == 0)) return 0;
  }
  return 1;
}
```

Figure 9.4
A result-parallel program in Linda. This program is too fine-grained to run well on
current implementations. In practical terms it serves only as a first step: we can
derive efficient (but more complicated) primes finders from this simple version.
Some details may be obscure without reference to [23], but we include the whole
program here for concreteness.

In present day Linda implementations, tuple space operations are generally too costly to allow fine-grained result-parallel programs like the one in figure 9.4 to run efficiently. But this style of program is interesting nonetheless, for two reasons. First, a result-parallel solution is often a good first step towards the development of a more efficient version using some other method. Second, as implementation techniques and multi-computer architectures improve (both are improving steadily), result-parallel programs should become more widely useful in practice than they are at present. (Using the master-worker technique, we can build a highly efficient Linda primes-finder; we return to this point below.) Result-parallel programming is difficult to impossible in CSP and Occam. These languages don't allow the dynamic creation of processes, and don't allow processes to "turn into" data objects.

Back to "eval." We referred above to the fact that Linda identifies processes and data objects. Linda might have provided a conventional "create process" operation, but `eval` creates a "live tuple" instead, which resolves eventually into an ordinary passive tuple. Why do things this way? This form of process creation is clearly useful in writing result-parallel programs. Result parallelism depends on the idea that processes are merely data objects under development. Processes that turn into data objects are useful in other program styles as well. In some master-worker programs, for example, the master must be informed when all workers have finished, so that it can terminate the computation or start the next phase. Worker processes become data tuples upon termination; a master process that has created n workers can execute a series of n in statements to remove the data-tuple residue of each worker. These `in`'s won't complete until every worker has terminated (a live tuple can't be removed until it has turned into a passive data tuple); hence the master knows, when all `in`'s have been completed, that every worker has terminated.

Linda's `eval` has a somewhat more general motivation as well: `eval` means that a process under evaluation has a certain shape—corresponds to a particular object (a live tuple) that occurs within a particular collection of objects (a tuple space). These facts lay the necessary foundations for expanded versions of Linda (not the implemented language but its successors, now under development). In the expanded and generalized version, the tuple space operations can be used to manipulate active

processes as well as passive data objects, computations can be organized into a hierarchy of many tuple spaces, and tuple spaces themselves
become first class objects.

9.5.2   Elegance at What Cost?

Linda is clearly a more flexible and general coordination language than
the coordination elements of CSP and Occam. So why would anybody
program in Occam?

Occam is a lower-level language than Linda—but its "low levelness"
means that it can be implemented simply and efficiently. When a programmer happens to have an application that can be neatly expressed
as a static network, and this network can be conveniently mapped to
an array of Transputers, Occam is an attractive programming vehicle.
Why? Because (1) the resulting program will be highly efficient, and (2)
since the application is tailor-made for Occam, it will be easy to express
in Occam—why look further?

Linda is the higher-level alternative—but as a result, it's far trickier than
Occam to implement. This is particularly true on distributed-memory
multi-computers and on networks. Occam provides only message passing, but Linda's tuple space is a kind of shared memory, and supporting
a tuple space in the absence of a *physically*-shared memory in which to
keep it presents a formidable implementation problem.

This problem has been solved, to the extent that a wide variety of Linda
programs perform well not only on shared-memory multi-computers but
on distributed machines and on networks. For example: consider the
agenda-parallel version of the primes finder discussed above (the most
efficient version). Running on all sixty-four nodes of an Intel iPSC/2 hypercube (a non-shared-memory machine), the C.Linda program finishes
roughly fifty-two and a half times faster than an efficient C program
performing the same computation sequentially—an excellent result in
terms of reasonable performance expectations. The identical program
with a larger grain size (in this case, the grain size designates the size of
the interval to be searched for primes) shows good performance even on
a local area network, where communication is substantially slower that
it is in a multi-computer.

Clearly Linda *can* be implemented efficiently. Nonetheless, for programmers willing to make the necessary sacrifices in expressivity, and in the time necessary to hand-configure programs for a particular machine, an Occam program will almost certainly be more efficient than a Linda program performing exactly the same kind of network computation. Is the gain in efficiency under these circumstances worth the cost in convenience and expressivity? Efficiency is extremely important in parallel programming: not merely running but running *fast* is the whole point. Convenience and expressivity, however, are also particularly important here: parallel programs can be somewhat more complex to develop, debug and understand than conventional sequential programs. As in any contest between low-level efficiency and high-level power, the final choice depends on circumstances, and it can only be subjective.

9.6   Readings

Basic Readings. [62] is the classic paper on CSP. [20] provides an introduction to C.Linda and its programming method. [23] is a more extensive survey of parallel programming techniques.

Suggested Readings. A recent paper by Bal, Steiner and Tanenbaum [9] is an excellent and extremely comprehensive survey of parallel languages.

[61] is a textbook devoted to CSP. [89] gives an overview of Occam. [26] is a formal treatment of parallel programming with emphasis on CSP.

[49] was the first widely read report on Linda. Distributed data structures were first introduced in [24]. [22] presents an implementation of Linda on the S/Net, a bus-based multicomputer; [16] discusses the implementation of Linda on an Intel iPSC/2 hypercube.

9.7   Exercises

1. Matrix multiplication is defined as follows: the product of a matrix A of size $n \times m$ and another matrix B of size $m \times n$, is a matrix C of size $n \times l$ whose elements are defined by the following equation:

$$C_{i,j} = \sum_{k=1}^{m} A_{i,k} * B_{k,j}$$

   (a) Sketch an Occam program to this problem. (b) Sketch C.Linda solutions to this problem using (i) result, (ii) agenda and (iii) specialist parallelism. Which solution is preferable under which circumstances?

2. Given a pool of n patients and m doctors $(n > m)$, patients become sick randomly and arrive at the doctors' office to be cured. A patient sees the first available doctor for a random amount of time. Once cured, the patient returns to the pool of well people until he gets sick again. If no doctor is available, patients are placed in a single FIFO (first-in, first-out) queue to wait for the next available doctor; likewise, if no patient is waiting, doctors are placed in a single FIFO queue to wait for the next patient. All events are nondeterministic; there are no global communications, no global synchronization, and no global knowledge. (a) Sketch the design of a program to simulate this problem in C.Linda and CSP. (b) Based on your answer, which model appears better suited for expressing the non-determinism required in this problem? Why?

3. The dining-philosophers problem is stated by Hoare [62, p.673] as follows: n philosophers spend their lives eating and thinking. The philosophers share a common dining room where there is a circular table surrounded by five chairs, each belonging to one philosopher. In the center of the table there is a large bowl of spaghetti, and the table is laid with five forks. When feeling hungry, a philosopher enters the dining room, sits in his chair, picks up the fork to his left. In order to eat the spaghetti, he realizes he must pick up the fork on his right as well. When he has finished, he puts down both forks, and leaves the room. (a) Sketch solutions to this problem in (i) Occam and (ii) Linda. (b) Compare your solutions to the ones

given in [62] and [20]. (c) In what significant ways do the solutions given in these languages differ?

4. (a) The Hamming numbers are defined to be the set of integers which can be expressed in the form:

$$2^a \times 3^b \times 5^c$$

(for integers $a,b,c \geq 0$). Assuming a stream of integers I of length n, formulate a solution to this problem in (i) C.Linda and (ii) Occam.

(b) The extended Hamming numbers are defined as follows: given a finite sequence of primes $\{A, B, C, D, \ldots\}$ and an integer n as input, output in increasing magnitude without duplication all integers less than or equal to n of the form:

$$A^i \times B^j \times C^k \times D^l \ldots$$

Sketch solutions to this problem in (i) C.Linda and (ii) Occam. Based on your answers, which language appears to best support stream-based computation? Why?

5. (a) Show how we can model a CSP-style synchronous communication in C.Linda. (b) Is it possible (in practical terms) to model Linda-style asynchronous communication in Occam? If yes, sketch a solution; if no, why not?

6. In what ways do tuples and the matching procedure facilitate parallelism? In what ways do they hinder it?

7. List three significant implementation problems posed by C.Linda but not by Occam. Can you sketch possible solutions to these problems?

10 Conclusion

To start, we ask each of our six Hero Languages to take a bow: the classical languages Fortran, Algol 60 and Lisp; their distinguished successors Pascal, Simula 67 and Scheme. And honorable mention to Algol 68 and Smalltalk—intriguing, important and original designs.

Having traced the evolution of programming languages from the start through the present, we can summarize their history in a few paragraphs:

Algol 60 established the foundations of language and program structure by discovering that programs could be conceived as recursively-structured objects—just like the algebraic expressions out of which formulas and proofs are built, just like the electronic circuitry out of which modern computers are built. Of course, Algol programs are not the *same as* either of these; they are a new kind of structure, with its own rules. Algol 60 discovered that a software machine could be conceived in terms of a kind of grid or latticework overlaid on computational space-time; some regions have names and hold values or templates, others are anonymous and contain sequences of executable statements. Lisp hints broadly at another fundamental language idea: that function definitions (in effect templates) can themselves be treated as data objects, as values. But there is a crucial limitation in the Algol 60 worldview: Algol's structural vision stops at the threshold of the data object world; we can't drop one of its elegant recursive structures into a named region and treat it as a data object. An array is an ordered sequence of regions, but it has nothing in common with a block, even though a block is also an ordered sequence of regions. We can't drop a block into a named region (giving a record or a module or a data system), we can't use templates to instantiate named blocks (no classes, no "record types"), and the parallelism latent in the idea of a block and of unsequenced parameter evaluation goes unrealized.

Filling in the blank spots in the Algol worldview becomes the (unacknowledged) *key theme in the subsequent evolution of language design.* How can we provide for the records, for the user-extensible template- or type-systems that Algol left out? Cobol and PL/I suggest partial approaches,

Algol 68 and Pascal fully worked-out schemes. How can we provide for
the classes, the data systems and (at base the same thing) the higher-
order functions that Algol left out? Simula 67, Smalltalk and the object-
oriented world explore one approach, CLU and other abstract-typing
languages explore another, Scheme and functional languages explore a
third. How can we provide for the modules that Algol left out? Ada
develops one approach. How can we provide for parallelism? CSP and
many other parallel languages have some suggestions. But *all* of this
power and expressivity (excepting only the coordination aspects of parallelism) would have been part of Algol if the Algol design hadn't con-
jured up a fundamental separation between the structure of programs
and of data objects.

Obviously many other highly significant themes develop in tandem with
this most important one. The dynamic data structures developed in
Lisp, the interpreter-based environment pioneered by Lisp and developed further by APL and by Smalltalk, the security-based view of types
developed in Pascal and in abstract-typing languages, the spectrum
of parameter-passing strategies developed by the Classical Languages
and investigated and fine-tuned in subsequent designs, the meaning of
"lambda" phrases from Lisp through Scheme, the (irreconcilable?) difference in viewpoint between those who esteem simplicity and conceptual
economy and those who shrug their shoulders over these "purely subjective" points—these are all important stories, many still unfolding.

A great deal has been accomplished by language designers during the
brief history of this field. Modern languages are likely to be substantially
more powerful (and more efficiently implemented) than earlier ones. The
breakthroughs represented by designs like Simula 67 and Scheme have
brought about new standards of elegance and expressivity, and have
inspired the construction of powerful and (sometimes) beautiful new
structures in software.

And yet: for all this progress to date, the field of programming language
design is young and (as one might expect) immature. Significant areas
of indecision and confusion remain. More research, more experience and
(above all) more pondering will be necessary before these are cleared up.

There are many important open questions. We know (in some cases,
anyway) what the static, source-text version of a program looks like,

but what should a *running* program look like?—how does it relate to the source version? Such questions are increasingly important in the context of computing environments that can support sophisticated visualization-based debugging tools. They are important in another, related way besides: given some program that executes continuously, what information can we glean from the running program itself about its current state? Can we take a snapshot of a running program and study it, or move the program (via snapshot) to another system?

Security, testing and debugging are perennial questions. The detailed study and testing of simplified computer models can be helpful to structural engineers: can we build simplified computer models of *software* structures for analysis and testing? How can we use visualization to make testing and analysis of existing programs more thorough? Would "artificial reality"—techniques that allow users to look at three-dimensional computer-generated scenes though miniature eyeglass-mounted displays—be useful? Would it be helpful to "walk around" *inside* an executing program? What are the most effective ways to apply the techniques of artificial intelligence and expert systems to program development and debugging—can they be integrated into a programming language framework?

Can we develop modern languages for *realtime* applications, a demanding field whose practitioners must often still rely on low-level languages and programming methods?

What's the best approach to building libraries of re-usable software? Might expert systems act as librarians, selecting appropriate routines from a large collection, if necessary customizing them for some new application?

It may be that the questions of greatest immediate significance are the ones that deal with *coordination*: What's the best way to build programs by gluing together *active* components? What if the components are written in heterogeneous languages, or running in heterogeneous computing environments? How do we write such a program, set it up, visualize it, debug and test it, control it as it executes? What can compilers do to support such environments? What are the most effective tools for writing parallel programs? How can we place *interpreters* in a parallel or distributed environment?

How can we rationalize the messy, complicated, inconsistent and poorly-integrated programming languages we so often rely on today? What *is* a program? For those who are satisfied with the "programs are mathematical expressions" answer, fine: your search is over. The rest of us (who are unwilling to erase the conceptual distinction between the description and the thing itself) still face a conceptual puzzle, as we try to fathom the character and structure of this evanescent, endlessly flexible species of machinery.

The ISM model represents one way to approach the problems of rational and integrated language structure, and the shape and structure of programs both as source text and as working machines. It's not that the ISM has all the answers or represents the "ultimate solution" (or even a demonstrably *correct* solution) to the problems we've raised in this book. But the ISM model *does* serve to underline the fact that many views of this field are still possible, and *ipso facto* that we have not settled on the ultimate or the "right" one. In the ISM, by way of summary and conclusion, a program is a structure that is laid out on a virtual line or a plane or some other "computational surface"; this surface is carved up into regions, and any of the regions may have names. All regions execute simultaneously—the entire surface "develops" like a photographic image—and the result is the *same* surface, but in "developed" form. Expressions have been replaced by values, but the structure is otherwise unchanged. There is no Algol Wall of any sort. All data structures follow the same rules; a "program" is merely a data structure whose constituent values have yet to be determined.

The ISM model might be implemented directly (a final, rather challenging, exercise)—but of course, the model described here is merely the shell of a language, with many details unspecified. A direct implementation would require considerable creativity. Symmetric Lisp[71] represents one way to embody the ISM in a complete programming language. Symmetric Lisp isn't really a Lisp at all, nor is it the only way to turn the ISM into a language, nor is it guaranteed to be "better" than any other language discussed in this book. But readers may want to compare it to the other designs we've discussed here.

Programming language design is a young field; there are many *basic* things we don't know. But of course there is, today, much exciting and innovative work in programming languages we well. The field continues to draw strength from the worldwide company of inspired builders who see, in software, the great medium of the age.

Bibliography

[1] Harold Abelson and Gerald Sussman. *Structure and Interpretation of Computer Programs*. MIT Press, Cambridge, Mass., 1985.

[2] H. Adams. *Mont-Saint-Michel and Chartres*. Doubleday Anchor, Garden City, NY, 1959. Originally published by the American Institute of Architects, 1913.

[3] Gul Agha. *Actors: A Model of Concurrent Computation in Distributed Systems*. MIT Press, Cambridge, Mass., 1986.

[4] Alfred Aho, Ravi Sethi, and Jeffrey Ullman. *Compilers: Principles, Techniques and Tools*. Addison-Wesley, Reading, Mass., 1987.

[5] John W. Backus. Can Programming be Liberated from the Von Neumann Style: A Functional Style and Its Algebra of Programs. *Communications of the ACM*, 21(8):613–640, 1978.

[6] John W. Backus *et al.* The FORTRAN Automatic Coding System. In *Proceedings of the Western Joint Computer Conference*, February 1957.

[7] John W. Backus and W.P. Heising. FORTRAN. *IEEE Transactions on Electronic Computers*, EC-13(4):382–385, August 1964.

[8] Henry Baker. List Processing in Real Time on a Serial Computer. *Communications of the ACM*, 21(4):280–294, April 1978.

[9] Henri Bal, J.G. Stenier, and Andrew Tanenbaum. Programming Languages for Distributed Computing Systems. *ACM Computing Surveys*, 21(3), September 1989.

[10] Henk Barendregt. *The Lambda Calculus*. North-Holland, Amsterdam, 1981.

[11] J.G.P. Barnes. An Overview of Ada. *Software Practice and Experience*, 10:851–887, 1980.

[12] R.W. Bemer. A Politico-Social History of Algol. In *Annual Review of Automatic Programming-5*, pages 151–238. Pergamon Press, 1969.

[13] David Billington. *The Tower and the Bridge*. Princeton University Press, 1983.

[14] Richard Bird and Philip Wadler. *Introduction to Functional Programming*. Prentice-Hall, New York, 1988.

[15] G. M. Birtwistle *et al*. *Simula Begin*. Auerbach Publishers, Philadelphia, Penn., 1973.

[16] Robert Bjornson, Nick Carriero, and David Gelernter. The Implementation and Performance of a Hypercube Linda. Technical Report RR-520, Yale University, Dept. of Computer Science, January 1989.

[17] Adrienne Bloss, Paul Hudak, and Jonathan Young. An Optimizing Compiler for a Modern Functional Language. *The Computer Journal*, 2(32), April 1989.

[18] Luca Cardelli. Basic Polymorphic Typechecking. *Science of Computer Programming*, 8:147–172, 1987.

[19] Luca Cardelli and Peter Wegner. On Understanding Types, Data Abstraction, and Polymorphism. *ACM Computing Surveys*, 17(4):471–522, 1985.

[20] Nicholas Carriero and David Gelernter. Linda in Context. *Communications of the ACM*, 32(4):444–458, April 1989.

[21] Nick Carriero and David Gelernter. The S/Net's Linda Kernel. In *ACM Symposium on Operating Systems Principles*, pages 160–161, December 1985.

[22] Nick Carriero and David Gelernter. The S/Net's Linda Kernel. *ACM Transactions on Computer Systems*, 4(2):110–129, May 1986.

[23] Nick Carriero and David Gelernter. How to Write Parallel Programs: A Guide to the Perplexed. *ACM Computing Surveys*, 21(3), September 1989. Also published as Yale University Technical Report, YALEU/DCS/RR-628.

[24] Nick Carriero, David Gelernter, and Jerry Leichter. Distributed Data Structures in Linda. In 13th *ACM Symposium on Principles of Programming Languages Conf.*, January 1986.

[25] Craig Chambers and David Ungar. Customization: Optimizing Compiler Technology for SELF, A Dynamically-Typed Object-Oriented Programming Language. In *ACM SIGPLAN '89 Conference on Programming Language Design and Implementation*, pages 146–160, June 1989.

[26] K. Mani Chandy and Jayadev Misra. *Parallel Program Design: A Foundation.* Addison-Wesley, Reading, Mass., 1988.

[27] Alonzo Church. *The Calculi of Lambda-Conversion.* Princeton University Press, Princeton, New Jersey, 1941.

[28] William Clinger *et al.* The Revised Revised Revised Report on Scheme or An UnCommon Lisp. Technical Report AI-TM 848, MIT Artificial Intelligence Laboratory, 1985.

[29] William F. Clocksin and Christopher S. Mellish. *Programming in Prolog.* Springer-Verlag, Berlin, 1981.

[30] Doug Cooper and Michael Clancy. *Oh! Pascal!* W.W Norton & Company, New York, 1985.

[31] Arvind and David Culler. *Dataflow Architectures*, volume 1, pages 225–253. Annual Reviews Inc., 1986.

[32] Josephy Cunningham. Why COBOL? *Communications of the ACM*, 5(5):236–253, 1962.

[33] O.J. Dahl and C.A.R. Hoare. Hierarchical program structures. In *Structured Programming.* Academic Press, 1972.

[34] O.J. Dahl, B. Myhruhaug, and K. Nygaard. The Simula67 Base Common Base Language. Technical Report S-22, Norwegian Computing Center, 1970.

[35] Scott Danforth and Chris Tomlinson. Type Theories and Object-Oriented Programming. *ACM Computing Surveys*, 20(1):29–72, 1988.

[36] Peter Deutsch and Allan Schiffman. Efficient Implementation of the Smalltalk-80 System. In 10th *ACM Symposium on Principles of Programming Languages Conf.*, pages 297–302, 1983.

[37] Edsger W. Dijkstra. Go To Statement Considered Harmful. *Communications of the ACM*, 11(8):538, 1968.

[38] Edsger W. Dijkstra. Guarded Commands, Nondeterminacy and Formal Derivation of Programs. *Communications of the ACM*, 18(8):453–457, August 1975.

[39] J.J. Dongarra, D.C. Sorenson, and P. Brewer. Tools and Methodology for Programming Parallel Processors. In M. Wright, editor, *Aspects of Computation on Asynchronous Processors*, pages 125–138. North-Holland, 1988.

[40] J. Dongarra, *ed. Experimental Parallel Computer Architecture.* North-Holland, Amsterdam, 1987.

[41] R. Kent Dybvig. *The Scheme Programming Language.* Prentice-Hall, Inc., Englewood Cliffs, New Jersey, 1987.

[42] A.D. Falkoff and K.E. Iverson. *APL/360 Manual.* I.B.M Corporation, 1966.

[43] A.D. Falkoff and K.E. Iverson. The Design of APL. *IBM Journal of Research and Development*, 17(4):324–334, July 1973.

[44] Jean Ferrante, K.J. Ottenstein, and J.D. Warren. The Program Dependence Graph and its Use in Optimization. *ACM Transactions on Programming Languages and Systems*, 9(3):319–349, July 1987.

[45] R.P. Feynman, R.B. Leighton, and M. Sands. *The Feynman Lectures on Physics.* Addison-Wesley, Reading, Mass., 1963.

[46] Gottlob Frege. Begriffsschrift, A Formula Language, Modeled upon that of Arithmetic, for Pure Thought. In *From Frege to Gödel: A Source Book in Mathematical Logic*, pages 1–82. Harvard University Press, 1967. Translated by S. Bauer-Mengelberg.

[47] Daniel Friedman and Christopher Haynes. Constraining Control. In *12th ACM Symposium on Principles of Programming Languages Conf.*, pages 245–254, January 1985.

[48] Daniel Friedman, Chris Haynes, and Eugene Kohlbecker. Programming With Continuations. In *Program Transformations and Programming Environments*, pages 263–274. Springer-Verlag, New York, 1985.

[49] David Gelernter. Generative Communication in Linda. *ACM Transactions on Programming Languages and Systems*, pages 80–112, January 1985.

[50] David Gelernter. *An Integrated Microcomputer Network for Experiments in Distributed Programming*. PhD thesis, State University of New York, Stony Brook, 1982.

[51] Adele Goldberg and David Robson. *Smalltalk-80: The Language and its Implementation*. Addison-Wesley Press, Reading, Mass., 1983.

[52] R. Greenblatt, T. Knight, J. Holloway, D. Moon, and D. Weinreb. The LISP Machine. In *Interactive Programming Environments*, pages 326–352. McGraw-Hill, 1984.

[53] A. Nico Habermann. Critical Comments on the Programming Language Pascal. *Acta Informatica*, 3:47–57, 1973.

[54] Per Brinch Hansen. Distributed Processes: A Concurrent Programming Concept. *Communications of the ACM*, 21(11), 1978.

[55] Per Brinch Hansen. The Programming Language Concurrent Pascal. *IEEE Transactions on Software Engineering*, 1(2):199–206, 1975.

[56] G. Henderson. *Chartres*. Penguin Books, 1968.

[57] Peter Henderson. *Functional Programming: Application and Implementation*. Prentice/Hall International, Englewood Cliffs, New Jersey, 1980.

[58] Carl Hewitt. Viewing Control Structures as Patterns of Passing Messages. *Journal of Artificial Intelligence*, 8(3):323–364, 1977.

[59] Daniel Hillis. *The Connection Machine.* MIT Press, Cambridge, Mass., 1985.

[60] C.A.R. Hoare *et al.* The Laws of Programming. *Communications of the ACM*, 30(8):672–686, August 1987.

[61] C.A.R. Hoare. *Communicating Sequential Processes.* Prentice-Hall, London, 1984.

[62] C.A.R. Hoare. Communicating Sequential Processes. *Communications of the ACM*, 21(8):666–677, August 1978.

[63] C.A.R. Hoare. Monitors: An Operating System Structuring Concept. *Communications of the ACM*, 17(10):549–557, October 1974.

[64] C.A.R. Hoare. Record Handling. In *Programming Languages*, pages 291–347. Academic Press, 1968.

[65] C.A.R. Hoare. A Contribution to the Development of Algol. *Communications of the ACM*, 9(6):413–431, June 1966.

[66] Ellis Horowitz. *Programming Languages: A Grand Tour.* Computer Science Press, Rockville, Maryland, 1983.

[67] John Hughes. Why Functional Programming Matters. *The Computer Journal*, 32(2):98–107, 1989.

[68] Daniel Ingalls. The Smalltalk-76 Programming System: Design and Implementation. In *Fifth ACM Symposium on Principles of Programming Languages Conf.*, pages 9–16, January 1978.

[69] INMOS Limited. *OCCAM 2 Reference Manual*, 1988. Published by Prentice-Hall, Englewood-Cliffs, New Jersey.

[70] Kenneth Iverson. *A Programming Language.* John Wiley and Sons, New York, 1962.

[71] Suresh Jagannathan. A Programming Language Supporting First-Class, Parallel Environments. Technical Report LCS-TR 434, Massachusetts Institute of Technology, December 1988.

[72] Kathleen Jensen and Niklaus Wirth. *Pascal User Manual and Report.* Springer-Verlag, New York, 1974.

[73] Simon Peyton Jones. *The Implementation of Functional Programming Languages*. Prentice-Hall, Englewood Cliffs, New Jersey, 1987.

[74] Brian W. Kernighan and D. M. Ritchie. *The C Programming Language*. Prentice-Hall, Englewood Cliffs, New Jersey, 1978.

[75] Stephen Kleene. *Introduction to MetaMathematics*. Von Nostrand, Princeton, 1950.

[76] Donald Knuth. An Empirical Study of FORTRAN Programs. *Software Practice and Experience*, 1(2):105–133, 1971.

[77] D. Knuth. The Remaining Troublespots in Algol 60. *Communications of the ACM*, 10(10):611–618, October 1967.

[78] Peter Kogge. *The Architecture of Pipelined Computers*. McGraw-Hill, 1981.

[79] R. Kowalski. Algorithms = Logic + Control. *Communications of the ACM*, 22(7):424–436, July 1979.

[80] David Kranz, R. Kelsey, Jonathan Rees, Paul Hudak, J. Philbin, and N. Adams. ORBIT: An Optimizing Compiler for Scheme. *ACM SIGPLAN Notices*, 21(7):219–233, July 1986.

[81] David Kuck *et al.* Dependence Graphs and Compiler Optimization. In *Eighth ACM Symposium on Principles of Programming Languages Conf.*, pages 207–218, January 1981.

[82] Peter J. Landin. The Mechanical Evaluation of Languages. *Computer Journal*, 6(4):308–320, January 1964.

[83] H.W. Lawson, Jr. PL/I List Processing. *Communications of the ACM*, 10(6):358–367, June 1967.

[84] C.H Lindsey and S.G. Van Der Meulen. *An Informal Introduction to Algol 68*. North-Holland, Amsterdam, 1971.

[85] Barbara Liskov *et al.* *CLU Reference Manual*. Springer-Verlag, Berlin, 1981.

[86] Barbara Liskov, Alan Synder, Russell Atkinson, and Craig Schaffert. Abstraction Mechanisms in CLU. *Communications of the ACM*, 20(8):564–576, August 1977.

[87] Barbara Liskov and Stephen Zilles. Specification Techniques for Data Abstractions. *IEEE Transactions on Software Engineering*, 1(1):7–19, 1975.

[88] John W. Lloyd. *The Foundations of Logic Programming*. Springer-Verlag, New York, 1984.

[89] David May. OCCAM. *ACM SIPLAN Notices*, 18(4):69–79, April 1983.

[90] John McCarthy *et al*. *Lisp 1.5 Programmer's Manual*. MIT Press, Cambridge, Mass., 1962.

[91] John McCarthy. Recursive Functions of Symbolic Expressions and Their Computation by Machine, Part I. *Communications of the ACM*, 3(4):184–195, 1960.

[92] J. McPhee. *The Control of Nature*. Farrar Straus Giroux, 1989.

[93] R. Milne and C. Strachey. *A Theory of Programming Language Semantics*. Chapman and Hall, London, 1976.

[94] Robin Milner. A Proposal for Standard ML. In *Proceedings of the ACM Symposium on Lisp and Functional Programming*, pages 184–193, 1984.

[95] Robin Milner. A Theory of Type Polymorphism in Programming. *Journal of Computer and System Sciences*, 17:348–375, December 1978.

[96] David Moon. *The MACLISP Reference Manual*. Laboratory of Computer Science, Massachusetts Institute of Technology, 1978.

[97] James Morris. Real Programming in Functional Languages. In *Functional Programming and its Applications: An Advanced Course*. Cambridge University Press, 1982.

[98] Peter Naur and M. Woodger (Eds.). Revised Report on the Algorithmic Language Algol 60. *Communications of the ACM*, pages 1–20, June 1963.

[99] Rishiyur Nikhil. ID Reference Manual (Version 88.0). Technical report, MIT, 1988. Computation Structures Group Technical Report.

[100] R. Nisbet. *Prejudices: A Philosophical Dictionary*. Harvard University Press, Cambridge, Mass., 1982.

[101] David Padua and Michael J. Wolfe. Advanced Compiler Optimizations for Supercomputers. *Communications of the ACM*, 29(12):1184–1201, December 1986.

[102] David L. Parnas. A Technique for Software Module Specification with Examples. *Communications of the ACM*, 15(5):330–336, May 1972.

[103] James L. Peterson. Petri Nets. *ACM Computing Surveys*, 9(3):223–250, 1977.

[104] G. J. Popek *et al.* Notes on the Design of Euclid. In *Language Design for Reliable Software Conf.*, pages 11–18, 1977. Also appears as ACM SIGPLAN Notice, volume 3, number 12.

[105] George Radin and H. Paul Rogoway. NPL: Highlights of a New Programming Language. *Communications of the ACM*, 8(1):9–17, January 1965.

[106] Jonathan A. Rees and Norman I. Adams. T: A Dialect of Lisp or, LAMBDA: The Ultimate Software Tool. In *Proceedings of the ACM Symposium on Lisp and Functional Programming*, pages 114–122, 1982.

[107] M. Richards. BCPL: A Tool for Compiler Writing and Systems Programming. In *Proceedings of the 1969 Joint Computer Conference*, 1969.

[108] John A. Robinson. A Machine-Oriented Logic Based on the Resolution Principle. *Journal of the ACM*, 12:23–44, 1965.

[109] Jean Sammet. *Programming Languages: History and Fundamentals.* Prentice-Hall, Englewood-Cliffs, New Jersey, 1969.

[110] David Schmidt. *Denotational Semantics.* Allyn and Bacon, Newton, Mass., 1986.

[111] Ehud Shapiro, *ed. Concurrent Prolog Collected Papers.* MIT Press, Cambridge, Mass., 1987.

[112] Ehud Shapiro. Concurrent Prolog: A Progress Report. *IEEE Computer*, 19(8):44–59, 1986.

[113] Mary Shaw *et al.* Abstraction and Verification in Alphard: Defining and Specifying Iteration and Generators. In *Language Design for Reliable Software Conf.*, 1977. Also appears as ACM SIGPLAN Notice, volume 3, number 12.

[114] SIGPLAN. *Proceedings of the History of Programming Languages.* ACM SIGPLAN, 1978. Also appears as ACM SIGPLAN Notice, volume 13, number 8, August, 1978.

[115] Guy Steele, Jr. *Common Lisp: The Language.* Digital Press, 1984.

[116] Guy Steele, Jr. An Overview of Common Lisp. In *Proceedings of the ACM Symposium on Lisp and Functional Programming*, pages 98–107, 1982.

[117] Guy Steele, Jr. and Gerald Sussman. The Art of the Interpreter, or the Modularity Complex. Technical Report AI-TM 453, MIT Artificial Intelligence Laboratory, 1978.

[118] Guy Steele, Jr. Rabbit: A Compiler for Scheme. Master's thesis, Massachusetts Institute of Technology, 1978.

[119] Guy Steele, Jr. and Gerald Sussman. Lambda: The Ultimate Imperative. Technical Report AI-TM 353, MIT Artificial Intelligence Laboratory, 1976.

[120] Guy Steele, Jr. Lambda: The Ultimate Declarative. Technical Report AI-TM 379, MIT Artificial Intelligence Laboratory, 1976.

[121] Leon Sterling and Ehud Shapiro. *The Art of Prolog.* MIT Press, Cambridge, Mass., 1986.

[122] Joseph Stoy. *Denotational Semantics: The Scott-Stratchey Approach to Programming Language Theory.* MIT Press, Cambridge, Mass., 1977.

[123] Norihisa Suzuki and Minoru Terada. Creating Efficient Systems for Object-Oriented Languages. In 10th *ACM Symposium on Principles of Programming Languages Conf.*, 1983.

[124] Warren Teitelman *et al. The InterLISP Reference Manual.* Xerox Palo Alto Research Center, 1978.

[125] David A. Turner. Miranda: A Non-Strict Functional Language with Polymorphic Types. In *1985 Proceedings on Functional Programming Languages and Computer Architecture*, pages 1–16. Springer-Verlag, September 1985. Lecture Notes on Computer Science, Number 201.

[126] David Turner. Recursion Equations as a Programming Language. In *Functional Programming and its Applications: An Advanced Course*, pages 1–28. Cambridge University Press, 1982.

[127] Steven H. Valentine. Comparative Notes on PL/I and Algol 68. *Computer Journal*, 17:325–331, 1974.

[128] A. van Wijnagaarden *et al.* Revised Report on the Algorithmic Language Algol 68. *Acta Informatica*, 5:1–236, 1975.

[129] David H. Warren. Logic Programming and Compiler Writing. *Software Practice and Experience*, 10(2):97–127, February 1980.

[130] Peter Wegner. On the Unification of Data and Abstraction in Ada. In 10th *ACM Symposium on Principles of Programming Languages Conf.*, pages 256–264, January 1983.

[131] J. Welsh, W. Sneeringer, and C.A.R. Hoare. Ambiguities and Insecurities in Pascal. *Software Practice and Experience*, 7:685–696, 1977.

[132] Patrick Winston and Berthold K.P. Horn. *Lisp.* Addison-Wesley, Reading, Mass., 1984.

[133] Niklaus Wirth. Program Development by Stepwise Refinement. *Communications of the ACM*, 144):221–227, 1971.

[134] Niklaus Wirth. *Programming in Modula-2.* Springer-Verlag, Berlin, 1985.

[135] Niklaus Wirth. Modula: A Language for Modular Multiprogramming. *Software–Practice and Experience*, 7:3–35, 1977.

[136] Niklaus Wirth. An Assessment of the Programming Language Pascal. *IEEE Transactions on Software Engineering*, pages 192–198, 1975.

[137] Niklaus Wirth. The Programming Language PASCAL. *Acta Informatica*, 1:35–63, 1971.

Index

U

V

W

XYZ

The MIT Press, with Peter Denning as general consulting editor, publishes computer science books in the following series:

ACM Doctoral Dissertation Award and Distinguished Dissertation Series

Artificial Intelligence
Patrick Winston, founding editor
J. Michael Brady, Daniel G. Bobrow, and Randall Davis, editors

Charles Babbage Institute Reprint Series for the History of Computing
Martin Campbell-Kelly, editor

Computer Systems
Herb Schwetman, editor

Explorations with Logo
E. Paul Goldenberg, editor

Foundations of Computing
Michael Garey and Albert Meyer, editors

History of Computing
I. Bernard Cohen and William Aspray, editors

Information Systems
Michael Lesk, editor

Logic Programming
Ehud Shapiro, editor; Koichi Furukawa, Jean-Louis Lassez, Fernando Pereira, and David H. D. Warren, associate editors

The MIT Press Electrical Engineering and Computer Science Series

Research Monographs in Parallel and Distributed Processing
Christopher Jesshope and David Klappholz, editors

Scientific and Engineering Computation
Janusz Kowalik, editor

Technical Communication
Ed Barrett, editor